Eight Modern Essayists

THIRD EDITION

Eight Modern Essayists

Third Edition

William Smart
Sweet Briar College

ST. MARTIN'S PRESS, NEW YORK

Library of Congress Catalog Card Number: 80–50175

Manufactured in the United States of America.
432
fed
For information, write St. Martin's Press, Inc.,
175 Fifth Avenue, New York, N. Y. 10010

cover design: Mies Hora
typography: Murray Fleminger

ISBN: 0–312–23976–9

ACKNOWLEDGMENTS

"Notes on the English Character," "My Wood," and "Voltaire's Laboratory" from *Abinger Harvest,* copyright 1936, 1964 by E. M. Forster. Reprinted by permission of Harcourt Brace Jovanovich, Inc., and Edwin Arnold (Publishers) Ltd.

"Not Listening to Music" and "What I Believe" copyright 1939, 1967 by E. M. Forster. Reprinted from his volume *Two Cheers for Democracy* by permission of Harcourt Brace Jovanovich, Inc., and Edwin Arnold (Publishers) Ltd.

"Professions for Women" and "The Death of the Moth" from *The Death of the Moth and Other Essays* by Virginia Woolf, copyright 1942 by Harcourt Brace Jovanovich, Inc.; renewed 1970 by Marjorie T. Parsons, Executrix. Reprinted by permission of Harcourt Brace Jovanovich, Inc., the author's Literary Estate, and The Hogarth Press.

"How Should One Read a Book?" from *The Second Common Reader* by Virginia Woolf, copyright 1932 by Harcourt Brace Jovanovich, Inc.; renewed 1960 by Leonard Woolf. Reprinted by permission of Harcourt Brace Jovanovich, Inc., the author's Literary Estate, and The Hogarth Press.

Excerpt from "A Sketch of the Past" in *Moments of Being* by Virginia Woolf, copyright © 1976 by Quentin Bell and Angelica Garnett. Reprinted by permission of Harcourt Brace Jovanovich, Inc., the author's Literary Estate, and The Hogarth Press.

Acknowledgments and copyrights continue at the back of the book on pages 381–382, which constitute an extension of the copyright page.

FOR *Juliana and Sarah*

Preface

> It is fit for the beginner and learner to study others and the best. For the mind and memory are more sharply exercised in comprehending another man's things than our own; and such as accustom themselves and are familiar with the best authors shall ever and anon find somewhat of them in themselves.
>
> —BEN JONSON
> "Of Style," 1640

The purpose of *Eight Modern Essayists* is to give students the opportunity to become familiar with the work of a few outstanding writers, in the belief that through such familiarity their own writing will greatly improve. Partly this occurs by a kind of osmosis, and partly it comes as a result of discovering that writers have distinct, personal styles and that there is no single, "correct" way that one must write. That is a very important lesson to learn, for it simultaneously both liberates and burdens the young writer. The burden is the responsibility to make the best use of the opportunity writing affords for having one's own say.

"Having one's own say"—*that* is the essential aim that all the writers in this book have in common, and it is an aim that the essay allows more than any other literary form. As Alfred Kazin has pointed out, the personal, informal essay is the most "open" form available to a writer. (See also Alexander Smith's "On the Writing of Essays" in the Appendix on Style at the rear of this book.) In the personal, informal essay the writer gets to speak in his own voice about the things that most interest him. Again to quote Kazin, "The really interesting and vital work in this form unmistakably declares itself . . . through the force of the writer's concern with the subject. It is this concern that makes a good essay."

The eight writers collected here are not necessarily the eight "best writers" of the twentieth century, but they are undeniably good. All but two of them are also novelists, and although they are probably best known for that, they also loved essays and wrote them throughout their lives.

Although only two of the essayists have been changed—Edmund Wilson and Norman Mailer have been replaced by Joan Didion and Lewis Thomas—this third edition of *Eight Modern Essayists* represents a major revision. There are twenty-three new essays. Three of the four Virginia Woolf selections are new, and there are three new selections from D. H. Lawrence and George Orwell. The Lawrence and White sections now contain six essays each, as do the sections by Joan Didion and Lewis Thomas. I am delighted to be able to add these two outstanding contemporary writers to the book, both of whom published collections of essays in 1979—Didion's *The White Album* and Thomas's *The Medusa and the Snail*—which proved by their large sales that essayists of the first rank can appeal to a very wide audience indeed. I am especially pleased to be adding Lewis Thomas, a noted biologist who writes exceedingly well about scientific matters, although his range is by no means limited to science. His inclusion adds a dimension to the book that none of the previous editions had and that I think should be most welcome.

The success of *Eight Modern Essayists* over the past fifteen years is quite gratifying, for it is a book that does not try to simplify the writing process or look for superficial inducements to entice students to take an interest in writing. Its aim has always been simply to present good writers in enough depth to allow familiarity, trusting that students will enjoy those writers and as a result work harder and more enthusiastically to become better writers themselves.

W. S.

Contents

Eight Modern Essayists

THIRD EDITION

E. M. Forster

Cecil Beaton/Photo Trend

EDWARD MORGAN FORSTER was born in London on January 1, 1879. On his father's side he was descended from an important banking family whose wealth and energies had for several generations been devoted to bringing about social reforms in areas such as relief for the poor and the abolition of slavery. They were, according to Forster, pious, respectable people, hard-working and generous, but for whom "poetry, mystery, passion, ecstasy, music" didn't count. "This indifference to the unseen seems to me the great defect in my great-grandfather's set. . . ." On his mother's side, on the other hand, his forebears were both less successful and more spontaneous: "they were devoid of public spirit, and they were averse to piety and quick to detect the falsity sometimes accompanying it." And it was with them and their wit and improvidence that Forster's sympathies always remained.

Two years after his father died in 1880, he and his mother—who had entered the family as a governess—moved to a house in Hertfordshire, and it was there, in rural England, that the happiest years of Forster's childhood were spent. In the background hovered his great-aunt, Marianne Thornton, the *grande dame* of his father's family, who claimed young Morgan as her favorite upon his father's death, and who now gave him the nickname The Important One. When Marianne Thornton died in 1887, she bequeathed her nephew a legacy of £8000, which Forster later called "the financial salvation of my life. Thanks to it, I was able to go to Cambridge—impossible otherwise, for I failed to win scholarships. After Cambridge I was able to travel for a couple of years, and traveling inclined me to write." Indeed, "she and no one else made my career as a writer possible."

Forster disliked Tonbridge, the public school he attended as a day-boy, but at King's College, Cambridge, which he entered in 1897, he found at last the atmosphere that brought out that combination of qualities he most admired: "Body and spirit, reason and emotion, work and play, architecture and scenery, laughter and seriousness, life and art—these pairs which are elsewhere contrasted were there fused into one. People and books reinforced one another, intelligence joined hands with affection, speculation became a passion, and discussion was made profound by love." In 1900 he took a classical degree, and in 1901 a degree in history.

The decade following Cambridge was the most active and productive of Forster's life. For a year and a half he traveled through Italy and Greece, then settled in London and began contributing to *The Independent Review*, a liberal journal founded by a group at Cambridge that included his friends G. Lowes Dickinson and Nathaniel Wedd. In quick succession he published four novels—*Where Angels Fear to Tread* (1905), *The Longest Journey* (1907), *A Room With a View* (1908), *Howard's End* (1910)—and his first collection of short stories, *The Celestial Omnibus* (1911). Also during this period he became associated with those writers and thinkers who would later be known as the "Bloomsbury group": Virginia and Leonard Woolf, Lytton Strachey, John Maynard Keynes, Roger Fry, and Clive and Vanessa Bell. Together they shared that same fusion of qualities—Life and Art—that had made Forster's years at Cambridge so delightful.

In 1913 he spent three months in India in the Hindu native state of Dewas Senior, "an amazing little state," as he wrote home, "which can have no parallel, except in a Gilbert and Sullivan opera." But more than with its comic opera aspects, Forster was impressed with the mysteries of India and began a novel that he was unable to complete. During World War I he was in Alexandria for three years as a noncombatant, then came back to London to serve for a short while as literary editor of the *Daily Herald*. Then, in 1921, he went back to Dewas State Senior as private secretary to the maharajah and, when he returned to England at the end of a year, was at last able to finish the book he had started nearly twelve years earlier. *A Passage to India* (1924) is not only Forster's most popular novel, but probably his best.

In 1927 Forster gave the Clark lectures at Trinity College, Cambridge; published under the title *Aspects of the Novel*, they have become a minor classic among books of criticism on the techniques of fiction. In the same year he was elected a Fellow of King's. His collected essays appeared in *Abinger Harvest* (1936) and *Two Cheers for Democracy* (1951), and in 1953 he published *The Hill of Devi*, a record of his visits to Dewas State Senior. In 1956 he published *Marianne Thornton*, a biography of his great-aunt. Forster spent the last twenty-five years of his life in Cambridge in rather scholarly seclusion, and died in 1970 at the age of ninety-one. A year later his long-awaited last novel, *Maurice*, written many years earlier, was finally published.

Two main ideas that one finds throughout Forster's novels and essays are that "poetry, mystery, passion, ecstasy, music" do indeed count, and that personal relationships are a good deal more important than public duty. His heroes are spontaneous, passionate, and occasionally cruel, but never cold or hypocritical. What they come in conflict with are members of the English middle classes who possess just the opposite characteristics. In the end neither side is the victor. But, if in nothing more than their juxtaposition, Forster managed to state his theme, which is: "Only connect the prose and the passion, and both will be exalted, and human love will soon be at its height" (*Howard's End*). For love is everything; nothing in the world is substantial but the relationships between people, ideas, and things: "Only connect . . ."

Like Erasmus and Montaigne, his spiritual ancestors, Forster was a true humanist whose plea was not for Heaven or Utopia, but simply "tolerance, good temper, and sympathy." And the modesty of his hopes for mankind can be detected immediately in the casual, off-hand style of his prose. His "unbuttoned manner," as Lionel Trilling once called it, is serious without being solemn. He believes what he says, but is fearful of the way beliefs solidify; therefore, his manner is slightly comic. If a few readers are put off by the voice, it is not because Forster was too urbane, but just the opposite: so civilized he didn't need to seem sophisticated.

NOTES ON THE ENGLISH CHARACTER

First note. I had better let the cat out of the bag at once and record my opinion that the character of the English is essentially middle class. There is a sound historical reason for this, for, since the end of the eighteenth century, the middle classes have been the dominant force in our community. They gained wealth by the Industrial Revolution, political power by the Reform Bill of 1832; they are connected with the rise and organization of the British Empire; they are responsible for the literature of the nineteenth century. Solidity, caution, integrity, efficiency. Lack of imagination, hypocrisy. These qualities characterize the middle classes in every country, but in England they are national characteristics also, because only in England have the middle classes been in power for one hundred and fifty years. Napoleon, in his rude way, called us "a nation of shopkeepers." We prefer to call ourselves "a great commercial nation"—it sounds more dignified—but the two phrases amount to the same. Of course there are other classes: there is an aristocracy, there are the poor. But it is on the middle classes that the eye of the critic rests—just as it rests on the poor in Russia and on the aristocracy in Japan. Russia is symbolized by the peasant or by the factory worker; Japan by the samurai; the national figure of England is Mr. Bull with his top hat, his comfortable clothes, his substantial stomach, and his substantial balance at the bank. Saint George may caper on banners and in the speeches of politicians, but it is John Bull who delivers the goods. And even Saint George—if Gibbon is correct—wore a top hat once; he was an army contractor and supplied indifferent bacon. It all amounts to the same in the end.

Second Note. Just as the heart of England is the middle classes, so the heart of the middle classes is the public school system. This extraordinary institution is local. It does not even exist all over the British Isles. It is unknown in Ireland, almost unknown in Scotland (countries excluded from my survey), and though it may inspire other great institutions—Aligarh, for example, and some of the schools in the United States—it remains unique, because it was created by the Anglo-Saxon middle classes, and can flourish only where they flourish. How perfectly it expresses their character—far better, for instance, than does the university, into which social and spiritual complexities have already entered. With its boarding-houses, its compulsory games, its system of prefects and fagging, its insistence on good form and on *esprit de corps*, it produces a type whose weight is out of all proportion to its numbers.

On leaving his school, the boy either sets to work at once—goes into the army or into business, or emigrates—or else proceeds to the university, and after three or four years there enters some other profession—becomes a barrister, doctor, civil servant, schoolmaster, or journalist. (If through some mishap he does not become a manual worker or an artist.) In all these careers his education, or the absence of it, influences him. Its memories influence him also. Many men look back on their school days as the happiest of their lives. They remember with regret that golden time when life, though hard, was not yet complex; when they all worked together and played together and thought together, so far as they thought at all: when they were taught that school is the world in miniature and believed that no one can love his country who does not love his school. And they prolong that time as best they can by joining their Old Boys' society; indeed, some of them remain Old Boys and nothing else for the rest of their lives. They attribute all good to the school. They worship it. They quote the remark that "the battle of Waterloo was won on the playing fields of Eton." It is nothing to them that the remark is inapplicable historically and was never made by the Duke of Wellington, and that the Duke of Wellington was an Irishman. They go on quoting it because it expresses their sentiments; they feel that if the Duke of Wellington didn't make it he ought to have, and if he wasn't an Englishman he ought to have been. And they go forth into a world that is not entirely composed of public-school men or even of Anglo-Saxons, but of men who are as various as the sands of the sea; into a world of whose richness and subtlety they have no conception. They go forth into it with well-developed bodies, fairly developed minds, and undeveloped hearts. And it is this undeveloped heart that is largely responsible for the difficulties of Englishmen abroad. An undeveloped heart—not a cold one. The difference is important, and on it my next note will be based.

For it is not that the Englishman can't feel—it is that he is afraid to feel. He has been taught at his public school that feeling is bad form. He must not express great joy or sorrow, or even open his mouth too wide when he talks—his pipe might fall out if he did. He must bottle up his emotions, or let them out only on a very special occasion.

Once upon a time (this is an anecdote) I went for a week's holiday on the Continent with an Indian friend. We both enjoyed ourselves and were sorry when the week was over, but on parting our behavior was absolutely different. He was plunged in despair. He felt that because the holiday was over all happiness was over until the world ended. He could not express his sorrow too much. But in me the Englishman came out strong. I reflected that we should meet again in a month or two, and could write in the interval if we had anything to say; and under these circumstances I could not see what there was to make a fuss about. It wasn't as if we were parting forever or dying. "Buck up," I said, "do buck up." He refused to buck up, and I left him plunged in gloom.

The conclusion of the anecdote is even more instructive. For when we met the next month our conversation threw a good deal of light on the English character. I began by scolding my friend. I told him that he had been wrong to feel and display so much emotion upon so slight an occasion; that it was inappropriate. The word "inappropriate" roused him to fury. "What?" he cried. "Do you measure out your emotions as if they were potatoes?" I did not like the simile of the potatoes, but after a moment's reflection I said, "Yes, I do; and what's more, I think I ought to. A small occasion demands a little emotion, just as a large occasion demands a great one. I would like my emotions to be appropriate. This may be measuring them like potatoes, but it is better than slopping them about like water from a pail, which is what you did." He did not like the simile of the pail. "If those are your opinions, they part us forever," he cried, and left the room. Returning immediately, he added: "No

—but your whole attitude toward emotion is wrong. Emotion has nothing to do with appropriateness. It matters only that it shall be sincere. I happened to feel deeply. I showed it. It doesn't matter whether I ought to have felt deeply or not."

This remark impressed me very much. Yet I could not agree with it, and said that I valued emotion as much as he did, but used it differently; if I poured it out on small occasions I was afraid of having none left for the great ones, and of being bankrupt at the crises of life. Note the word "bankrupt." I spoke as a member of a prudent middle-class nation, always anxious to meet my liabilities. But my friend spoke as an Oriental, and the Oriental has behind him a tradition, not of middle-class prudence but of kingly munificence and splendor. He feels his resources are endless, just as John Bull feels his are finite. As regards material resources, the Oriental is clearly unwise. Money isn't endless. If we spend or give away all the money we have, we haven't any more, and must take the consequences, which are frequently unpleasant. But, as regards the resources of the spirit, he may be right. The emotions may be endless. The more we express them, the more we may have to express.

> True love in this differs from gold and clay,
> That to divide is not to take away,

says Shelley. Shelley, at all events, believes that the wealth of the spirit is endless; that we may express it copiously, passionately, and always; and that we can never feel sorrow or joy too acutely.

In the above anecdote, I have figured as a typical Englishman. I will now descend from that dizzy and somewhat unfamiliar height, and return to my business of notetaking. A note on the *slowness* of the English character. The Englishman appears to be cold and unemotional because he is really slow. When an event happens, he may understand it quickly enough with his mind, but he takes quite a while to feel it. Once upon a time a coach, containing some Englishmen and some Frenchmen, was driving over the Alps. The horses ran away, and as they were dashing across a bridge the coach caught on the stonework, tottered, and nearly fell into the ravine below. The Frenchmen were frantic with terror: they screamed and gesticulated and flung themselves about, as Frenchmen would. The Englishmen sat quite calm. An hour later, the coach drew up at an inn to change horses, and by that time the situations were exactly reversed. The Frenchmen had forgotten all about the danger, and were chattering gaily; the Englishmen had just begun to feel it, and one had a nervous breakdown and was obliged to go to bed. We have here a clear physical difference between the two races—a difference that goes deep into character. The Frenchmen responded at once; the Englishmen responded in time. They were slow and they were also practical. Their instinct forbade them to throw themselves about in the coach, because it was more likely to tip over if they did. They had this extraordinary appreciation of *fact* that we shall notice again and again. When a disaster comes, the English instinct is to do what can be done first, and to postpone the feeling as long as possible. Hence they are splendid at emergencies. No doubt they are brave—no one will deny that—but bravery is partly an affair of the nerves, and the English nervous system is well equipped for meeting a physical emergency. It acts promptly and feels slowly. Such a combination is fruitful, and anyone who possesses it has gone a long way toward being brave. And when the action is over, then the Englishman can feel.

There is one more consideration—a most important one. If the English nature is cold, how is it that it has produced a great literature and a literature that is particularly great in poetry? Judged by its prose, English literature would not stand in the first rank. It is its poetry that raises it to the level of Greek, Persian, or French. And yet the English are supposed to be so unpoetical. How is this? The nation that produced the Elizabethan drama and the Lake Poets cannot be a cold, unpoetical nation. We can't get fire out of ice. Since literature always rests upon national character, there must be in the English nature hidden springs of fire to produce the fire we see. The warm sympathy, the romance, the imagination, that we look for in Englishmen whom we meet, and too often vainly look for, must exist in the nation as a whole, or we could not have this outburst of national song. An undeveloped heart—not a cold one.

The trouble is that the English nature is not at all easy to understand. It has a great air of simplicity, it advertises itself as simple, but the more we consider it, the greater the problems we shall encounter. People talk of the mysterious East, but the West also is mysterious. It has depths that do not reveal themselves at the first gaze. We know what the sea looks like from a distance: it is of one color, and level, and obviously cannot contain such creatures as fish. But if we look into the sea over the edge of a boat, we see a dozen colors, and depth below depth, and fish swimming in them. That sea is the English character—apparently imperturbable and even. The depths and the colors are the English romanticism and the English sensitiveness—we do not expect to find such things, but they exist. And—to continue my metaphor—the fish are the English emotions, which are always trying to get up to the surface, but don't quite know how. For the most part we see them moving far below, distorted and obscure. Now and then they succeed and we exclaim, "Why, the Englishman has emotions! He actually can feel!" And occasionally we see that beautiful creature the flying fish, which rises out of the water altogether into the air and the sunlight. English literature is a flying fish. It is a sample of the life that goes on day after day beneath the surface; it is a proof that beauty and emotion exist in the salt, inhospitable sea.

And now let's get back to terra firma. The Englishman's attitude toward criticism will give us another starting point. He is not annoyed by criticism. He listens or not as the case may be, smiles and passes on, saying, "Oh, the fellow's jealous"; "Oh, I'm used to Bernard Shaw; monkey tricks don't hurt me." It never occurs to him that the fellow may be accurate as well as jealous, and that he might do well to take the criticism to heart and profit by it. It never strikes him—except as a form of words—that he is capable of improvement; his self-complacency is abysmal. Other nations, both Oriental and European, have an uneasy feeling that they are not quite perfect. In consequence they resent criticism. It hurts them; and their snappy answers often mask a determination to improve themselves. Not so the Englishman. He has no uneasy feeling. Let the critics bark. And the "tolerant humorous attitude" with which he confronts them is not really humorous, because it is bounded by the titter and the guffaw.

Turn over the pages of *Punch.* There is neither wit, laughter, nor satire in our national jester—only the snigger of a suburban householder who can understand nothing that does not resemble himself. Week after week, under Mr. Punch's supervision, a man falls off his horse, or a colonel misses a golfball, or a little girl makes a mistake in her prayers. Week after week ladies show not too much of their legs, foreigners are deprecated, originality condemned. Week after week a bricklayer does not do as much work as he ought and a futurist does more than he need. It is all supposed to be so good-tempered and clean; it is also supposed to be funny. It is actually an outstanding example of our attitude toward criticism: the middle-class Englishman, with a smile on his clean-shaven lips, is engaged in admiring himself and ignoring the rest of mankind. If, in those colorless pages, he came across anything that really was funny—a drawing by Max Beerbohm, for instance—his smile would disappear, and he would say to himself, "The fellow's a bit of a crank," and pass on.

This particular attitude reveals such insensitiveness as to suggest a more serious charge: is the Englishman altogether indifferent to the things of the spirit? Let us glance for a moment at his religion—not, indeed, at his theology, which would not merit inspection, but at the action on his daily life of his belief in the unseen. Here again his attitude is practical. But an innate decency comes out: he is thinking of others rather than of himself. Right conduct is his aim. He asks of his religion that it shall make him a better man in daily life: that he shall be more kind, more just, more merciful, more desirous to fight what is evil and to protect what is good. No one could call this a low conception. It is, as far as it goes, a spiritual one. Yet—and this seems to me typical of the race—it is only half the religious idea. Religion is more than an ethical code with a divine sanction. It is also a means through which man may get into direct connection with the divine, and, judging by history, few Englishmen have succeeded in doing this. We have produced no series of prophets, as has Judaism or Islam. We have not even produced a Joan of Arc, or a Savonarola. We have produced few saints. In Germany the Reformation was due to the passionate conviction of Luther. In England it was due to palace intrigue. We can show a steady level of piety, a fixed determination to live decently according to our lights—little more.

Well, it is something. It clears us of the charge of being an unspiritual nation. That facile contrast between the spiritual East and the materialistic West can be pushed too far. The West also is spiritual. Only it expresses its belief, not in fasting and visions, not in prophetic rapture, but in the daily round, the common task. An incomplete expression, if you like. I agree. But the argument underlying these scattered notes is that the Englishman is an incomplete person. Not a cold or an unspiritual one. But undeveloped, incomplete.

The attitude of the average orthodox Englishman is often misunderstood. It is thought that he must know that a doctrine—say, like that of the Trinity—is untrue. Moslems in particular feel that his faith is a dishonest compromise between polytheism and monotheism. The answer to this criticism is that the average orthodox Englishman is no theologian. He regards the Trinity as a mystery that it is not his place to solve. "I find difficulties enough in daily life," he will say. "I concern myself with those. As for the Trinity, it is a doctrine handed down to me from my fathers, whom I respect, and I hope to hand it down to my sons, and that they will respect me. No doubt it is true, or it would not have been handed down. And no doubt the clergy could explain it to me if I asked them; but, like myself, they are busy men, and I will not take up their time."

In such an answer there is confusion of thought, if you like, but no conscious deceit, which is alien to the English nature. The Englishman's deceit is generally unconscious.

For I have suggested earlier that the English are sometimes hypocrites, and it is now my duty to develop this rather painful subject. Hypocrisy is the prime charge that is always brought against us. The Germans are called brutal, the Spanish cruel, the Americans superficial, and so on; but we are perfide Albion, the island of hypocrites, the people who have built up an Empire with a Bible in one hand, a pistol in the other, and financial concessions in both pockets. Is the charge true? I think it is; but while making it we must be quite clear as to what we mean by hypocrisy. Do we mean *conscious* deceit? Well, the English are comparatively guiltless of this; they have little of the Renaissance villain about them. Do we mean *unconscious* deceit? Muddleheadedness? Of this I believe them to be guilty. When an Englishman has been led into a course of wrong action, he has nearly always begun by muddling himself. A public-school education does not make for mental clearness, and he possesses to a very high degree the power of confusing his own mind. We have seen this tendency at work in the domain of theology; how does it work in the domain of conduct?

Jane Austen may seem an odd authority to cite, but Jane Austen has, within her limits, a marvelous insight into the English mind. Her range is limited, her characters never attempt any of the more scarlet sins. But she has a merciless eye for questions of conduct, and the classical example of two English people muddling themselves before they embark upon a wrong course of action is to be found in the opening chapters of *Sense and Sensibility*. Old Mr. Dashwood has just died. He has been twice married. By his first marriage he has a son, John; by his second marriage three daughters. The son is well off; the young ladies and their mother—for Mr. Dashwood's second wife survives him—are badly off. He has called his son to his death-bed and has solemnly adjured him to provide for the second family. Much moved, the young man promises, and mentally decides to give each of his sisters a thousand pounds; and then the comedy begins. For he announces his generous intention to his wife, and Mrs. John Dashwood by no means approves of depriving their own little boy of so large a sum. The thousand pounds are accordingly reduced to five hundred. But even this seems rather much. Might not an annuity to the stepmother be less of a wrench? Yes—but though less of a wrench it might be more of a drain, for "she is very stout and healthy, and scarcely forty." An occasional present of fifty pounds will be better, "and will, I think, be amply discharging my promise to my father." Or, better still, an occasional present of fish. And in the end nothing is done, nothing; the four impecunious ladies are not even helped in the moving of their furniture.

Well, are the John Dashwoods hypocrites? It depends upon our definition of hypocrisy. The young man could not see his evil impulses as they gathered force and gained on him. And even his wife, though a worse character, is also self-deceived. She reflects that old Mr. Dashwood may have been out of his mind at his death. She thinks of her own little boy—and surely a mother ought to think of her own child. She has muddled herself so completely that in one sentence she can refuse the ladies the income that would enable them to keep a carriage and in the next can say that they will not be keeping a carriage and so will have no expenses. No doubt men and women in other lands can muddle themselves, too, yet the state of mind of Mr. and Mrs. John Dashwood seems to me typical of England. They are slow —they take time even to do wrong; whereas people in other lands do wrong quickly.

There are national faults as there are national diseases, and perhaps one can draw a parallel between them. It has always impressed me that the national diseases of England should be cancer and consumption—slow, insidious, pretending to be something else; while the diseases proper to the South should be cholera and plague, which strike at a man when he is perfectly well and may leave him a corpse by evening. Mr. and Mrs. John Dashwood are moral consumptives. They collapse gradually without realizing what the disease is. There is nothing dramatic or violent about their sin. You cannot call them villains.

Here is the place to glance at some of the other charges that have been brought against the English as a nation. They have, for instance, been accused of treachery, cruelty, and fanaticism. In these charges I have never been able to see the least point, because treachery and cruelty are conscious sins. The man knows he is doing wrong, and does it deliberately, like Tartuffe or Iago. He betrays his friend because he wishes to. He tortures his prisoners because he enjoys seeing the blood flow. He worships the Devil because he prefers evil to good. From villainies such as these the average Englishman is free. His character, which prevents his rising to certain heights, also prevents him from sinking to these depths. Because he doesn't produce mystics he doesn't produce villains either; he gives the world no prophets, but no anarchists, no fanatics—religious or political.

Of course there are cruel and treacherous people in England—one has only to look at the police courts—and examples of public infamy can be found, such as the Amritsar massacre. But one does not look at the police courts or the military mind to find the soul of any nation; and the more English people one meets the more convinced one becomes that the charges as a whole are untrue. Yet foreign critics often make them. Why? Partly because they are annoyed with certain genuine defects in the English character, and in their irritation throw in cruelty in order to make the problem simpler. Moral indignation is always agreeable, but nearly always misplaced. It is indulged in both by the English and by the critics of the English. They all find it great fun. The drawback is that while they are amusing themselves the world becomes neither wiser nor better.

The main point of these notes is that the English character is incomplete. No national character is complete. We have to look for some qualities in one part of the world and others in another. But the English character is incomplete in a way that is particularly annoying to the foreign observer. It has a bad surface—self-complacent, unsympathetic, and reserved. There is plenty of emotion further down, but it never gets used. There is plenty of brain power, but it is more often used to confirm prejudices than to dispel them. With such an equipment the Englishman cannot be popular. Only I would repeat: there is little vice in him and no real coldness. It is the machinery that is wrong.

I hope and believe myself that in the next twenty years we shall see a great change, and that the national character will alter into something that is less unique but more lovable. The supremacy of the middle classes is probably ending. What new element the working classes will introduce one cannot say, but at all events they will not have been educated at public schools. And whether these notes praise or blame the English character—that is only incidental. They are the notes of a student who is trying to get at the truth and would value the assistance of others. I believe myself that the truth is great and that it shall prevail. I have no faith in official caution and reticence. The cats are all out of their bags, and diplomacy cannot recall them. The nations *must* understand one another, and quickly; and without the interposition of their governments, for the shrinkage of the globe is throwing them into one another's arms. To that understanding these notes are a feeble contribution—notes on the English character as it has struck a novelist.

1920

MY WOOD

A few years ago I wrote a book which dealt in part with the difficulties of the English in India. Feeling that they would have had no difficulties in India themselves, the Americans read the book freely. The more they read it the better it made them feel, and a check to the author was the result. I bought a wood with the check. It is not a large wood—it contains scarcely any trees, and it is intersected, blast it, by a public footpath. Still, it is the first property that I have owned, so it is right that other people should participate in my shame, and should ask themselves, in accents that will vary in horror, this very important question: What is the effect of property upon the character? Don't let's touch economics; the effect of private ownership upon the community as a whole is another question—a more important question, perhaps, but another one. Let's keep to psychology. If you own things, what's their effect on you? What's the effect on me of my wood?

In the first place, it makes me feel heavy. Property does have this effect. Property produces men of weight, and it was a man of weight who failed to get into the Kingdom of Heaven. He was not wicked, that unfortunate millionaire in the parable, he was only stout; he stuck out in front, not to mention behind, and as he wedged himself this way and that in the crystalline entrance and bruised his well-fed flanks, he saw beneath him a comparatively slim camel passing through the eye of a needle and being woven into the robe of God. The Gospels all through couple stoutness and slowness. They point out what is perfectly obvious, yet seldom realized: that if you have a lot of things you cannot move a lot, that furniture requires dusting, dusters require servants, servants require insurance stamps, and the whole tangle of them makes you think twice before you accept an invitation to dinner or go for a bathe in the Jordan. Sometimes the Gospels proceed further and say with Tolstoy that property is sinful; they approach the difficult ground of asceticism here, where I cannot follow them. But as to the immediate effects of property on people, they just show straightforward logic. It produces men of weight. Men of weight cannot, by definition, move like the lightning from the East unto the West, and the ascent of a fourteen-stone bishop into a pulpit is thus the exact antithesis of the coming of the Son of Man. My wood makes me feel heavy.

In the second place, it makes me feel it ought to be larger.

The other day I heard a twig snap in it. I was annoyed at first, for I thought that someone was blackberrying, and depreciating the value of the undergrowth. On coming nearer, I saw it was not a man who had trodden on the twig and snapped it, but a bird, and I felt pleased. My bird. The bird was not equally pleased. Ignoring the relation between us, it took fright as soon as it saw the shape of my face, and flew straight over the boundary hedge into a field, the property of Mrs. Henessy, where it sat down with a loud squawk. It had become Mrs. Henessy's bird. Something seemed grossly amiss here, something that would not have occurred had the wood been larger. I could not afford to buy Mrs. Henessy out, I dared not murder her, and limitations of this sort beset me on every side. Ahab did not want that vineyard—he only needed it to round off his property, preparatory to plotting a new curve—and all the land around my wood has become necessary to me in order to round off the wood. A boundary protects. But—poor little thing—the boundary ought in its turn to be protected. Noises on the edge of it. Children throw stones. A little more, and then a little more, until we reach the sea. Happy Canute! Happier Alexander! And after all, why should even the world be the limit of possession? A rocket containing a Union Jack, will, it is hoped, be shortly fired at the moon. Mars. Sirius. Beyond which . . . But these immensities ended by saddening me. I could not suppose that my wood was the destined nucleus of universal dominion—it is so small and contains no mineral wealth beyond the blackberries. Nor was I comforted when Mrs. Henessy's bird took alarm for the second time and flew clean away from us all, under the belief that it belonged to itself.

In the third place, property makes its owner feel that he ought to do something to it. Yet he isn't sure what. A restlessness comes over him, a vague sense that he has a personality to express—the same sense which, without any vagueness, leads the artist to an act of creation. Sometimes I think I will cut down such trees as remain in the wood, at other times I want to fill up the gaps between them with new trees. Both impulses are pretentious and empty. They are not honest movements towards moneymaking or beauty. They spring from a foolish desire to express myself and from an inability to enjoy what I have got. Creation, property, enjoyment form a sinister trinity in the human mind. Creation and enjoyment are both very very good, yet they are often unattainable without a material basis, and at such moments property pushes itself in as a substitute, saying, "Accept me instead–I'm good enough for all three." It is not enough. It is, as Shakespeare said of lust, "The expense of spirit in a waste of shame": it is "Before, a joy proposed; behind, a dream." Yet we don't know how to shun it. It is forced on us by our economic system as the alternative to starvation. It is also forced on us by an internal defect in the soul, by the feeling that in property may lie the germs of self-development and of exquisite or heroic deeds. Our life on earth is, and ought to be, material and carnal. But we have not yet learned to manage our materialism and carnality properly; they are still entangled with the desire for ownership, where (in the words of Dante) "Possession is one with loss."

And this brings us to our fourth and final point: the blackberries.

Blackberries are not plentiful in this meagre grove, but they are easily seen from the public footpath which traverses it, and all too easily gathered. Foxgloves, too–people will pull up the foxgloves, and ladies of an educational tendency even grub for toadstools to show them on the Monday in class. Other ladies, less educated, roll down the bracken in the arms of their gentlemen friends. There is paper, there are tins. Pray, does my wood belong to me or doesn't it? And, if it does, should I not own it best by allowing no one else to walk there? There is a wood near Lyme Regis, also cursed by a public footpath, where the owner has not hesitated on this point. He has built high stone walls each side of the path, and has spanned it by bridges, so that the public circulate like termites while he gorges on the blackberries unseen. He really does own his wood, this able chap.

Dives in Hell did pretty well, but the gulf dividing him from Lazarus could be traversed by vision, and nothing traverses it here. And perhaps I shall come to this in time. I shall wall in and fence out until I really taste the sweets of property. Enormously stout, endlessly avaricious, pseudo-creative, intensely selfish, I shall weave upon my forehead the quadruple crown of possession until those nasty Bolshies come and take it off again and thrust me aside into the outer darkness.

1926

VOLTAIRE'S LABORATORY

1. How They Weighed Fire

During the spring of 1737 the iron foundries in a remote district of Lorraine were often visited by a thin middle-aged man with a notebook. He would weigh out two pounds of iron, have them heated till they were red-hot, and then weigh them again. He repeated the experiment, increasing the amount until he had weighed up to a thousand pounds. Three cauldrons were next prepared under his directions, they were placed on scales, so that their weight could be estimated, and then molten metal was poured into them from the furnace, a hundred pounds into the first cauldron, thirty-five pounds into the second, twenty-five into the third, and when the cauldrons were cold the mass was weighed again. As the title of this article suggests, the thin, middle-aged man is Voltaire, but what on earth is he doing in an iron foundry? Wait a minute. Here comes a still more remarkable figure.

The newcomer is a lady of about thirty, with a long thin face, a commanding nose, and greenish eyes. Her appearance is masculine but not mannish; in spite of her earnest mien she is gay and charming, she dresses well, and is very kindhearted. It will be easy to make fun of her. For she, too, holds a notebook in her hand, in which she enters the weights of the hot and cold iron. She is quite as keen as Voltaire, and even more serious. She has taken up science, not because it is fashionable and brings her into contact with celebrities, but because she hopes to discover the nature of the universe. Facts, facts! A theory may come later—if there is one. She gives up acting, dancing, games, in order to do experiments. Voltaire calls her "divine Emilie." She is his mistress, Madame du Châtelet, and she owns Cirey, the great house where he is stopping.

On returning to Cirey, the investigators separate, and Voltaire goes to his own suite, which contains half a dozen ground-floor rooms, beautifully furnished; passing through a tiny antechamber, and a bedroom of crimson velvet, he comes to the long gallery, and sits down there. The long gallery is lacquered in yellow, with panels of Indian paper; it is ornamented with statues, one of which, a statue of Love, conceals the stove; there are cupboards full of books and scientific instruments; there are windows opening into the garden or onto the chapel—so that without disturbing himself too much he can hear Mass. At the end is a camera obscura and another room, not yet in order. Voltaire drinks a cup of coffee. Establishing himself at a superb writing-desk, he takes up his pen in despair. For he is going in for a prize competition on the subject of the Nature and Propagation of Fire, and he has been unable to find out whether fire weighs anything. Since fire is an element, one expects it to weigh something, yet the hot iron at the foundry was only occasionally heavier than the cold: sometimes it was the same weight and sometimes actually lighter. Nor is this all: other problems connected with fire are equally obscure. If he shuts up burning coals in a metal box, sometimes they continue to burn, at other times they go out. If he prepares sections of little trees and places them on a red-hot surface, the time in which they are reduced to ashes varies considerably, although they are exactly the same thickness and size, and even come from the same plantation. "I then repeated this experiment with vegetables"; but the vegetables burned unevenly too. An experiment with objects painted different colours had been more satisfactory: black objects got hot quicker than green ones, yellow than white; but even here there were exceptions, and all he can do is to add to the Laws of Fire a supplementary law to the effect that they do not always work.

"My dear Abbé, we are surrounded by uncertainties," he writes to his agent in Paris. "To discover the least scrap of truth entails endless labour," and he implores the Abbé to inquire of people who are likely to know whether fire really does weigh anything; also whether a burning glass has a normal effect on objects in a vacuum; also, is it true that Persian naphtha of the best quality flames under water; also he wants writing-paper of various sizes, sealing wax, an astrolabe, two globes on stands, thermometers, barometers, earthenware pans, retorts, crucibles; also a complete sportsman's outfit—gun, costume; also face-powder, hair-powder, scent, nail-scissors, sponges, two very large pots of orange-flower pomatum; also a young priest who will officiate in the chapel, and knows a little chemistry besides; and a young mathematician who knows astronomy; also he does *not* want the publications of the French Academy, but the publications of the Academy of Sciences: the good Abbé has confused the two institutions, and sent the wrong volumes, so that Voltaire feels like the man who ordered eighteen swans for his ornamental water, and received eighteen monkeys by mistake; also—also—the list of wants rolls on; what, meantime, is Madame du Châtelet doing at her end of the house?

She, too, is entering for the prize competition on the Nature and Propagation of Fire, but she has not told her lover this. It is to be a surprise. An indefatigable inquirer, she has visited foundries and scorched vegetables until she is left with very little time for the actual writing, and has to dip her hand constantly in cold water, it aches so. Her suite is even more gorgeous than his: everything matches in blue and yellow, down to the little dog's basket, the bed is covered with blue satin, Veroneses and Watteaus adorn the walls, her writing table, inlaid with amber, was the gift of Prince Frederick of Prussia, her bathroom is tiled, and paved with marble, the chandeliers are exquisite, a looking-glass door leads from the bedroom into the library. Far into the night she writes; so does Voltaire; and between them slumbers the dilapidated central portion of the house, possibly occupied by her husband.

Life at Cirey was certainly comic, but before we have our good laugh at it we had better remind ourselves that Voltaire and Madame du Châtelet were abreast of their age, and their science relatively no more absurd than our own—indeed, it may well prove to be less absurd, for they were highly intelligent. We find them funny because we know more, but if we patronize them for not knowing more it is we who become funny. For example, their difficulties over fire were shared by all their contemporaries. Chemistry now informs us that fire is not an element, but a state through which bodies are passing, and which is likely to be accompanied by certain reactions: under some conditions, when they are heated, they give out gas, and so get lighter; under other conditions they generate solid oxide, and so get heavier. In a hundred years' time chemistry will inform us of something else. The eighteenth century had not discovered even what we know, so the experiments at the foundry seemed to give contradictory results. Moreover, the apparatus was hopelessly inaccurate; however good a pendulum clock the Abbé sent from Paris, and however carefully he packed it, it still could not record the exact times two cauliflowers took to burn. "My dear Abbé, we are surrounded by uncertainties." The uncertainties thrilled him, he dashed hither and thither to put them right and took genuine pleasure in the complexity of the universe.

It has been well said that Voltaire is not a journalist but a newspaper. Every sort of activity gets mentioned in his columns. The literary side is strongest, but science jottings constantly appear, and first become prominent during his exile in England. He picked up in England many scraps that moved his respect or mirth: inoculation; a woman who bore rabbits; an Irishman who saw worms through a microscope in mutton broth. But it was not until he returned to France and fell under Madame du Châtelet's influence that his interests concentrated. She inclined him to the subjects she herself had studied—that is to say to physics and to astronomy—and his chief scientific work, an exposition of Newton's theory, was composed under her protection. He presented the theory accurately, criticized it intelligently, and has the undivided credit of introducing Newton to the French public. Orthodoxy was alarmed; it had invested in the whirlwinds of Descartes as a suitable basis for the physical universe, and resented the possibility of gravitation. On account of gravitation, and on account of other laxities, which included an improper poem on Joan of Arc, Voltaire kept away from Paris. He was not yet the very great Voltaire who quarrelled with Frederick the Great and avenged Calas. But he was a considerable figure, tragedian, poet, wit, philosopher, and now science was to place her metallic wreath a little crookedly upon his brows.

He and his hostess had arrived at Cirey earlier in that same year, 1737. They had driven by night and through the snow, and the wheel had come off the carriage on Voltaire's side, so that Madame du Châtelet, her maid, and a quantity of luggage fell on him. At the same moment, all the menservants fell off the box. It was long before the luggage, the maid, the mistress, and the great man could be progressively extracted, and he uttered a series of short, sharp shrieks. As so often happened, he was enjoying himself. Cushions were spread in the frozen road, and he and Madame du Châtelet sat on them and pointed out to one another the glories of the night sky. "The stars shone brilliantly," one of their servants writes. "Not a tree, not a house disturbed the expanse of the horizon. M. de Voltaire and Madame du Châtelet were in ecstasies: wrapped in furs, they discussed the nature and the orbits of the stars and their destination in space while their teeth chattered. If only they had had a telescope, their joy would have been complete." There they sat, half laughing and wholly serious, until the carriage could be repaired and take them on to their home.

When they got there, they evolved a routine which both impressed and annoyed their visitors. They took themselves seriously, in which they were fully justified, and they were obliged to organize their work, or it would not have got done. Eleven in the morning and nine at night were the only hours in the twenty-four when they were certain to be visible. At eleven there was coffee in Voltaire's gallery; in the evening came the great event—supper—occasionally marred by a quarrel. After supper, if all had gone well, Voltaire showed the magic lantern, or directed a telescope at the moon, or played tricks with prisms, being screamingly funny all the time, or read Joan of Arc aloud in the marble bathroom, or had plays performed in a barn. Science was much discussed, also religion; at no time of his life was he either an atheist or an agnostic, he believed firmly in God, provided God is given nothing to do, and he always insisted that physics must rest upon metaphysics, and that metaphysics are divine. When the party broke up, they retired to their work, and somewhere or other in the house, well looked after but seldom seen, slept her little boy. The variety, the vigour of Cirey is most impressive; the imagination flits from room to room until it wearies, and fails even to reach the huge woods which shut in the domain, and the peasants whose labour supported it. What stands out in the end is the laboratory work. That the experiments were primitive, ill-directed, and unsuccessful did not trouble the investigators, and need not trouble us if we understand what they felt: they saw a new world opening in every direction and asking to be interpreted.

Madame du Châtelet was certainly a most remarkable creature—tiresome, but not too tiresome, and therefore an ideal mate for a very tiresome man. "Venus-Newton," Frederick of Prussia calls her, while Madame du Deffand insinuates that she was only Newton because she could not be Venus, and also accuses her of spending more on her dresses than on her underthings—gravest of charges that one woman of quality can bring against another. Voltaire adored her. She irritated him, but he also irritated her, which he enjoyed doing, and they were too affectionate and gay to subside into sourness. The relationship between them is very odd: it included emotion, and lasted twelve years, yet it cannot be classed among famous love-affairs. He was not a lover—he had all the ingredients that make up love, such as tenderness, pity, lust, selfishness, unselfishness, but they never combined: he was a chemical experiment, which, if love be the desired result, may be said to have failed. Madame du Châtelet was more normal, and it was she in the end who tired of the liaison, or rather tried for an additional one which ended in a ghastly catastrophe. With their tragedy I am not concerned here: at the moment I visualize them they were wholly in accord, and in accord with her husband, and now that the eighteenth century is no longer here to sneer or the nineteenth century to lecture, they are perhaps coming into their own. What kept them together was their interest in outside things—science, the drama, philosophy, art. They can never have said—at least I cannot imagine them ever saying—"What is this? What has brought us so close? We had better not inquire, lest it vanish away." They were held by their common interests, and so the nerve-storms that occasionally swept over them left no wreckage behind.

Neither he nor she obtained the prize for the Nature and Propagation of Fire. The judges complimented him on being a poet and her on being a lady, but appear to have been slightly shocked by the number of facts they mentioned, and divided the prize between three other competitors, who confined themselves to theory. In the opinion of modern authorities, the award ought to have been made to Madame du Châtelet: her essay is much the best.

2. Troublesome Molluscs

Thirty years have passed, and Voltaire, now at the height of his fame, holds a pair of scissors in one hand and a slug in the other. Let me repeat: in the one hand he holds a large brown slug, and in the other a pair of scissors. The slug is of Swiss extraction, and comes off one of his estates, where it has been eating the lettuces. *Ecrasez l'infame?* But no: he reserves it for another purpose. Looking into its face, he surveys the gloomy unresponsive snout which is all a slug offers, he compares it with the face of a snail, so much more piquant, and both with the face of a man. All three are different, but all are faces, and he does not know whether he trembles at the edge of a great discovery or of a joke. Beneath him are the blue waters of the Lake Leman, beyond them the walls of Mont Blanc, he stands with one foot in Genevan territory to escape the French, and the other in France, to be safe from the Swiss. He stands triumphant, all his possessions are around him, thousands of his trees grow, his contented peasantry work, his invalid cousin dozes, the bells of the church he built chime—and he cuts off the slug's head.

His niece, Madame Denis, keeps house for him now—or rather houses, for he possesses three. Awkward and torpid, Madame Denis holds at bay the ambassadors, savants, mountebanks, princesses, who have come from all over Europe to see her uncle. He is researching, he must not be disturbed. The scissors approach again, and a second slug is decapitated, and a third, until there are twelve. Nor does this conclude the gruesome tale: in a box hard by seethes a clot of headless snails. Voltaire surveys his victims with affability. He does not like the slugs much, but has great sympathy with the snails, he finds their courtships gallant if curious, their contours intelligent, and their taste delightful. Nevertheless, he continues to snip off their heads. It is Science. He is trying to find out whether heads grow again.

Once more, the results are conflicting. As in the case of fire, it is as if all nature combines to conceal the truth. Slugs behave differently to snails, which might be expected, but they also behave differently among themselves. All molluscs lack earnestness of purpose, so to speak—sometimes they die when their heads are removed, sometimes they grow fresh heads and live, sometimes they live without heads. Voltaire is delighted, but puzzled. On the whole, slugs grow new heads, snails don't; though snails when mutilated merely between the horns repair the damage more frequently than do slugs whose heads have been removed entirely. What may we deduce from this? Well—not much, and at the end of one of his solemn works (his *Questions on the Encyclopaedia*) he suddenly exclaims, "Retraction! I retract the scissors with which I cut off the snails' heads." For they had grown in 1772 but not in 1773, and what can one build on such creatures? He can only say that Nature is always admirable, and that what we call "Nature" is really an art that we have not yet understood. "All is art, from the Zodiac down to my snails."

To retract and to relinquish are, however, different things, and Voltaire had the happy idea of turning his failures into a joke, and fathering them on the unfortunate clergy. He invents a charming monk, Père l'Escarbotier, who is also a cook, and causes him to pour out his difficulties to Père Elie, who is a Doctor in Theology in another convent. The correspondence between the two is superb. "People used only to talk about Jesuits, but now they are completely occupied with snails," begins Père l'Escarbotier with modest pride, and he goes on to describe his own inconclusive experiments in the kitchen; he has often mentioned them in his sermons: "I could compare certain of my snails only to Saint Denis, who, after his head had been cut off, carried it tenderly for six miles in his arms." Père Elie receives this miracle in silence. In a second letter the reverend cook asks what, when the heads are cut off, happens to the souls. He replies to this readily enough: the question is simple, though it requires a different answer in the case of snails and of slugs, for the souls of snails are in their heads, but slugs have their souls anywhere. But a third letter, raising the question of a "vital germ," from which all species have developed, elicits a sharp rebuke; Père Elie reminds Père l'Escarbotier that "corruption is the mother of all things" and warns him against heretical speculations which lead to no good. "Adieu!" he concludes, on a kinder note. "May the snails who are set beneath you and the insects who accompany you ever bless your reverence." And there is a further conclusion as from the pen of Voltaire himself: "We must marvel and be silent." Gaily and charmingly he has turned his foolish scientific experiments into a humorous pamphlet: he has begun as a goose and ended as a mockingbird.

Since Madame du Châtelet's death he had taken science less seriously. He had never married, and his niece urged him towards the drama, if anywhere, for she enjoyed acting. Now and then the old ardour would break out: he would wonder whether Hannibal had really dissolved the Alps with hot vinegar, as the historian Livy reports, so he heated some vinegar and poured it on a piece of Mont Blanc. As soon as Mont Blanc adequately cracked, his mind was at rest, and he went on to other matters. The fact is that his seriousness was taking another direction: all his wit and wisdom were being marshalled for his struggle against the Church. He believed in God, he even built a church: but he loathed the Church, and the depth of his hatred appears in the extraordinary difficulties into which he got over sea-shells.

Sea-shells do not, to the outsider, seem more troublesome than other molluscs, but Voltaire regarded them from a very special point of view: they were traitors, who attempted to demonstrate the truth of revealed religion instead of advancing the cause of Liberty, as natural objects should. Had they remained in the sea, all would have been well, but straying from their proper element they appeared in large heaps in the middle of Touraine and elsewhere, or in fossil forms, or on the tops of mountains. Why, you may ask, did this disconcert Voltaire? Why, because it suggested that they had been left when the waters of the Flood subsided, so that Genesis was true. He could not allow this, and he set out with his usual energy and ingenuity to put shells in their places. He had not been trained by the Jesuits for nothing, and the arguments he brought forward are rather too conclusive to be convincing.

In the first place, he argued that the shells in question are not from the sea at all, but are either the shells of fresh-water oysters or the property of his old friends the snails. "In a rainy year, there are more snails in a space of thirty miles than there are men in the whole earth," and this being so, the deposits in Touraine and elsewhere can be easily accounted for. Then he argues that the shells were engendered spontaneously in the earth, "and grew just as stones do." A correspondent of his, a gentleman who had property near Chinon, had actually watched empty shells growing; twice in eighty years a heavy crop had been produced, they were microscopic at first, and gradually swelled and stuck against one another until they formed a soft stone, suitable for building; there were five or six species of these empty shells, and since the tenants and neighbours of the gentleman had seen them too, doubt was impossible. Indeed, we can all of us watch the process for ourselves, for the reason that the so-called Ammonite fossils vary in size: the curves of their spirals must obviously increase the longer they lie in the earth. And, finally, let us grant, for the sake of argument, that all the above arguments are false, and that the shells which have given such support to superstition really did originate in the sea. No matter—all is not lost: they can still be accounted for in three ways. Firstly, since so many of them are cockles, they may have dropped from the hats of Palmers who were going to the shrine of St. James at Compostella in the Middle Ages. Secondly, since so many are edible, they may be the debris of picnic parties. And thirdly, since so many of them are different, they may have come from the collections of dead conchologists. To this last argument—which leaves us almost more breathless than its companions—Voltaire returns more than once. He was vexed by the bones of a reindeer and of a hippopotamus which were found near Etampes. "Are we to conclude from this," he asks, "that the Nile and Lapland once shared the Orleans-Paris road?" Surely, it is simpler to suppose that the bones once adorned the cabinet of a connoisseur!

His anxiety over shells led him ever further than we should expect. He feared that if once a flood was admitted Noah's ark would come sailing in, and consequently had to ridicule all theories of the universe that emphasized water. There was the fish Oannes, who came out of the Euphrates to preach to the Babylonians. There was Thales, who thought that the stars lived on mist. There was Buffon, who ascribes mountains to the action of waves. There was Maillet, who deduced from a heap of shells at Cairo that Egypt had once been under the sea and the Egyptians fish. Voltaire mocks them all indiscriminately. "In spite of the present passion for genealogies, there are not many people who would claim descent from a turbot or a cod." Then the coral insects strike his eye, and seeing that they may give trouble he makes short work of their claims. They must not be allowed to build coral reefs, or the land will appear once to have been under the sea. "Certainly, one does find little insects in coral, but where does one not find little insects? Old walls are full of them, but no one supposes that they build the old walls. So is old cheese—but no one argues that the cheese has been made by the mites." One way and another, the sea is prevented from encroaching on human destiny; not even in the name of science may it cover the earth, lest when the waters decrease Mount Ararat should appear and our race again enter into bondage. Voltaire's attitude here is, in a cruder form, the attitude of certain unorthodox people today, who are disquieted by the work of Eddington and Jeans, because of the support for Christianity that may be extracted from it. He hated religion, having witnessed the misery it caused, and he was not detached enough to admit that because a thing is baneful it is not necessarily untrue. Indeed, he was not detached at all, and if we think he was we misread both him and his age; he loved freedom, not truth, so that when the coral insects appeared to be helping the Jesuits he used casuistry to discredit them. Never, never, if he could help it, should Noah's ark sail over the world again. And if he had lived today, and been told that in the opinion of many biologists all life, including human life, had a marine or intertidal origin, he would once more bring up his armoury and produce arguments which, alas! we should no longer find devastating. For Voltaire, today, would seem a much smaller figure than he was in the eighteenth century; we should admire his personality, fear his tongue, and adore his short stories, but dismiss his "serious" utterances as journalism.

Probably he could have been an eminent scientist if he liked —he was intelligent enough for anything, and while he was under Madame du Châtelet's influence he showed powers of application: his treatise on Newton proves this. But after her death he became desultory and a tease; his mistrust of theories led him to the theory that other people's conclusions must be wrong. He was hampered by his need of fun; both scientists and their pursuits can be irresistibly amusing, and Voltaire was not the man to check his own mirth. He came, he saw, he laughed, and the slugs and snails that might have led a serious anatomist towards the discovery of the pharyngeal ring, suggested instead a correspondence between two comic monks.

Nevertheless, he did science one good turn: he impressed the general public with her importance. This is all that a literary man can do for science, and perhaps only a literary man can do it. The expert scientist is too conscious of the difficulties of his subject; he knows that he can only communicate his discoveries to us by simplifying and therefore falsifying them, and that even when he can state a fact correctly we receive it incorrectly, because we cannot relate it to the thousands of other facts relevant. The literary man has no such misgivings. His imagination is touched by the infinite variety of the natural world; he reads books about it, skipping the statistics, he forgets most of what he does read, and perhaps he performs a few experiments in order to grasp the meaning of research. Then, in the course of his other activities, he writes about science, with a spurious lucidity that makes the expert smile. Spurious, but stimulating; the public does realize, from the remarks of such men as Lucretius, Voltaire, Charles Kingsley, Samuel Butler, Mr. Aldous Huxley, Mr. Gerald Heard, that something is happening. It does get a misty idea of the expanding empire of mankind.

"Certainly, one must admit that Nature is varied," said the traveller.

"Yes, Nature is like a bed of flowers, where—"

"Oh, never mind the bed of flowers!"

"She is," the secretary continued, "like an assemblage of blondes and of brunettes, whose tresses—"

"Oh, bother the blondes and brunettes!"

"Well, she is like a picture gallery, where the features—"

"No, no; Nature is like Nature; why introduce similes?"

"To amuse you!" the secretary replied.

"I don't want to be amused," said the traveller; "I want to learn!"

In this passage—it comes from his charming fantasy *Micromegas*—Voltaire neatly contrasts the literary man and the scientist. The literary man loves images, and as soon as he has found a vivid one, his interest in the truth it is supposed to illustrate is apt to cease. But the scientist knows that Nature is Nature. Voltaire himself was literary, yet he had enough sense of science to perceive his own limitations, and though he amuses us and is amused by hot iron and slugs, he has realized—perhaps through Madame du Châtelet—that the universe has not been created for our stylistic exercises. For what, then, has it been created? He cannot say; *"cultiver son jardin"* is a reaction, not a reply. But he could ask the question, he could cause others to ask it, and if "popular interest in science" has any importance (for my own part, I think it has immense importance), he must be honoured as an early popularizer.

1931

NOT LISTENING TO MUSIC

Listening to music is such a muddle that one scarcely knows how to start describing it. The first point to get clear in my own case is that during the greater part of every performance I do not attend. The nice sounds make me think of something else. I wool-gather most of the time, and am surprised that others don't. Professional critics can listen to a piece as consistently and as steadily as if they were reading a chapter in a novel. This seems to me an amazing feat, and probably they only achieve it through intellectual training; that is to say, they find in the music the equivalent of a plot; they are following the ground bass or expecting the theme to re-enter in the dominant, and so on, and this keeps them on the rails. But I fly off every minute: after a bar or two I think how musical I am, or of something smart I might have said in conversation; or I wonder what the composer—dead a couple of centuries—can be feeling as the flames on the altar still flicker up; or how soon an H.E. bomb would extinguish them. Not to mention more obvious distractions: the tilt of the soprano's chin or chins; the antics of the conductor, that impassioned beetle, especially when it is night time and he waves his shards; the affectation of the pianist when he takes a top note with difficulty, as if he too were a soprano; the backs of the chairs; the bumps on the ceiling; the extreme physical ugliness of the audience. A classic audience is surely the plainest collection of people anywhere assembled for any common purpose; contributing my quota, I have the right to point this out. Compare us with a gang of navvies or with an office staff, and you will be appalled. This, too, distracts me.

What do I hear during the intervals when I do attend? Two sorts of music. They melt into each other all the time, and are not easy to christen, but I will call one of them "music that reminds me of something," and the other "music itself." I used to be very fond of music that reminded me of something, and especially fond of Wagner. With Wagner I always knew where I was; he never let the fancy roam; he ordained that one phrase should recall the ring, another the sword, another the blameless fool and so on; he was as precise in his indications as an oriental dancer. Since he is a great poet, that did not matter, but I accepted his leitmotiv system much too reverently and forced it on to other composers whom it did not suit, such as Beethoven and Franck. I thought that music must be the better for having a meaning. I think so still, but am less clear as to what "a meaning" is. In those days it was either a non-musical object, such as a sword or a blameless fool, or a non-musical emotion, such as fear, lust, or resignation. When music reminded me of something which was not music, I supposed it was getting me somewhere. "How like Monet!" I thought when listening to Debussy, and "How like Debussy!" when looking at Monet. I translated sounds into colors, saw the piccolo as apple-green, and the trumpets as scarlet. The arts were to be enriched by taking in one another's washing.

I still listen to some music this way. For instance, the slow start of Beethoven's Seventh Symphony invokes a gray-green tapestry of hunting scenes, and the slow movements of his Fourth Piano Concerto (the dialogue between piano and orchestra) reminds me of the dialogue between Orpheus and the Furies in Gluck. The climax of the first movement of the Appassionata (the "più allegro") seems to me sexual, although I can detect no sex in the Kreutzer, nor have I come across anyone who could, except Tolstoy. That disappointing work, Brahms' Violin Concerto, promises me clear skies at the opening, and only when the violin has squealed up in the air for page after page is the promise falsified. Wolf's "Ganymed" does give me sky—stratosphere beyond stratosphere. In these cases and in many others music reminds me of something non-musical, and I fancy that to do so is part of its job. Only a purist would condemn all visual parallels, all emotional labelings, all programs.

Yet there is a danger. Music that reminds does open the door to that imp of the concert hall, inattention. To think of a gray-green tapestry is not very different from thinking of the backs of the chairs. We gather a superior wool from it, still we do wool-gather, and the sounds slip by blurred. The sounds! It is for them that we come, and the closer we can get up against them the better. So I do prefer "music itself" and listen to it and for it as far as possible. In this connection, I will try to analyze a mishap that has recently overtaken the Coriolanus Overture. I used to listen to the Coriolanus for "itself," conscious when it passed of something important and agitating, but not defining further. Now I learn that Wagner, endorsed by Sir Donald Tovey, has provided it with a Program: the opening bars indicate the hero's decision to destroy the Volscii, then a sweet tune for female influence, then the dotted-quaver-restlessness of indecision. This seems indisputable, and there is no doubt that this was, or was almost, Beethoven's intention. All the same, I have lost my Coriolanus. Its largeness and freedom have gone. The exquisite sounds have been hardened like a road that has been tarred for traffic. One has to go somewhere down them, and to pass through the same domestic crisis to the same military impasse, each time the overture is played.

Music is so very queer that an amateur is bound to get muddled when writing about it. It seems to be more "real" than anything, and to survive when the rest of civilization decays. In these days I am always thinking of it with relief. It can never be ruined or nationalized. So that the music which is untrammeled and untainted by reference is obviously the best sort of music to listen to; we get nearer the center of reality. Yet though it is untainted, it is never abstract; it is not like mathematics, even when it uses them. The Goldberg Variations, the last Beethoven Sonata, the Franck Quartet, the Schumann Piano Quintet and the Fourth Symphonies of Tchaikovsky and of Brahms certainly have a message. Though what on earth is it? I shall get tied up trying to say. There's an insistence in music—expressed largely through rhythm; there's a sense that it is trying to push across at us something which is neither an esthetic pattern nor a sermon. That's what I listen for specially.

So music that is itself seems on the whose better than music that reminds. And now to end with an important point: my own performances upon the piano. These grow worse yearly, but never will I give them up. For one thing, they compel me to attend—no wool-gathering or thinking myself clever here—and they drain off all non-musical matter. For another thing, they teach me a little about construction. I see what becomes of a phrase, how it is transformed or returned, sometimes bottom upward, and get some notion of the relation of keys. Playing Beethoven, as I generally do, I grow familiar with his tricks, his impatience, his sudden softness, his dropping of a tragic theme one semitone, his love, when tragic, for the key of C minor, and his aversion to the key of B major. This gives me a physical approach to Beethoven which cannot be gained through the slough of "appreciation." Even when people play as badly as I do, they should continue: it will help them to listen.

1939

WHAT I BELIEVE

I do not believe in Belief. But this is an age of faith, and there are so many militant creeds that, in self-defense, one has to formulate a creed of one's own.Tolerance, good temper and sympathy are no longer enough in a world which is rent by religious and racial persecution, in a world where ignorance rules, and science, who ought to have ruled, plays the subservient pimp. Tolerance, good temper and sympathy—they are what matter really, and if the human race is not to collapse they must come to the front before long. But for the moment they are not enough, their action is no stronger than a flower, battered beneath a military jack-boot. They want stiffening, even if the process coarsens them. Faith, to my mind, is a stiffening process, a sort of mental starch, which ought to be applied as sparingly as possible. I dislike the stuff. I do not believe in it, for its own sake, at all. Herein I probably differ from most people, who believe in Belief, and are only sorry they cannot swallow even more than they do. My law-givers are Erasmus and Montaigne, not Moses and St. Paul. My temple stands not upon Mount Moriah but in that Elysian Field where even the immoral are admitted. My motto is: "Lord, I disbelieve—help thou my unbelief."

I have, however, to live in an Age of Faith—the sort of epoch I used to hear praised when I was a boy. It is extremely unpleasant really. It is bloody in every sense of the word. And I have to keep my end up in it. Where do I start?

With personal relationships. Here is something comparatively solid in a world full of violence and cruelty. Not absolutely solid, for Psychology has split and shattered the idea of a "Person," and has shown that there is something incalculable in each of us, which may at any moment rise to the surface and destroy our normal balance. We don't know what we are like. We can't know what other people are like. How, then, can we put any trust in personal relationships, or cling to them in the gathering political storm? In theory we cannot. But in practice we can and do.

Though A is not unchangeably A or B unchangeably B, there can still be love and loyalty between the two. For the purpose of living one has to assume that the personality is solid, and the "self" is an entity, and to ignore all contrary evidence. And since to ignore evidence is one of the characteristics of faith, I certainly can proclaim that I believe in personal relationships.

Starting from them, I get a little order into the contemporary chaos. One must be fond of people and trust them if one is not to make a mess of life, and it is therefore essential that they should not let one down. They often do. The moral of which is that I must, myself, be as reliable as possible, and this I try to be. But reliability is not a matter of contract—that is the main difference between the world of personal relationships and the world of business relationships. It is a matter for the heart, which signs no documents. In other words, reliability is impossible unless there is a natural warmth. Most men possess this warmth, though they often have bad luck and get chilled. Most of them, even when they are politicians, *want* to keep faith. And one can, at all events, show one's own little light here, one's own poor little trembling flame, with the knowledge that it is not the only light that is shining in the darkness, and not the only one which the darkness does not comprehend. Personal relations are despised today. They are regarded as bourgeois luxuries, as products of a time of fair weather which is now past, and we are urged to get rid of them, and to dedicate ourselves to some movement or cause instead. I hate the idea of causes, and if I had to choose between betraying my country and betraying my friend, I hope I should have the guts to betray my country. Such a choice may scandalize the modern reader, and he may stretch out his patriotic hand to the telephone at once and ring up the police. It would not have shocked Dante, though. Dante places Brutus and Cassius in the lowest circle of Hell because they had chosen to betray their friend Julius Caesar rather than their country Rome. Probably one will not be asked to make such an agonizing choice. Still, there lies at the back of every creed something terrible and hard for which the worshipper may one day be required to suffer, and there is even a terror and a hardness in this creed of personal relationships, urbane and mild though it sounds. Love and loyalty to an individual can run counter to the claims of the State. When they do—down with the State, say I, which means that the State would down me.

This brings me along to Democracy, "even Love, the Beloved Republic, which feeds upon Freedom and lives." Democracy is not a Beloved Republic really, and never will be. But it is less hateful than other contemporary forms of government, and to that extent it deserves our support. It does start from the assumption that the individual is important, and that all types are needed to make a civilization. It does not divide its citizens into the bossers and the bossed—as an efficiency-regime tends to do. The people I admire most are those who are sensitive and want to create something or discover something, and do not see life in terms of power, and such people get more of a chance under a democracy than elsewhere. They found religions, great or small, or they produce literature and art, or they do disinterested scientific research, or they may be what is called "ordinary people," who are creative in their private lives, bring up their children decently, for instance, or help their neighbors. All these people need to express themselves; they cannot do so unless society allows them liberty to do so, and the society which allows them most liberty is a democracy.

Democracy has another merit. It allows criticism, and if there is not public criticism there are bound to be hushed-up scandals. That is why I believe in the Press, despite all its lies and vulgarity, and why I believe in Parliament. Parliament is often sneered at because it is a Talking Shop. I believe in it *because* it is a talking shop. I believe in the Private Member who makes himself a nuisance. He gets snubbed and is told that he is cranky or ill-informed, but he does expose abuses which would otherwise never have been mentioned, and very often an abuse gets put right just by being mentioned. Occasionally, too, a well-meaning public official starts losing his head in the cause of efficiency, and thinks himself God Almighty. Such officials are particularly frequent in the Home Office. Well, there will be questions about them in Parliament sooner or later, and then they will have to mind their steps. Whether Parliament is either a representative body or an efficient one is questionable, but I value it because it criticizes and talks, and because its chatter gets widely reported.

So Two Cheers for Democracy: one because it admits variety and two because it permits criticism. Two cheers are quite enough: there is no occasion to give three. Only Love the Beloved Republic deserves that.

What about Force, though? While we are trying to be sensitive and advanced and affectionate and tolerant, an unpleasant question pops up: does not all society rest upon force? If a government cannot count upon the police and the army, how can it hope to rule? And if an individual gets knocked on the head or sent to a labor camp, of what significance are his opinions?

This dilemma does not worry me as much as it does some. I realize that all society rests upon force. But all the great creative actions, all the decent human relations, occur during the intervals when force has not managed to come to the front. These intervals are what matter. I want them to be as frequent and as lengthy as possible, and I call them "civilization." Some people idealize force and pull it into the foreground and worship it, instead of keeping it in the background as long as possible. I think they make a mistake, and I think that their opposites, the mystics, err even more when they declare that force does not exist. I believe that it exists, and that one of our jobs is to prevent it from getting out of its box. It gets out sooner or later, and then it destroys us and all the lovely things which we have made. But it is not out all the time, for the fortunate reason that the strong are so stupid. Consider their conduct for a moment in the Niebelung's Ring. The giants there have the guns, or in other words the gold; but they do nothing with it, they do not realize that they are all-powerful, with the result that the catastrophe is delayed and the castle of Walhalla, insecure but glorious, fronts the storms. Fafnir, coiled round his hoard, grumbles and grunts; we can hear him under Europe today; the leaves of the wood already tremble, and the Bird calls its warnings uselessly. Fafnir will destroy us, but by a blessed dispensation he is stupid and slow, and creation goes on just outside the poisonous blast of his breath. The Nietzschean would hurry the monster up, the mystic would say he did not exist, but Wotan, wiser than either, hastens to create warriors before doom declares itself. The Valkyries are symbols not only of courage but of intelligence; they represent the human spirit snatching its opportunity while the going is good, and one of them even finds time to love. Brünnhilde's last song hymns the recurrence of love, and since it is the privilege of art to exaggerate, she goes even further, and proclaims the love which is eternally triumphant and feeds upon freedom, and lives.

So that is what I feel about force and violence. It is, alas! the ultimate reality on this earth, but it does not always get to the front. Some people call its absences "decadence"; I call them "civilization" and find in such interludes the chief justification for the human experiment. I look the other way until fate strikes me. Whether this is due to courage or to cowardice in my own case I cannot be sure. But I know that if men had not looked the other way in the past, nothing of any value would survive. The people I respect most behave as if they were immortal and as if society was eternal. Both assumptions are false: both of them must be accepted as true if we are to go on eating and working and loving, and are to keep open a few breathing holes for the human spirit. No millennium seems likely to descend upon humanity; no better and stronger League of Nations will be instituted; no form of Christianity and no alternative to Christianity will bring peace to the world or integrity to the individual; no "change of heart" will occur. And yet we need not despair, indeed, we cannot despair; the evidence of history shows us that men have always insisted on behaving creatively under the shadow of the sword; that they have done their artistic and scientific and domestic stuff for the sake of doing it, and that we had better follow their example under the shadow of the aeroplanes. Others, with more vision or courage than myself, see the salvation of humanity ahead, and will dismiss my conception of civilization as paltry, a sort of tip-and-run game. Certainly it is presumptuous to say that we *cannot* improve, and that Man, who has only been in power for a few thousand years, will never learn to make use of his power. All I mean is that, if people continue to kill one another as they do, the world cannot get better than it is, and that since there are more people than formerly, and their means for destroying one another superior, the world may well get worse. What is good in people—and consequently in the world—is their insistence on creation, their belief in friendship and loyalty for their own sakes; and though Violence remains and is, indeed, the major partner in this muddled establishment, I believe that creativeness remains too, and will always assume direction when violence sleeps. So, though I am not an optimist, I cannot agree with Sophocles that it were better never to have been born. And although, like Horace, I see no evidence that each batch of births is superior to the last, I leave the field open for the more complacent view. This is such a difficult moment to live in, one cannot help getting gloomy and also a bit rattled, and perhaps short-sighted.

In search of a refuge, we may perhaps turn to hero-worship. But here we shall get no help, in my opinion. Hero-worship is a dangerous vice, and one of the minor merits of a democracy is that it does not encourage it, or produce that unmanageable type of citizen known as the Great Man. It produces instead different kinds of small men—a much finer achievement. But people who cannot get interested in the variety of life, and cannot make up their own minds, get discontented over this, and they long for a hero to bow down before and to follow blindly. It is significant that a hero is an integral part of the authoritarian stock-in-trade today. An efficiency-regime cannot be run without a few heroes stuck about it to carry off the dullness—much as plums have to be put into a bad pudding to make it palatable. One hero at the top and a smaller one each side of him is a favorite arrangement, and the timid and the bored are comforted by the trinity, and, bowing down, feel exalted and strengthened.

No, I distrust Great Men. They produce a desert of uniformity around them and often a pool of blood too, and I always feel a little man's pleasure when they come a cropper. Every now and then one reads in the newspapers some such statement as: "The coup d'état appears to have failed, and Admiral Toma's whereabouts is at present unknown." Admiral Toma had probably every qualification for being a Great Man—an iron will, personal magnetism, dash, flair, sexlessness—but fate was against him, so he retires to unknown whereabouts instead of parading history with his peers. He fails with a completeness which no artist and no lover can experience, because with them the process of creation is itself an achievement, whereas with him the only possible achievement is success.

I believe in aristocracy, though—if that is the right word, and if a democrat may use it. Not an aristocracy of power, based upon rank and influence, but an aristocracy of the sensitive, the considerate and the plucky. Its members are to be found in all nations and classes, and all through the ages, and there is a secret understanding between them when they meet. They represent the true human tradition, the one permanent victory of our queer race over cruelty and chaos. Thousands of them perish in obscurity, a few are great names. They are sensitive for others as well as for themselves, they are considerate without being fussy, their pluck is not swankiness but the power to endure, and they can take a joke. I give no examples—it is risky to do that—but the reader may as well consider whether this is the type of person he would like to meet and to be, and whether (going farther with me) he would prefer that this type should *not* be an ascetic one. I am against asceticism myself. I am with the old Scotsman who wanted less chastity and more delicacy. I do not feel that my aristocrats are a real aristocracy if they thwart their bodies, since bodies are the instruments through which we register and enjoy the world. Still, I do not insist. This is not a major point. It is clearly possible to be sensitive, considerate and plucky and yet be an ascetic too, if anyone possesses the first three qualities, I will let him in! On they go—an invincible army, yet not a victorious one. The aristocrats, the elect, the chosen, the Best People—all the words that describe them are false, and all attempts to organize them fail. Again and again Authority, seeing their value, has tried to net them and to utilize them as the Egyptian Priesthood or the Christian Church or the Chinese Civil Service or the Group Movement, or some other worthy stunt. But they slip through the net and are gone; when the door is shut, they are no longer in the room; their temple, as one of them remarked, is the Holiness of the Heart's Affection, and their kingdom, though they never possess it, is the wide-open world.

With this type of person knocking about, and constantly crossing one's path if one has eyes to see or hands to feel, the experiment of earthly life cannot be dismissed as a failure. But it may well be hailed as a tragedy, the tragedy being that no device has been found by which these private decencies can be transmitted to public affairs. As soon as people have power they go crooked and sometimes dotty as well, because the possession of power lifts them into a region where normal honesty never pays. For instance, the man who is selling newspapers outside the Houses of Parliament can safely leave his papers to go for a drink and his cap beside them: anyone who takes a paper is sure to drop a copper into the cap. But the men who are inside the Houses of Parliament—they cannot trust one another like that, still less can the Government they compose trust other governments. No caps upon the pavement here, but suspicion, treachery and armaments. The more highly public life is organized the lower does its morality sink; the nations of today behave to each other worse than they ever did in the past, they cheat, rob, bully and bluff, make war without notice, and kill as many women and children as possible; whereas primitive tribes were at all events restrained by taboos. It is a humiliating outlook—though the greater the darkness, the brighter shine the little lights, reassuring one another, signalling: "Well, at all events, I'm still here. I don't like it very much, but how are you?" Unquenchable lights of my aristocracy! Signals of the invincible army! "Come along—anyway, let's have a good time while we can." I think they signal that too.

The Saviour of the future—if ever he comes—will not preach a new Gospel. He will merely utilize my aristocracy, he will make effective the good will and the good temper which are already existing. In other words, he will introduce a new technique. In economics, we are told that if there was a new technique of distribution, there need be no poverty, and people would not starve in one place while crops were being ploughed under in another. A similar change is needed in the sphere of morals and politics. The desire for it is by no means new; it was expressed, for example, in theological terms by Jacopone da Todi over six hundred years ago. "*Ordina questo amore, O tu che m'ami,*" he said; "O thou who lovest me—set this love in order." His prayer was not granted, and I do not myself believe that it ever will be, but here, and not through a change of heart, is our probable route. Not by becoming better, but by ordering and distributing his native goodness, will Man shut up Force into its box, and so gain time to explore the universe and to set his mark upon it worthily. At present he only explores it at odd moments, when Force is looking the other way, and his divine creativeness appears as a trivial by-product, to be scrapped as soon as the drums beat and the bombers hum.

Such a change, claim the orthodox, can only be made by Christianity, and will be made by it in God's good time: man always has failed and always will fail to organize his own goodness, and it is presumptuous of him to try. This claim—solemn as it is—leaves me cold. I cannot believe that Christianity will ever cope with the present worldwide mess, and I think that such influence as it retains in modern society is due to the money behind it, rather than to its spiritual appeal. It was a spiritual force once, but the indwelling spirit will have to be restated if it is to calm the waters again, and probably restated in a non-Christian form. Naturally a lot of people, and people who are not only good but able and intelligent, will disagree here; they will vehemently deny that Christianity has failed, or they will argue that its failure proceeds from the wickedness of men, and really proves its ultimate success. They have Faith, with a large F. My faith has a very small one, and I only intrude it because these are strenuous and serious days, and one likes to say what one thinks while speech is comparatively free: it may not be free much longer.

The above are the reflections of an individualist and a liberal who has found liberalism crumbling beneath him and at first felt ashamed. Then, looking around, he decided there was no special reason for shame, since other people, whatever they felt, were equally insecure. And as for individualism—there seems no way of getting off this, even if one wanted to. The dictator-hero can grind down his citizens till they are all alike, but he cannot melt them into a single man. That is beyond his power. He can order them to merge, he can incite them to mass-antics, but they are obliged to be born separately, and to die separately, and, owing to these unavoidable termini, will always be running off the totalitarian rails. The memory of birth and the expectation of death always lurk within the human being, making him separate from his fellows and consequently capable of intercourse with them. Naked I came into the world, naked I shall go out of it! And a very good thing too, for it reminds me that I am naked under my shirt, whatever its color.

1939

Virginia Woolf

PERHAPS NO ENGLISH WRITER ever grew up as surrounded by books, writers, and the affluence that makes culture possible as Virginia Woolf. At the time of her birth (in London in 1882) her father, Leslie Stephen, was already distinguished as a philosopher, critic, and editor of the *Cornhill Magazine*. His first wife had been Thackeray's youngest daughter; his second, Virginia's mother, was descended from French nobility. Meredith, Hardy, and Henry James were his close friends, as was James Russell Lowell, who accepted the invitation to be Virginia's godfather by sending along some verses that expressed the wish that "the child would be/ A sample of heredity." Later that same year Leslie Stephen was named editor of the *Dictionary of National Biography*, and it was in the presence of that enormous undertaking that Virginia was educated. Instead of being sent to school, she was simply turned loose in her father's library, and the breadth of the knowledge she gained therein reveals itself in nearly all her essays.

Books, though, were not the whole of her education, and for the rest one must look to St. Ives in Cornwall, where the Stephen family went for its summer holidays. There, close by the sea, Virginia and the other Stephen children, Thoby, Vanessa, and Adrian—along with the children from their mother's first marriage—spent many happy days picnicking, boating, and playing games. In *To the Lighthouse* (1927) Virginia Woolf describes their summers in Cornwall with great fidelity.

When Sir Leslie died in 1904, the four Stephen children gave up the house at Hyde Park Gate and moved to 46 Gordon Square, Bloomsbury. Soon Thoby's friends, Lytton Strachey and Clive Bell, started coming around to carry on the discussions they had begun at Cambridge under the name of the "Midnight Society." And thus began what has since been known as the "Bloomsbury Group," by no means a formal organization, but merely a gathering of friends who believed (as their Cambridge mentor, G. E. Moore, had declared in his *Principia Ethica*) that the appreciation of beauty and the need for personal relationships were man's supreme endeavors.

After Thoby died of typhoid in Greece in 1906 and Vanessa married Clive Bell a year later, Virginia and Adrian moved to Fitzroy Square, a short distance away, and the Thursday night meetings followed them. New friends began coming—among them the art critic Roger Fry, the economist John Maynard Keynes, and E. M. Forster—until, by the late nineteen-twenties, the group was so famous that the word Bloomsbury had become synonymous with high brow. Nor was it always used as a compliment; D. H. Lawrence called the "Bloomsberries" gilded youth, beetles that stung like scorpions.

In 1912 Virginia Stephen married Leonard Woolf, a socialist and political writer who had been one of Thoby's friends at Cambridge, and three years later she published her first novel, *The Voyage Out.* Then, in 1917, with no other intention than that of printing a few short works by themselves and their friends, purely for the fun of it, the Woolfs bought a hand printing press and set it up in the dining room of their house in Richmond. The first book they produced contained two stories, one by Virginia and the other by Leonard; a little later they published *Prelude* by Katherine Mansfield and *Poems 1919* by T. S. Eliot. What had started out as a lark suddenly became a successful business, and over the years that followed The Hogarth Press became famous as a publisher of new writers. Undoubtedly, the Woolfs made their greatest mistake as editors when they refused to publish Joyce's *Ulysses.*

In 1919 they bought the cottage Monks House in the village of Rodmell, near the River Ouse, in Sussex, and there they spent their weekends and holidays for the next twenty-two years. In March 1941, in a state of depression brought on both by the war and the fear that she might lose her mind and be a burden on her husband, Virginia Woolf committed suicide by drowning herself in the Ouse. Later, her husband revealed that she had suffered several nervous breakdowns earlier in her life, going back as far as her mother's death in 1895.

Along with Joyce and Proust, Virginia Woolf is one of the great innovators of the modern novel, directing the reader's attention away from a sequence of outward actions and toward the complex inner lives of her characters. In her most successful novels—*Jacob's Room* (1922), *Mrs. Dalloway* (1925), *To the Lighthouse* (1927), *The Waves* (1931), and *Between the Acts* (published posthumously in 1941)—almost nothing happens on the surface of her characters' lives. Instead, the action all takes place in their heads, in their responses both to each other and to the objects they are surrounded by. Time, also, changes: the chronological time of outward actions—in which morning is separated from night by a sequence of events or "actions"—is replaced by the *real* time of an alert consciousness; morning to night becomes a sequence of impressions, intuitions, memories, anticipations. In short, the conflicts between the characters all take place within their sensibilities, and because of that, the novels make large demands on the reader's perceptions.

However difficult and annoying her novels may be, as an essayist Virginia Woolf is always perfectly lucid. Seldom does she abandon her father's advice "to write in the fewest possible words, as clearly as possible, exactly what one meant." Moreover, she obviously benefited from the more than two hundred book reviews she wrote for the *Times Literary Supplement* from 1905 until a few years before her death. And yet she was never a formal, systematic critic, but rather a common reader, personal and subjective, who read "for his own pleasure rather than to impart knowledge or correct the opinions of others." And one notices that the books she loved the best and wrote the most engagingly about were not especially the classics, but all those memoirs, letters, biographies, and autobiographies of the obscure, all those "rubbish-heaps," as she put it, of "vanished moments and forgotten lives told in faltering and feeble accents. . . ." For Virginia Woolf was a novelist even when she was writing essays, and it made little difference to her if her characters came from real life or the pages of a book. All she wanted was to illuminate those lives, make them stand before us in all their vitality and confusion. Nothing else really mattered to her. "If one wishes to better the world," she once wrote, "one must, paradoxically enough, withdraw and spend more and more time fashioning one's sentences to perfection in solitude."

PROFESSIONS FOR WOMEN *

When your secretary invited me to come here, she told me that your Society is concerned with the employment of women and she suggested that I might tell you something about my own professional experiences. It is true I am a woman; it is true I am employed; but what professional experiences have I had? It is difficult to say. My profession is literature; and in that profession there are fewer experiences for women than in any other, with the exception of the stage—fewer, I mean, that are peculiar to women. For the road was cut many years ago—by Fanny Burney, by Aphra Behn, by Harriet Martineau, by Jane Austen, by George Eliot—many famous women, and many more unknown and forgotten, have been before me, making the path smooth, and regulating my steps. Thus, when I came to write, there were very few material obstacles in my way. Writing was a reputable and harmless occupation. The family peace was not broken by the scratching of a pen. No demand was made upon the family purse. For ten and sixpence one can buy paper enough to write all the plays of Shakespeare—if one has a mind that way. Pianos and models, Paris, Vienna and Berlin, masters and mistresses, are not needed by a writer. The cheapness of writing paper is, of course, the reason why women have succeeded as writers before they have succeeded in the other professions.

But to tell you my story—it is a simple one. You have only got to figure to yourselves a girl in a bedroom with a pen in her hand. She had only to move that pen from left to right—from ten o'clock to one. Then it occurred to her to do what is simple and cheap enough after all—to slip a few of those pages into an envelope, fix a penny stamp in the corner, and drop the envelope into the red box at the corner. It was thus that I became a journalist; and my effort was rewarded on the first day

* A paper read to The Women's Service League.

of the following month—a very glorious day it was for me—by a letter from an editor containing a cheque for one pound ten shillings and sixpence. But to show you how little I deserve to be called a professional woman, how little I know of the struggles and difficulties of such lives, I have to admit that instead of spending that sum upon bread and butter, rent, shoes and stockings, or butcher's bills, I went out and bought a cat—a beautiful cat, a Persian cat, which very soon involved me in bitter disputes with my neighbours.

What could be easier than to write articles and to buy Persian cats with the profits? But wait a moment. Articles have to be about something. Mine, I seem to remember, was about a novel by a famous man. And while I was writing this review, I discovered that if I were going to review books I should need to do battle with a certain phantom. And the phantom was a woman, and when I came to know her better I called her after the heroine of a famous poem, The Angel in the House. It was she who used to come between me and my paper when I was writing reviews. It was she who bothered me and wasted my time and so tormented me that at last I killed her. You who come of a younger and happier generation may not have heard of her—you may not know what I mean by the Angel in the House. I will describe her as shortly as I can. She was intensely sympathetic. She was immensely charming. She was utterly unselfish. She excelled in the difficult arts of family life. She sacrificed herself daily. If there was chicken, she took the leg; if there was a draught she sat in it—in short she was so constituted that she never had a mind or a wish of her own, but preferred to sympathize always with the minds and wishes of others. Above all—I need not say it—she was pure. Her purity was supposed to be her chief beauty—her blushes, her great grace. In those days—the last of Queen Victoria—every house had its Angel. And when I came to write I encountered her with the very first words. The shadow of her wings fell on my page; I heard the rustling of her skirts in the room. Directly, that is to say, I took my pen in hand to review that novel by a famous man, she slipped behind me and whispered: "My dear, you are a young woman. You are writing about a book that has been written by a man. Be sympathetic; be tender; flatter; deceive;

use all the arts and wiles of our sex. Never let anybody guess that you have a mind of your own. Above all, be pure." And she made as if to guide my pen. I now record the one act for which I take some credit to myself, though the credit rightly belongs to some excellent ancestors of mine who left me a certain sum of money—shall we say five hundred pounds a year?—so that it was not necessary for me to depend solely on charm for my living. I turned upon her and caught her by the throat. I did my best to kill her. My excuse, if I were to be had up in a court of law, would be that I acted in self-defence. Had I not killed her she would have killed me. She would have plucked the heart out of my writing. For, as I found, directly I put pen to paper, you cannot review even a novel without having a mind of your own, without expressing what you think to be the truth about human relations, morality, sex. And all these questions, according to the Angel in the House, cannot be dealt with freely and openly by women; they must charm, they must conciliate, they must—to put it bluntly—tell lies if they are to succeed. Thus, whenever I felt the shadow of her wing or the radiance of her halo upon my page, I took up the inkpot and flung it at her. She died hard. Her fictitious nature was of great assistance to her. It is far harder to kill a phantom than a reality. She was always creeping back when I thought I had despatched her. Though I flatter myself that I killed her in the end, the struggle was severe; it took much time that had better have been spent upon learning Greek grammar; or in roaming the world in search of adventures. But it was a real experience; it was an experience that was bound to befall all women writers at that time. Killing the Angel in the House was part of the occupation of a woman writer.

But to continue my story. The Angel was dead; what then remained? You may say that what remained was a simple and common object—a young woman in a bedroom with an inkpot. In other words, now that she had rid herself of falsehood, that young woman had only to be herself. Ah, but what is "herself"? I mean, what is a woman? I assure you, I do not know. I do not believe that you know. I do not believe that anybody can know until she has expressed herself in all the arts and professions open to human skill. That indeed is one of the reasons why I have come here—out of respect for you, who are in process of showing us by your experiments what a woman is, who are in process of providing us, by your failures and successes, with that extremely important piece of information.

But to continue the story of my professional experiences. I made one pound ten and six by my first review; and I bought a Persian cat with the proceeds. Then I grew ambitious. A Persian cat is all very well, I said; but a Persian cat is not enough. I must have a motor car. And it was thus that I became a novelist —for it is a very strange thing that people will give you a motor car if you will tell them a story. It is a still stranger thing that there is nothing so delightful in the world as telling stories. It is far pleasanter than writing reviews of famous novels. And yet, if I am to obey your secretary and tell you my professional experiences as a novelist, I must tell you about a very strange experience that befell me as a novelist. And to understand it you must try to imagine a novelist's state of mind. I hope I am not giving away professional secrets if I say that a novelist's chief desire is to be as unconscious as possible. He has to induce in himself a state of perpetual lethargy. He wants life to proceed with the utmost quiet and regularity. He wants to see the same faces, to read the same books, to do the same things day after day, month after month, while he is writing, so that nothing may break the illusion in which he is living—so that nothing may disturb or disquiet the mysterious nosings about, feelings round, darts, dashes and sudden discoveries of that very shy and illusive spirit, the imagination. I suspect that this state is the same both for men and women. Be that as it may, I want you to imagine me writing a novel in a state of trance. I want you to figure to yourselves a girl sitting with a pen in her hand, which for minutes, and indeed for hours, she never dips into the inkpot. The image that comes to my mind when I think of this girl is the image of a fisherman lying sunk in dreams on the verge of a deep lake with a rod held out over the water. She was letting her imagination sweep unchecked round every rock and cranny of the world that lies submerged in the depths of our unconscious being. Now came the experience, the experience that I believe to be far commoner with women writers than with men. The line raced through the girl's fingers. Her imagination had rushed away. It had sought the pools, the depths, the dark places where the largest fish slumber. And then there was a smash. There was an explosion. There was foam and confusion. The imagination had dashed itself against something hard. The girl was roused from her dream. She was indeed in a state of the most acute and difficult distress. To speak without figure she had thought of something, something about the body, about the passions which it was unfitting for her as a woman to say. Men, her reason told her, would be shocked. The consciousness of what men will say of a woman who speaks the truth about her passions had roused her from her artist's state of unconsciousness. She could write no more. The trance was over. Her imagination could work no longer. This I believe to be a very common experience with women writers—they are impeded by the extreme conventionality of the other sex. For though men sensibly allow themselves great freedom in these respects, I doubt that they realize or can control the extreme severity with which they condemn such freedom in women.

These then were two very genuine experiences of my own. These were two of the adventures of my professional life. The first—killing the Angel in the House—I think I solved. She died. But the second, telling the truth about my own experiences as a body, I do not think I solved. I doubt that any woman has solved it yet. The obstacles against her are still immensely powerful—and yet they are very difficult to define. Outwardly, what is simpler than to write books? Outwardly, what obstacles are there for a woman rather than for a man? Inwardly, I think, the case is very different; she has still many ghosts to fight, many prejudices to overcome. Indeed it will be a long time still, I think, before a woman can sit down to write a book without finding a phantom to be slain, a rock to be dashed against. And if this is so in literature, the freest of all professions for women, how is it in the new professions which you are now for the first time entering?

Those are the questions that I should like, had I time, to ask you. And indeed, if I have laid stress upon these professional experiences of mine, it is because I believe that they are, though in different forms, yours also. Even when the path is nominally open—when there is nothing to prevent a woman from being a doctor, a lawyer, a civil servant—there are many phantoms and obstacles, as I believe, looming in her way. To discuss and define them is I think of great value and importance; for thus only can the labour be shared, the difficulties be solved. But besides this, it is necessary also to discuss the ends and the aims for which we are fighting, for which we are doing battle with these formidable obstacles. Those aims cannot be taken for granted; they must be perpetually questioned and examined. The whole position, as I see it—here in this hall surrounded by women practising for the first time in history I know not how many different professions—is one of extraordinary interest and importance. You have won rooms of your own in the house hitherto exclusively owned by men. You are able, though not without great labour and effort, to pay the rent. You are earning your five hundred pounds a year. But this freedom is only a beginning; the room is your own, but it is still bare. It has to be furnished; it has to be decorated; it has to be shared. How are you going to furnish it, how are you going to decorate it? With whom are you going to share it, and upon what terms? These, I think are questions of the utmost importance and interest. For the first time in history you are able to ask them; for the first time you are able to decide for yourselves what the answers should be. Willingly would I stay and discuss those questions and answers—but not tonight. My time is up; and I must cease.

1931

HOW SHOULD ONE READ A BOOK? *

In the first place, I want to emphasize the note of interrogation at the end of my title. Even if I could answer the question for myself, the answer would apply only to me and not to you. The only advice, indeed, that one person can give another about

* A paper read at a school.

reading is to take no advice, to follow your own instincts, to use your own reason, to come to your own conclusions. If this is agreed between us, then I feel at liberty to put forward a few ideas and suggestions because you will not allow them to fetter that independence which is the most important quality that a reader can possess. After all, what laws can be laid down about books? The battle of Waterloo was certainly fought on a certain day; but is *Hamlet* a better play than *Lear*? Nobody can say. Each must decide that question of himself. To admit authorities, however heavily furred and gowned, into our libraries and let them tell us how to read, what to read, what value to place upon what we read, is to destroy the spirit of freedom which is the breath of those sanctuaries. Everywhere else we may be bound by laws and conventions—there we have none.

But to enjoy freedom, if the platitude is pardonable, we have of course to control ourselves. We must not squander our powers, helplessly and ignorantly, squirting half the house in order to water a single rose-bush; we must train them, exactly and powerfully, here on the very spot. This, it may be, is one of the first difficulties that faces us in a library. What is "the very spot"? There may well seem to be nothing but a conglomeration and huddle of confusion. Poems and novels, histories and memoirs, dictionaries and blue-books; books written in all languages by men and women of all tempers, races, and ages jostle each other on the shelf. And outside the donkey brays, the women gossip at the pump, the colts gallop across the fields. Where are we to begin? How are we to bring order into this multitudinous chaos and so get the deepest and widest pleasure from what we read?

It is simple enough to say that since books have classes—fiction, biography, poetry—we should separate them and take from each what is right that each should give us. Yet few people ask from books what books can give us. Most commonly we come to books with blurred and divided minds, asking of fiction that it shall be true, of poetry that it shall be false, of biography that it shall be flattering, of history that it shall enforce our own prejudices. If we could banish all such preconceptions when we read, that would be an admirable beginning. Do not dictate to your author; try to become him. Be his fellow-worker and accomplice. If you hang back, and reserve and criticize at first, you are preventing yourself from getting the fullest possible value from what you read. But if you open your mind as widely as possible, then signs and hints of almost imperceptible fineness, from the twist and turn of the first sentences, will bring you into the presence of a human being unlike any other. Steep yourself in this, acquaint yourself with this, and soon you will find that your author is giving you, or attempting to give you, something far more definite. The thirty-two chapters of a novel—if we consider how to read a novel first—are an attempt to make something as formed and controlled as a building: but words are more impalpable than bricks; reading is a longer and more complicated process than seeing. Perhaps the quickest way to understand the elements of what a novelist is doing is not to read, but to write; to make your own experiment with the dangers and difficulties of words. Recall, then, some event that has left a distinct impression on you—how at the corner of the street, perhaps, you passed two people talking. A tree shook; an electric light danced; the tone of the talk was comic, but also tragic; a whole vision, an entire conception, seemed contained in that moment.

But when you attempt to reconstruct it in words, you will find that it breaks into a thousand conflicting impressions. Some must be subdued; others emphasized; in the process you will lose, probably, all grasp upon the emotion itself. Then turn from your blurred and littered pages to the opening pages of some great novelist—Defoe, Jane Austen, Hardy. Now you will be better able to appreciate their mastery. It is not merely that we are in the presence of a different person—Defoe, Jane Austen, or Thomas Hardy—but that we are living in a different world. Here, in *Robinson Crusoe*, we are trudging a plain highroad; one thing happens after another; the fact and the order of the fact is enough. But if the open air and adventure mean everything to Defoe they mean nothing to Jane Austen. Hers is the drawing-room, and people talking, and by the many mirrors of their talk revealing their characters. And if, when we have accustomed ourselves to the drawing-room and its reflections, we turn to Hardy, we are once more spun round. The moors are round us and the stars are above our heads. The other side of the mind is now exposed—the dark side that comes uppermost in solitude, not the light side that shows in company. Our relations are not towards people, but towards Nature and destiny. Yet different as these worlds are, each is consistent with itself. The maker of each is careful to observe the laws of his own perspective, and however great a strain they may put upon us they will never confuse us, as lesser writers so frequently do, by introducing two different kinds of reality into the same book. Thus to go from one great novelist to another—from Jane Austen to Hardy, from Peacock to Trollope, from Scott to Meredith—is to be wrenched and uprooted; to be thrown this way and then that. To read a novel is a difficult and complex art. You must be capable not only of great fineness of perception, but of great boldness of imagination if you are going to make use of all that the novelist—the great artist—gives you.

But a glance at the heterogeneous company on the shelf will show you that writers are very seldom "great artists"; far more often a book makes no claim to be a work of art at all. These biographies and autobiographies, for example, lives of great men, of men long dead and forgotten, that stand cheek by jowl with the novels and poems, are we to refuse to read them because they are not "art"? Or shall we read them, but read them in a different way, with a different aim? Shall we read them in the first place to satisfy that curiosity which possesses us sometimes when in the evening we linger in front of a house where the lights are lit and the blinds not yet drawn, and each floor of the house shows us a different section of human life in being? Then we are consumed with curiosity about the lives of these people—the servants gossiping, the gentlemen dining, the girl dressing for a party, the old woman at the window with her knitting. Who are they, what are they, what are their names, their occupations, their thoughts, and adventures?

Biographies and memoirs answer such questions, light up innumerable such houses; they show us people going about their daily affairs, toiling, failing, succeeding, eating, hating, loving, until they die. And sometimes as we watch, the house fades and the iron railings vanish and we are out at sea; we are hunting, sailing, fighting; we are among savages and soldiers; we are taking part in great campaigns. Or if we like to stay here in England, in London, still the scene changes; the street narrows; the house becomes small, cramped, diamond-paned, and malodorous. We see a poet, Donne, driven from such a house because the walls were so thin that when the children cried their voices cut through them. We can follow him, through the paths that lie in the pages of books, to Twickenham; to Lady Bedford's Park, a famous meeting-ground for nobles and poets; and then turn our steps to Wilton, the great house under the downs, and hear Sidney read the *Arcadia* to his sister; and ramble among the very marshes and see the very herons that figure in that famous romance; and then again travel north with that other Lady Pembroke, Anne Clifford, to her wild moors, or plunge into the city and control our merriment at the sight of Gabriel Harvey in his black velvet suit arguing about poetry with Spenser. Nothing is more fascinating than to grope and stumble in the alternate darkness and splendor of Elizabethan London. But there is no staying there. The Temples and the Swifts, the Harleys and the St. Johns beckon us on; hour upon hour can be spent disentangling their quarrels and deciphering their characters; and when we tire of them we can stroll on, past a lady in black wearing diamonds, to Samuel Johnson and Goldsmith and Garrick; or cross the channel, if we like, and meet Voltaire and Diderot, Madame du Deffand; and so back to England and Twickenham —how certain places repeat themselves and certain names!— where Lady Bedford had her Park once and Pope lived later, to Walpole's home at Strawberry Hill. But Walpole introduces us to such a swarm of new acquaintances, there are so many houses to visit and bells to ring that we may well hesitate for a moment, on the Miss Berrys' doorstep, for example, when behold, up comes Thackeray; he is the friend of the woman whom Walpole loved; so that merely by going from friend to friend, from garden to garden, from house to house, we have passed from one end of English literature to another and wake to find ourselves here again in the present, if we can so differentiate this moment from all that have gone before. This, then, is one of the ways in which we can read these lives and letters; we can make them light up the many windows of the past; we can watch the famous dead in their familiar habits and fancy sometimes that we are very close and can surprise their secrets, and sometimes we may pull out a play or a poem that they have written and see whether it reads differently in the presence of the author. But this again rouses other questions. How far, we must ask ourselves, is a book influenced by its writer's life—how far is it safe to let the man interpret the writer? How far shall we resist or give way to the sympathies and antipathies that the man himself rouses in us—so sensitive are words, so receptive of the character of the author? These are questions that press upon us when we read lives and letters, and we must answer them for ourselves, for nothing can be more fatal than to be guided by the preferences of others in a matter so personal.

But also we can read such books with another aim, not to throw light on literature, not to become familiar with famous people, but to refresh and exercise our own creative powers. Is there not an open window on the right hand of the bookcase? How delightful to stop reading and look out! How stimulating the scene is, in its unconsciousness, its irrelevance, its perpetual movement—the colts galloping round the field, the woman filling her pail at the well, the donkey throwing back his head and emitting his long, acrid moan. The greater part of any library is nothing but the record of such fleeting moments in the lives of men, women, and donkeys. Every literature, as it grows old, has its rubbish-heap, its record of vanished moments and forgotten lives told in faltering and feeble accents that have perished. But if you give yourself up to the delight of rubbish-reading you will be surprised, indeed you will be overcome, by the relics of human life that have been cast out to molder. It may be one letter—but what a vision it gives! It may be a few sentences—but what vistas they suggest! Sometimes a whole story will come together with such beautiful humor and pathos and completeness that it seems as if a great novelist had been at work, yet it is only an old actor, Tate Wilkinson, remembering the strange story of Captain Jones; it is only a young subaltern serving under Arthur Wellesley and falling in love with a pretty girl at Lisbon; it is only Maria Allen letting fall her sewing in the empty drawing-room and sighing how she wishes she had taken Dr. Burney's good advice and had never eloped wth her Rishy. None of this has any value; it is negligible in the extreme; yet how absorbing it is now and again to go through the rubbish-heaps and find rings and scissors and broken noses buried in the huge past and try to piece them together while the colt gallops round the field, the woman fills her pail at the well, and the donkey brays.

But we tire of rubbish-reading in the long run. We tire of searching for what is needed to complete the half-truth which is all that the Wilkinsons, the Bunburys, and the Maria Allens are able to offer us. They had not the artist's power of mastering and eliminating; they could not tell the whole truth even about their own lives; they have disfigured the story that might have been so shapely. Facts are all that they can offer us, and facts are a very inferior form of fiction. Thus the desire grows upon us to have done with half-statements and approximations; to cease from searching out the minute shades of human character, to enjoy the greater abstractness, the purer truth of fiction. Thus we create the mood, intense and generalized, unaware of detail, but stressed by some regular, recurrent beat, whose natural expression is poetry; and that is the time to read poetry when we are almost able to write it.

> Western wind, when wilt thou blow?
> The small rain down can rain.
> Christ, if my love were in my arms,
> And I in my bed again!

The impact of poetry is so hard and direct that for the moment there is no other sensation except that of the poem itself. What profound depths we visit then—how sudden and complete is our immersion! There is nothing here to catch hold of; nothing to stay us in our flight. The illusion of fiction is gradual; its effects are prepared; but who when they read these four lines stops to ask who wrote them, or conjures up the thought of Donne's house or Sidney's secretary; or enmeshes them in the intricacy of the past and the succession of generations? The poet is always our contemporary. Our being for the moment is centered and constricted, as in any violent shock of personal emotion. Afterwards, it is true, the sensation begins to spread in wider rings through our minds; remoter senses are reached; these begin to sound and to comment and we are aware of echoes and reflections. The intensity of poetry covers an immense range of emotion. We have only to compare the force and directness of

I shall fall like a tree, and find my grave,
 Only remembering that I grieve,

with the wavering modulation of

Minutes are numbered by the fall of sands,
As by an hour glass; the span of time
Doth waste us to our graves, and we look on it;
An age of pleasure, revelled out, comes home
At last, and ends in sorrow; but the life,
Weary of riot, numbers every sand,
Wailing in sighs, until the last drop down,
So to conclude calamity in rest,

or place the meditative calm of

 whether we be young or old,
Our destiny, our being's heart and home,
Is with infinitude, and only there;
With hope it is, hope that can never die,
Effort, and expectation, and desire,
And something evermore about to be,

beside the complete and inexhaustible loveliness of

The moving Moon went up the sky,
And no where did abide:
Softly she was going up,
And a star or two beside–

or the splendid fantasy of

And the woodland haunter
Shall not cease to saunter
 When, far down some glade,
Of the great world's burning,
One soft flame upturning
Seems, to his discerning,
 Crocus in the shade.

to bethink us of the varied art of the poet; his power to make us at once actors and spectators; his power to run his hand into character as if it were a glove, and be Falstaff or Lear; his power to condense, to widen, to state, once and for ever.

"We have only to compare"—with those words the cat is out of the bag, and the true complexity of reading is admitted. The first process, to receive impressions with the utmost understanding, is only half the process of reading; it must be completed, if we are to get the whole pleasure from a book, by another. We must pass judgment upon these multitudinous impressions; we must make of these fleeting shapes one that is hard and lasting. But not directly. Wait for the dust of reading to settle; for the conflict and the questioning to die down; walk, talk, pull the dead petals from a rose, or fall asleep. Then suddenly without our willing it, for it is thus that Nature undertakes these transitions, the book will return, but differently. It will float to the top of the mind as a whole. And the book as a whole is different from the book received currently in separate phrases. Details now fit themselves into their places. We see the shape from start to finish; it is a barn, a pig-sty, or a cathedral. Now then we can compare book with book as we compare building with building. But this act of comparison means that our attitude has changed; we are no longer the friends of the writer, but his judges; and just as we cannot be too sympathetic as friends, so as judges we cannot be too severe. Are they not criminals, books that have wasted our time and sympathy; are they not the most insidious enemies of society, corrupters, defilers, the writers of false books, faked books, books that fill the air with decay and disease? Let us then be severe in our judgments; let us compare each book with the greatest of its kind. There they hang in the mind the shapes of the books we have read solidified by the judgments we have passed on them—*Robinson Crusoe, Emma, The Return of the Native*. Compare the novels with these—even the latest and least of novels has a right to be judged with the best. And so with poetry—when the intoxication of rhythm has died down and the splendor of words has faded a visionary shape will return to us and this must be compared with *Lear*, with *Phèdre*, with *The Prelude*; or if not with these, with whatever is the best or seems to us to be the best in its own kind. And we may be sure that the newness of new poetry and fiction is its most superficial quality and that we have only to alter slightly, not to recast, the standards by which we have judged the old.

It would be foolish, then, to pretend that the second part of reading, to judge, to compare, is as simple as the first—to open the mind wide to the fast flocking of innumerable impressions. To continue reading without the book before you, to hold one shadow-shape against another, to have read widely enough and with enough understanding to make such comparisons alive and illuminating—that is difficult; it is still more difficult to press further and to say, "Not only is the book of this sort, but it is of this value; here it fails; here it succeeds; this is bad; that is good." To carry out this part of a reader's duty needs such imagination, insight, and learning that it is hard to conceive any one mind sufficiently endowed; impossible for the most self-confident to find more than the seeds of such powers in himself. Would it not be wiser, then, to remit this part of reading and to allow the critics, the gowned and furred authorities of the library, to decide the question of the book's absolute value for us? Yet how impossible! We may stress the value of sympathy; we may try to sink our own identity as we read. But we know that we cannot sympathize wholly or immerse ourselves wholly; there is always a demon in us who whispers, "I hate, I love," and we cannot silence him. Indeed, it is precisely because we hate and we love that our relation with the poets and novelists is so intimate that we find the presence of another person intolerable. And even if the results are abhorrent and our judgments are wrong, still our taste, the nerve of sensation that sends shocks through us, is our chief illuminant; we learn through feeling; we cannot suppress our own idiosyncrasy without impoverishing it. But as time goes on perhaps we can train our taste; perhaps we can make it submit to some control. When it has fed greedily and lavishly upon books of all sorts—poetry, fiction, history, biography—and has stopped reading and looked for long spaces upon the variety, the incongruity of the living world, we shall find that it is changing a little; it is not so greedy, it is more reflective. It will begin to bring us not merely judgments on particular books, but it will tell us that there is a quality common to certain books. Listen, it will say, what shall we call *this*? And it will read us perhaps

Lear and then perhaps the *Agamemnon* in order to bring out that common quality. Thus, with our taste to guide us, we shall venture beyond the particular book in search of qualities that group books together; we shall give them names and thus frame a rule that brings order into our perceptions. We shall gain a further and a rarer pleasure from that discrimination. But as a rule only lives when it is perpetually broken by contact with the books themselves—nothing is easier and more stultifying than to make rules which exist out of touch with facts, in a vacuum—now at last, in order to steady ourselves in this difficult attempt, it may be well to turn to the very rare writers who are able to enlighten us upon literature as an art. Coleridge and Dryden and Johnson, in their considered criticism, the poets and novelists themselves in their unconsidered sayings, are often surprisingly relevant; they light up and solidify the vague ideas that have been tumbling in the misty depths of our minds. But they are only able to help us if we come to them laden with questions and suggestions won honestly in the course of our own reading. They can do nothing for us if we herd ourselves under their authority and lie down like sheep in the shade of a hedge. We can only understand their ruling when it comes in conflict with our own and vanquishes it.

If this is so, if to read a book as it should be read calls for the rarest qualities of imagination, insight, and judgment, you may perhaps conclude that literature is a very complex art and that it is unlikely that we shall be able, even after a lifetime of reading, to make any valuable contribution to its criticism. We must remain readers; we shall not put on the further glory that belongs to those rare beings who are also critics. But still we have our responsibilities as readers and even our importance. The standards we raise and the judgments we pass steal into the air and become part of the atmosphere which writers breathe as they work. An influence is created which tells upon them even if it never finds its way into print. And that influence, if it were well instructed, vigorous and individual and sincere, might be of great value now when criticism is necessarily in abeyance; when books pass in review like the procession in a shooting-gallery, and the critic has only one second in which to load and aim and shoot and may well be pardoned if he mistakes rabbits for tigers, eagles for barndoor fowls, or misses altogether and wastes his shot upon some peaceful cow grazing in a further field. If behind the erratic gunfire of the press the author felt that there was another kind of criticism, the opinion of people reading for the love of reading, slowly and unprofessionally, and judging with great sympathy and yet with great severity, might this not improve the quality of his work? And if by our means books were to become stronger, richer, and more varied, that would be an end worth reaching.

Yet who reads to bring about an end however desirable? Are there not some pursuits that we practice because they are good in themselves, and some pleasures that are final? And is not this among them? I have sometimes dreamt, at least, that when the Day of Judgment dawns and the great conquerors and lawyers and statesmen come to receive their rewards—their crowns, their laurels, their names carved indelibly upon imperishable marble—the Almighty will turn to Peter and will say, not without a certain envy when He sees us coming with our books under our arms, "Look, these need no reward. We have nothing to give them here. They have loved reading."

1932

THE DEATH OF THE MOTH

Moths that fly by day are not properly to be called moths; they do not excite that pleasant sense of dark autumn nights and ivy-blossom which the commonest yellow-underwing asleep in the shadow of the curtain never fails to rouse in us. They are hybrid creatures, neither gay like butterflies nor sombre like their own species. Nevertheless the present specimen, with his narrow hay-coloured wings, fringed with a tassel of the same colour, seemed to be content with life. It was a pleasant morning, mid-September, mild, benignant, yet with a keener breath than that of the summer months. The plough was already scoring the field opposite the window, and where the share had been, the earth was pressed flat and gleamed with moisture. Such vigour came rolling in from the fields and the down beyond that it was difficult to keep the eyes strictly turned upon the book. The rooks too were keeping one of their annual festivities; soaring round the tree tops until it looked as if a vast net with thousands of black knots in it had been cast up into the air; which, after a few moments sank slowly down upon the trees until every twig seemed to have a knot at the end of it. Then, suddenly, the net would be thrown into the air again in a wider circle this time, with the utmost clamour and vociferation, as though to be thrown into the air and settle slowly down upon the tree tops were a tremendously exciting experience.

The same energy which inspired the rooks, the ploughmen, the horses, and even, it seemed, the lean bare-backed downs, sent the moth fluttering from side to side of his square of the window-pane. One could not help watching him. One was, indeed, conscious of a queer feeling of pity for him. The possibilities of pleasure seemed that morning so enormous and so various that to have only a moth's part in life, and a day moth's at that, appeared a hard fate, and his zest in enjoying his meagre opportunities to the full, pathetic. He flew vigorously to one corner of his compartment, and, after waiting there a second, flew across to the other. What remained for him but to fly to a third corner and then to a fourth? That was all he could do, in spite of the size of the downs, the width of the sky, the far-off smoke of houses, and the romantic voice, now and then, of a steamer out at sea. What he could do he did. Watching him, it seemed as if a fibre, very thin but pure, of the enormous energy of the world had been thrust into his frail and diminutive body. As often as he crossed the pane, I could fancy that a thread of vital light became visible. He was little or nothing but life.

Yet, because he was so small, and so simple a form of the energy that was rolling in at the open window and driving its way through so many narrow and intricate corridors in my own brain and in those of other human beings, there was something marvelous as well as pathetic about him. It was as if someone had taken a tiny bead of pure life and decking it as lightly as possible with down and feathers, had set it dancing and zigzagging to show us the true nature of life. Thus displayed one could not get over the strangeness of it. One is apt to forget all about life, seeing it humped and bossed and garnished and cumbered so that it has to move with the greatest circumspection and dignity. Again, the thought of all that life might have been had he been born in any other shape caused one to view his simple activities with a kind of pity.

After a time, tired by his dancing apparently, he settled on the window ledge in the sun, and, the queer spectacle being at an end, I forgot about him. Then, looking up, my eye was caught by him. He was trying to resume his dancing, but seemed either so stiff or so awkward that he could only flutter to the bottom of the window-pane; and when he tried to fly across it he failed. Being intent on other matters I watched these futile attempts for a time without thinking, unconsciously waiting for him to resume his flight, as one waits for a machine, that has stopped momentarily, to start again without considering the reason of its failure. After perhaps a seventh attempt he slipped from the wooden ledge and fell, fluttering his wings, onto his back on the widow sill. The helplessness of his attitude roused me. It flashed upon me he was in difficulties; he could no longer raise himself; his legs struggled vainly. But, as I stretched out a pencil, meaning to help him to right himself, it came over me that the failure and awkwardness were the approach of death. I laid the pencil down again.

The legs agitated themselves once more. I looked as if for the enemy against which he struggled. I looked out of doors. What had happened there? Presumably it was midday, and work in the fields had stopped. Stillness and quiet had replaced the previous animation. The birds had taken themselves off to feed in the brooks. The horses stood still. Yet the power was there all the same, massed outside indifferent, impersonal, not attending to anything in particular. Somehow it was opposed to the little hay-coloured moth. It was useless to try to do anything. One could only watch the extraordinary efforts made by those tiny legs against an oncoming doom which could, had it chosen, have submerged an entire city, not merely a city, but masses of human beings; nothing, I knew had any chance against death. Nevertheless after a pause of exhaustion the legs fluttered again. It was superb this last protest, and so frantic that he succeeded at last in righting himself. One's sympathies, of course, were all on the side of life. Also, when there was nobody to care or to know, this gigantic effort on the part of an insignificant little moth, against a power of such magnitude, to retain what no one else valued or desired to keep, moved one strangely. Again, somehow, one saw life, a pure bead. I lifted the pencil again, useless though I knew it to be. But even as I did so, the unmistakable tokens of death showed themselves. The body relaxed, and instantly grew stiff. The struggle was over. The insignificant little creature now knew death. As I looked at the dead moth, this minute wayside triumph of so great a force over so mean an antagonist filled me with wonder. Just as life had been strange a few minutes before, so death was now as strange. The moth having righted himself now lay most decently and uncomplainingly composed. O yes, he seemed to say, death is stronger than I am.

1942

A SKETCH OF THE PAST

Two days ago—Sunday 16th April 1939 to be precise—Nessa said that if I did not start writing my memoirs I should soon be too old. I should be eighty-five, and should have forgotten—witness the unhappy case of Lady Strachey. As it happens that I am sick of writing Roger's life, perhaps I will spend two or three mornings making a sketch.* There are several difficulties. In the first place, the enormous number of things I can remember; in the second, the number of different ways in which memoirs can be written. As a great memoir reader, I know many different ways.

* VW was at work on *Roger Fry: A Biography*.

But if I begin to go through them and to analyse them and their merits and faults, the mornings—I cannot take more than two or three at most—will be gone. So without stopping to choose my way, in the sure and certain knowledge that it will find itself—or if not it will not matter—I begin: the first memory.

This was of red and purple flowers on a black ground—my mother's dress; and she was sitting either in a train or in an omnibus, and I was on her lap. I therefore saw the flowers she was wearing very close; and can still see purple and red and blue, I think, against the black; they must have been anemones, I suppose. Perhaps we were going to St Ives; more probably, for from the light it must have been evening, we were coming back to London. But it is more convenient artistically to suppose that we were going to St Ives, for that will lead to my other memory, which also seems to be my first memory, and in fact it is the most important of all my memories. If life has a base that it stands upon, if it is a bowl that one fills and fills and fills—then my bowl without a doubt stands upon this memory. It is of lying half asleep, half awake, in bed in the nursery at St Ives. It is of hearing the waves breaking, one, two, one, two, and sending a splash of water over the beach; and then breaking, one, two, one, two, behind a yellow blind. It is of hearing the blind draw its little acorn across the floor as the wind blew the blind out. It is of lying and hearing this splash and seeing this light, and feeling, it is almost impossible that I should be here; of feeling the purest ecstasy I can conceive.

I could spend hours trying to write that as it should be written, in order to give the feeling which is even at this moment very strong in me. But I should fail (unless I had some wonderful luck); I dare say I should only succeed in having the luck if I had begun by describing Virginia herself.

Here I come to one of the memoir writer's difficulties—one of the reasons why, though I read so many, so many are failures. They leave out the person to whom things happened. The reason is that it is so difficult to describe any human being. So they say: "This is what happened"; but they do not say what the person was like to whom it happened. And the events mean very little unless we know first to whom they happened. Who was I then? Adeline Virginia Stephen, the second daughter of Leslie and

Julia Prinsep Stephen, born on 25th January 1882, descended from a great many people, some famous, others obscure; born into a large connection, born not of rich parents, but of well-to-do parents, born into a very communicative, literate, letter writing, visiting, articulate, late nineteenth century world; so that I could if I liked to take the trouble, write a great deal here not only about my mother and father but about uncles and aunts, cousins and friends. But I do not know how much of this, or what part of this, made me feel what I felt in the nursery at St Ives. I do not know how far I differ from other people. That is another memoir writer's difficulty. Yet to describe oneself truly one must have some standard of comparison; was I clever, stupid, good looking, ugly, passionate, cold—? Owing partly to the fact that I was never at school, never competed in any way with children of my own age, I have never been able to compare my gifts and defects with other people's. But of course there was one external reason for the intensity of this first impression: the impression of the waves and the acorn on the blind; the feeling, as I describe it sometimes to myself, of lying in a grape and seeing through a film of semi-transparent yellow—it was due partly to the many months we spent in London. The change of nursery was a great change. And there was the long train journey; and the excitement. I remember the dark; the lights; the stir of the going up to bed.

But to fix my mind upon the nursery—it had a balcony; there was a partition, but it joined the balcony of my father's and mother's bedroom. My mother would come out onto her balcony in a white dressing gown. There were passion flowers growing on the wall; they were great starry blossoms, with purple streaks, and large green buds, part empty, part full.

If I were a painter I should paint these first impressions in pale yellow, silver, and green. There was the pale yellow blind; the green sea; and the silver of the passion flowers. I should make a picture that was globular; semi-transparent. I should make a picture of curved petals; of shells; of things that were semi-transparent; I should make curved shapes, showing the light through, but not giving a clear outline. Everything would be large and dim; and what was seen would at the same time be heard; sounds would come through this petal or leaf—sounds indistinguishable from sights. Sound and sight seem to make equal parts of these first impressions. When I think of the early morning in bed I also hear the caw of rooks falling from a great height. The sound seems to fall through an elastic, gummy air; which holds it up; which prevents it from being sharp and distinct. The quality of the air above Talland House seemed to suspend sound, to let it sink down slowly, as if it were caught in a blue gummy veil. The rooks cawing is part of the waves breaking—one, two, one, two—and the splash as the wave drew back and then it gathered again, and I lay there half awake, half asleep, drawing in such ecstasy as I cannot describe.

The next memory—all these colour-and-sound memories hang together at St Ives—was much more robust; it was highly sensual. It was later. It still makes me feel warm; as if everything were ripe; humming; sunny; smelling so many smells at once; and all making a whole that even now makes me stop—as I stopped then going down to the beach; I stopped at the top to look down at the gardens. They were sunk beneath the road. The apples were on a level with one's head. The gardens gave off a murmur of bees; the apples were red and gold; there were also pink flowers; and grey and silver leaves. The buzz, the croon, the smell, all seemed to press voluptuously against some membrane; not to burst it; but to hum round one such a complete rapture of pleasure that I stopped, smelt; looked. But again I cannot describe that rapture. It was rapture rather than ecstasy.

The strength of these pictures—but sight was always then so much mixed with sound that picture is not the right word—the strength anyhow of these impressions makes me again digress. Those moments—in the nursery, on the road to the beach—can still be more real than the present moment. This I have just tested. For I got up and crossed the garden. Percy was digging the asparagus bed; Louie was shaking a mat in front of the bedroom door. But I was seeing them through the sight I saw here—the nursery and the road to the beach. At times I can go back to St Ives more completely than I can this morning. I can reach a state where I seem to be watching things happen as if I were there. That is, I suppose, that my memory supplies what I had forgotten, so that it seems as if it were happening independently, though I am really making it happen. In certain favourable moods, memories—what one has forgotten—come to the top. Now if this is so, is it not possible—I often wonder—that things we have felt with great intensity have an existence independent of our minds; are in fact still in existence? And if so, will it not be possible, in time, that some device will be invented by which we can tap them? I see it—the past—as an avenue lying behind; a long ribbon of scenes, emotions. There at the end of the avenue still, are the garden and the nursery. Instead of remembering here a scene and there a sound, I shall fit a plug into the wall; and listen in to the past. I shall turn up August 1890. I feel that strong emotion must leave its trace; and it is only a question of discovering how we can get ourselves again attached to it, so that we shall be able to live our lives through from the start.

But the peculiarity of these two strong memories is that each was very simple. I am hardly aware of myself, but only of the sensation. I am only the container of the feeling of ecstasy, of the feeling of rapture. Perhaps this is characteristic of all childhood memories; perhaps it accounts for their strength. Later we add to feelings much that makes them more complex; and therefore less strong; or if not less strong, less isolated, less complete. But instead of analysing this, here is an instance of what I mean—my feeling about the looking-glass in the hall.

There was a small looking-glass in the hall at Talland House. It had, I remember, a ledge with a brush on it. By standing on tiptoe I could see my face in the glass. When I was six or seven perhaps, I got into the habit of looking at my face in the glass. But I only did this if I was sure that I was alone. I was ashamed of it. A strong feeling of guilt seemed naturally attached to it. But why was this so? One obvious reason occurs to me—Vanessa and I were both what was called tomboys; that is, we played cricket, scrambled over rocks, climbed trees, were said not to care for clothes and so on. Perhaps therefore to have been found looking in the glass would have been against our tomboy code. But I think that my feeling of shame went a great deal deeper. I am almost inclined to drag in my grandfather—Sir James, who once smoked a cigar, liked it, and so threw away his cigar and never smoked another. I am almost inclined to think that I inherited a streak of the puritan, of the Clapham Sect. At any rate, the looking-glass shame has lasted all my life, long after the tomboy phase was over.

I cannot now powder my nose in public. Everything to do with dress—to be fitted, to come into a room wearing a new dress—still frightens me; at least makes me shy, self-conscious, uncomfortable. "Oh to be able to run, like Julian Morrell, all over the garden in a new dress", I thought not many years ago at Garsington; when Julian undid a parcel and put on a new dress and scampered round and round like a hare. Yet femininity was very strong in our family. We were famous for our beauty—my mother's beauty, Stella's beauty, gave me as early as I can remember, pride and pleasure. What then gave me this feeling of shame, unless it were that I inherited some opposite instinct? My father was spartan, ascetic, puritanical. He had I think no feeling for pictures; no ear for music; no sense of the sound of words. This leads me to think that my—I would say "our" if I knew enough about Vanessa, Thoby and Adrian—but how little we know even about brothers and sisters—this leads me to think that my natural love for beauty was checked by some ancestral dread. Yet this did not prevent me from feeling ecstasies and raptures spontaneously and intensely and without any shame or the least sense of guilt, so long as they were disconnected with my own body. I thus detect another element in the shame which I had in being caught looking at myself in the glass in the hall. I must have been ashamed or afraid of my own body. Another memory, also of the hall, may help to explain this. There was a slab outside the dining room door for standing dishes upon. Once when I was very small Gerald Duckworth lifted me onto this, and as I sat there he began to explore my body. I can remember the feel of his hand going under my clothes; going firmly and steadily lower and lower. I remember how I hoped that he would stop; how I stiffened and wriggled as his hand approached my private parts. But it did not stop. His hand explored my private parts too. I remember resenting, disliking it—what is the word for so dumb and mixed a feeling? It must have been strong, since I still recall it. This seems to show that a feeling about certain parts of the body; how they must not be touched; how it is wrong to allow them to be touched; must be instinctive. It proves that Virginia Stephen was not born on the 25th January 1882, but was born many thousands of years ago; and had from the very first to encounter instincts already acquired by thousands of ancestresses in the past.

And this throws light not merely on my own case, but upon the problem that I touched on the first page; why it is so difficult to give any account of the person to whom things happen. The person is evidently immensely complicated. Witness the incident of the looking-glass. Though I have done my best to explain why I was ashamed of looking at my own face I have only been able to discover some possible reasons; there may be others; I do not suppose that I have got at the truth; yet this is a simple incident; and it happened to me personally; and I have no motive for lying about it. In spite of all this, people write what they call "lives" of other people; that is, they collect a number of events, and leave the person to whom it happened unknown. Let me add a dream; for it may refer to the incident of the looking-glass. I dreamt that I was looking in a glass when a horrible face—the face of an animal—suddenly showed over my shoulder. I cannot be sure if this was a dream, or if it happened. Was I looking in the glass one day when something in the background moved, and seemed to me alive? I cannot be sure. But I have always remembered the other face in the glass, whether it was a dream or a fact, and that it frightened me.

These then are some of my first memories. But of course as an account of my life they are misleading, because the things one does not remember are as important; perhaps they are more important. If I could remember one whole day I should be able to describe, superficially at least, what life was like as a child. Unfortunately, one only remembers what is exceptional. And there seems to be no reason why one thing is exceptional and another not. Why have I forgotten so many things that must have been, one would have thought, more memorable than what I do remember? Why remember the hum of bees in the garden going down to the beach, and forget completely being thrown naked by father into the sea? (Mrs Swanwick says she saw that happen.)

This leads to a digression, which perhaps may explain a little of my own psychology; even of other people's. Often when I have been writing one of my so-called novels I have been baffled by this same problem; that is, how to describe what I call in my private shorthand—"non-being". Every day includes much more non-being than being. Yesterday for example, Tuesday the 18th of April was [as] it happened a good day; above the average in "being". It was fine; I enjoyed writing these first pages; my head was relieved of the pressure of writing about Roger; I walked over Mount Misery and along the river; and save that the tide was out, the country, which I notice very closely always, was coloured and shaded as I like—there were the willows, I remember, all plumy and soft green and purple against the blue. I also read Chaucer with pleasure; and began a book—the memoirs of Madame de la Fayette—which interested me. These separate moments of being were however embedded in many more moments of non-being. I have already forgotten what Leonard and I talked about at lunch; and at tea; although it was a good day the goodness was embedded in a kind of nondescript cotton wool. This is always so. A great part of every day is not lived consciously. One walks, eats, sees things, deals with what has to be done; the broken vacuum cleaner; ordering dinner; writing orders to Mabel; washing; cooking dinner; bookbinding. When it is a bad day the proportion of non-being is much larger. I had a slight temperature last week; almost the whole day was non-being. The real novelist can somehow convey both sorts of being. I think Jane Austen can; and Trollope; perhaps Thackeray and Dickens and Tolstoy. I have never been able to do both. I tried—in *Night and Day*; and in *The Years*. But I will leave the literary side alone for the moment.

As a child then, my days, just as they do now, contained a large proportion of this cotton wool, this non-being. Week after week passed at St Ives and nothing made any dint upon me. Then, for no reason that I know about, there was a sudden violent shock; something happened so violently that I have remembered it all my life. I will give a few instances. The first: I was fighting with Thoby on the lawn. We were pommelling each other with our fists. Just as I raised my fist to hit him, I felt: why hurt another person? I dropped my hand instantly, and stood there, and let him beat me. I remember the feeling. It was a feeling of hopeless sadness. It was as if I became aware of something terrible; and of my own powerlessness. I slunk off alone, feeling horribly depressed. The second instance was also in the garden at St Ives. I was looking at the flower bed by the front door; "That is the whole", I said. I was looking at a plant with a spread of leaves; and it seemed suddenly plain that the flower itself was a part of the earth; that a ring enclosed what was the flower; and that was the real flower; part earth; part flower. It was a thought I put away as being likely to be very useful to me later. The third case was also at St Ives. Some people called Valpy had been staying at St Ives, and had left. We were waiting at dinner one night, when somehow I overheard my father or my mother say that Mr Valpy had killed himself. The next thing I remember is being in the garden at night and walking on the path by the apple tree. It seemed to me that the apple tree was connected with the horror of Mr Valpy's suicide. I could not pass it. I stood there looking at the grey-green creases of the bark—it was a moonlit night—in a trance of horror. I seemed to be dragged down, hopelessly, into some pit of absolute despair from which I could not escape. My body seemed paralysed.

These are three instances of exceptional moments. I often tell them over, or rather they come to the surface unexpectedly. But now that for the first time I have written them down, I realise something that I have never realised before. Two of these moments ended in a state of despair. The other ended, on the contrary, in a state of satisfaction. When I said about the flower "That is the whole", I felt that I had made a discovery. I felt that I had put away in my mind something that I should go back [to], to turn over and explore. It strikes me now that this was a profound difference. It was the difference in the first place between despair and satisfaction. This difference I think arose from the fact that I was quite unable to deal with the pain of discovering that people hurt each other; that a man I had seen had killed himself. The sense of horror held me powerless. But in the case of the flower I found a reason; and was thus able to deal with the sensation. I was not powerless. I was conscious—if only at a distance—that I should in time explain it. I do not know if I was older when I saw the flower than I was when I had the other two experiences. I only know that many of these exceptional moments brought with them a peculiar horror and a physical collapse; they seemed dominant; myself passive. This suggests that as one gets older one has a greater power through reason to provide an explanation; and that this explanation blunts the sledge-hammer force of the blow. I think this is true, because though I still have the peculiarity that I receive these sudden shocks, they are now always welcome; after the first surprise, I always feel instantly that they are particularly valuable. And so I go on to suppose that the shock-receiving capacity is what makes me a writer. I hazard the explanation that a shock is at once in my case followed by the desire to explain it. I feel that I have had a blow; but it is not, as I thought as a child, simply a blow from an enemy hidden behind the cotton wool of daily life; it is or will become a revelation of some order; it is a token of some real thing behind appearances; and I make it real by putting it into words. It is only by putting it into words that I make it whole; this wholeness means that it has lost its power to hurt me; it gives me, perhaps because by doing so I take away the pain, a great delight to put the severed parts together. Perhaps this is the strongest pleasure known to me. It is the rapture I get when in writing I seem to be discovering what belongs to what; making a scene come right; making a character come together. From this I reach what I might call a philosophy; at any rate it is a constant idea of mine; that behind the cotton wool is hidden a pattern; that we—I mean all human beings—are connected with this; that the whole world is a work of art; that we are parts of the work of art. *Hamlet* or a Beethoven quartet is the truth about this vast mass that we call the world. But there is no Shakespeare, there is no Beethoven; certainly and emphatically there is no God; we are the words; we are the music; we are the thing itself. And I see this when I have a shock.

This intuition of mine—it is so instinctive that it seems given to me, not made by me—has certainly given its scale to my life ever since I saw the flower in the bed by the front door at St Ives. If I were painting myself I should have to find some—rod, shall I say—something that would stand for the conception. It proves that one's life is not confined to one's body and what one says and does; one is living all the time in relation to certain background rods or conceptions. Mine is that there is a pattern hid behind the cotton wool. And this conception affects me every day. I prove this, now, by spending the morning writing, when I might be walking, running a shop, or learning to do something that will be useful if war comes. I feel that by writing I am doing what is far more necessary than anything else.

All artists I suppose feel something like this. It is one of the obscure elements in life that has never been much discussed. It is left out in almost all biographies and autobiographies, even of artists. Why did Dickens spend his entire life writing stories? What was his conception? I bring in Dickens partly because I am reading *Nicholas Nickleby* at the moment; also partly because it struck me, on my walk yesterday, that these moments of being of mine were scaffolding in the background; were the invisible and silent part of my life as a child. But in the foreground there were of course people; and these people were very like characters in Dickens. They were caricatures; they were very simple; they were immensely alive. They could be made with three strokes of the pen, if I could do it. Dickens owes his astonishing power to make characters alive to the fact that he saw them as a child sees them; as I saw Mr Wolstenholme; C. B. Clarke, and Mr Gibbs.

I name these three people because they all died when I was a child. Therefore they have never been altered. I see them exactly as I saw them then. Mr Wolstenholme was a very old gentleman who came every summer to stay with us. He was brown; he had a beard and very small eyes in fat cheeks; and he fitted into a brown wicker beehive chair as if it had been his nest. He used to sit in this beehive chair smoking and reading. He had only one characteristic—that when he ate plum tart he spurted the juice through his nose so that it made a purple stain on his grey moustache. This seemed enough to cause us perpetual delight. We called him "The Wooly One". By way of shading him a little I remember that we had to be kind to him because he was not happy at home; that he was very poor, yet once gave Thoby half a crown; that he had a son who was drowned in Australia; and I know too that he was a great mathematician. He never said a word all the time I knew him. But he still seems to me a complete character; and whenever I think of him I begin to laugh.

Mr Gibbs was perhaps less simple. He wore a tie ring; had a bald, benevolent head; was dry; neat; precise; and had folds of skin under his chin. He made father groan—"why can't you go—why can't you go?" And he gave Vanessa and myself two ermine skins, with slits down the middle out of which poured endless wealth—streams of silver. I also remember him lying in bed, dying; husky; in a night shirt; and showing us drawings by Retzsch. The character of Mr Gibbs also seems to me complete and amuses me very much.

As for C. B. Clarke, he was an old botanist; and he said to my father "All you young botanists like Osmunda." He had an aunt aged eighty who went for a walking tour in the New Forest. That is all—that is all I have to say about these three old gentlemen. But how real they were! How we laughed at them! What an immense part they played in our lives!

One more caricature comes into my mind; though pity entered into this one. I am thinking of Justine Nonon. She was immensely old. Little hairs sprouted on her long bony chin. She was a hunchback; and walked like a spider, feeling her way with her long dry fingers from one chair to another. Most of the time she sat in the arm-chair beside the fire. I used to sit on her knee; and her knee jogged up and down; and she sang in a hoarse cracked voice "Ron ron ron—et plon plon plon—" and then her knee gave and I was tumbled onto the floor. She was French; she had been with the Thackerays. She only came to us on visits. She lived by herself at Shepherd's Bush; and used to bring Adrian a glass jar of honey. I got the notion that she was extremely poor; and it made me uncomfortable that she brought this honey, because I felt she did it by way of making her visit acceptable. She said too: "I have come in my carriage and pair" —which meant the red omnibus. For this too I pitied her; also because she began to wheeze; and the nurses said she would not live much longer; and soon she died. That is all I know about her; but I remember her as if she were a completely real person, with nothing left out, like the three old men.

1939

D. H. Lawrence

DAVID HERBERT LAWRENCE was born in the village of Eastwood in Nottinghamshire on September 11, 1885. His father was an uneducated miner with strong, uninhibited instincts, and his mother, who had been a schoolteacher before her marriage, came from a respectable, middle-class Nottingham family. Unhappy in her marriage to a man who lacked refinement and gentility, Lawrence's mother focused all her love and attention on her children, determined that they should rise in the world. Her favorite was Bertie, as she called the youngest and most delicate of her three sons, and in him she nurtured all the qualities opposite those of her husband. She taught him to sew and to cook, to detest the coarse vitality of his father, and finally, when he began to develop relationships with girls, to feel guilty about his infidelity to his mother.

From 1898 to 1901 Lawrence attended the Nottingham High School on scholarship, then went to work for a surgical goods manufacturer in Nottingham. But that winter he fell ill with pneumonia—the beginning of lung ailments that would last for the rest of his life—and had to come home, where his mother nursed him back to health. The following fall he began teaching at a school in Eastwood and continued to do so until 1906, when he became a student in the Teacher's Training Department of University College, Nottingham (having received the highest grade in all of England and Scotland in the King's Scholarship Examination). Upon receiving his teacher's certificate in 1908 Lawrence went to Croydon, outside London, where he taught school until 1911 and wrote his first two novels, *The White Peacock* and *The Trespasser.*

Up until this point in his life Lawrence was a rather unexceptional young writer—sensitive and "literary," but not particularly original or forceful. But then a series of events occurred from which he emerged drastically changed. In the winter of 1910 his mother died and Lawrence sank into a great depression. Not long afterward he had another attack of pneumonia and had to give up teaching. Then he began to write the highly autobiographical novel *Sons and Lovers.* And finally, in the spring of 1912, he fell in love with Frieda von Richthofen, the wife of one of his former teachers at Nottingham, and six weeks later she left her husband and three children to go with Lawrence to the continent.

For the next two years he and Frieda traveled about Austria and Italy, rarely staying in one place for more than a few months, and Lawrence began the enormous outpouring of novels, short stories, and poems that would continue—as would the incessant traveling—for the rest of his life. In 1914 Frieda's husband granted her a divorce and they returned to England and were married. Because of the outbreak of World War I, they had to remain in England for the next five years, and it became a period of mounting unhappiness for Lawrence: the war itself depressed him extremely; in 1915 his novel *The Rainbow* was suppressed for being obscene; and in 1917 they were ordered to move out of Cornwall because—Frieda being German—they were suspected of being German spies. Growing more and more disillusioned with the moral hypocrisy of England, Lawrence began formulating ideas for a Utopian community in which he and his friends could live in harmony and love. Nevertheless, despite the justifications he had for being depressed and unproductive, Lawrence wrote during this period a book of travel sketches, *Twilight in Italy*, a collection of poems entitled *Look! We Have Come Through!*, and one of his finest novels, *Women in Love.*

As soon as the war was over and they could get passports, the Lawrences left for Italy, and thereafter returned to England only for brief visits. For the next eleven years Lawrence wandered the globe looking for a place where he felt comfortable, but never finding it. He went to Ceylon, Australia, a ranch in New Mexico, Mexico, and then back to England; he repeated most of this cycle and returned, ultimately, to an Italian village outside Florence, where he wrote his final novel, the misunderstood and long-censured *Lady Chatterley's Lover.* In the spring of 1930, at the age of forty-four, D. H. Lawrence died of tuberculosis at Vence, France; five years later his body was exhumed and cremated, and Frieda took his ashes back to their ranch in the Sangre de Cristo mountains above Taos, New Mexico, where she placed them in a small chapel.

Though his career as a writer spanned only twenty years, Lawrence published nearly fifty books; and though the quality is uneven, it is remarkable that he produced as much exceptionally good writing in as many different genres as he actually did. His excellence as a novelist and short story writer often obscures the fact that he was also a fine poet and essayist and that he wrote some of the best descriptions of places ("travel books") there are, and that he was one of the most perceptive—and exciting—critics of literature in the twentieth century. He also wrote extensively on psychology, religion, and a variety of moral and philosophical issues.

Many readers find Lawrence a very disturbing writer. A demonic quality keeps emerging from his work that makes them uneasy. He's too passionate, too intense, too Pan-like. At times, reading Lawrence, it is almost like being in a forest at night, feeling the eyes of animals watching you in the dark. Lawrence believed in the power of the unconscious—one's darkest, most passionate feelings—and wanted to give them at least equal importance with the daytime qualities of the rational mind. As he once wrote, "My great religion is a belief in the blood, the flesh, as being wiser than the intellect. We can go wrong in our minds. But what our blood feels and believes and says, is always true."

F. R. Leavis called Lawrence "the great creative genius of our age, and one of the greatest figures in English literature." Whether or not one agrees with that, there is little questioning the fact that he introduced into English literature a new level of appreciation of the emotional side of life. It wasn't until after his mother was dead and he was free of her genteel aspirations for middle-class respectability that Lawrence came to see that she had been wrong, that the true flame, the vital fire, had not been in her but in his father—that tender, instinctual man who seldom thought, but who had virtually a tactile relationship with nature, darkness, and the living blood. For Lawrence, such pure physicality became the necessary antidote to the industrialism, intellectual sterility, and emotional deadness of life in the twentieth century.

ADOLF

When we were children our father often worked on the night-shift. Once it was spring-time, and he used to arrive home, black and tired, just as we were downstairs in our nightdresses. Then night met morning face to face, and the contact was not always happy. Perhaps it was painful to my father to see us gaily entering upon the day into which he dragged himself soiled and weary. He didn't like going to bed in the spring morning sunshine.

But sometimes he was happy, because of his long walk through the dewy fields in the first daybreak. He loved the open morning, the crystal and the space, after a night down pit. He watched every bird, every stir in the trembling grass, answered the whinnying of the pewits and tweeted to the wrens. If he could, he also would have whinnied and tweeted and whistled in a native language that was not human. He liked non-human things best.

One sunny morning we were all sitting at table when we heard his heavy slurring walk up the entry. We became uneasy. His was always a disturbing presence, trammelling. He passed the window darkly, and we heard him go into the scullery and put down his tin bottle. But directly he came into the kitchen. We felt at once that he had something to communicate. No one spoke. We watched his black face for a second.

"Give me a drink," he said.

My mother hastily poured out his tea. He went to pour it out into his saucer. But instead of drinking he suddenly put something on the table among the teacups. A tiny brown rabbit! A small rabbit, a mere morsel, sitting against the bread as still as if it were a made thing.

"A rabbit! A young one! Who gave it you, father?"

But he laughed enigmatically, with a sliding motion of his yellow-grey eyes, and went to take off his coat. We pounced on the rabbit.

"Is it alive? Can you feel its heart beat?"

My father came back and sat down heavily in his armchair. He dragged his saucer to him, and blew his tea, pushing out his red lips under his black moustache.

"Where did you get it, father?"

"I picked it up," he said, wiping his naked forearm over his mouth and beard.

"Where?"

"It is a wild one!" came my mother's quick voice.

"Yes, it is."

"Then why did you bring it?" cried my mother.

"Oh, we wanted it," came our cry.

"Yes, I've no doubt you did—" retorted my mother. But she was drowned in our clamour of questions.

On the field path my father had found a dead mother rabbit and three dead little ones—this one alive, but unmoving.

"But what had killed them, daddy?"

"I couldn't say, my child. I s'd think she'd aten something."

"Why did you bring it!" again my mother's voice of condemnation. "You know what it will be."

My father made no answer, but we were loud in protest.

"He must bring it. It's not big enough to live by itself. It would die," we shouted.

"Yes, and it will die now. And then there'll be *another* outcry."

My mother set her face against the tragedy of dead pets. Our hearts sank.

"It won't die, father, will it? Why will it? It won't."

"I s'd think not," said my father.

"You know well enough it will. Haven't we had it all before!" said my mother.

"They dunna always pine," replied my father testily.

But my mother reminded him of other little wild animals he had brought, which had sulked and refused to live, and brought storms of tears and trouble in our house of lunatics.

Trouble fell on us. The little rabbit sat on our lap, unmoving, its eye wide and dark. We brought it milk, warm milk, and held it to its nose. It sat as still as if it was far away, retreated down some deep burrow, hidden, oblivious. We wetted its mouth and whiskers with drops of milk. It gave no sign, did not even shake off the wet white drops. Somebody began to shed a few secret tears.

"What did I say?" cried my mother. "Take it and put it down in the field."

Her command was in vain. We were driven to get dressed for school. There sat the rabbit. It was like a tiny obscure cloud. Watching it, the emotions died out of our breast. Useless to love it, to yearn over it. Its little feelings were all ambushed. They must be circumvented. Love and affection were a trespass upon it. A little wild thing, it became more mute and asphyxiated still in its own arrest, when we approached with love. We must not love it. We must circumvent it, for its own existence.

So I passed the order to my sister and my mother. The rabbit was not to be spoken to, nor even looked at. Wrapping it in a piece of flannel I put it in an obscure corner of the cold parlour, and put a saucer of milk before its nose. My mother was forbidden to enter the parlour whilst we were at school.

"As if I should take any notice of your nonsense," she cried affronted. Yet I doubt if she ventured into the parlour.

At midday, after school, creeping into the front room, there we saw the rabbit still and unmoving in the piece of flannel. Strange grey-brown neutralization of life, still living! It was a sore problem to us.

"Why won't it drink its milk, mother?" we whispered. Our father was asleep.

"It prefers to sulk its life away, silly little thing." A profound problem. Prefers to sulk its life away! We put young dandelion leaves to its nose. The sphinx was not more oblivious. Yet its eye was bright.

At tea-time, however, it had hopped a few inches, out of its flannel, and there it sat again, uncovered, a little solid cloud of muteness, brown, with unmoving whiskers. Only its side palpitated slightly with life.

Darkness came; my father set off to work. The rabbit was still unmoving. Dumb despair was coming over the sisters, a threat of tears before bedtime. Clouds of my mother's anger gathered as she muttered against my father's wantonness.

Once more the rabbit was wrapped in the old pit-singlet. But now it was carried into the scullery and put under the copper fire-place, that it might imagine itself inside a burrow. The saucers were placed about, four or five, here and there on the floor, so that if the little creature *should* chance to hop abroad, it could not fail to come upon some food. After this my mother was allowed to take from the scullery what she wanted and then she was forbidden to open the door.

When morning came and it was light, I went downstairs. Opening the scullery door, I heard a slight scuffle. Then I saw dabbles of milk all over the floor and tiny rabbit-droppings in the saucers. And there the miscreant, the tips of his ears showing behind a pair of boots. I peeped at him. He sat bright-eyed and askance, twitching his nose and looking at me while not looking at me.

He was alive—very much alive. But still we were afraid to trespass much on his confidence.

"Father!" My father was arrested at the door. "Father, the rabbit's alive."

"Back your life it is," said my father.

"Mind how you go in."

By evening, however, the little creature was tame, quite tame. He was christened Adolf. We were enchanted by him. We couldn't really love him, because he was wild and loveless to the end. But he was an unmixed delight.

We decided he was too small to live in a hutch—he must live at large in the house. My mother protested, but in vain. He was so tiny. So we had him upstairs, and he dropped his tiny pills on the bed and we were enchanted.

Adolf made himself instantly at home. He had the run of the house, and was perfectly happy, with his tunnels and his holes behind the furniture.

We loved him to take meals with us. He would sit on the table humping his back, sipping his milk, shaking his whiskers and his tender ears, hopping off and hobbling back to his saucer, with an air of supreme unconcern. Suddenly he was alert. He hobbled a few tiny paces, and reared himself up inquisitively at the sugar basin. He fluttered his tiny fore-paws, and then reached and laid them on the edge of the basin, whilst he craned his thin neck and peeped in. He trembled his whiskers at the sugar, then did his best to lift down a lump.

"*Do* you think I will have it! Animals in the sugar pot!" cried my mother, with a rap of her hand on the table.

Which so delighted the electric Adolf that he flung his hind-quarters and knocked over a cup.

"It's your own fault, mother. If you left him alone—"

He continued to take tea with us. He rather liked warm tea. And he loved sugar. Having nibbled a lump, he would turn to the butter. There he was shooed off by our parent. He soon learned to treat her shooing with indifference. Still, she hated him to put his nose in the food. And he loved to do it. And one day between them they overturned the cream-jug. Adolf deluged his little chest, bounced back in terror, was seized by his little ears by my mother and bounced down on the hearth-rug. There he shivered in momentary discomfort, and suddenly set off in a wild flight to the parlour.

This last was his happy hunting ground. He had cultivated the bad habit of pensively nibbling certain bits of cloth in the hearth rug. When chased from this pasture he would retreat under the sofa. There he would twinkle in Buddhist meditation until suddenly, no one knew why, he would go off like an alarm clock. With a sudden bumping scuffle he would whirl out of the room, going through the doorway with his little ears flying. Then we would hear his thunderbolt hurtling in the parlour, but before we could follow, the wild streak of Adolf would flash past us, on an electric wind that swept him round the scullery and carried him back, a little mad thing, flying possessed like a ball round the parlour. After which ebullition he would sit in a corner composed and distant, twitching his whiskers in abstract meditation. And it was in vain we questioned him about his outbursts. He just went off like a gun, and was as calm after it as a gun that smokes placidly.

Alas, he grew up rapidly. It was almost impossible to keep him from the outer door.

One day, as we were playing by the stile, I saw his brown shadow loiter across the road and pass into the field that faced the houses. Instantly a cry of "Adolf!"—a cry he knew full well. And instantly a wind swept him away down the sloping meadow, his tail twinkling and zigzagging through the grass. After him we pelted. It was a strange sight to see him, ears back, his little loins so powerful, flinging the world behind him. We ran ourselves out of breath, but could not catch him. Then somebody headed him off, and he sat with sudden unconcern, twitching his nose under a bunch of nettles.

His wanderings cost him a shock. One Sunday morning my father had just been quarrelling with a pedlar, and we were hearing the aftermath indoors, when there came a sudden unearthly scream from the yard. We flew out. There sat Adolf cowering under a bench, whilst a great black and white cat glowered intently at him, a few yards away. Sight not to be forgotten. Adolf rolling back his eyes and parting his strange muzzle in another scream, the cat stretching forward in a slow elongation.

Ha, how we hated that cat! How we pursued him over the chapel wall and across the neighbours' gardens.

Adolf was still only half grown.

"Cats!" said my mother. "Hideous detestable animals, why do people harbour them?"

But Adolf was becoming too much for her. He dropped too many pills. And suddenly to hear him clumping downstairs when she was alone in the house was startling. And to keep him from the door was impossible. Cats prowled outside. It was worse than having a child to look after.

Yet we would not have him shut up. He became more lusty, more callous than ever. He was a strong kicker, and many a scratch on face and arms did we owe to him. But he brought his own doom on himself. The lace curtains in the parlour—my mother was rather proud of them—fell on the floor very full. One of Adolf's joys was to scuffle wildly through them as though through some foamy undergrowth. He had already torn rents in them.

One day he entangled himself altogether. He kicked, he whirled round in a mad nebulous inferno. He screamed—and brought down the curtain-rod with a smash, right on the best beloved pelargonium, just as my mother rushed in. She extricated him, but she never forgave him. And he never forgave either. A heartless wildness had come over him.

Even we understood that he must go. It was decided, after a long deliberation, that my father should carry him back to the wildwoods. Once again he was stowed into the great pocket of the pit-jacket.

"Best pop him i' th' pot," said my father, who enjoyed raising the wind of indignation.

And so, next day, our father said that Adolf, set down on the edge of the coppice, had hopped away with utmost indifference, neither elated nor moved. We heard it and believed. But many, many were the heartsearchings. How would the other rabbits receive him? Would they smell his tameness, his humanized degradation, and rend him? My mother pooh-poohed the extravagant idea.

However, he was gone, and we were rather relieved. My father kept an eye open for him. He declared that several times passing the coppice in the early morning, he had seen Adolf peeping through the nettle-stalks. He had called him, in an odd, high-voiced, cajoling fashion. But Adolf had not responded. Wildness gains so soon upon its creatures. And they become so contemptuous then of our tame presence. So it seemed to me. I myself would go to the edge of the coppice, and call softly. I myself would imagine bright eyes between the nettle-stalks, flash of a white, scornful tail past the bracken. That insolent white tail, as Adolf turned his flank on us! It reminded me always of a certain rude gesture, and a certain unprintable phrase, which may not even be suggested.

But when naturalists discuss the meaning of the rabbit's white tail, that rude gesture and still ruder phrase always come to my mind. Naturalists say that the rabbit shows his white tail in order to guide his young safely after him, as a nursemaid's flying strings are the signal to her toddling charges to follow on. How nice and naïve! I only know that my Adolf wasn't naïve. He used to whisk his flank at me, push his white feather in my eye, and say "*Merde!*" It's a rude word—but one which Adolf was always semaphoring at me, flag-wagging it with all the derision of his narrow haunches.

That's a rabbit all over—insolence, and the white flag of spiteful derision. Yes, and he keeps his flag flying to the bitter end, sporting, insolent little devil that he is. See him running for his life. Oh, how his soul is fanned to an ecstasy of fright, a fugitive whirlwind of panic. Gone mad, he throws the world behind him, with astonishing hind legs. He puts back his head and lays his ears on his sides and rolls the white of his eyes in sheer ecstatic agony of speed. He knows the awful approach behind him; bullet or stoat. He knows! He knows, his eyes are turned back almost into his head. It is agony. But it is also ecstasy. Ecstasy! See the insolent white flag bobbing. He whirls on the magic wind of terror. All his pent-up soul rushes into agonized electric emotion of fear. He flings himself on, like a falling star swooping into extinction. White heat of the agony of fear. And at the same time, bob! bob! bob! goes the white tail, *merde! merde! merde!* it says to the pursuer. The rabbit can't help it. In his utmost extremity he still flings the insult at the pursuer. He is the inconquerable fugitive, the indomitable meek. No wonder the stoat becomes vindictive.

And if he escapes, this precious rabbit! Don't you see him sitting there, in his earthly nook, a little ball of silence and rabbit triumph? Don't you see the glint on his black eye? Don't you see, in his very immobility, how the whole world is *merde* to him? No conceit like the conceit of the meek. And if the avenging angel in the shape of the ghostly ferret steals down on him, there comes a shriek of terror out of that little hump of self-satisfaction sitting motionless in a corner. Falls the fugitive. But even fallen, his white feather floats. Even in death it seems to say: "I am the meek, I am the righteous, I am the rabbit. All you rest, you are evil doers, and you shall be *bien emmerdés*!"

1920

HYMNS IN A MAN'S LIFE

Nothing is more difficult than to determine what a child takes in, and does not take in, of its environment and its teaching. This fact is brought home to me by the hymns which I learned as a child, and never forgot. They mean to me almost more than the finest poetry, and they have for me a more permanent value, somehow or other.

It is almost shameful to confess that the poems which have meant most to me, like Wordsworth's *Ode to Immortality* and Keats' Odes, and pieces of *Macbeth* or *As You Like It* or *Midsummer Night's Dream,* and Goethe's lyrics, such as *Über allen Gipfeln ist Ruh,* and Verlaine's *Ayant poussé la porte qui chancelle* —all these lovely poems which after all give the ultimate shape to one's life; all these lovely poems woven deep into a man's consciousness, are still not woven so deep in me as the rather banal Nonconformist hymns that penetrated through and through my childhood.

Each gentle dove
And sighing bough
That makes the eve
So fair to me
Has something far
Diviner now
To draw me back
To Galilee.
O Galilee, sweet Galilee,
Where Jesus loved so much to be,
O Galilee, sweet Galilee,
Come sing thy songs again to me!

To me the word *Galilee* has a wonderful sound. The Lake of Galilee! I don't want to know where it is. I never want to go to Palestine. Galilee is one of those lovely, glamorous worlds, not places, that exist in the golden haze of a child's half-formed imagination. And in my man's imagination it is just the same. It has been left untouched. With regard to the hymns which had such a profound influence on my childish consciousness, there has been no crystallizing out, no dwindling into actuality, no hardening into the commonplace. They are the same to my man's experience as they were to me nearly forty years ago.

The moon, perhaps, has shrunken a little. One has been forced to learn about orbits, eclipses, relative distances, dead worlds, craters of the moon, and so on. The crescent at evening still startles the soul with its delicate flashing. But the mind works automatically and says: "Ah, she is in her first quarter. She is all there, in spite of the fact that we see only this slim blade. The earth's shadow is over her." And, willy-nilly, the intrusion of the mental processes dims the brilliance, the magic of the first apperception.

It is the same with all things. The sheer delight of a child's apperception is based on *wonder*; and deny it as we may, knowledge and wonder counteract one another. So that as knowledge increases wonder decreases. We say again: Familiarity breeds contempt. So that as we grow older, and become more familiar with phenomena, we become more contemptuous of them. But that is only partly true. It has taken some races of men thousands of years to become contemptuous of the moon, and to the Hindu the cow is still wondrous. It is not familiarity that breeds contempt: it is the assumption of knowledge. Anybody who looks at the moon and says, "I know all about that poor orb," is, of course, bored by the moon.

Now the great and fatal fruit of our civilization, which is a civilization based on knowledge, and hostile to experience, is boredom. All our wonderful education and learning is producing a grand sum-total of boredom. Modern people are inwardly thoroughly bored. Do as they may, they are bored.

They are bored because they experience nothing. And they experience nothing because the wonder has gone out of them. And when the wonder has gone out of a man he is dead. He is henceforth only an insect.

When all comes to all, the most precious element of life is wonder. Love is a great emotion, and power is power. But both love and power are based on wonder. Love without wonder is a sensational affair, and power without wonder is mere force and compulsion. The one universal element in consciousness which is fundamental to life is the element of wonder. You cannot help feeling it in a bean as it starts to grow and pulls itself out of its jacket. You cannot help feeling it in the glisten of the nucleus of the amoeba. You recognize it, willy-nilly, in an ant busily tugging at a straw; in a rook, as it walks the frosty grass.

They all have their own obstinate will. But also they all live with a sense of wonder. Plant consciousness, insect consciousness, fish consciousness, animal consciousness, all are related by one permanent element, which we may call the religious element inherent in all life, even in a flea: the sense of wonder. That is our sixth sense. And it is the *natural* religious sense.

Somebody says that mystery is nothing, because mystery is something you don't know, and what you don't know is nothing to you. But there is more than one way of knowing.

Even the real scientist works in the sense of wonder. The pity is, when he comes out of his laboratory he puts aside his wonder along with his apparatus, and tries to make it all perfectly didactic. Science in its true condition of wonder is as religious as any religion. But didactic science is as dead and boring as dogmatic religion. Both are wonderless and productive of boredom, endless boredom.

Now we come back to the hymns. They live and glisten in the depths of the man's consciousness in undimmed wonder, because they have not been subjected to any criticism or analysis. By the time I was sixteen I had criticized and got over the Christian dogma.

It was quite easy for me; my immediate forebears had already done it for me. Salvation, heaven, virgin birth, miracles, even the Christian dogmas of right and wrong—one soon got them adjusted. I never could really worry about them. Heaven is one of the instinctive dreams. Right and wrong is something you can't dogmatize about; it's not so easy. As for my soul, I simply don't and never did understand how I could "save" it. One can save one's pennies. But how can one save one's soul? One can only *live* one's soul. The business is to live, really alive. And this needs wonder.

So that the miracle of the loaves and fishes is just as good to me now as when I was a child. I don't care whether it is historically a fact or not. What does it matter? It is part of the genuine wonder. The same with all the religious teaching I had as a child, *apart* from the didacticism and sentimentalism. I am eternally grateful for the wonder with which it filled my childhood.

> Sun of my soul! Thou Saviour dear,
> It is not night if Thou be near—

That was the last hymn at the board school. It did not mean to me any Christian dogma or any salvation. Just the words, "Sun of my soul, thou Saviour dear," penetrated me with wonder and the mystery of twilight. At another time the last hymn was:

> Fair waved the golden corn
> In Canaan's pleasant land—

And again I loved "Canaan's pleasant land." The wonder of "Canaan," which could never be localized.

I think it was good to be brought up a Protestant: and among Protestants, a Nonconformist, and among Nonconformists, a Congregationalist. Which sounds pharisaic. But I should have missed bitterly a direct knowledge of the Bible, and a direct relation to Galilee and Canaan, Moab and Kedron, those places that never existed on earth. And in the Church of England one would hardly have escaped those snobbish hierarchies of class, which spoil so much for a child. And the Primitive Methodists, when I was a boy, were always having "revivals" and being "saved," and I always had a horror of being saved.

So, altogether, I am grateful to my "Congregational" upbringing. The Congregationalists are the oldest Nonconformists, descendants of the Oliver Cromwell Independents. They still had the Puritan tradition of no ritual. But they avoided the personal emotionalism which one found among the Methodists when I was a boy.

I liked our chapel, which was tall and full of light, and yet still; and colour-washed pale green and blue, with a bit of lotus pattern. And over the organ-loft, "O worship the Lord in the beauty of holiness," in big letters.

That was a favourite hymn, too:

> O worship the Lord, in the beauty of holiness,
> Bow down before Him, His glory proclaim;
> With gold of obedience and incense of lowliness
> Kneel and adore Him, the Lord is His name.

I don't know what the "beauty of holiness" is, exactly. It easily becomes cant, or nonsense. But if you don't think about it—and why should you?—it has a magic. The same with the whole verse. It is rather bad, really, "gold of obedience" and "incense of lowliness." But in me, to the music, it still produces a sense of splendour.

I am always glad we had the Bristol hymn-book, not Moody and Sankey. And I am glad our Scotch minister on the whole avoided sentimental messes such as "Lead, Kindly Light," or even "Abide With Me." He had a healthy preference for healthy hymns.

> At even, ere the sun was set,
> The sick, O Lord, around Thee lay.
> Oh, in what divers pains they met!
> Oh, in what joy they went away!

And often we had "Fight the good fight with all thy might."

In Sunday School I am eternally grateful to old Mr. Remington, with his round white beard and his ferocity. He made us sing! And he loved the martial hymns:

> Sound the battlecry,
> See, the foe is nigh.
> Raise the standard high
> For the Lord.

The ghastly sentimentalism that came like a leprosy over religion had not yet got hold of our colliery village. I remember when I was in Class II in the Sunday School, when I was about seven, a woman teacher trying to harrow us about the Crucifixion. And she kept saying: "And aren't you sorry for Jesus? Aren't you sorry?" And most of the children wept. I believe I shed a crocodile tear or two, but very vivid is my memory of saying to myself: "I don't *really* care a bit." And I could never go back on it. I never *cared* about the Crucifixion, one way or another. Yet the *wonder* of it penetrated very deep in me.

Thirty-six years ago men, even Sunday School teachers, still believed in the fight for life and the fun of it. "Hold the fort, for I am coming." It was far, far from any militarism or gun-fighting. But it was the battle-cry of a stout soul, and a fine thing too.

Stand up, stand up for Jesus,
Ye soldiers of the Cross.

Here is the clue to the ordinary Englishman—in the Nonconformist hymns.

1928

INSOUCIANCE

My balcony is on the east side of the hotel, and my neighbours on the right are a Frenchman, white-haired, and his white-haired wife; my neighbours on the left are two little white-haired English ladies. And we are all mortally shy of one another.

When I peep out of my room in the morning and see the matronly French lady in a purple silk wrapper, standing like the captain on the bridge surveying the morning, I pop in again before she can see me. And whenever I emerge during the day, I am aware of the two little white-haired ladies popping back like two white rabbits, so that literally I only see the whisk of their skirt-hems.

This afternoon being hot and thundery, I woke up suddenly and went out on the balcony barefoot. There I sat serenely contemplating the world, and ignoring the two bundles of feet of the two little ladies which protruded from their open doorways, upon the end of the two *chaises longues*. A hot, still afternoon! the lake shining rather glassy away below, the mountains rather sulky, the greenness very green, all a little silent and lurid, and two mowers mowing with scythes, downhill just near: *slush! slush!* sound the scythe-strokes.

The two little ladies become aware of my presence. I become aware of a certain agitation in the two bundles of feet wrapped in two discreet steamer rugs and protruding on the end of two *chaises longues* from the pair of doorways upon the balcony next me. One bundle of feet suddenly disappears; so does the other. Silence!

Then lo! with odd sliding suddenness a little white-haired lady in grey silk, with round blue eyes, emerges and looks straight at me, and remarks that it is pleasant now. A little cooler, say I, with false amiability. She quite agrees, and we speak of the men mowing; how plainly one hears the long breaths of the scythes.

By now we are *tête-à-tête*. We speak of cherries, strawberries, and the promise of the vine crop. This somehow leads to Italy, and to Signor Mussolini. Before I know where I am, the little white-haired lady has swept me off my balcony, away from the glassy lake, the veiled mountains, the two men mowing, and the cherry trees, away into the troubled ether of international politics.

I am not allowed to sit like a dandelion on my own stem. The little lady in a breath blows me abroad. And I was so pleasantly musing over the two men mowing: the young one, with long legs in bright blue cotton trousers, and with bare black head, swinging so lightly downhill, and the other, in black trousers, rather stout in front, and wearing a new straw hat of the boater variety, coming rather stiffly after, crunching the end of his stroke with a certain violent effort.

I was watching the curiously different motions of the two men, the young thin one in bright blue trousers, the elderly fat one in shabby black trousers that stick out in front, the different amount of effort in their mowing, the lack of grace in the elderly one, his jerky advance, the unpleasant effect of the new "boater" on his head—and I tried to interest the little lady.

But it meant nothing to her. The mowers, the mountains, the cherry trees, the lake, all the things that were *actually* there, she didn't care about. They even seemed to scare her off the balcony. But she held her ground, and instead of herself being scared away, she snatched me up like some ogress, and swept me off into the empty desert spaces of right and wrong, politics, Fascism and the rest.

The worst ogress couldn't have treated me more villainously. I don't care about right and wrong, politics, Fascism, abstract liberty, or anything else of the sort. I want to look at the mowers, and wonder why fatness, elderliness, and black trousers should inevitably wear a new straw hat of the boater variety, move in stiff jerks, shove the end of the scythe-strokes with a certain violence, and win my hearty disapproval, as contrasted with young long thinness, bright blue cotton trousers, a bare black head, and a pretty lifting movement at the end of the scythe-stroke.

Why do modern people almost invariably ignore the things that are actually present to them? Why, having come out from England to find mountains, lakes, scythe-mowers and cherry trees, does the little blue-eyed lady resolutely close her blue eyes to them all, now she's got them, and gaze away to Signor Mussolini, whom she hasn't got, and to Fascism, which is invisible anyhow? Why isn't she content to be where she is? Why can't she be happy with what she's got? Why must she *care*?

I see now why her round blue eyes are so round, so noticeably round. It is because she "cares." She is haunted by that mysterious bugbear of "caring." For everything on earth that doesn't concern her she "cares." She cares terribly because far-off, invisible, hypothetical Italians wear black shirts, but she doesn't care a rap that one elderly mower whose stroke she can hear, wears black trousers instead of bright blue cotton ones. Now if she would descend from the balcony and climb the glassy slope and say to the fat mower: "*Cher monsieur, pourquoi portez-vous les pantalons noirs?* Why, oh, why do you wear black trousers?"—then I should say: What an on-the-spot little lady!—But since she only torments me with international politics, I can only remark: What a tiresome off-the-spot old woman!

They care! They simply are eaten up with caring. They are so busy caring about Fascism or Leagues of Nations or whether France is right or whether Marriage is threatened, that they never know where they are. They certainly never live on the spot where they are. They inhabit abstract space, the desert void of politics, principles, right and wrong, and so forth. They are doomed to be abstract. Talking to them is like trying to have a human relationship with the letter x in algebra.

There simply is a deadly breach between actual living and this abstract caring. What is actual living? It is a question mostly of direct contact. There was a direct sensuous contact between me, the lake, mountains, cherry trees, mowers, and a certain invisible but noisy chaffinch in a clipped lime tree. All this was cut off by the fatal shears of that abstract word *Fascism*, and the little old lady next door was the Atropos who cut the thread of my actual life this afternoon. She beheaded me, and flung my head into abstract space. Then we are supposed to love our neighbours!

When it comes to living, we live through our instincts and our intuitions. Instinct makes me run from little over-earnest ladies; instinct makes me sniff the lime blossoms and reach for the darkest cherry. But it is intuition which makes me feel the uncanny glassiness of the lake this afternoon, the sulkiness of the mountains, the vividness of near green in thunder-sun, the young man in bright blue trousers lightly tossing the grass from the scythe, the elderly man in a boater stiffly shoving his scythe-strokes, both of them sweating in the silence of the intense light.

1928

MAKING PICTURES

One has to eat one's own words. I remember I used to assert, perhaps I even wrote it: Everything that can possibly be painted has been painted, every brush-stroke that can possibly be laid on canvas has been laid on. The visual arts are at a dead end. Then suddenly, at the age of forty, I begin painting myself and am fascinated.

Still, going through the Paris picture shops this year of grace, and seeing the Dufys and Chiricos, etc., and the Japanese Ito with his wish-wash nudes with pearl-button eyes, the same weariness comes over me. They are all so would-be, they make such efforts. They at least have nothing to paint. In the midst of them a graceful Fricsz flower-piece, or a blotting-paper Laurencin seems a masterpiece. At least here is a bit of *natural* expression in paint. Trivial enough, when compared to the big painters, but still, as far as they go, real.

What about myself, then! What am I doing, bursting into paint? I am a writer, I ought to stick to ink. I have found my medium of expression; why, at the age of forty, should I suddenly want to try another?

Things happen, and we have no choice. If Maria Huxley hadn't come rolling up to our house near Florence with four rather large canvases, one of which she had busted, and presented them to me because they had been abandoned in her house, I might never have started in on a real picture in my life. But those nice stretched canvases were too tempting. We had been painting doors and window-frames in the house, so there was a little stock of oil, turps, and colour in powder, such as one buys from an Italian drogheria. There were several brushes for house-painting. There was a canvas on which the unknown owner had made a start—mud-grey, with the beginnings of a red-haired man. It was a grimy and ugly beginning, and the young man who had made it had wisely gone no further. He certainly had had no inner compulsion: nothing in him, as far as paint was concerned, or if there was anything in him, it had stayed in, and only a bit of the mud-grey "group" had come out.

So for the sheer fun of covering a surface and obliterating that mud-grey, I sat on the floor with the canvas propped against a chair—and with my house-paint brushes and colours in little casseroles, I disappeared into that canvas. It is to me the most exciting moment—when you have a blank canvas and a big brush full of wet colour, and you plunge. It is just like diving in a pond—then you start frantically to swim. So far as I am concerned, it is like swimming in a baffling current and being rather frightened and very thrilled, gasping and striking out for all you're worth. The knowing eye watches sharp as a needle; but the picture comes clean out of instinct, intuition, and sheer physical action. Once the instinct and intuition gets into the brush-tip, the picture *happens*, if it is to be a picture at all.

At least, so my first picture happened—the one I have called "A Holy Family." In a couple of hours there it all was, man, woman, child, blue shirt, red shawl, pale room—all in the rough, but, as far as I am concerned, a picture. The struggling comes later. But the picture itself comes in the first rush, or not at all. It is only when the picture has come into being that one can struggle and make it *grow* to completion.

Ours is an excessively conscious age. We *know* so much, we feel so little. I have lived enough among painters and around studios to have had all the theories—and how contradictory they are—rammed down my throat. A man has to have a gizzard like an ostrich to digest all the brass-tacks and wire nails of modern art theories. Perhaps all the theories, the utterly indigestible theories, like nails in an ostrich's gizzard, do indeed help to grind small and make digestible all the emotional and aesthetic pabulum that lies in an artist's soul. But they can serve no other purpose. Not even corrective. The modern theories of art make real pictures impossible. You only get these expositions, critical ventures in paint, and fantastic negations. And the bit of fantasy that may lie in the negation—as in a Dufy or a Chirico—is just the bit that has escaped theory and perhaps saves the picture. Theorize, theorize all you like—but when you start to paint, shut your theoretic eyes and go for it with instinct and intuition.

Myself, I have always loved pictures, the pictorial art. I never went to an art school, I have had only one real lesson in painting in all my life. But of course I was thoroughly drilled in "drawing," the solid-geometry sort, and the plaster-cast sort, and the pin-wire sort. I think the solid-geometry sort, with all the elementary laws of perspective, was valuable. But the pin-wire sort and the plaster-cast light-and-shade sort was harmful. Plaster-casts and pin-wire outlines were always so repulsive to me, I quite early decided I "couldn't draw." I couldn't draw, so I could never do anything on my own. When I did paint jugs of flowers or bread and potatoes, or cottages in a lane, copying from Nature, the result wasn't very thrilling. Nature was more or less of a plaster-cast to me—those plaster-cast heads of Minerva or figures of Dying Gladiators which so unnerved me as a youth. The "object," be it what it might, was always slightly repulsive to me once I sat down in front of it, to paint it. So, of course, I decided I couldn't really paint. Perhaps I can't. But I verily believe I can make pictures, which is to me all that matters in this respect. The art of painting consists in making pictures—and so many artists accomplish canvases without coming within miles of painting a picture.

I learnt to paint from copying other pictures—usually reproductions, sometimes even photographs. When I was a boy, how I concentrated over it! Copying some perfectly worthless scene reproduction in some magazine. I worked with almost dry watercolour, stroke by stroke, covering half a square-inch at a time, each square-inch perfect and completed, proceeding in a kind of mosaic advance, with no idea at all of laying on a broad wash. Hours and hours of intense concentration, inch-by-inch progress, in a method entirely wrong—and yet those copies of mine managed, when they were finished, to have a certain something that delighted me: a certain glow of life, which was beauty to me. A picture lives with the life you put into it. If you put no *life* into it—no thrill, no concentration of delight or exaltation of visual discovery—then the picture is dead like so many canvases, no matter how much thorough and scientific work is put into it. Even if you only copy a purely banal reproduction of an old bridge, some sort of keen, delighted awareness of the old bridge or of its atmosphere, or the image it has kindled inside you, can go over on to the paper and give a certain touch of life to a banal conception.

It needs a certain purity of spirit to be an artist, of any sort. The motto which should be written over every School of Art is: "Blessed are the pure in spirit, for theirs is the kingdom of heaven." But by "pure in spirit" we mean pure in spirit. An artist may be a profligate and, from the social point of view, a scoundrel. But if he can paint a nude woman, or a couple of apples, so that they are a living image, then he was pure in spirit, and, for the time being, his was the kingdom of heaven. This is the beginning of all art, visual or literary or musical: be pure in spirit. It isn't the same as goodness. It is much more difficult and nearer the divine. The divine isn't only good, it is all things.

One may see the divine in natural objects; I saw it to-day, in the frail, lovely little camellia flowers on long stems, here on the bushy and splendid flower-stalls of the Ramblas in Barcelona. They were different from the usual fat camellias, more like gardenias, poised delicately, and I saw them like a vision. So now, I could paint them. But if I had bought a handful, and started in to paint them "from nature," then I should have lost them. By staring at them I should have lost them. I have learnt by experience. It is personal experience only. Some men can only get at a vision by staring themselves blind, as it were: like Cézanne; but staring kills my vision. That's why I could never "draw" at school. One was supposed to draw what one stared at.

The only thing one can look into, stare into, and see only vision, is the vision itself: the visionary image. That is why I am glad I never had any training but the self-imposed training of copying other men's pictures. As I grew more ambitious, I copied Leader's landscapes, and Frank Brangwyn's cartoon-like pictures, then Peter de Wint and Girtin water-colours. I can never be sufficiently grateful for the series of English water-colour painters, published by the *Studio* in eight parts, when I was a youth. I had only six of the eight parts, but they were invaluable to me. I copied them with the greatest joy, and found some of them extremely difficult. Surely I put as much labour into copying from those water-colour reproductions as most modern art students put into all their years of study. And I had enormous profit from it. I not only acquired a considerable technical skill in handling water-colour—let any man try copying the English water-colour artists, from Paul Sandby and Peter de Wint and Girtin, up to Frank Brangwyn and the impressionists like Brabazon, and he will see how much skill he requires—but also I developed my visionary awareness. And I believe one can only develop one's visionary awareness by close contact with the vision itself: that is, by knowing pictures, real vision pictures, and by dwelling on them, and really dwelling in them. It is a great delight, to dwell in a picture. But it needs a purity of spirit, a sloughing of vulgar sensation and vulgar interest, and above all, vulgar contact, that few people know how to perform. Oh, if art schools only taught that! If, instead of saying: This drawing is wrong, incorrect, badly drawn, etc., they would say: Isn't this in bad taste? isn't it insensitive? isn't that an insentient curve with none of the delicate awareness of life in it?—But art is treated all wrong. It is treated as if it were a science, which it is not. Art is a form of religion, minus the Ten Commandment business, which is sociological. Art is a form of supremely delicate awareness and atonement—meaning at-oneness, the state of being at one with the object.

But is the great atonement in delight?—for I can never look on art save as a form of delight.

All my life I have from time to time gone back to paint, because it gave me a form of delight that words can never give. Perhaps the joy in words goes deeper and is for that reason more unconscious. The *conscious* delight is certainly stronger in paint. I have gone back to paint for real pleasure—and by paint I mean copying, copying either in oils or waters. I think the greatest pleasure I ever got came from copying Fra Angelico's "Flight into Egypt" and Lorenzetti's big picture of the Thebaid, in each case working from photographs and putting in my own colour; or perhaps even more a Carpaccio picture in Venice. Then I *really* learned what life, what powerful life has been put into every curve, every motion of a great picture. Purity of spirit, sensitive awareness, intense eagerness to portray an inward vision, how it all comes. The English water-colours are frail in comparison—and the French and the Flemings are shallow. The great Rembrandt I never tried to copy, though I loved him intensely, even more than I do now; and Rubens I never tried, though I always liked him so much, only he seemed so spread out. But I have copied Peter de Hooch, and Vandyck and others that I forget. Yet none of them gave me the deep thrill of the Italians, Carpaccio, or the lovely "Death of Procris" in the National Gallery, or that "Wedding" with the scarlet legs, in the Uffizi, or a Giotto from Padua. I must have made many copies in my day, and got endless joy out of them.

Then suddenly, by having a blank canvas, I discovered I could make a picture myself. That is the point, to make a picture on a blank canvas. And I was forty before I had the real courage to try. Then it became an orgy, making pictures.

I have learnt now not to work from objects, not to have models, not to have a technique. Sometimes, for a water-colour, I have worked direct from a model. But it always spoils the *picture*. I can only use a model when the picture is already made; then I can look at the model to get some detail which the vision failed me with, or to modify something which I *feel* is unsatisfactory and I don't know why. Then a model may give a suggestion. But at the beginning, a model only spoils the picture. The picture must all come out of the artist's inside, awareness of forms and figures. We can call it memory, but it is more than memory. It is the image as it lives in the consciousness, alive like a vision, but unknown. I believe many people have in their consciousness, living images that would give them the greatest joy to bring out. But they don't know how to go about it. And teaching only hinders them.

To me, a picture has delight in it, or it isn't a picture. The saddest pictures of Piero della Francesca or Sodoma or Goya, have still that indescribable delight that goes with the real picture. Modern critics talk a lot about ugliness, but I never saw a real picture that seemed to me ugly. The theme may be ugly, there may be a terrifying, distressing, almost repulsive quality, as in El Greco. Yet it is all, in some strange way, swept up in the delight of a picture. No artist, even the gloomiest, ever painted a picture without the curious delight in image-making.

1929

NOTTINGHAM AND THE MINING COUNTRYSIDE

I was born nearly forty-four years ago, in Eastwood, a mining village of some three thousand souls, about eight miles from Nottingham, and one mile from the small stream, the Erewash, which divides Nottinghamshire from Derbyshire. It is hilly country, looking west to Crich and towards Matlock, sixteen miles away, and east and northeast towards Mansfield and the Sherwood Forest district. To me it seemed, and still seems, an extremely beautiful countryside, just between the red sandstone and the oak-trees of Nottingham, and the cold limestone, the ash-trees, the stone fences of Derbyshire. To me, as a child and a young man, it was still the old England of the forest and agricultural past; there were no motor-cars, the mines were, in a sense, an accident in the landscape, and Robin Hood and his merry men were not very far away.

The string of coal-mines of B.W. & Co. had been opened some sixty years before I was born, and Eastwood had come into being as a consequence. It must have been a tiny village at the beginning of the nineteenth century, a small place of cottages and fragmentary rows of little four-room miners' dwellings, the homes of the old colliers of the eighteenth century, who worked in the bits of mines, foot-rill mines with an opening in the hill-side into which the miners walked, or windlass mines, where the men were wound up one at a time, in a bucket, by a donkey. The windlass mines were still working when my father was a boy—and the shafts of some were still there, when I was a boy.

But somewhere about 1820 the company must have sunk the first big shaft—not very deep—and installed the first machinery of the real industrial colliery. Then came my grandfather, a young man trained to be a tailor, drifting from the south of England, and got the job of company tailor for the Brinsley mine. In those days the company supplied the men with the thick flannel vests, or singlets, and the moleskin trousers lined at the top with flannel, in which the colliers worked. I remember the great rolls of coarse flannel and pit-cloth which stood in the corner of my grandfather's shop when I was a small boy, and the big, strange old sewing-machine, like nothing else on earth, which sewed the massive pit-trousers. But when I was only a child the company discontinued supplying the men with pit-clothes.

My grandfather settled in an old cottage down in a quarry-bed, by the brook at Old Brinsley, near the pit. A mile away, up at Eastwood, the company built the first miners' dwellings—it must be nearly a hundred years ago. Now Eastwood occupies a lovely position on a hilltop, with the steep slope towards Derbyshire and the long slope towards Nottingham. They put up a new church, which stands fine and commanding, even if it has no real form, looking across the awful Erewash Valley at the church of Heanor, similarly commanding, away on a hill beyond. What opportunities, what opportunities! These mining villages *might* have been like the lovely hill-towns of Italy, shapely and fascinating. And what happened?

Most of the little rows of dwellings of the old-style miners were pulled down, and dull little shops began to rise along the Nottingham Road, while on the down-slope of the north side the company erected what is still known as the New Buildings, or the Square. These New Buildings consist of two great hollow squares of dwellings planked down on the rough slope of the hill, little four-room houses with the "front" looking outward into the grim, blank street, and the "back," with a tiny square brick yard, a low wall, and a w.c. and ash-pit, looking into the desert of the square, hard, uneven, jolting black earth tilting rather steeply down, with these little back yards all round, and openings at the corners. The squares were quite big, and absolutely desert, save for the posts for clothes lines, and people passing, children playing on the hard earth. And they were shut in like a barracks enclosure, very strange.

Even fifty years ago the squares were unpopular. It was "common" to live in the Square. It was a little less common to live in the Breach, which consisted of six blocks of rather more pretentious dwellings erected by the company in the valley below, two rows of three blocks, with an alley between. And it was most "common," most degraded of all to live in Dakins Row, two rows of the old dwellings, very old, black, four-roomed little places, that stood on the hill again, not far from the Square.

So the place started. Down the steep street between the squares, Scargill Street, the Wesleyans' chapel was put up, and I was born in the little corner shop just above. Across the other side the Square the miners themselves built the big, barn-like Primitive Methodist chapel. Along the hill-top ran the Nottingham Road, with its scrappy, ugly mid-Victorian shops. The little market-place, with a superb outlook, ended the village on the Derbyshire side, and was just left bare, with the Sun Inn on one side, the chemist across, with the gilt pestle-and-mortar, and a shop at the other corner, the corner of Alfreton Road and Nottingham Road.

In this queer jumble of the old England and the new, I came into consciousness. As I remember, little local speculators already began to straggle dwellings in rows, always in rows, across the fields: nasty red-brick, flat-faced dwellings with dark slate roofs. The bay-window period only began when I was a child. But most of the country was untouched.

There must be three or four hundred company houses in the squares and the streets that surround the squares, like a great barracks wall. There must be sixty or eighty company houses in the Breach. The old Dakins Row will have thirty to forty little holes. Then counting the old cottages and rows left with their old gardens down the lanes and along the twitchells, and even in the midst of Nottingham Road itself, there were houses enough for the population, there was no need for much building. And not much building went on when I was small.

We lived in the Breach, in a corner house. A field-path came down under a great hawthorn hedge. On the other side was the brook, with the old sheep-bridge going over into the meadows. The hawthorn hedge by the brook had grown tall as tall trees, and we used to bathe from there in the dipping-hole, where the sheep were dipped, just near the fall from the old mill-dam, where the water rushed. The mill only ceased grinding the local corn when I was a child. And my father, who always worked in Brinsley pit, and who always got up at five o'clock, if not at four, would set off in the dawn across the fields at Coney Grey, and hunt for mushrooms in the long grass, or perhaps pick up a skulking rabbit, which he would bring home at evening inside the lining of his pit-coat.

So that the life was a curious cross between industrialism and the old agricultural England of Shakespeare and Milton and Fielding and George Eliot. The dialect was broad Derbyshire, and always "thee" and "thou." The people lived almost entirely by instinct, men of my father's age could not really read. And the pit did not mechanize men. On the contrary. Under the butty system, the miners worked underground as a sort of intimate community, they knew each other practically naked, and with curious close intimacy, and the darkness and the underground remoteness of the pit "stall," and the continual presence of danger, made the physical, instinctive, and intuitional contact between men very highly developed, a contact almost as close as touch, very real and very powerful. This physical awareness and intimate *togetherness* was at its strongest down pit. When the men came up into the light, they blinked. They had, in a measure, to change their flow. Nevertheless they brought with them above ground the curious dark intimacy of the mine, the naked sort of contact, and if I think of my childhood, it is always as if there was a lustrous sort of inner darkness, like the gloss of coal, in which we moved and had our real being. My father loved the pit. He was hurt badly, more than once, but he would never stay away. He loved the contact, the intimacy, as men in the war loved the intense male comradeship of the dark days. They did not know what they had lost till they lost it. And I think it is the same with the young colliers of today.

Now the colliers had also an instinct of beauty. The colliers' wives had not. The colliers were deeply alive, instinctively. But they had no daytime ambition, and no daytime intellect. They avoided, really, the rational aspect of life. They preferred to take life instinctively and intuitively. They didn't even care very profoundly about wages. It was the women, naturally, who nagged on this score. There was a big discrepancy, when I was a boy, between the collier who saw, at the best, only a brief few hours of daylight—often no daylight at all during the winter weeks—and the collier's wife, who had all the day to herself when the man was down pit.

The great fallacy is, to pity the man. He didn't dream of pitying himself, till agitators and sentimentalists taught him to. He was happy: or more than happy, he was fulfilled. Or he was fulfilled on the receptive side, not on the expressive. The collier went to the pub and drank in order to continue his intimacy with his mates. They talked endlessly, but it was rather of wonders and marvels, even in politics, than of facts. It was hard facts, in the shape of wife, money, and nagging home necessities, which they fled away from, out of the house to the pub, and out of the house to the pit.

The collier fled out of the house as soon as he could, away from the nagging materialism of the woman. With the women it was always: This is broken, now you've got to mend it! or else: We want this, that and the other, and where is the money coming from? The collier didn't know and didn't care very deeply—his life was otherwise. So he escaped. He roved the countryside with his dog, prowling for a rabbit, for nests, for mushrooms, anything. He loved the countryside, just the indiscriminating feel of it. Or he loved just to sit on his heels and watch—anything or nothing. He was not intellectually interested. Life for him did not consist in facts, but in a flow. Very often, he loved his garden. And very often he had a genuine love of the beauty of flowers. I have known it often and often, in colliers.

Now the love of flowers is a very misleading thing. Most women love flowers as possessions, and as trimmings. They can't look at a flower, and wonder a moment, and pass on. If they see a flower that arrests their attention, they must at once pick it, pluck it. Possession! A possession! Something added on to *me*! And most of the so-called love of flowers today is merely this reaching out of possession and egoism: something I've *got*: something that embellishes *me*. Yet I've seen many a collier stand in his back garden looking down at a flower with that odd, remote sort of contemplation which shows a *real* awareness of the presence of beauty. It would not even be admiration, or joy, or delight, or any of those things which so often have a root in the possessive instinct. It would be a sort of contemplation: which shows the incipient artist.

The real tragedy of England, as I see it, is the tragedy of ugliness. The country is so lovely: the man-made England is so vile. I know that the ordinary collier, when I was a boy, had a peculiar sense of beauty, coming from his intuitive and instinctive consciousness, which was awakened down pit. And the fact that he met with just cold ugliness and raw materialism when he came up into daylight, and particularly when he came to the Square or the Breach, and to his own table, killed something in him, and in a sense spoiled him as a man. The woman almost invariably nagged about material things. She was taught to do it; she was encouraged to do it. It was a mother's business to see that her sons "got on," and it was the man's business to provide the money. In my father's generation, with the old wild England behind them, and the lack of education, the man was not beaten down. But in my generation, the boys I went to school with, colliers now, have all been beaten down, what with the din-din-dinning of Board Schools, books, cinemas, clergymen, the whole national and human consciousness hammering on the fact of material prosperity above all things.

The men are beaten down, there is prosperity for a time, in their defeat—and then disaster looms ahead. The root of all disaster is disheartenment. And men are disheartened. The men of England, the colliers in particular, are disheartened. They have been betrayed and beaten.

Now though perhaps nobody knew it, it was ugliness which really betrayed the spirit of man, in the nineteenth century. The great crime which the moneyed classes and promoters of industry committed in the palmy Victorian days was the condemning of the workers to ugliness, ugliness, ugliness: meanness and formless and ugly surroundings, ugly ideals, ugly religion, ugly hope, ugly love, ugly clothes, ugly furniture, ugly houses, ugly relationship between workers and employers. The human soul needs actual beauty even more than bread. The middle classes jeer at the colliers for buying pianos—but what is a piano, often as not, but a blind reaching out for beauty. To the woman it is a possession and a piece of furniture and something to feel superior about. But see the elderly colliers trying to learn to play, see them listening with queer alert faces to their daughter's execution of *The Maiden's Prayer,* and you will see a blind, unsatisfied craving for beauty. It is far more deep in the men than the women. The women want show. The men want beauty, and still want it.

If the company, instead of building those sordid and hideous Squares, then, when they had that lovely site to play with, there on the hill top: if they had put a tall column in the middle of the small market-place, and run three parts of a circle of arcade round the pleasant space, where people could stroll or sit, and with handsome houses behind! If they had made big, substantial houses, in apartments of five or six rooms, and with handsome entrances. If above all, they had encouraged song and dancing—for the miners still sang and danced—and provided handsome space for these. If only they had encouraged some form of beauty in dress, some form of beauty in interior life—furniture, decoration. If they had given prizes for the handsomest chair or table, the loveliest scarf, the most charming room that the men or women could make! If only they had done this, there would never have been an industrial problem. The industrial problem arises from the base forcing of all human energy into a competition of mere acquisition.

You may say the working man would not have accepted such a form of life: the Englishman's home is his castle, etc., etc.—"my own little home." But if you can hear every word the next-door people say, there's not much castle. And if you can see everybody in the square if they go to the w.c.! And if your one desire is to get out of your "castle" and your "own little home"!—well, there's not much to be said for it. Anyhow, it's only the woman who idolizes "her own little home"—and it's always the woman at her worst, her most greedy, most possessive, most mean. There's nothing to be said for the "little home" any more: a great scrabble of ugly pettiness over the face of the land.

As a matter of fact, till 1800 the English people were strictly a rural people—very rural. England has had towns for centuries, but they have never been real towns, only clusters of village streets. Never the real *urbs*. The English character has failed to develop the real *urban* side of a man, the civic side. Siena is a bit of a place, but it is a real city, with citizens intimately connected with the city. Nottingham is a vast place sprawling towards a million, and it is nothing more than an amorphous agglomeration. There *is* no Nottingham, in the sense that there is Siena. The Englishman is stupidly undeveloped, as a citizen. And it is partly due to his "little home" stunt, and partly to his acceptance of hopeless paltriness in his surrounding. The new cities of America are much more genuine cities, in the Roman sense, than is London or Manchester. Even Edinburgh used to be more of a true city than any town England ever produced.

That silly little individualism of "the Englishman's home is his castle" and "my own little home" is out of date. It would work almost up to 1800, when every Englishman was still a villager, and a cottager. But the industrial system has brought a great change. The Englishman still likes to think of himself as a "cottager"—"my home, my garden." But it is puerile. Even the farm labourer today is psychologically a town-bird. The English are town-birds through and through, today, as the inevitable result of their complete industrialization. Yet they don't know how to build a city, how to think of one, or how to live in one. They are all suburban, pseudo-cottagy, and not one of them knows how to be truly urban—the citizen as the Romans were citizens—or the Athenians—or even the Parisians, till the war came.

And this is because we have frustrated that instinct of community which would make us unite in pride and dignity in the bigger gesture of the citizen, not the cottager. The great city means, beauty, dignity, and a certain splendour. This is the side of the Englishman that has been thwarted and shockingly betrayed. England is a mean and petty scrabble of paltry dwellings called "homes." I believe in their heart of hearts all Englishmen loathe their little homes—but not the women. What we want is a bigger gesture, a greater scope, a certain splendour, a certain grandeur, and beauty, big beauty. The American does far better than we, in this.

And the promoter of industry, a hundred years ago, dared to perpetrate the ugliness of my native village. And still more monstrous, promoters of industry today are scrabbling over the face of England with miles and square miles of red-brick "homes," like horrible scabs. And the men inside these little red rat-traps get more and more helpless, being more and more humiliated, more and more dissatisfied, like trapped rats. Only the meaner sort of women go on loving the little home which is no more than a rat-trap to her man.

Do away with it all, then. At no matter what cost, start in to alter it. Never mind about wages and industrial squabbling. Turn the attention elsewhere. Pull down my native village to the last brick. Plan a nucleus. Fix the focus. Make a handsome gesture of radiation from the focus. And then put up big buildings, handsome, that sweep to a civic centre. And furnish them with beauty. And make an absolute clean start. Do it place by place. Make a new England. Away with little homes! Away with scrabbling pettiness and paltriness. Look at the contours of the land, and build up from these, with a sufficient nobility. The English may be mentally or spiritually developed. But as citizens of splendid cities they are more ignominious than rabbits. And they nag, nag, nag all the time about politics and wages and all that, like mean narrow housewives.

1930

WHY THE NOVEL MATTERS

We have curious ideas of ourselves. We think of ourselves as a body with a spirit in it, or a body with a soul in it, or a body with a mind in it. *Mens sana in corpore sano.* The years drink up the wine, and at last throw the bottle away, the body, of course, being the bottle.

It is a funny sort of superstition. Why should I look at my hand, as it so cleverly writes these words, and decide that it is a mere nothing compared to the mind that directs it? Is there really any huge difference between my hand and my brain? Or my mind? My hand is alive, it flickers with a life of its own. It meets all the strange universe in touch, and learns a vast number of things, and knows a vast number of things. My hand, as it writes these words, slips gaily along, jumps like a grasshopper to dot an *i*, feels the table rather cold, gets a little bored if I write too long, has its own rudiments of thought, and is just as much *me* as is my brain, my mind, or my soul. Why should I imagine that there is a *me* which is more *me* than my hand is? Since my hand is absolutely alive, me alive.

Whereas, of course, as far as I am concerned, my pen isn't alive at all. My pen *isn't me* alive. Me alive ends at my fingertips.

Whatever is me alive is me. Every tiny bit of my hands is alive, every little freckle and hair and fold of skin. And whatever is me alive is me. Only my fingernails, those ten little weapons between me and an inanimate universe, they cross the mysterious Rubicon between me alive and things like my pen, which are not alive, in my own sense.

So, seeing my hand is all alive, and me alive, wherein is it just a bottle, or a jug, or a tin can, or a vessel of clay, or any of the rest of that nonsense? True, if I cut it it will bleed, like a can of cherries. But then the skin that is cut, and the veins that bleed, and the bones that should never be seen, they are all just as alive as the blood that flows. So the tin can business, or vessel of clay, is just bunk.

And that's what you learn, when you're a novelist. And that's what you are very liable *not* to know, if you're a parson, or a philosopher, or a scientist, or a stupid person. If you're a parson, you talk about souls in heaven. If you're a novelist, you know that paradise is in the palm of your hand, and on the end of your nose, because both are alive; and alive, and man alive, which is more than you can say, for certain, of paradise. Paradise is after life, and I for one am not keen on anything that is *after* life. If you are a philosopher, you talk about infinity, and the pure spirit which knows all things. But if you pick up a novel, you realize immediately that infinity is just a handle to this self-same jug of a body of mine; while as for knowing, if I find my finger in the fire, I know that fire burns, with a knowledge so emphatic and vital, it leaves Nirvana merely a conjecture. Oh, yes, my body, me alive, *knows*, and knows intensely. And as for the sum of all knowledge, it can't be anything more than an accumulation of all things I know in the body, and you, dear reader, know in the body.

These damned philosophers, they talk as if they suddenly went off in steam, and were then much more important than they are when they're in their shirts. It is nonsense. Every man, philosopher included, ends in his own finger-tips. That's the end of his man alive. As for the words and thoughts and sighs and aspirations that fly from him, they are so many tremulations in the ether, and not alive at all. But if the tremulations reach another man alive, he may receive them into his life, and his life may take on a new colour, like a chameleon creeping from a brown rock on to a green leaf. All very well and good. It still doesn't alter the fact that the so-called spirit, the message or teaching of the philosopher or the saint, isn't alive at all, but just a tremulation upon the ether, like a radio message. All this spirit stuff is just tremulations upon the ether. If you, as man alive, quiver from the tremulation of the ether into new life, that is because you are man alive, and you take sustenance and stimulation into your alive man in a myriad ways. But to say that the message, or the spirit which is communicated to you, is more important than your living body, is nonsense. You might as well say that the potato at dinner was more important.

Nothing is important but life. And for myself, I can absolutely see life nowhere but in the living. Life with a capital L is only man alive. Even a cabbage in the rain is cabbage alive. All things that are alive are amazing. And all things that are dead are subsidiary to the living. Better a live dog than a dead lion. But better a live lion than a live dog. *C'est la vie!*

It seems impossible to get a saint, or a philosopher, or a scientist, to stick to this simple truth. They are all, in a sense, renegades. The saint wishes to offer himself up as spiritual food for the multitude. Even Francis of Assisi turns himself into a sort of angel-cake, of which anyone may take a slice. But an angel-cake is rather less than man alive. And poor St. Francis might well apologize to his body, when he is dying: "Oh, pardon me, my body, the wrong I did you through the years!" It was no wafer, for others to eat.

The philosopher, on the other hand, because he can think, decides that nothing but thoughts matter. It is as if a rabbit, because he can make little pills, should decide that nothing but little pills matter. As for the scientist, he has absolutely no use for me so long as I am man alive. To the scientist, I am dead. He puts under the microscope a bit of dead me, and calls it me. He takes me to pieces, and says first one piece, and then another piece, is me. My heart, my liver, my stomach have all been scientifically me, according to the scientist; and nowadays I am either a brain, or nerves, or glands, or something more up-to-date in the tissue line.

Now I absolutely flatly deny that I am a soul, or a body, or a mind, or an intelligence, or a brain, or a nervous system, or a bunch of glands, or any of the rest of these bits of me. The whole is greater than the part. And therefore, I, who am man alive, am greater than my soul, or spirit, or body, or mind or consciousness, or anything else that is merely a part of me. I am a man, and alive. I am man alive, and as long as I can, I intend to go on being man alive.

For this reason I am a novelist. And being a novelist, I consider myself superior to the saint, the scientist, the philosopher, and the poet, who are all great masters of different bits of man alive, but never get the whole hog.

The novel is the one bright book of life. Books are not life. They are only tremulations on the ether. But the novel as a tremulation can make the whole man alive tremble. Which is more than poetry, philosophy, science, or any other book-tremulation can do.

The novel is the book of life. In this sense, the Bible is a great confused novel. You may say, it is about God. But it is really about man alive. Adam, Eve, Sarai, Abraham, Isaac, Jacob, Samuel, David, Bath-Sheba, Ruth, Esther, Solomon, Job, Isaiah, Jesus, Mark, Judas, Paul, Peter: what is it but man alive, from start to finish? Man alive, not mere bits. Even the Lord is another man alive, in a burning bush, throwing the tablets of stone at Moses's head.

I do hope you begin to get my idea, why the novel is supremely important, as a tremulation on the ether. Plato makes the perfect ideal being tremble in me. But that's only a bit of me. Perfection is only a bit, in the strange make-up of man alive. The Sermon on the Mount makes the selfless spirit of me quiver. But that, too, is only a bit of me. The Ten Commandments set the old Adam shivering in me, warning me that I am a thief and a murderer, unless I watch it. But even the old Adam is only a bit of me.

I very much like all these bits of me to be set trembling with life and the wisdom of life. But I do ask that the whole of me shall tremble in its wholeness, some time or other.

And this, of course, must happen in me, living.

But as far as it can happen from a communication, it can only happen when a whole novel communicates itself to me. The Bible —but *all* the Bible—and Homer, and Shakespeare: these are the supreme old novels. These are all things to all men. Which means that in their wholeness they affect the whole man alive, which is the man himself, beyond any part of him. They set the whole tree trembling with a new access of life, they do not just stimulate growth in one direction.

I don't want to grow in any one direction any more. And, if I can help it, I don't want to stimulate anybody else into some particular direction. A particular direction ends in a *cul-de-sac*. We're in a *cul-de-sac* at present.

I don't believe in any dazzling revelation, or in any supreme Word. "The grass withereth, the flower fadeth, but the Word of the Lord shall stand for ever." That's the kind of stuff we've drugged ourselves with. As a matter of fact, the grass withereth, but comes up all the greener for that reason, after the rains. The flower fadeth, and therefore the bud opens. But the Word of the Lord, being man-uttered and a mere vibration on the ether, becomes staler and staler, more and more boring, till at last we turn a deaf ear and it ceases to exist, far more finally than any withered grass. It is grass that renews its youth like the eagle, not any Word.

We should ask for no absolutes, or absolute. Once and for all and for ever, let us have done with the ugly imperialism of any absolute. There is no absolute good, there is nothing absolutely right. All things flow and change, and even change is not absolute. The whole is a strange assembly of apparently incongruous parts, slipping past one another.

Me, man alive, I am a very curious assembly of incongruous parts. My yea! of today is oddly different from my yea! of yesterday. My tears of tomorrow will have nothing to do with my tears of a year ago. If the one I love remains unchanged and unchanging, I shall cease to love her. It is only because she changes and startles me into change and defies my inertia, and is herself staggered in her inertia by my changing, that I can continue to love her. If she stayed put, I might as well love the pepper-pot.

In all this change, I maintain a certain integrity. But woe betide me if I try to put my finger on it. If I say of myself, I am this, I am that!—then, if I stick to it, I turn into a stupid fixed thing like a lamp-post. I shall never know wherein lies my integrity, my individuality, my me. I *can* never know it. It is useless to talk about my ego. That only means that I have made up an *idea* of myself, and that I am trying to cut myself out to pattern. Which is no good. You can cut your cloth to fit your coat, but you can't clip bits off your living body, to trim it down to your idea. True, you can put yourself into ideal corsets. But even in ideal corsets, fashions change.

Let us learn from the novel. In the novel, the characters can do nothing but *live*. If they keep on being good, according to pattern, or bad, according to pattern, or even volatile, according to pattern, they cease to live, and the novel falls dead. A character in a novel has got to live, or it is nothing.

We, likewise, in life have got to live, or we are nothing.

What we mean by living is, of course, just as indescribable as what we mean by *being*. Men get ideas into their heads, of what they mean by Life, and they proceed to cut life out to pattern.

Voc. simulacrum of life

Sometimes they go into the desert to seek God, sometimes they go into the desert to seek cash, sometimes it is wine, woman, and song, and again it is water, political reform, and votes. You never know what it will be next: from killing your neighbour with hideous bombs and gas that tears the lungs, to supporting a Foundlings Home and preaching infinite Love, and being co-respondent in a divorce.

In all this wild welter, we need some sort of guide. It's no good inventing Thou Shalt Nots!

What then? Turn truly, honourably to the novel, and see wherein you are man alive, and wherein you are dead man in life. You may love a woman as man alive, and you may be making love to a woman as sheer dead man in life. You may eat your dinner as man alive, or as a mere masticating corpse. As man alive you may have a shot at your enemy. But as a ghastly simulacrum of life you may be firing bombs into men who are neither your enemies nor your friends, but just things you are dead to. Which is criminal, when the things happen to be alive.

To be alive, to be man alive, to be whole man alive: that is the point. And at its best, the novel, and the novel supremely, can help you. It can help you not to be dead man in life. So much of a man walks about dead and a carcass in the street and house, today: so much of women is merely dead. Like a pianoforte with half the notes mute.

But in the novel you can see, plainly, when the man goes dead, the woman goes inert. You can develop an instinct for life, if you will, instead of a theory of right and wrong, good and bad.

In life, there is right and wrong, good and bad, all the time. But what is right in one case is wrong in another. And in the novel you see one man becoming a corpse, because of his so-called goodness, another going dead because of his so-called wickedness. Right and wrong is an instinct: but an instinct of the whole consciousness in a man, bodily, mental, spiritual at once. And only in the novel are *all* things given full play, or at least, they may be given full play, when we realize that life itself, and not inert safety, is the reason for living. For out of the full play of all things emerges the only thing that is anything, the wholeness of a man, the wholeness of a woman, man alive, and live woman.

1925

George Orwell

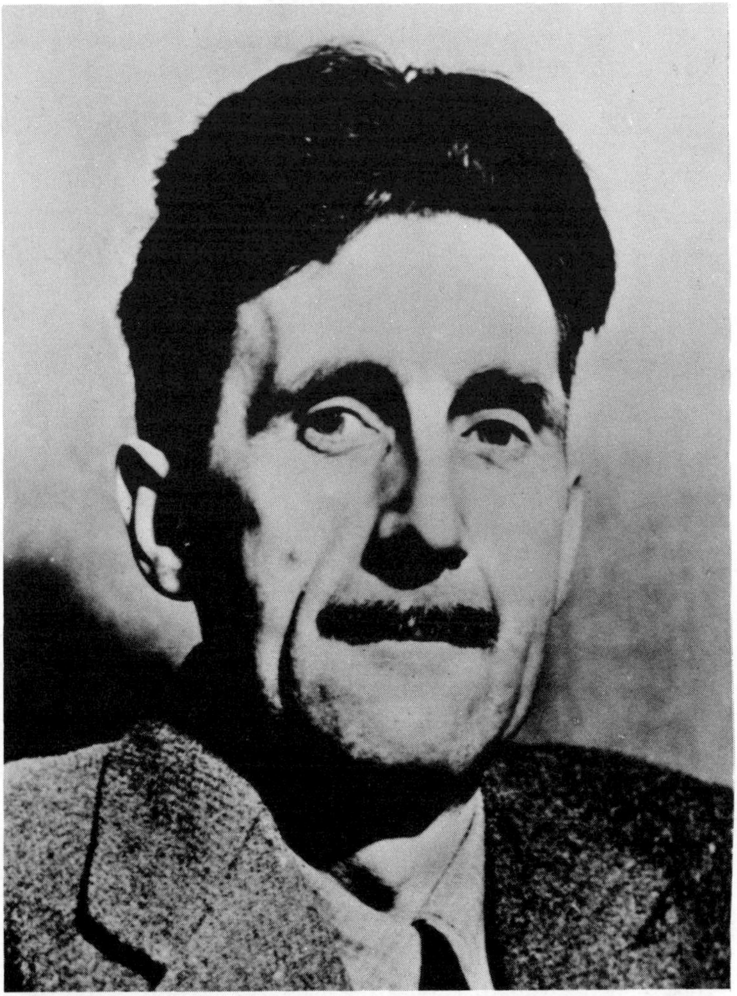

BORN AT MOTIHARI, BENGAL, in 1903, the son of a minor official in the Bengal Civil Service, George Orwell attended private schools in England on scholarships from the age of eight until he was graduated from Eton in 1921. But then, instead of going on to one of the universities as might have been expected, Orwell took the advice of a tutor who suggested that he "see something of the world" and joined the Indian Imperial Police. For five years he was a police officer in Burma, then resigned, as he said, "mainly because I could not go on any longer serving an imperialism which I had come to regard as very largely a racket."

For the next year and a half he lived in Paris on his savings and tried to write, but with little success. When his money ran out in the summer of 1929, he got his first taste of poverty as a *plongeur* (dishwasher) in a Paris restaurant, then as a tramp and day-laborer in London and the south of England. Indeed, being a tramp, sleeping in doss-houses, and eating hand-me-out meals so stimulated Orwell's imagination (and perhaps the psychic needs of an acute class-consciousness from having been a scholarship boy in exclusive schools) that even after he became a schoolteacher, and later a clerk in a London book shop, he continued to dress up in old clothes and go "on the bum" on weekends. In 1933 he published his first book, *Down and Out in Paris and London*, a vivid account of his experiences during the summer of 1929, and for the first time used the pseudonym "George Orwell." As with most other writers who have taken pen-names, the purpose was to keep a secret—in this case from his former Eton schoolmates: that he had once been "down and out." Though he published poetry and many book reviews during the next three years under his real name, Eric Blair, he continued to use the name "Orwell" for his books (the novels *Burmese*

Days, A Clergyman's Daughter, and *Keep the Aspidistra Flying*).

Between the summer of 1936 and the spring of 1937 Orwell underwent a great metamorphosis. Until then he had been a rather shabby, "serious"—but conventional—young poet on the fringes of the London literati, a very Gissing-like, unsuccessful writer, not at all interested in politics. But then a number of things happened. First, Victor Gollancz commissioned him to go to the north of England and observe the lives of the unemployed coal miners and to write a book about it, which the Left Book Club, a socialist organization, would publish (*The Road to Wigan Pier*). Next, he got married, which meant he had to start earning a bit more money. Then John Lehmann invited him to submit something for a new magazine he was editing, and Orwell wrote his first real *essay* (as opposed to book review or reportage): he called it "Shooting an Elephant." And finally, in December, 1936, he left for the Spanish Civil War.

At the time that he arrived in Barcelona, Orwell was so naive about politics that he had only the vaguest notion which faction of the Left (the Republican, or Socialist, side) he wished to join. He was interested in the war mainly as a *war*, not as a battle of political ideologies. But his experiences over the next four months changed everything. To put it very simply, what Orwell discovered was that politics was all lies: that the Tory-dominated British press was distorting the truth about what was happening in Spain; and that the Soviets, who were presumably on the side of the workers, were in fact maneuvering to bring about a socialist defeat. As Orwell wrote many years later, "The Spanish war and other events in 1936-37 turned the scale and thereafter I knew where I stood. Every line of serious work that I have written since 1936 has been written, directly or indirectly, against totalitarianism and *for* democratic socialism, as I understand it." In April, 1937, Orwell was severely wounded while fighting on the Aragon front and was lucky to get out of Spain alive. When he got back to England he wrote the first of his important books, *Homage to Catalonia* (1938).

If the political events he observed in Spain were the turning point of Orwell's intellectual life, his near death might be called its psychological equivalent, for after 1936 Eric Blair vanished:

no more poetry, no more *belles lettres* book reviews, and only one more conventional novel, *Coming Up for Air* (1939). "George Orwell" became George Orwell, a fiercely dedicated political journalist. But even that doesn't describe the writer who emerged from Spain, for Orwell was more than a mere journalist; he became a devil's advocate of twentieth-century liberalism, an iconoclast in the temples of socialism and communism. His last two books, *Animal Farm* (1945) and *1984* (1949), must be read not as novels nor even strictly as satires—though of course *Animal Farm is* a satire—but as Arguments in the service of truth and human freedom.

Orwell died of tuberculosis in 1950, a few months after finishing *1984*. Looking back over his work, the critic V. S. Pritchett declared that Orwell had been "the conscience of his generation," a claim one might examine by reading Orwell's *Collected Essays, Journalism and Letters*, published in 1968 in four volumes.

Orwell was never a member of any political organization. Though he approved of many aspects of socialism, he was never a socialist. Though he defended the rights of the poor and oppressed, and occasionally (as in *1984*) sentimentalized their virtues, he never thought that their limited consciousness was the desired goal of man. Orwell believed in only one thing: honesty—or as he said in one of his essays, the "power of facing unpleasant facts." What he had discovered in Spain in 1937 was that objective truth could cease to exist, that the people who controlled the means of communication could—and *did*—alter it at will, and therefore, as his friend Arthur Koestler has said, history was dead. This, then, was Orwell's great perception, and it was his fear that this sort of "thought-control" was happening not only in the "totalitarian" countries but the "democracies" as well that underlay everything he wrote during the last thirteen years of his life.

As a writer, Orwell's rules were very simple: be clear, be concrete, and avoid all frills and mannerisms. But even these rules, as fine as they are, go only part way in explaining the particular forcefulness of his writing. To understand the rest, one must recall Joseph Conrad's credo: "My task, which I am trying to achieve is, by the power of the written word, to make you hear, to make you feel—it is, above all, to make you *see*." Hearing, feeling, seeing—that is precisely what we are doing when we read George Orwell, and because of it we shall go on reading him for a long time to come.

SHOOTING AN ELEPHANT

In Moulmein, in lower Burma, I was hated by large numbers of people—the only time in my life that I have been important enough for this to happen to me. I was sub-divisional police officer of the town, and in an aimless, petty kind of way anti-European feeling was very bitter. No one had the guts to raise a riot, but if a European woman went through the bazaars alone somebody would probably spit betel juice over her dress. As a police officer I was an obvious target and was baited whenever it seemed safe to do so. When a nimble Burman tripped me up on the football field and the referee (another Burman) looked the other way, the crowd yelled with hideous laughter. This happened more than once. In the end the sneering yellow faces of young men that met me everywhere, the insults hooted after me when I was at a safe distance, got badly on my nerves. The young Buddhist priests were the worst of all. There were several thousands of them in the town and none of them seemed to have anything to do except stand on street corners and jeer at Europeans.

All this was perplexing and upsetting. For at that time I had already made up my mind that imperialism was an evil thing and the sooner I chucked up my job and got out of it the better. Theoretically—and secretly, of course—I was all for the Burmese and all against their oppressors, the British. As for the job I was doing, I hated it more bitterly than I can perhaps make clear. In a job like that you see the dirty work of Empire at close quarters. The wretched prisoners huddling in the stinking cages of the lock-ups, the gray, cowed faces of the long-term convicts, the scarred buttocks of the men who had been flogged with bamboos—all these oppressed me with an intolerable sense of guilt. But I could get nothing into perspective. I was young and ill educated and I had had to think out my problems in the utter silence that is imposed on every Englishman in the East. I did not even know that the British Empire is dying, still less did I know that it is a great deal better than the younger empires that are going to supplant it. All I knew was that I was stuck between my hatred of the empire I served and my rage against the evil-spirited little beasts who tried to make my job impossible. With one part of my mind I thought of the British Raj as an unbreakable tyranny, as something clamped down, in *saecula saeculorum*, upon the will of prostrate peoples; with another part I thought that the greatest joy in the world would be to drive a bayonet into a Buddhist priest's guts. Feelings like these are the normal by-products of imperialism; ask any Anglo-Indian official, if you can catch him off duty.

One day something happened which in a roundabout way was enlightening. It was a tiny incident in itself; but it gave me a better glimpse than I had had before of the real nature of imperialism—the real motives for which despotic governments act. Early one morning the sub-inspector at a police station the other end of the town rang me up on the 'phone and said that an elephant was ravaging the bazaar. Would I please come and do something about it? I did not know what I could do, but I wanted to see what was happening and I got on to a pony and started out. I took my rifle, an old .44 Winchester and much too small to kill an elephant, but I thought the noise might be useful *in terrorem*. Various Burmans stopped me on the way and told me about the elephant's doings. It was not, of course, a wild elephant, but a tame one which had gone "must." It had been chained up, as tame elephants always are when their attack of "must" is due, but on the previous night it had broken its chain and escaped. Its mahout, the only person who could manage it when it was in that state, had set out in pursuit, but had taken the wrong direction and was now twelve hours' journey away, and in the morning the elephant had suddenly reappeared in the town. The Burmese population had no weapons and were quite helpless against it. It had already destroyed somebody's bamboo hut, killed a cow and raided some fruit-stalls and devoured the stock; also it had met the municipal rubbish van and, when the driver jumped out and took to his heels, had turned the van over and inflicted violences upon it.

The Burmese sub-inspector and some Indian constables were waiting for me in the quarter where the elephant had been seen.

It was a very poor quarter, a labyrinth of squalid bamboo huts, thatched with palm-leaf, winding all over a steep hillside. I remember that it was a cloudy, stuffy morning at the beginning of the rains. We began questioning the people as to where the elephant had gone and, as usual, failed to get any definite information. That is invariably the case in the East; a story always sounds clear enough at a distance, but the nearer you get to the scene of events the vaguer it becomes. Some of the people said that the elephant had gone in one direction, some said that he had gone in another, some professed not even to have heard of any elephant. I had almost made up my mind that the whole story was a pack of lies, when we heard yells a little distance away. There was a loud, scandalized cry of "Go away, child! Go away this instant!" and an old woman with a switch in her hand came round the corner of a hut, violently shooing away a crowd of naked children. Some more women followed, clicking their tongues and exclaiming; evidently there was something that the children ought not to have seen. I rounded the hut and saw a man's dead body sprawling in the mud. He was an Indian, a black Dravidian coolie, almost naked, and he could not have been dead many minutes. The people said that the elephant had come suddenly upon him round the corner of the hut, caught him with its trunk, put its foot on his back and ground him into the earth. This was the rainy season and the ground was soft, and his face had scored a trench a foot deep and a couple of yards long. He was lying on his belly with arms crucified and head sharply twisted to one side. His face was coated with mud, the eyes wide open, the teeth bared and grinning with an expression of unendurable agony. (Never tell me, by the way, that the dead look peaceful. Most of the corpses I have seen looked devilish.) The friction of the great beast's foot had stripped the skin from his back as neatly as one skins a rabbit. As soon as I saw the dead man I sent an orderly to a friend's house nearby to borrow an elephant rifle. I had already sent back the pony, not wanting it to go mad with fright and throw me if it smelt the elephant.

The orderly came back in a few minutes with a rifle and five cartridges, and meanwhile some Burmans had arrived and told us that the elephant was in the paddy fields below, only a few hundred yards away. As I started forward practically the whole population of the quarter flocked out of the houses and followed me. They had seen the rifle and were all shouting excitedly that I was going to shoot the elephant. They had not shown much interest in the elephant when he was merely ravaging their homes, but it was different now that he was going to be shot. It was a bit of fun to them, as it would be to an English crowd; besides they wanted the meat. It made me vaguely uneasy. I had no intention of shooting the elephant—I had merely sent for the rifle to defend myself if necessary—and it is always unnerving to have a crowd following you. I marched down the hill, looking and feeling a fool, with the rifle over my shoulder and an ever-growing army of people jostling at my heels. At the bottom, when you got away from the huts, there was a metalled road and beyond that a miry waste of paddy fields a thousand yards across, not yet ploughed but soggy from the first rains and dotted with coarse grass. The elephant was standing eight yards from the road, his left side toward us. He took not the slightest notice of the crowd's approach. He was tearing up bunches of grass, beating them against his knees to clean them, and stuffing them into his mouth.

I had halted on the road. As soon as I saw the elephant I knew with perfect certainty that I ought not to shoot him. It is a serious matter to shoot a working elephant—it is comparable to destroying a huge and costly piece of machinery—and obviously one ought not to do it if it can possibly be avoided. And at that distance, peacefully eating, the elephant looked no more dangerous than a cow. I thought then and I think now that his attack of "must" was already passing off; in which case he would merely wander harmlessly about until the mahout came back and caught him. Moreover, I did not in the least want to shoot him. I decided that I would watch him for a little while to make sure that he did not turn savage again, and then go home.

But at that moment I glanced round at the crowd that had followed me. It was an immense crowd, two thousand at the least and growing every minute. It blocked the road for a long distance on either side. I looked at the sea of yellow faces above the garish clothes—faces all happy and excited over this bit of fun, all certain that the elephant was going to be shot. They were watching me as they would watch a conjurer about to perform a trick. They did not like me, but with the magical rifle in my hands I was momentarily worth watching. And suddenly I realized that I should have to shoot the elephant after all. The people expected it of me and I had got to do it; I could feel their two thousand wills pressing me forward, irresistibly. And it was at this moment, as I stood there with the rifle in my hands, that I first grasped the hollowness, the futility of the white man's dominion in the East. Here was I, the white man with his gun, standing in front of the unarmed native crowd—seemingly the leading actor of the piece; but in reality I was only an absurd puppet pushed to and fro by the will of those yellow faces behind. I perceived in this moment that when the white man turns tyrant it is his own freedom that he destroys. He becomes a sort of hollow, posing dummy, the conventionalized figure of a sahib. For it is the condition of his rule that he shall spend his life in trying to impress the "natives," and so in every crisis he has got to do what the "natives" expect of him. He wears a mask, and his face grows to fit it. I had got to shoot the elephant. I had committed myself to doing it when I sent for the rifle. A sahib has got to act like a sahib; he has got to appear resolute, to know his own mind and do definite things. To come all that way, rifle in hand, with two thousand people marching at my heels, and then to trail feebly away, having done nothing—no, that was impossible. The crowd would laugh at me. And my whole life, every white man's life in the East, was one long struggle not to be laughed at.

But I did not want to shoot the elephant. I watched him beating his bunch of grass against his knees with that preoccupied grandmotherly air that elephants have. It seemed to me that it would be murder to shoot him. At that age I was not squeamish about killing animals, but I had never shot an elephant and never wanted to. (Somehow it always seems worse to kill a *large* animal.) Besides, there was the beast's owner to be considered. Alive, the elephant was worth at least a hundred pounds; dead, he would only be worth the value of his tusks, five pounds, possibly. But I had got to act quickly. I turned to some experienced-looking Burmans who had been there when we arrived, and asked them how the elephant had been behaving. They all said the same thing: he took no notice of you if you left him alone, but he might charge if you went too close to him.

It was perfectly clear to me what I ought to do. I ought to walk up to within, say, twenty-five yards of the elephant and test his behavior. If he charged, I could shoot; if he took no notice of me, it would be safe to leave him until the mahout came back. But also I knew that I was going to do no such thing. I was a poor shot with a rifle and the ground was soft mud into which one would sink at every step. If the elephant charged and I missed him, I should have about as much chance as a toad under a steam-roller. But even then I was not thinking particularly of my own skin, only of the watchful yellow faces behind. For at that moment, with the crowd watching me, I was not afraid in the ordinary sense, as I would have been if I had been alone. A white man mustn't be frightened in front of "natives"; and so, in general, he isn't frightened. The sole thought in my mind was that if anything went wrong those two thousand Burmans would see me pursued, caught, trampled on, and reduced to a grinning corpse like that Indian up the hill. And if that happened it was quite probable that some of them would laugh. That would never do. There was only one alternative. I shoved the cartridges into the magazine and lay down on the road to get a better aim.

The crowd grew very still, and a deep, low, happy sigh, as of people who see the theater curtain go up at last, breathed from innumerable throats. They were going to have their bit of fun after all. The rifle was a beautiful German thing with cross-hair sights. I did not then know that in shooting an elephant one would shoot to cut an imaginary bar running from ear-hole to ear-hole. I ought, therefore, as the elephant was sideways on, to have aimed straight at his ear-hole; actually I aimed several inches in front of this, thinking the brain would be further forward.

When I pulled the trigger I did not hear the bang or feel the kick—one never does when a shot goes home—but I heard the devillish roar of glee that went up from the crowd. In that instant, in too short a time, one would have thought, even for the bullet to get there, a mysterious, terrible change had come over the elephant. He neither stirred, nor fell, but every line of his body had altered. He looked suddenly stricken, shrunken, immensely old, as though the frightful impact of the bullet had paralyzed him without knocking him down. At last, after what seemed a long time—it might have been five seconds, I dare say—he sagged flabbily to his knees. His mouth slobbered. An enormous senility seemed to have settled upon him. One could have imagined him thousands of years old. I fired again into the same spot. At the second shot he did not collapse but climbed with desperate slowness to his feet and stood weakly upright, with legs sagging and head drooping. I fired a third time. That was the shot that did for him. You could see the agony of it jolt his whole body and knock the last remnant of strength from his legs. But in falling he seemed for a moment to rise, for as his hind legs collapsed beneath him he seemed to tower upward like a huge rock toppling, his trunk reaching skyward like a tree. He trumpeted, for the first and only time. And then down he came, his belly toward me, with a crash that seemed to shake the ground even where I lay.

I got up. The Burmans were already racing past me across the mud. It was obvious that the elephant would never rise again, but he was not dead. He was breathing very rhythmically with long rattling gasps, his great mound of a side painfully rising and falling. His mouth was wide open—I could see far down into caverns of pale pink throat. I waited a long time for him to die, but his breathing did not weaken. Finally I fired my two remaining shots into the spot where I thought his heart must be. The thick blood welled out of him like red velvet, but still he did not die. His body did not even jerk when the shots hit him, the tortured breathing continued without a pause. He was dying, very slowly and in great agony, but in some world remote from me where not even a bullet could damage him further. I felt that I had got to put an end to that dreadful noise. It seemed dreadful to see the great beast lying there, powerless to move and yet powerless to die, and not even to be able to finish him. I sent back for my small rifle and poured shot after shot into his heart and down his throat. They seemed to make no impression. The tortured gasps continued as steadily as the ticking of a clock.

In the end I could not stand it any longer and went away. I

heard later that it took him half an hour to die. Burmans were bringing dahs and baskets even before I left, and I was told they had stripped his body almost to the bones by the afternoon.

Afterward, of course, there were endless discussions about the shooting of the elephant. The owner was furious, but he was only an Indian and could do nothing. Besides, legally I had done the right thing, for a mad elephant has to be killed, like a mad dog, if its owner fails to control it. Among the Europeans opinion was divided. The older men said I was right, the younger men said it was a damn shame to shoot an elephant for killing a coolie, because an elephant was worth more than any damn Coringhee coolie. And afterward I was very glad that the coolie had been killed; it put me legally in the right and it gave me a sufficient pretext for shooting the elephant. I often wondered whether any of the others grasped that I had done it solely to avoid looking a fool.

1936

MARRAKECH

As the corpse went past the flies left the restaurant table in a cloud and rushed after it, but they came back a few minutes later.

The little crowd of mourners—all men and boys, no women—threaded their way across the market-place between the piles of pomegranates and the taxis and the camels, wailing a short chant over and over again. What really appeals to the flies is that the corpses here are never put into coffins, they are merely wrapped in a piece of rag and carried on a rough wooden bier on the shoulders of four friends. When the friends get to the burying-ground they hack an oblong hole a foot or two deep, dump the body in it and fling over it a little of the dried-up, lumpy earth, which is like broken brick. No gravestone, no name, no identifying mark of any kind. The burying-ground is merely a huge waste of hummocky earth, like a derelict building-lot. After a month or two no one can even be certain where his own relatives are buried.

When you walk through a town like this—two hundred thousand inhabitants, of whom at least twenty thousand own literally nothing except the rags they stand up in—when you see how the people live, and still more how easily they die, it is always difficult to believe that you are walking among human beings. All colonial empires are in reality founded upon that fact. The people have brown faces—besides, there are so many of them! Are they really the same flesh as yourself? Do they even have names? Or are they merely a kind of undifferentiated brown stuff, about as individual as bees or coral insects? They rise out of the earth, they sweat and starve for a few years, and then they sink back into the nameless mounds of the graveyard and nobody notices that they are gone. And even the graves themselves soon fade back into the soil. Sometimes, out for a walk, as you break your way through the prickly pear, you notice that it is rather bumpy underfoot, and only a certain regularity in the bumps tells you that you are walking over skeletons.

I was feeding one of the gazelles in the public gardens.

Gazelles are almost the only animals that look good to eat when they are still alive, in fact, one can hardly look at their hindquarters without thinking of mint sauce. The gazelle I was feeding seemed to know that this thought was in my mind, for though it took the piece of bread I was holding out it obviously did not like me. It nibbled rapidly at the bread, then lowered its head and tried to butt me, then took another nibble and then butted again. Probably its idea was that if it could drive me away the bread would somehow remain hanging in mid-air.

An Arab navvy working on the path nearby lowered his heavy hoe and sidled towards us. He looked from the gazelle to the bread and from the bread to the gazelle, with a sort of quiet amazement, as though he had never seen anything quite like this before. Finally he said shyly in French:

"*I* could eat some of that bread."

I tore off a piece and he stowed it gratefully in some secret place under his rags. This man is an employee of the Municipality.

When you go through the Jewish quarters you gather some idea of what the medieval ghettoes were probably like. Under their Moorish rulers the Jews were only allowed to own land in certain restricted areas, and after centuries of this kind of treatment they have ceased to bother about overcrowding. Many of the streets are a good deal less than six feet wide, the houses are completely windowless, and sore-eyed children cluster everywhere in unbelievable numbers, like clouds of flies. Down the centre of the street there is generally running a little river of urine.

In the bazaar huge families of Jews, all dressed in the long black robe and little black skull-cap, are working in dark fly-infested booths that look like caves. A carpenter sits cross-legged at a prehistoric lathe, turning chair-legs at lightning speed. He works the lathe with a bow in his right hand and guides the chisel with his left foot, and thanks to a lifetime of sitting in this position his left leg is warped out of shape. At his side his grandson, aged six, is already starting on the simpler parts of the job.

I was just passing the coppersmiths' booths when somebody noticed that I was lighting a cigarette. Instantly, from the dark holes all round, there was a frenzied rush of Jews, many of them old grandfathers with flowing grey beards, all clamouring for a cigarette. Even a blind man somewhere at the back of one of the booths heard a rumour of cigarettes and came crawling out, groping in the air with his hand. In about a minute I had used up the whole packet. None of these people, I suppose, works less than twelve hours a day, and every one of them looks on a cigarette as a more or less impossible luxury.

As the Jews live in self-contained communities they follow the same trades as the Arabs, except for agriculture. Fruit-sellers, potters, silversmiths, blacksmiths, butchers, leather-workers, tailors, water-carriers, beggars, porters—whichever way you look you see nothing but Jews. As a matter of fact there are thirteen thousand of them, all living in the space of a few acres. A good job Hitler isn't here. Perhaps he is on his way, however. You hear the usual dark rumours about the Jews, not only from the Arabs but from the poorer Europeans.

"Yes, *mon vieux*, they took my job away from me and gave it to a Jew. The Jews! They're the real rulers of this country, you know. They've got all the money. They control the banks, finance —everything."

"But," I said, "isn't it a fact that the average Jew is a labourer working for about a penny an hour?"

"Ah, that's only for show! They're all moneylenders really. They're cunning, the Jews."

In just the same way, a couple of hundred years ago, poor old women used to be burned for witchcraft when they could not even work enough magic to get themselves a square meal.

All people who work with their hands are partly invisible, and the more important the work they do, the less visible they are. Still, a white skin is always fairly conspicuous. In northern Europe, when you see a labourer ploughing a field, you probably give him a second glance. In a hot country, anywhere south of Gibraltar or east of Suez, the chances are that you don't even see him. I have noticed this again and again. In a tropical landscape one's eye takes in everything except the human beings. It takes in the dried-up soil, the prickly pear, the palm-tree and the distant mountain, but it always misses the peasant hoeing at his patch. He is the same colour as the earth, and a great deal less interesting to look at.

It is only because of this that the starved countries of Asia and Africa are accepted as tourist resorts. No one would think of running cheap trips to the Distressed Areas. But where the human beings have brown skins their poverty is simply not noticed. What does Morocco mean to a Frenchman? An orange-grove or a job in government service. Or to an Englishman? Camels, castles, palm-trees, Foreign Legionnaires, brass trays and bandits. One could probably live here for years without noticing that for nine-tenths of the people the reality of life is an endless, back-breaking struggle to wring a little food out of an eroded soil.

Most of Morocco is so desolate that no wild animal bigger than a hare can live on it. Huge areas which were once covered with forest have turned into a treeless waste where the soil is exactly like broken-up brick. Nevertheless a good deal of it is cultivated, with frightful labour. Everything is done by hand. Long lines of women, bent double like inverted capital Ls, work their way slowly across the field, tearing up the prickly weeds with their hands, and the peasant gathering lucerne for fodder pulls it up stalk by stalk instead of reaping it, thus saving an inch or two on each stalk. The plough is a wretched wooden thing, so frail that one can easily carry it on one's shoulder, and fitted underneath with a rough iron spike which stirs the soil to a depth of about four inches. This is as much as the strength of the animals is equal to. It is usual to plough with a cow and a donkey yoked together. Two donkeys would not be quite strong enough, but on the other hand two cows would cost a little more to feed. The peasants possess no harrows, they merely plough the soil several times over in different directions, finally leaving it in rough furrows, after which the whole field has to be shaped with hoes into small oblong patches, to conserve water. Except for a day or two after the rare rainstorms there is never enough water. Along the edges of the fields channels are hacked out to a depth of thirty or forty feet to get at the tiny trickles which run through the subsoil.

Every afternoon a file of very old women passes down the road outside my house, each carrying a load of firewood. All of them are mummified with age and the sun, and all of them are tiny. It seems to be generally the case in primitive communities that the women, when they get beyond a certain age, shrink to the size of children. One day a poor old creature who could not have been more than four feet tall crept past me under a vast load of wood. I stopped her and put a five-sou piece (a little more than a farthing) into her hand. She answered with a shrill wail, almost a scream, which was partly gratitude but mainly surprise. I suppose that from her point of view, by taking any notice of her, I seemed almost to be violating a law of nature. She accepted her status as an old woman, that is to say as a beast of burden. When a family is travelling it is quite usual to see a father and a grown-up son riding ahead on donkeys, and an old woman following on foot, carrying the baggage.

But what is strange about these people is their invisibility. For several weeks, always at about the same time of day, the file of old women had hobbled past the house with their firewood, and though they had registered themselves on my eyeballs I cannot truly say that I had seen them. Firewood was passing—that was how I saw it. It was only that one day I happened to be walking behind them, and the curious up-and-down motion of a load of wood drew my attention to the human being underneath it. Then for the first time I noticed the poor old earth-coloured bodies, bodies reduced to bones and leathery skin, bent double under the crushing weight. Yet I suppose I had not been five minutes on Moroccan soil before I noticed the overloading of the donkeys and was infuriated by it. There is no question that the donkeys are damnably treated. The Moroccan donkey is hardly bigger than a St Bernard dog, it carries a load which in the British army would be considered too much for a fifteen-hands mule, and very often its pack-saddle is not taken off its back for weeks together. But what is peculiarly pitiful is that it is the most willing creature on earth, it follows its master like a dog and does not need either bridle or halter. After a dozen years of devoted work it suddenly drops dead, whereupon its master tips it into the ditch and the village dogs have torn its guts out before it is cold.

This kind of thing makes one's blood boil, whereas—on the whole—the plight of the human beings does not. I am not commenting, merely pointing to a fact. People with brown skins are next door to invisible. Anyone can be sorry for the donkey with its galled back, but it is generally owing to some kind of accident if one even notices the old woman under her load of sticks.

As the storks flew northward the Negroes were marching southward—a long, dusty column, infantry, screw-gun batteries and then more infantry, four or five thousand men in all, winding up the road with a clumping of boots and a clatter of iron wheels.

They were Senegalese, the blackest Negroes in Africa, so black that sometimes it is difficult to see whereabouts on their necks the hair begins. Their splendid bodies were hidden in reach-me-down khaki uniforms, their feet squashed into boots that looked like blocks of wood, and every tin hat seemed to be a couple of sizes too small. It was very hot and the men had marched a long way. They slumped under the weight of their packs and the curiously sensitive black faces were glistening with sweat.

As they went past a tall, very young Negro turned and caught my eye. But the look he gave me was not in the least the kind of look you might expect. Not hostile, not contemptuous, not sullen, not even inquisitive. It was the shy, wide-eyed Negro look, which actually is a look of profound respect. I saw how it was. This wretched boy, who is a French citizen and has therefore been dragged from the forest to scrub floors and catch syphilis in garrison towns, actually has feelings of reverence before a white skin. He has been taught that the white race are his masters, and he still believes it.

But there is one thought which every white man (and in this connection it doesn't matter twopence if he calls himself a Socialist) thinks when he sees a black army marching past. "How much longer can we go on kidding these people? How long before they turn their guns in the other direction?"

It was curious, really. Every white man there has this thought stowed somewhere or other in his mind. I had it, so had the other onlookers, so had the officers on their sweating chargers and the white NCOs marching in the ranks. It was a kind of secret which we all knew and were too clever to tell; only the Negroes didn't know it. And really it was almost like watching a flock of cattle to see the long column, a mile or two miles of armed men, flowing peacefully up the road, while the great white birds drifted over them in the opposite direction, glittering like scraps of paper.

1939

HOW THE POOR DIE

In the year 1929 I spent several weeks in the Hôpital X, in the fifteenth *arrondissement* of Paris. The clerks put me through the usual third-degree at the reception desk, and indeed I was kept answering questions for some twenty minutes before they would let me in. If you have ever had to fill up forms in a Latin country you will know the kind of questions I mean. For some days past I had been unequal to translating Réaumur into Fahrenheit, but I know that my temperature was round about 103, and by the end of the interview I had some difficulty in standing on my feet. At my back a resigned little knot of patients, carrying bundles done up in coloured handkerchiefs, waited their turn to be questioned.

After the questioning came the bath—a compulsory routine for all newcomers, apparently, just as in prison or the workhouse. My clothes were taken away from me, and after I had sat shivering for some minutes in five inches of warm water I was given a linen nightshirt and a short blue flannel dressing-gown—no slippers, they had none big enough for me, they said—and led out into the open air. This was a night in February and I was suffering from pneumonia. The ward we were going to was 200 yards away and it seemed that to get to it you had to cross the hospital grounds. Someone stumbled in front of me with a lantern. The gravel path was frosty underfoot, and the wind whipped the nightshirt round my bare calves. When we got into the ward I was aware of a strange feeling of familiarity whose origin I did not succeed in pinning down till later in the night. It was a long, rather low, ill-lit room, full of murmuring voices and with three rows of beds surprisingly close together. There was a foul smell, faecal and yet sweetish. As I lay down I saw on a bed nearly opposite me a small, round-shouldered, sandy-haired man sitting half naked while a doctor and a student performed some strange operation on him. First the doctor produced from his black bag a dozen small glasses like wine glasses, then the student burned a match inside each glass to exhaust the air, then the glass was popped on to the man's back or chest and the vacuum drew up a huge yellow blister. Only after some moments did I realise what they were doing to him. It was something called cupping, a treatment which you can read about in old medical text-books but which till then I had vaguely thought of as one of those things they do to horses.

The cold air outside had probably lowered my temperature, and I watched this barbarous remedy with detachment and even a certain amount of amusement. The next moment, however, the doctor and the student came across to my bed, hoisted me upright and without a word began applying the same set of glasses, which had not been sterilised in any way. A few feeble protests that I uttered got no more response than if I had been an animal. I was very much impressed by the impersonal way in which the two men started on me. I had never been in the public ward of a hospital before, and it was my first experience of doctors who handle you without speaking to you, or, in a human sense, taking any notice of you. They only put on six glasses in my case, but after doing so they scarified the blisters and applied the glasses again. Each glass now drew out about a dessert-spoonful of dark-coloured blood. As I lay down again, humiliated, disgusted and frightened by the thing that had been done to me, I reflected that now at least they would leave me alone. But no, not a bit of it. There was another treatment coming, the mustard poultice, seemingly a matter of routine like the hot bath. Two slatternly nurses had already got the poultice ready, and they lashed it round my chest as tight as a strait jacket while some men who were wandering about the ward in shirt and trousers began to collect round my bed with half-sympathetic grins. I learned later that watching a patient have a mustard poultice was a favourite pastime in the ward. These things are normally applied for a quarter of an hour and certainly they are funny enough if you don't happen to be the person inside. For the first five minutes the pain is severe, but you believe you can bear it. During the second five minutes this belief evaporates, but the poultice is buckled at the back and you can't get it off. This is the period the onlookers most enjoy. During the last five minutes, I noted a sort of numbness supervenes. After the poultice had been removed a waterproof pillow packed with ice was thrust beneath my head and I was left alone. I did not sleep and to the best of my knowledge this was the only night of my life—I mean the only night spent in bed—in which I have not slept at all, not even a minute.

During my first hour in the Hôpital X, I had had a whole series of different and contradictory treatments, but this was misleading, for in general you got very little treatment at all, either good or bad, unless you were ill in some interesting and instructive way. At five in the morning the nurses came round, woke the patients and took their temperatures, but did not wash them. If you were well enough you washed yourself, otherwise you depended on the kindness of some walking patient. It was generally patients, too, who carried the bed-bottles and the grim bed-pan, nicknamed *la casserole*. At eight breakfast arrived, called army-fashion *la soupe*. It was soup, too, a thin vegetable soup with slimy hunks of bread floating about in it. Later in the day the tall, solemn, black-bearded doctor made his rounds, with an *interne* and a troop of students following at his heels, but there were about sixty of us in the ward and it was evident that he had other wards to attend to as well. There were many beds past which he walked day after day, sometimes followed by imploring cries. On the other hand if you had some disease with which the students wanted to familiarise themselves you got plenty of attention of a kind. I myself, with an exceptionally fine specimen of a bronchial rattle, sometimes had as many as a dozen students queueing up to listen to my chest. It was a very queer feeling—queer, I mean, because of their intense interest in learning their job, together with a seeming lack of any perception that the patients were human beings. It is strange to relate, but sometimes as some young student stepped forward to take his turn at manipulating you he would be actually tremulous with excitement, like a boy who has at last got his hands on some expensive piece of machinery. And then ear after ear—ears of young men, of girls, of Negroes—pressed against your back, relays of fingers solemnly but clumsily tapping, and not from any one of them did you get a word of conversation or a look direct in your face. As a non-paying patient, in the uniform nightshirt, you were primarily *a specimen*, a thing I did not resent but could never quite get used to.

After some days I grew well enough to sit up and study the surrounding patients. The stuffy room, with its narrow beds so close together that you could easily touch your neighbour's hand, had every sort of disease in it except, I suppose, acutely infectious cases. My right-hand neighbour was a little red-haired cobbler with one leg shorter than the other, who used to announce the death of any other patient (this happened a number of times, and my neighbour was always the first to hear of it) by whistling to me, exclaiming "*Numéro 43!*" (or whatever it was) and flinging his arms above his head. This man had not much wrong with him, but in most of the other beds within my angle of vision some squalid tragedy or some plain horror was being enacted. In the bed that was foot to foot with mine there lay, until he died (I didn't see him die—they moved him to another bed), a little weazened man who was suffering from I do not know what disease, but something that made his whole body so intensely sensitive that any movement from side to side, sometimes even the weight of the bed-clothes, would make him shout out with pain. His worst suffering was when he urinated, which he did with the greatest difficulty. A nurse would bring him the bed-bottle and then for a long time stand beside his bed, whistling, as grooms are said to do with horses, until at last with an agonised shriek of "*Je pisse!*" he would get started. In the bed next to him the sandy-haired man whom I had seen being cupped used to cough up blood-streaked mucus at all hours. My left-hand neighbour was a tall, flaccid-looking young man who used periodically to have a tube inserted into his back and astonishing quantities of frothy liquid drawn off from some part of his body. In the bed beyond that a veteran of the war of 1870 was dying, a handsome old man with a white imperial, round whose bed, at all hours when visiting was allowed, four elderly female relatives dressed all in black sat exactly like crows, obviously scheming for some pitiful legacy. In the bed opposite me in the further row was an old bald-headed man with drooping moustaches and greatly swollen face and body, who was suffering from some disease that made him urinate almost incessantly. A huge glass receptacle stood always beside his bed. One day his wife and daughter came to visit him. At the sight of them the old man's bloated face lit up with a smile of surprising sweetness, and as his daughter, a pretty girl of about twenty, approached the bed I saw that his hand was slowly working its way from under the bed-clothes. I seemed to see in advance the gesture that was coming—the girl kneeling beside the bed, the old man's hand laid on her head in his dying blessing. But no, he merely handed her the bed-bottle, which she promptly took from him and emptied into the receptacle.

About a dozen beds away from me was *numéro* 57—I think that was his number—a cirrhosis of the liver case. Everyone in the ward knew him by sight because he was sometimes the subject of a medical lecture. On two afternoons a week the tall, grave doctor would lecture in the ward to a party of students, and on more than one occasion old *numéro* 57 was wheeled on a sort of trolley into the middle of the ward, where the doctor would roll back his nightshirt, dilate with his fingers a huge flabby protuberance on the man's belly—the diseased liver, I suppose—and explain solemnly that this was a disease attributable to alcoholism, commoner in the wine-drinking countries. As usual he neither spoke to his patient nor gave him a smile, a nod or any kind of recognition. While he talked, very grave and upright, he would hold the wasted body beneath his two hands, sometimes giving it a gentle roll to and fro, in just the attitude of a woman handling a rolling-pin. Not that *numéro* 57 minded this kind of thing. Obviously he was an old hospital inmate, a regular exhibit at lectures, his liver long since marked down for a bottle in some pathological museum. Utterly uninterested in what was said about him, he would lie with his colourless eyes gazing at nothing, while the doctor showed him off like a piece of antique china. He was a man of about sixty, astonishingly shrunken. His face, pale as vellum, had shrunken away till it seemed no bigger than a doll's.

One morning my cobbler neighbour woke me by plucking at my pillow before the nurses arrived. "*Numéro 57!*"—he flung his arms above his head. There was a light in the ward, enough to see by. I could see old *numéro* 57 lying crumpled up on his side, his face sticking out over the side of the bed, and towards me. He had died some time during the night, nobody knew when. When the nurses came they received the news of his death indifferently and went about their work. After a long time, an hour or more, two other nurses marched in abreast like soldiers, with a great clumping of sabots, and knotted the corpse up in the sheets, but it was not removed till some time later. Meanwhile, in the better light, I had had time for a good look at *numéro 57*. Indeed I lay on my side to look at him. Curiously enough he was the first dead European I had seen. I had seen dead men before, but always Asiatics and usually people who had died violent deaths. *Numéro 57*'s eyes were still open, his mouth also open, his small face contorted into an expression of agony. What most impressed me however was the whiteness of his face. It had been pale before, but now it was little darker than the sheets. As I gazed at the tiny, screwed-up face it struck me that this disgusting piece of refuse, waiting to be carted away and dumped on a slab in the dissecting room, was an example of "natural" death, one of the things you pray for in the Litany. There you are, then, I thought, that's what is waiting for you, twenty, thirty, forty years hence: that is how the lucky ones die, the ones who live to be old. One wants to live, of course, indeed one only stays alive by virtue of the fear of death, but I think now, as I thought then, that it's better to die violently and not too old. People talk about the horrors of war, but what weapon has man invented that even approaches in cruelty some of the commoner diseases? "Natural" death, almost by definition, means something slow, smelly and painful. Even at that, it makes a difference if you can achieve it in your own home and not in a public institution. This poor old wretch who had just flickered out like a candle-end was not even important enough to have anyone watching by his deathbed. He was merely a number, then a "subject" for the students' scalpels. And the sordid publicity of dying in such a place! In the Hôpital X the beds were very close together and there were no screens. Fancy, for instance, dying like the little man whose bed was for a while foot to foot with mine, the one who cried out when the bedclothes touched him! I dare say *Je pisse!* were his last recorded words. Perhaps the dying don't bother about such things—that at least would be the standard answer: nevertheless dying people are often more or less normal in their minds till within a day or so of the end.

In the public wards of a hospital you see horrors that you don't seem to meet with among people who manage to die in their own homes, as though certain diseases only attacked people at the lower income levels. But it is a fact that you would not in any English hospitals see some of the things I saw in the Hôpital X. This business of people just dying like animals, for instance, with nobody standing by, nobody interested, the death not even noticed till the morning—this happened more than once. You certainly would not see that in England, and still less would you see a corpse left exposed to the view of the other patients. I remember that once in a cottage hospital in England a man died while we were at tea, and though there were only six of us in the ward the nurses managed things so adroitly that the man was dead and his body removed without our even hearing about it till tea was over. A thing we perhaps underrate in England is the advantage we enjoy in having large numbers of well-trained and rigidly-disciplined nurses. No doubt English nurses are dumb enough, they may tell fortunes with tea-leaves, wear Union Jack badges and keep photographs of the Queen on their mantelpieces, but at least they don't let you lie unwashed and constipated on an unmade bed, out of sheer laziness. The nurses at the Hôpital X still had a tinge of Mrs Gamp about them, and later, in the military hospitals of Republican Spain, I was to see nurses almost too ignorant to take a temperature. You wouldn't, either, see in England such dirt as existed in the Hôpital X. Later on, when I was well enough to wash myself in the bathroom, I found that there was kept there a huge packing-case into which the scraps of food and dirty dressings from the ward were flung, and the wainscottings were infested by crickets.

When I had got back my clothes and grown strong on my legs I fled from the Hôpital X, before my time was up and without waiting for a medical discharge. It was not the only hospital I have fled from, but its gloom and bareness, its sickly smell and, above all, something in its mental atmosphere stand out in my memory as exceptional. I had been taken there because it was the hospital belonging to my *arrondissement*, and I did not learn till after I was in it that it bore a bad reputation. A year or two later the celebrated swindler, Madame Hanaud, who was ill while on remand, was taken to the Hôpital X, and after a few days of it she managed to elude her guards, took a taxi and drove back to the prison, explaining that she was more comfortable there. I have no doubt that the Hôpital X was quite untypical of French hospitals even at that date. But the patients, nearly all of them working men, were surprisingly resigned. Some of them seemed to find the conditions almost comfortable, for at least two were destitute malingerers who found this a good way of getting through the winter. The nurses connived because the malingerers made themselves useful by doing odd jobs. But the attitude of the majority was: of course this is a lousy place, but what else do you expect? It did not seem strange to them that you should be woken at five and then wait three hours before starting the day on watery soup, or that people should die with no one at their bedside, or even that your chance of getting medical attention should depend on catching the doctor's eye as he went past. According to their traditions that was what hospitals were like. If you are seriously ill, and if you are too poor to be treated in your own home, then you must go into hospital, and once there you must put up with harshness and discomfort, just as you would in the army. But on top of this I was interested to find a lingering belief in the old stories that have now almost faded from memory in England—stories, for instance, about doctors cutting you open out of sheer curiosity or thinking it funny to start operating before you were properly "under". There were dark tales about a little operating room said to be situated just beyond the bathroom. Dreadful screams were said to issue from this room. I saw nothing to confirm these stories and no doubt they were all nonsense, though I did see two students kill a sixteen-year-old boy, or nearly kill him (he appeared to be dying when I left the hospital, but he may have recovered later) by a mischievous experiment which they probably could not have tried on a paying patient. Well within living memory it used to be believed in London that in some of the big hospitals patients were killed off to get dissection subjects. I didn't hear this tale repeated at the Hôpital X, but I should think some of the men there would have found it credible. For it was a hospital in which not the methods, perhaps, but something of the atmosphere of the nineteenth century had managed to survive, and therein lay its peculiar interest.

During the past fifty years or so there has been a great change in the relationship between doctor and patient. If you look at almost any literature before the later part of the nineteenth century, you find that a hospital is popularly regarded as much the same thing as a prison, and an old-fashioned, dungeon-like prison at that. A hospital is a place of filth, torture and death, a sort of antechamber to the tomb. No one who was not more or less destitute would have thought of going into such a place for treatment. And especially in the early part of the last century, when medical science had grown bolder than before without being any more successful, the whole business of doctoring was looked on with horror and dread by ordinary people. Surgery, in particular, was believed to be no more than a peculiarly gruesome form of sadism, and dissection, possible only with the aid of body-snatchers, was even confused with necromancy. From the nineteenth century you could collect a large horror-literature connected with doctors and hospitals. Think of poor old George III, in his dotage, shrieking for mercy as he sees his surgeons approaching to "bleed him till he faints"! Think of the conversations of Bob Sawyer and Benjamin Allen, which no doubt are hardly parodies, or the field hospitals in *La Débâcle* and *War and Peace,* or that shocking description of an amputation in Melville's *Whitejacket*! Even the names given to doctors in nineteenth-century English fiction, Slasher, Carver, Sawyer, Fillgrave and so on, and the generic nickname "sawbones", are about as grim as they are comic. The anti-surgery tradition is perhaps best expressed in Tennyson's poem "The Children's Hospital!", which is essentially a pre-chloroform document though it seems to have been written as late as 1880. Moreover, the outlook which Tennyson records in this poem had a lot to be said for it. When you consider what an operation without anaesthetics must have been like, what it notoriously *was* like, it is difficult not to suspect the motives of people who would undertake such things. For these bloody horrors which the students so eagerly looked forward to ("A magnificent sight if Slasher does it!") were admittedly more or less useless: the patient who did not die of shock usually died of gangrene, a result which was taken for granted. Even now doctors can be found whose motives are questionable. Anyone who has had much illness, or who has listened to medical students talking, will know what I mean. But anaesthetics were a turning-point, and disinfectants were another. Nowhere in the world, probably, would you now see the kind of scene described by Axel Munthe in *The Story of San Michele,* when the sinister surgeon in top-hat and frock-coat, his starched shirtfront spattered with blood and pus, carves up patient after patient with the same knife and flings the severed limbs into a pile beside the table. Moreover, national health insurance has partly done away with the idea that a working-class patient is a pauper who deserves little consideraton. Well into this century it was usual for "free" patients at the big hospitals to have their teeth extracted with no anaesthetic. They didn't pay, so why should they have an anaesthetic—that was the attitude. That too has changed.

And yet every institution will always bear upon it some lingering memory of its past. A barrack-room is still haunted by the ghost of Kipling, and it is difficult to enter a workhouse without being reminded of *Oliver Twist.* Hospitals began as a kind of casual ward for lepers and the like to die in, and they continued as places where medical students learned their art on the bodies of the poor. You can still catch a faint suggestion of their history in their characteristically gloomy architecture. I would be far from complaining about the treatment I have received in any English hospital, but I do know that it is a sound instinct that warns people to keep out of hospitals if possible, and especially out of the public wards. Whatever the legal position may be, it is unquestionable that you have far less control over your own treatment, far less certainty that frivolous experiments will not be tried on you, when it is a case of "accept the discipline or get out". And it is a great thing to die in your own bed, though it is better still to die in your boots. However great the kindness and the efficiency, in every hospital death there will be some cruel, squalid detail, something perhaps too small to be told but leaving terribly painful memories behind, arising out of the haste, the crowding, the impersonality of a place where every day people are dying among strangers.

The dread of hospitals probably still survives among the very poor and in all of us it has only recently disappeared. It is a dark patch not far beneath the surface of our minds. I have said earlier that, when I entered the ward at the Hôpital X, I was conscious of a strange feeling of familiarity. What the scene reminded me of, of course, was the reeking, pain-filled hospitals of the nineteenth century, which I had never seen but of which I had a traditional knowledge. And something, perhaps the black-clad doctor with his frowsy black bag, or perhaps only the sickly smell, played the queer trick of unearthing from my memory that poem of Tennyson's, "The Children's Hospital", which I had not thought of for twenty years. It happened that as a child I had it read aloud to me by a sick-nurse whose own working life might have stretched back to the time when Tennyson wrote the poem. The horrors and sufferings of the old-style hospitals were a vivid memory to her. We had shuddered over the poem together, and then seemingly I had forgotten it. Even its name would probably have recalled nothing to me. But the first glimpse of the ill-lit, murmurous room, with the beds so close together, suddenly roused the train of thought to which it belonged, and in the night that followed I found myself remembering the whole story and atmosphere of the poem, with many of its lines complete.

1946

WHY I WRITE

From a very early age, perhaps the age of five or six, I knew that when I grew up I should be a writer. Between the ages of about seventeen and twenty-four I tried to abandon this idea, but I did so with the consciousness that I was outraging my true nature and that sooner or later I should have to settle down and write books.

I was the middle child of three, but there was a gap of five years on either side, and I barely saw my father before I was eight. For this and other reasons I was somewhat lonely, and I soon developed disagreeable mannerisms which made me unpopular throughout my schooldays. I had the lonely child's habit of making up stories and holding conversations with imaginary persons, and I think from the very start my literary ambitions were mixed up with the feeling of being isolated and undervalued. I knew that I had a facility with words and a power of facing unpleasant facts, and I felt that this created a sort of private world in which I could get my own back for my failure in everyday life. Nevertheless the volume of serious—i.e. seriously intended—writing which I produced all through my childhood and boyhood would not amount to half a dozen pages. I wrote my first poem at the age of four or five, my mother taking it down to dictation. I cannot remember anything about it except that it was about a tiger and the tiger had "chair-like teeth"—a good enough phrase, but I fancy the poem was a plagiarism of Blake's "Tiger, Tiger". At eleven, when the war of 1914–18 broke out, I wrote a patriotic poem which was printed in the local newspaper, as was another, two years later, on the death of Kitchener. From time to time, when I was a bit older, I wrote bad and usually unfinished "nature poems" in the Georgian style. I also, about twice, attempted a short story which was a ghastly failure. That was the total of the would-be serious work that I actually set down on paper during all those years.

However, throughout this time I did in a sense engage in literary activities. To begin with there was the made-to-order stuff which I produced quickly, easily and without much pleasure to myself. Apart from school work, I wrote *vers d'occasion*, semi-comic poems which I could turn out at what now seems to me astonishing speed—at fourteen I wrote a whole rhyming play, in imitation of Aristophanes, in about a week—and helped to edit school magazines, both printed and in manuscript. These magazines were the most pitiful burlesque stuff that you could imagine, and I took far less trouble with them than I now would with the cheapest journalism. But side by side with all this, for fifteen years or more, I was carrying out a literary exercise of a quite different kind: this was the making up of a continuous "story" about myself, a sort of diary existing only in the mind.

I believe this is a common habit of children and adolescents. As a very small child I used to imagine that I was, say, Robin Hood, and picture myself as the hero of thrilling adventures, but quite soon my "story" ceased to be narcissistic in a crude way and became more and more a mere description of what I was doing and the things I saw. For minutes at a time this kind of thing would be running through my head: "He pushed the door open and entered the room. A yellow beam of sunlight, filtering through the muslin curtains, slanted on to the table, where a matchbox, half open, lay beside the inkpot. With his right hand in his pocket he moved across to the window. Down in the street a tortoiseshell cat was chasing a dead leaf," etc etc. This habit continued till I was about twenty-five, right through my non-literary years. Although I had to search, and did search, for the right words, I seemed to be making this descriptive effort almost against my will, under a kind of compulsion from outside. The "story" must, I suppose, have reflected the styles of the various writers I admired at different ages, but so far as I remember it always had the same meticulous descriptive quality.

When I was about sixteen I suddenly discovered the joy of mere words, i.e. the sounds and associations of words. The lines from *Paradise Lost,*

> So hee with difficulty and labour hard
> Moved on: with difficulty and labour hee,

which do not now seem to me so very wonderful, sent shivers down my backbone; and the spelling "hee" for "he" was an added pleasure. As for the need to describe things, I knew all about it already. So it is clear what kind of books I wanted to write, in so far as I could be said to want to write books at that time. I wanted to write enormous naturalistic novels with unhappy endings, full of detailed descriptions and arresting similes, and also full of purple passages in which words were used partly for the sake of their sound. And in fact my first completed novel, *Burmese Days,* which I wrote when I was thirty but projected much earlier, is rather that kind of book.

I give all this background information because I do not think one can assess a writer's motives without knowing something of his early development. His subject matter will be determined by the age he lives in—at least this is true in tumultuous, revolutionary ages like our own—but before he ever begins to write he will have acquired an emotional attitude from which he will never completely escape. It is his job, no doubt, to discipline his temperament and avoid getting stuck at some immature stage, or in some perverse mood: but if he escapes from his early influences altogether, he will have killed his impulse to write. Putting aside the need to earn a living, I think there are four great motives for writing, at any rate for writing prose. They exist in different degrees in every writer, and in any one writer the proportions will vary from time to time, according to the atmosphere in which he is living. They are:

1. Sheer egoism. Desire to seem clever, to be talked about, to be remembered after death, to get your own back on grown-ups who snubbed you in childhood, etc. etc. It is humbug to pretend that this is not a motive, and a strong one. Writers share this characteristic with scientists, artists, politicians, lawyers, soldiers, successful businessmen—in short, with the whole top crust of humanity. The great mass of human beings are not acutely selfish. After the age of about thirty they abandon individual ambition—in many cases, indeed, they almost abandon the sense of being individuals at all—and live chiefly for others, or are simply smothered under drudgery. But there is also the minority of gifted, wilful people who are determined to live their own lives to the end, and writers belong in this class. Serious writers, I should say, are on the whole more vain and self-centered than journalists, though less interested in money.

2. Aesthetic enthusiasm. Perception of beauty in the external world, or, on the other hand, in words and their right arrangement. Pleasure in the impact of one sound on another, in the firmness of good prose or the rhythm of a good story. Desire to share an experience which one feels is valuable and ought not to be missed. The aesthetic motive is very feeble in a lot of writers, but even a pamphleteer or a writer of textbooks will have pet words and phrases which appeal to him for non-utilitarian reasons; or he may feel strongly about typography, width of margins, etc. Above

the level of a railway guide, no book is quite free from aesthetic considerations.

3. Historical impulse. Desire to see things as they are, to find out true facts and store them up for the use of posterity.

4. Political purpose—using the word "political" in the widest possible sense. Desire to push the world in a certain direction, to alter other people's idea of the kind of society that they should strive after. Once again, no book is genuinely free from political bias. The opinion that art should have nothing to do with politics is itself a political attitude.

It can be seen how these various impulses must war against one another, and how they must fluctuate from person to person and from time to time. By nature—taking your "nature" to be the state you have attained when you are first adult—I am a person in whom the first three motives would outweigh the fourth. In a peaceful age I might have written ornate or merely descriptive books, and might have remained almost unaware of my political loyalties. As it is I have been forced into becoming a sort of pamphleteer. First I spent five years in an unsuitable profession (the Indian Imperial Police, in Burma), and then I underwent poverty and the sense of failure. This increased my natural hatred of authority and made me for the first time fully aware of the existence of the working classes, and the job in Burma had given me some understanding of the nature of imperialism: but these experiences were not enough to give me an accurate political orientation. Then came Hitler, the Spanish civil war, etc. By the end of 1935 I had still failed to reach a firm decision. I remember a little poem that I wrote at that date, expressing my dilemma:

A happy vicar I might have been
Two hundred years ago,
To preach upon eternal doom
And watch my walnuts grow;

But born, alas, in an evil time,
I missed that pleasant haven,
For the hair has grown on my upper lip
And the clergy are all clean-shaven.

And later still the times were good,
We were so easy to please,
We rocked our troubled thoughts to sleep
On the bosoms of the trees.

All ignorant we dared to own
The joys we now dissemble;
The greenfinch on the apple bough
Could make my enemies tremble.

But girls' bellies and apricots,
Roach in a shaded stream,
Horses, ducks in flight at dawn,
All these are a dream.

It is forbidden to dream again;
We maim our joys or hide them;
Horses are made of chromium steel
And little fat men shall ride them.

I am the worm who never turned,
The eunuch without a harem;
Between the priest and the commissar
I walk like Eugene Aram;

And the commissar is telling my fortune
While the radio plays,
But the priest has promised an Austin Seven,
For Duggie always pays.

I dreamed I dwelt in marble halls,
And woke to find it true;
I wasn't born for an age like this;
Was Smith? Was Jones? Were you?

The Spanish war and other events in 1936–37 turned the scale and thereafter I knew where I stood. Every line of serious work that I have written since 1936 has been written, directly or indirectly, *against* totalitarianism and *for* democratic Socialism, as I understand it. It seems to me nonsense, in a period like our own, to think that one can avoid writing of such subjects. Everyone writes of them in one guise or another. It is simply a question of which side one takes and what approach one follows. And the more one is conscious of one's political bias, the more chance one has of acting politically without sacrificing one's aesthetic and intellectual integrity.

What I have most wanted to do throughout the past ten years is to make political writing into an art. My starting point is always a feeling of partisanship, a sense of injustice. When I sit down to write a book, I do not say to myself, "I am going to produce a work of art." I write it because there is some lie that I want to expose, some fact to which I want to draw attention, and my initial concern is to get a hearing. But I could not do the work of writing a book, or even a long magazine article, if it were not also an aesthetic experience. Anyone who cares to examine my work will see that even when it is downright propaganda it contains much that a full-time politician would consider irrelevant. I am not able, and I do not want, completely to abandon the world-view that I acquired in childhood. So long as I remain alive and well I shall continue to feel strongly about prose style, to love the surface of the earth, and to take pleasure in solid objects and scraps of useless information. It is no use trying to suppress that side of myself. The job is to reconcile my ingrained likes and dislikes with the essentially public, non-individual activities that this age forces on all of us.

It is not easy. It raises problems of construction and of language, and it raises in a new way the problem of truthfulness. Let me give just one example of the cruder kind of difficulty that arises. My book about the Spanish civil war, *Homage to Catalonia,* is, of course, a frankly political book, but in the main it is written with a certain detachment and regard for form. I did try very hard in it to tell the whole truth without violating my literary instincts. But among other things it contains a long chapter, full of newspaper quotations and the like, defending the Trotskyists who were accused of plotting with Franco. Clearly such a chapter, which after a year or two would lose its interest for any ordinary reader, must ruin the book. A critic whom I respect read me a lecture about it. "Why did you put in all that stuff?" he said. "You've turned what might have been a good book into journalism." What he said was true, but I could not have done otherwise. I happened to know, what very few people in England had been allowed to know, that innocent men were being falsely accused. If I had not been angry about that I should never have written the book.

In one form or another this problem comes up again. The problem of language is subtler and would take too long to discuss. I will only say that of late years I have tried to write less picturesquely and more exactly. In any case I find that by the time you have perfected any style of writing, you have always outgrown it. *Animal Farm* was the first book in which I tried, with full consciousness of what I was doing, to fuse political purpose and artistic purpose into one whole. I have not written a novel for seven years, but I hope to write another fairly soon. It is bound to be a failure, every book is a failure, but I know with some clarity what kind of book I want to write.

Looking back through the last page or two, I see that I have made it appear as though my motives in writing were wholly public-spirited. I don't want to leave that as the final impression. All writers are vain, selfish and lazy, and at the very bottom of their motives there lies a mystery. Writing a book is a horrible, exhausting struggle, like a long bout of some painful illness. One would never undertake such a thing if one were not driven on by some demon whom one can neither resist nor understand. For all one knows that demon is simply the same instinct that makes a baby squall for attention. And yet it is also true that one can write nothing readable unless one constantly struggles to efface one's own personality. Good prose is like a window pane. I cannot say with certainty which of my motives are the strongest, but I know which of them deserve to be followed. And looking back through my work, I see that it is invariably where I lacked a *political* purpose that I wrote lifeless books and was betrayed into purple passages, sentences without meaning, decorative adjectives and humbug generally.

1946

POLITICS AND THE ENGLISH LANGUAGE

Most people who bother with the matter at all would admit that the English language is in a bad way, but it is generally assumed that we cannot by conscious action do anything about it. Our civilization is decadent and our language—so the argument runs—must inevitably share in the general collapse. It follows that any struggle against the abuse of language is a sentimental archaism, like preferring candles to electric light or hansom cabs to aeroplanes. Underneath this lies the half-conscious belief that language is a natural growth and not an instrument which we shape for our own purposes.

Now, it is clear that the decline of a language must ultimately have political and economic causes: it is not due simply to the bad influence of this or that individual writer. But an effect can become a cause, reinforcing the original cause and producing the same effect in an intensified form, and so on indefinitely. A man may take to drink because he feels himself to be a failure, and then fail all the more completely because he drinks. It is rather the same thing that is happening to the English language. It becomes ugly and inaccurate because our thoughts are foolish, but the slovenliness of our language makes it easier for us to have foolish thoughts. The point is that the process is reversible. Modern English, especially written English, is full of bad habits which spread by imitation and which can be avoided if one is willing to take the necessary trouble. If one gets rid of these habits one can think more clearly, and to think clearly is a necessary first step toward political regeneration: so that the fight against bad English is not frivolous and is not the exclusive concern of professional writers. I will come back to this presently, and I hope that by that time the meaning of what I have said here will have become clearer. Meanwhile, here are five specimens of the English language as it is now habitually written.

These five passages have not been picked out because they are especially bad—I could have quoted far worse if I had chosen—but because they illustrate various of the mental vices from which we now suffer. They are a little below the average, but are fairly representative samples. I number them so that I can refer back to them when necessary:

(1) I am not, indeed, sure whether it is not true to say that the Milton who once seemed not unlike a seventeenth-century Shelley had not become, out of an experience ever more bitter in each year, more alien [*sic*] to the founder of that Jesuit sect which nothing could induce him to tolerate.

Professor Harold Laski
(Essay in *Freedom of Expression*)

(2) Above all, we cannot play ducks and drakes with a native battery of idioms which prescribes such egregious collocations of vocables as the Basic *put up with* for *tolerate* or *put at a loss* for *bewilder*.

Professor Lancelot Hogben (*Interglossa*)

(3) On the one side we have the free personality: by definition it is not neurotic, for it has neither conflict nor dream. Its desires, such as they are, are transparent, for they are just what institutional approval keeps in the forefront of consciousness; another institutional pattern would alter their number and intensity; there is little in them that is natural, irreducible, or culturally dangerous. But *on the other side,* the social bond itself is nothing but the mutual reflection of these self-secure integrities. Recall the definition of love. Is not this the very picture of a small academic? Where is there a place in this hall of mirrors for either personality or fraternity?

Essay on psychology in *Politics* (New York)

(4) All the "best people" from the gentlemen's clubs, and all the frantic fascist captains, united in common hatred of Socialism and bestial horror of the rising tide of the mass revolutionary movement, have turned to acts of provocation, to foul incendiarism, to medieval legends of poisoned wells, to legalize their own destruction of proletarian organizations, and rouse the agitated petty-bourgeoisie to chauvinistic fervor on behalf of the fight against the revolutionary way out of the crisis.

Communist pamphlet

(5) If a new spirit *is* to be infused into this old country, there is one thorny and contentious reform which must be tackled, and that is the humanization and galvanization of the B.B.C. Timidity here will bespeak canker and atrophy of the soul. The heart of Britain may be sound and of strong beat, for instance, but the British lion's roar at present is like that of Bottom in Shakespeare's *Midsummer Night's Dream*—as gentle as any sucking dove. A virile new Britain cannot continue indefinitely to be traduced in the eyes, or rather ears, of the world by the effete languors of Langham Place, brazenly masquerading as "standard English." When the Voice of Britain is heard at nine o'clock, better far and infinitely less ludicrous to hear aitches honestly dropped than the present priggish, inflated, inhibited, school-ma'amish arch braying of blameless bashful mewing maidens!

Letter in *Tribune*

Each of these passages has faults of its own, but, quite apart from avoidable ugliness, two qualities are common to all of them. The first is staleness of imagery; the other is lack of precision. The writer either has a meaning and cannot express it, or he inadvertently says something else, or he is almost indifferent as to whether his words mean anything or not. This mixture of vagueness and sheer incompetence is the most marked characteristic of modern English prose, and especially of any kind of political writing. As soon as certain topics are raised, the concrete melts into the abstract and no one seems able to think of turns of speech that are not hackneyed: prose consists less and less of *words* chosen for the sake of their meaning, and more and more of *phrases* tacked together like the sections of a prefabricated henhouse. I list below, with notes and examples, various of the tricks by means of which the work of prose-construction is habitually dodged:

Dying metaphors. A newly invented metaphor assists thought by evoking a visual image, while on the other hand a metaphor which is technically "dead" (e.g. *iron resolution*) has in effect reverted to being an ordinary word and can generally be used without loss of vividness. But in between these two classes there is a huge dump of worn-out metaphors which have lost all evocative power and are merely used because they save people the trouble of inventing phrases for themselves. Examples are: *Ring the changes on, take up the cudgels for, toe the line, ride roughshod over, stand shoulder to shoulder with, play into the hands of, no axe to grind, grist to the mill, fishing in troubled waters, on the order of the day, Achilles' heel, swan song, hotbed.* Many of these are used without knowledge of their meaning (what is a "rift," for instance?), and incompatible metaphors are frequently mixed, a sure sign that the writer is not interested in what he is saying. Some metaphors now current have been twisted out of their original meaning without those who use them ever being aware of the fact. For example, *toe the line* is sometimes written *tow the line*. Another example is *the hammer and the anvil,* now always used with the implication that the anvil gets the worst of it. In real life it is always the anvil that breaks the hammer, never the other way about: a writer who stopped to think what he was saying would be aware of this, and would avoid perverting the original phrase.

Operators or *verbal false limbs.* These save the trouble of picking out appropriate verbs and nouns, and at the same time pad each sentence with extra syllables which give it an appearance of symmetry. Characteristic phrases are *render inoperative, militate against, make contact with, be subjected to, give rise to, give grounds for, have the effect of, play a leading part (role) in, make itself felt, take effect, exhibit a tendency to, serve the purpose of,* etc., etc. The key-note is the elimination of simple verbs. Instead of being a single word, such as *break, stop, spoil, mend, kill,* a verb becomes a *phrase,* made up of a noun or adjective tacked on to some general-purpose verb such as *prove, serve, form, play, render.* In addition, the passive voice is wherever possible used in preference to the active, and noun constructions are used instead of gerunds (*by examination of* instead of *by examining*). The range of verbs is further cut down by means of the *-ize* and *de-* formations, and the banal statements are given an appearance of profundity by means of the *not un-* formation. Simple conjunctions and prepositions are replaced by such phrases as *with respect to, having regard to, the fact that, by dint of, in view of, in the interests of, on the hypothesis that;* and the ends of sentences are saved from anticlimax by such resounding commonplaces as *greatly to be desired, cannot be left out of account, a development to be expected in the near future, deserving of serious consideration, brought to a satisfactory conclusion,* and so on and so forth.

Pretentious diction. Words like *phenomenon, element, individual* (as noun), *objective, categorical, effective, virtual, basic, primary, promote, constitute, exhibit, exploit, utilize, eliminate, liquidate,* are used to dress up simple statement and give an air of scientific impartiality to biased judgments. Adjectives like *epoch-making, epic, historic, unforgettable, triumphant, age-old, inevitable, inexorable, veritable,* are used to dignify the sordid processes of international politics, while writing that aims at glorifying war usually takes on an archaic color, its characteristic words being: *realm, throne, chariot, mailed fist, trident, sword, shield, buckler, banner, jackboot, clarion.* Foreign words and expressions such as *cul de sac, ancien régime, deus ex machina, mutatis mutandis, status quo, gleichschaltung, weltanschauung,* are used to give an air of culture and elegance. Except for the useful abbreviations *i.e., e.g.,* and *etc.,* there is no real need for any of the hundreds of foreign phrases now current in English. Bad writers, and especially scientific, political, and sociological writers, are nearly always haunted by the notion that Latin or Greek words are grander than Saxon ones, and unnecessary words like *expedite, ameliorate, predict, extraneous, deracinated, clandestine, subaqueous,* and hundreds of others constantly gain ground from their Anglo-Saxon opposite numbers.* The jargon peculiar to Marxist writing (*hyena, hangman, cannibal, petty bourgeois, these gentry, lackey, flunkey, mad dog, White Guard,* etc.) consists largely of words and phrases translated from Russian, German, or French; but the normal way of coining a new word is to use a Latin or Greek root with the appropriate affix and, where necessary, the -ize formation. It is often easier to make up words of this kind (*deregionalize, impermissible, extra-*

* An interesting illustration of this is the way in which the English flower names which were in use till very recently are being ousted by Greek ones, *snapdragon* becoming *antirrhinum, forget-me-not* becoming *myosotis,* etc. It is hard to see any practical reason for this change of fashion: it is probably due to an instinctive turning away from the more homely word and a vague feeling that the Greek word is scientific.

marital, nonfragmentary and so forth) than to think up the English words that will cover one's meaning. The result, in general, is an increase in slovenliness and vagueness.

Meaningless words. In certain kinds of writing, particularly in art criticism and literary criticism, it is normal to come across long passages which are almost completely lacking in meaning.* Words like *romantic, plastic, values, human, dead, sentimental, natural, vitality,* as used in art criticism, are strictly meaningless, in the sense that they not only do not point to any discoverable object, but are hardly ever expected to do so by the reader. When one critic writes, "The outstanding feature of Mr. X's work is its living quality," while another writes, "The immediately striking thing about Mr. X's work is its peculiar deadness," the reader accepts this as a simple difference of opinion. If words like *black* and *white* were involved, instead of the jargon words *dead* and *living,* he would see at once that language was being used in an improper way. Many political words are similarly abused. The word *Fascism* has now no meaning except in so far as it signifies "something not desirable." The words *democracy, socialism, freedom, patriotic, realistic, justice,* have each of them several different meanings which cannot be reconciled with one another. In the case of a word like *democracy,* not only is there no agreed definition, but the attempt to make one is resisted from all sides. It is almost universally felt that when we call a country democratic we are praising it: consequently the defenders of every kind of régime claim that it is a democracy, and fear that they might have to stop using the word if it were tied down to any one meaning. Words of this kind are often used in a consciously dishonest way. That is, the person who uses them has his own private definition, but allows his hearer to think he means something quite different. Statements like *Marshal Pétain was a true patriot, The Soviet press is the freest in the world, The Cath-*

* Example: "Comfort's catholicity of perception and image, strangely Whitmanesque in range, almost the exact opposite in aesthetic compulsion, continues to evoke that trembling atmospheric accumulative hinting at a cruel, an inexorably serene timelessness. . . . Wrey Gardiner scores by aiming at simple bull's-eyes with precision. Only they are not so simple, and through this contented sadness runs more than the surface bittersweet of resignation." (*Poetry Quarterly.*)

olic Church is opposed to persecution, are almost always made with intent to deceive. Other words used in variable meanings, in most cases more or less dishonestly, are: *class, totalitarian, science, progressive, reactionary, bourgeois, equality.*

Now that I have made this catalogue of swindles and perversions, let me give another example of the kind of writing that they lead to. This time it must of its nature be an imaginary one. I am going to translate a passage of good English into modern English of the worst sort. Here is a well-known verse from *Ecclesiastes*:

> I returned and saw under the sun, that the race is not to the swift, nor the battle to the strong, neither yet bread to the wise, nor yet riches to men of understanding, nor yet favor to men of skill; but time and chance happeneth to them all.

Here it is in modern English:

> Objective consideration of contemporary phenomena compels the conclusion that success or failure in competitive activities exhibits no tendency to be commensurate with innate capacity, but that a considerable element of the unpredictable must invariably be taken into account.

This is a parody, but not a very gross one. Exhibit (3), above, for instance, contains several patches of the same kind of English. It will be seen that I have not made a full translation. The beginning and ending of the sentence follow the original meaning fairly closely, but in the middle the concrete illustrations—race, battle, bread—dissolve into the vague phrase "success or failure in competitive activities." This had to be so, because no modern writer of the kind I am discussing—no one capable of using phrases like "objective consideration of contemporary phenomena"—would ever tabulate his thoughts in that precise and detailed way. The whole tendency of modern prose is away from concreteness. Now analyze these two sentences a little more closely. The first contains forty-nine words but only sixty syllables, and all its words are those of everyday life. The second contains thirty-eight words of ninety syllables: eighteen of its words are from Latin roots and one from Greek. The first sentence contains six vivid images, and only one phrase ("time and chance") that could be called vague. The second contains not a single fresh, arresting phrase, and in spite of its ninety syllables it gives only a shortened version of the meaning contained in the first. Yet without a doubt it is the second kind of sentence that is gaining ground in modern English. I do not want to exaggerate. This kind of writing is not yet universal, and outcrops of simplicity will occur here and there in the worst-written page. Still, if you or I were told to write a few lines on the uncertainty of human fortunes, we should probably come much nearer to my imaginary sentence than to the one from *Ecclesiastes.*

As I have tried to show, modern writing at its worst does not consist in picking out words for the sake of their meaning and inventing images in order to make the meaning clearer. It consists in gumming together long strips of words which have already been set in order by someone else, and making the results presentable by sheer humbug. The attraction of this way of writing is that it is easy. It is easier—even quicker, once you have the habit—to say *In my opinion it is not an unjustifiable assumption that* than to say *I think.* If you use ready-made phrases, you not only don't have to hunt about for words; you also don't have to bother with the rhythms of your sentences, since these phrases are generally so arranged as to be more or less euphonious. When you are composing in a hurry—when you are dictating to a stenographer, for instance, or making a public speech—it is natural to fall into a pretentious, Latinized style. Tags like *a consideration which we should do well to bear in mind* or *a conclusion to which all of us would readily assent* will save many a sentence from coming down with a bump. By using stale metaphors, similes, and idioms, you save much mental effort, at the cost of leaving your meaning vague, not only for your reader but for yourself. This is the significance of mixed metaphors. The sole aim of a metaphor is to call up a visual image. When these images clash—as in *The Fascist octopus has sung its swan song, the jackboot is thrown into the melting pot*—it can be taken as certain that the writer is not seeing a mental image of the objects he is naming; in other words he is not really thinking. Look again at the examples I gave at the beginning of this essay.

Professor Laski (1) uses five negatives in fifty-three words. One of these is superfluous, making nonsense of the whole passage, and in addition there is the slip—*alien* for akin—making further nonsense, and several avoidable pieces of clumsiness which increase the general vagueness. Professor Hogben (2) plays ducks and drakes with a battery which is able to write prescriptions, and, while disapproving of the everyday phrase *put up with*, is unwilling to look *egregious* up in the dictionary and see what it means; (3), if one takes an uncharitable attitude towards it, is simply meaningless: probably one could work out its intended meaning by reading the whole of the article in which it occurs. In (4), the writer knows more or less what he wants to say, but an accumulation of stale phrases chokes him like tea leaves blocking a sink. In (5), words and meaning have almost parted company. People who write in this manner usually have a general emotional meaning—they dislike one thing and want to express solidarity with another—but they are not interested in the detail of what they are saying. A scrupulous writer, in every sentence that he writes, will ask himself at least four questions, thus: What am I trying to say? What words will express it? What image or idiom will make it clearer? Is this image fresh enough to have an effect? And he will probably ask himself two more: Could I put it more shortly? Have I said anything that is avoidably ugly? But you are not obliged to go to all this trouble. You can shirk it by simply throwing your mind open and letting the ready-made phrases come crowding in. They will construct your sentences for you—even think your thoughts for you, to a certain extent—and at need they will perform the important service of partially concealing your meaning even from yourself. It is at this point that the special connection between politics and the debasement of language becomes clear.

In our time it is broadly true that political writing is bad writing. Where it is not true, it will generally be found that the writer is some kind of rebel, expressing his private opinions and not a "party line." Orthodoxy, of whatever color, seems to demand a lifeless, imitative style. The political dialects to be found in pamphlets, leading articles, manifestoes, White Papers and the speeches of undersecretaries do, of course, vary from party to party, but they are all alike in that one almost never finds in them a fresh, vivid, home-made turn of speech. When one watches some tired hack on the platform mechanically repeating the familiar phrases—*bestial atrocities, iron heel, bloodstained tyranny, free peoples of the world, stand shoulder to shoulder*—one often has a curious feeling that one is not watching a live human being but some kind of dummy: a feeling which suddenly becomes stronger at moments when the light catches the speaker's spectacles and turns them into blank discs which seem to have no eyes behind them. And this is not altogether fanciful. A speaker who uses that kind of phraseology has gone some distance towards turning himself into a machine. The appropriate noises are coming out of his larynx, but his brain is not involved as it would be if he were choosing his words for himself. If the speech he is making is one that he is accustomed to make over and over again, he may be almost unconscious of what he is saying, as one is when one utters the responses in church. And this reduced state of consciousness, if not indispensable, is at any rate favorable to political conformity.

In our time, political speech and writing are largely the defense of the indefensible. Things like the continuance of British rule in India, the Russian purges and deportations, the dropping of the atom bombs on Japan, can indeed be defended, but only by arguments which are too brutal for most people to face, and which do not square with the professed aims of political parties. Thus political language has to consist largely of euphemism, question-begging and sheer cloudy vagueness. Defenseless villages are bombarded from the air, the inhabitants driven out into the countryside, the cattle machine-gunned, the huts set on fire with incendiary bullets: this is called *pacification.* Millions of peasants are robbed of their farms and sent trudging along the roads with no more than they can carry: this is called *transfer of population* or *rectification of frontiers.* People are imprisoned for years without trial, or shot in the back of the neck or sent to die of scurvy in Arctic lumber camps: this is called *elimination of unreliable elements.* Such phraseology is needed if one wants to name things without calling up mental pictures of them. Consider for instance some comfortable English professor defending

Russian totalitarianism. He cannot say outright, "I believe in killing off your opponents when you can get good results by doing so." Probably, therefore, he will say something like this:

"While freely conceding that the Soviet régime exhibits certain features which the humanitarian may be inclined to deplore, we must, I think, agree that a certain curtailment of the right to political opposition is an unavoidable concomitant of transitional periods, and that the rigors which the Russian people have been called upon to undergo have been amply justified in the sphere of concrete achievement."

The inflated style is itself a kind of euphemism. A mass of Latin words falls upon the facts like soft snow, blurring the outlines and covering up all the details. The great enemy of clear language is insincerity. When there is a gap between one's real and one's declared aims, one turns as it were instinctively to long words and exhausted idioms, like a cuttlefish squirting out ink. In our age there is no such thing as "keeping out of politics." All issues are political issues, and politics itself is a mass of lies, evasions, folly, hatred and schizophrenia. When the general atmosphere is bad, language must suffer. I should expect to find—this is a guess which I have not sufficient knowledge to verify—that the German, Russian and Italian languages have all deteriorated in the last ten or fifteen years, as a result of dictatorship.

But if thought corrupts language, language can also corrupt thought. A bad usage can spread by tradition and imitation, even among people who should and do know better. The debased language that I have been discussing is in some ways very convenient. Phrases like *a not unjustifiable assumption, leaves much to be desired, would serve no good purpose, a consideration which we should do well to bear in mind,* are a continuous temptation, a packet of aspirins always at one's elbow. Look back through this essay, and for certain you will find that I have again and again committed the very faults I am protesting against. By this morning's post I have received a pamphlet dealing with conditions in Germany. The author tells me that he "felt impelled" to write it. I open it at random, and here is almost the first sentence that I see: "[The Allies] have an opportunity not only of achieving a radical transformation of Germany's social and political structure in such a way as to avoid a nationalistic reaction in Germany itself, but at the same time of laying the foundations of a co-operative and unified Europe." You see, he "feels impelled" to write—feels, presumably, that he has something new to say—and yet his words, like cavalry horses answering the bugle, group themselves automatically into the familiar dreary pattern. This invasion of one's mind by ready-made phrases (*lay the foundations, achieve a radical transformation*) can only be prevented if one is constantly on guard against them, and every such phrase anaesthetizes a portion of one's brain.

I said earlier that the decadence of our language is probably curable. Those who deny this would argue, if they produced an argument at all, that language merely reflects existing social conditions, and that we cannot influence its development by any direct tinkering with words and constructions. So far as the general tone or spirit of a language goes, this may be true, but it is not true in detail. Silly words and expressions have often disappeared, not through any evolutionary process but owing to the conscious action of a minority. Two recent examples were *explore every avenue* and *leave no stone unturned*, which were killed by the jeers of a few journalists. There is a long list of flyblown metaphors which could similarly be got rid of if enough people would interest themselves in the job; and it should also be possible to laugh the *not un-* formation out of existence,* to reduce the amount of Latin and Greek in the average sentence, to drive out foreign phrases and strayed scientific words, and, in general, to make pretentiousness unfashionable. But all these are minor points. The defense of the English language implies more than this, and perhaps it is best to start by saying what it does *not* imply.

To begin with it has nothing to do with archaism, with the salvaging of obsolete words and turns of speech, or with the setting up of a "standard English" which must never be departed from. On the contrary, it is especially concerned with the scrapping of every word or idiom which has outworn its usefulness. It has nothing to do with correct grammar and syntax, which are

* One can cure oneself of the *not un-* formation by memorizing this sentence: *A not unblack dog was chasing a not unsmall rabbit across a not ungreen field.*

of no importance so long as one makes one's meaning clear, or with the avoidance of Americanisms, or with having what is called a "good prose style." On the other hand it is not concerned with fake simplicity and the attempt to make written English colloquial. Nor does it even imply in every case preferring the Saxon word to the Latin one, though it does imply using the fewest and shortest words that will cover one's meaning. What is above all needed is to let the meaning choose the word, and not the other way about. In prose, the worst thing one can do with words is to surrender to them. When you think of a concrete object, you think wordlessly, and then, if you want to describe the thing you have been visualizing you probably hunt about till you find the exact words that seem to fit it. When you think of something abstract you are more inclined to use words from the start, and unless you make a conscious effort to prevent it, the existing dialect will come rushing in and do the job for you, at the expense of blurring or even changing your meaning. Probably it is better to put off using words as long as possible and get one's meaning as clear as one can through pictures or sensations. Afterward one can choose—not simply *accept*—the phrases that will best cover the meaning, and then switch round and decide what impression one's words are likely to make on another person. This last effort of the mind cuts out all stale or mixed images, all prefabricated phrases, needless repetitions, and humbug and vagueness generally. But one can often be in doubt about the effect of a word or a phrase, and one needs rules that one can rely on when instinct fails. I think the following rules will cover most cases:

(i) Never use a metaphor, simile, or other figure of speech which you are used to seeing in print.

(ii) Never use a long word where a short one will do.

(iii) If it is possible to cut a word out, always cut it out.

(iv) Never use the passive where you can use the active.

(v) Never use a foreign phrase, a scientific word, or a jargon word if you can think of an everyday English equivalent.

(vi) Break any of these rules sooner than say anything outright barbarous.

These rules sound elementary, and so they are, but they demand a deep change of attitude in anyone who has grown used to writing in the style now fashionable. One could keep all of them and still write bad English, but one could not write the kind of stuff that I quoted in those five specimens at the beginning of this article.

I have not here been considering the literary use of language, but merely language as an instrument for expressing and not for concealing or preventing thought. Stuart Chase and others have come near to claiming that all abstract words are meaningless, and have used this as a pretext for advocating a kind of political quietism. Since you don't know what Fascism is, how can you struggle against Fascism? One need not swallow such absurdities as this, but one ought to recognize that the present political chaos is connected with the decay of language, and that one can probably bring about some improvement by starting at the verbal end. If you simplify your English, you are freed from the worst follies of orthodoxy. You cannot speak any of the necessary dialects, and when you make a stupid remark its stupidity will be obvious, even to yourself. Political language—and with variations this is true of all political parties, from Conservatives to Anarchists—is designed to make lies sound truthful and murder respectable, and to give an appearance of solidity to pure wind. One cannot change this all in a moment, but one can at least change one's own habits, and from time to time one can even, if one jeers loudly enough, send some worn-out and useless phrase—some *jackboot*, *Achilles' heel*, *hotbed*, *melting pot*, *acid test*, *veritable inferno*, or other lump of verbal refuse—into the dustbin where it belongs.

1946

E. B. White

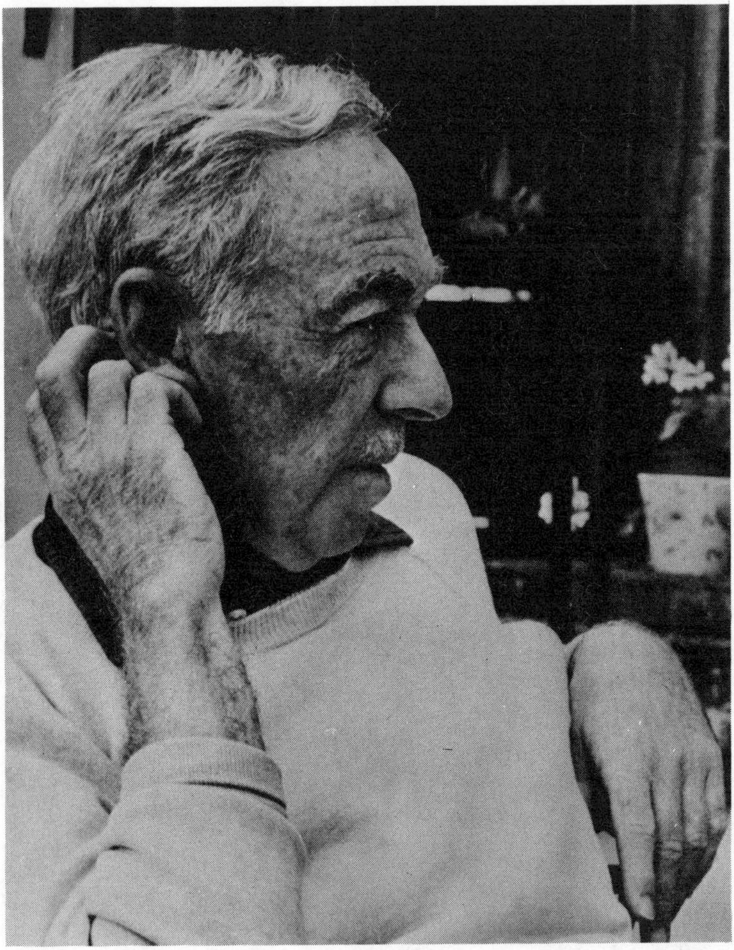

Photo: Donald E. Johnson

THE YOUNGEST OF SIX CHILDREN, E. B. White was born in Mt. Vernon, New York, on July 11, 1899. At the time, Mt. Vernon was still a small town—certainly not the beginning of suburbia that it is today—and White's father, who was prospering as a piano manufacturer, had moved his family up from Brooklyn because he thought Mt. Vernon would be a better place to raise children. As it turned out, it was almost perfect. Their house was large, the streets were shady, and the town was as peaceful as an upper-middle-class suburb could be at the turn of the century. "There was," White has written, describing their house, "an iron vase on the lawn and a copy of *Wet Days at Edgewood* on the library table." Years later, he recalled the things he did: "I rode my bicycle sitting backward on the handle bars, I made up poems, I played selections from *Aïda* on the piano. In winter, I tended goal in the hockey games on the frozen pond in the dell." To such idyllic pastimes was added, in 1905, a camp on one of the Belgrade lakes in Maine, and each August for many years thereafter the family went there for its summer vacation. Indeed, one gathers from his writings that there were few catastrophes in White's childhood more serious than hay fever, and from that he is still a sufferer. In 1917 he graduated from Mt. Vernon High School, and the following fall he entered Cornell University.

Unlike their cousins, the novelists, the American humorists of this century seem more or less to have taken to college, and White was no exception. He joined a fraternity, got gentlemanly marks in his courses, rode a motorcycle, and spent two months during his sophomore year as a private in the U.S. Army. (Enlisting only a few weeks before the Armistice, he got no farther than the campus drill field and faced no enemy worse than a flu epidemic, "which I met stoically with a bag of licorice drops.") His real interest, however, was writing, and in his senior year he was editor-in-chief of the *Cornell Daily Sun*.

After his graduation in 1921, White tried his hand for a while at various jobs in New York City, but was dissatisfied and restless. Then, in March of 1922, he and a friend decided to head West in White's Model T Ford. It was a leisurely trip, and when they arrived in Seattle six months later, White took a job as a reporter with the Seattle *Times*. But poetry, not journalism, was the thing he had his eye on in those days, and when the job fell through the following summer, it was with relief that he began looking around for something to do. What turned up was a steamer on its way to Alaska and Siberia, and White determined to go with it. With the last of his money he bought a one-way ticket as far as Skagway, and trusted that once on board he could get a job that would take him the full round trip. Luckily, he did, and that fall he returned to New York City.

For the next two years he worked in an advertising agency and tried to write poetry, but without much success. Then, in 1925, *The New Yorker* was founded, and very soon White was submitting poems and sketches. Harold Ross, the editor, was so impressed that he asked White to come to work, which he did, and for the next eleven years his wit and good sense did much to make the magazine the success that it was. He not only wrote many of the "Notes and Comments" that appeared in the "Talk of the Town," but also thought up the witty captions and taglines that turned normal space-fillers into capsule editorials on the absurdities of both man and the press. Even though most of his work during those years was unsigned, the recurrent style was unmistakable to anyone who read *The New Yorker* regularly. In 1929 White published his first two books: *The Lady Is Cold*, a collection of light verse, and *Is Sex Necessary?*, a spoof on scientific sex literature written in collaboration with his office mate, James Thurber.

In 1937, "desiring," he said, "to simplify my life," E. B. White left New York and moved his family to a salt water farm in North Brooklin, Maine. The following summer he began a regular monthly column for *Harper's Magazine* entitled "One Man's Meat," and it was soon apparent that an aspect of his character that had hitherto remained largely hidden was beginning to emerge. The essays that he sent down from Maine revealed a depth one wouldn't have expected from his earlier *New Yorker* pieces. The wit and clear sight into the nature of things were still there, but with a difference. No longer were they being exercised for the sake of cleverness alone—the thing one regrets about much of the work of Benchley, Sullivan, and even Thurber at times—but more seriously, as a means of revealing not merely man's absurdities, but his virtues as well. White, it turned out, could be as serious as he could be clever. Although *Quo Vadimus? or The Case for the Bicycle,* a collection of sketches that had appeared in *The New Yorker,* was published in 1939, the sort of humor that it contained was already a thing of the past. In 1943 he wrote the last of his columns for *Harper's* and returned to New York City, where he resumed the writing of *The New Yorker's* editorial page. The magazine's staff had been depleted by the war, and Ross had asked him to help. A few years later he moved back to Maine and began writing his "Letters from the East" (and other points of the compass) for *The New Yorker*; and Maine is where he still lives.

Altogether White has written twelve books and either edited or collaborated on four others. Two of the most charming are children's stories that take their place alongside such modern classics as *The Wind in the Willows* and the Pooh books: *Stuart Little* (1945) and *Charlotte's Web* (1952). In 1941 he and his wife, Katharine S. White, edited *A Subtreasury of American Humor,* and in 1959 he revised, introduced, and wrote a chapter on style for a grammar handbook he had used as a student at Cornell. To everyone's surprise, *The Elements of Style,* by William Strunk, Jr., and E. B. White, became a national best-seller. White's best essays appear in three collections: *One Man's Meat* (1944), *The Second Tree from the Corner* (1954), and *The Points of My Compass* (1962). In 1970 White published a third children's book, *The Trumpet of the Swan,* and in 1977 he was awarded a Pulitzer Prize Special Citation in Letters for his lifetime's work.

The themes that White comes back to in essay after essay are, first, that the natural is preferable to the artificial or mechanical, and, secondly, that even though time moves on apace and things constantly change, the larger patterns of Nature are recurrent. The first idea is generally presented as a lament for the past, and thus the imperceptive reader often comes away with the impression that White is a nostalgic reactionary. Read closely, however, the essays are quite clear in their scorn for sentimentality, and whatever homage is paid the past proves to be not a love for the simple and uncomplicated, but just the opposite, a love of the excitement and adventure that is inseparable from physical hardships. As our material goods and comforts increase, White would say, we lose touch with reality; we are dehumanized; we become no better than the machine we created; indeed, worse (see "The Hour of Letdown" in *The Second Tree from the Corner*). Fortunately, however, there is always Nature, and no matter how furiously we hack away at her, in the end she is victorious. These beliefs, and the proof of his life, place White directly in the tradition of his fellow New Englanders, Thoreau and Frost.

"With some writers," White wrote in *The Elements of Style*, "style not only reveals the spirit of the man, it reveals his identity, as surely as would his fingerprints." Then he added, a little later, "The approach to style is by way of plainness, simplicity, orderliness, sincerity." Taken together, the two statements—however simple they appear on the surface—imply an extremely subtle attitude toward style. "How," one might ask, "am I to do both at the same time—be plain, simple, orderly, and sincere, and yet reveal the complexities of my identity?" No easy, practicable answer is given, for White knows that it is a problem that can be solved only by each solitary writer in his own unending struggle to make the words he sets down on paper approach the temper of his thought. But he does tell us two important things. The first is a belief: "The whole duty of a writer is to please and satisfy himself, and the true writer always plays to an audience of one." And the second is a method: "I write by ear, always with difficulty and seldom with any exact notion of what is taking place under the hood." In short, style, E. B. White would say, is a matter of character, intuition, faith, mystery . . . and hard work.

THE WORLD OF TOMORROW

I wasn't really prepared for the World's Fair last week, and it certainly wasn't prepared for me. Between the two of us there was considerable of a mixup.

The truth is that my ethmoid sinuses broke down on the eve of Fair Day, and this meant I had to visit the Fair carrying a box of Kleenex concealed in a copy of the *Herald Tribune*. When you can't breathe through your nose, Tomorrow seems strangely like the day before yesterday. The Fair, on its part, was having trouble too. It couldn't find its collar button. Our mutual discomfort established a rich bond of friendship between us, and I realize that the World's Fair and myself actually both need the same thing—a nice warm day.

The road to Tomorrow leads through the chimney pots of Queens. It is a long, familiar journey, through Mulsified Shampoo and Mobilgas, through Bliss Street, Kix, Astring-O-Sol, and the Majestic Auto Seat Covers. It winds through Textene, Blue Jay Corn Plasters; through Musterole and the delicate pink blossoms on the fruit trees in the ever-hopeful back yards of a populous borough, past Zemo, Alka-Seltzer, Baby Ruth, past Iodent and the Fidelity National Bank, by trusses, belts, and the clothes that fly bravely on the line under the trees with the new little green leaves in Queens' incomparable springtime. Suddenly you see the first intimation of the future, of man's dream—the white ball and spire—and there is the ramp and the banners flying from the pavilions and the brave hope of a glimpsed destination. Except for the Kleenex, I might have been approaching the lists at Camelot, for I felt that perhaps here would be the tournament all men wait for, the field of honor, the knights and the ladies under these bright banners, beyond these great walls. A closer inspection, however, on the other side of the turnstile, revealed that it was merely Heinz jousting with Beech-Nut—the same old contest on a somewhat larger field, with accommodations for more spectators, and rather better facilities all round.

The place is honeycombed with streets—broad, gusty streets, with tulips bending to the gale and in the air the sound of distant choirs. There are benches all along for the weary and the halt, but though science's failure to cope with the common cold had embittered my heart and slowed my steps, the ball and spire still beckoned me on. It was not particularly surprising, somehow, when at last after so many months of anticipation and after so much of actual travail and suffering, when at last I arrived, paper handkerchiefs in hand, at the very threshold of Tomorrow, when I finally presented myself there at the base of the white phallus, face to face with the girl in the booth behind the little bars behind the glass window with the small round hole, expectant, ready to see at last what none had ever seen, Tomorrow—it was not, somehow, particularly surprising to see the window close in my face and hear a bald contemporary voice say, "There will be a short wait of a few minutes, please."

That's the way it is with the future. Even after Grover Whalen has touched it with his peculiar magic, there is still a short wait.

The lady behind me was not surprised either, but she seemed apprehensive.

"Anything wrong in there?" she asked testily.

"No, Madam," said the guard. "Just some minor difficulty in the Perisphere."

The lady was not satisfied. "Is there anything in there to scare you?" she asked, looking at the Perisphere rolling motionless in the gray vapors that have hung for centuries above the Flushing Meadows.

"No, Madam," he replied. "The longest escalator in the world moves very slowly."

I clocked the wait. It was twenty minutes. Not bad, for a man who's waited all his life.

Much depends, when you ascend into the interior of the Perisphere, on the moment at which you happen to arrive at the top of the escalator and teeter off in a sidewise direction onto one of the two great moving rings that turn endlessly above the City of Man. If you arrive just as day has faded into night, and without any advance information about being shunted from an upward moving stairway onto a sidewise moving balcony, the experience is something that stays with you. I was lucky. The City of Man, when it first broke on my expectant sight, was as dark as a hall bedroom, and for a second or two I didn't catch on that I myself was in motion—except celestially. If I hadn't recognized Mr. Kaltenborn's electric voice, I would have felt lonelier than perhaps the situation warranted.

"As day fades into night," he said, with the majestic huskiness which science has given speech, "each man seeks home, for here are children, comfort, neighbors, recreation—the good life of the well-planned city."

Trembling in violet light beneath me, there it was—the towers, now to the adjusted eye dimly visible—"a brave new world [such a big voice you have, Grandpa!] built by united hands and hearts. Here brain and brawn, faith and courage, are linked in high endeavor as men march on toward unity and peace. Listen! From office, farm, and factory they come with joyous song."

I don't know how long it takes in there. Ten minutes, maybe. But when I emerged from the great ball, to begin the descent of the Helicline, it had come on to rain.

To be informative about the Fair is a task for someone with a steadier nose than mine. I saw all as in a dream, and I cherish the dream and have put it away in lavender. The great size of the place has been a temporary disadvantage these first few days, when the draftiness, the chill, the disorder, the murky bath of canned reverence in which many of the commercial exhibits are steeped have conspired to give the place the clammy quality of a seaside resort in mid-November. But this same great size, come the first warm, expansive days, will suddenly become the most valuable asset of the Fair. The refurbished ash heap, rising from its own smolder, is by far the biggest show that has even been assembled on God's earth, and it is going to be a great place to go on a fine summer night, a great place to go on a sunny spring morning. After all, nobody can embrace Culture in a topcoat.

The architecture is amusing enough, the buildings are big enough, to give the visitor that temporary and exalted feeling of being in the presence of something pretty special, something full of aspiration, something which at times is even exciting. And the exhibition is cock-eyed enough to fall, as it naturally does, in line with all carnivals, circuses, and wonderlands. The buildings (there are two hundred of them) have color and a certain dash, here and there a certain beauty. They are of the type that shows up best in strong light. Like any Miami Beach cottage, they look incredibly lovely in sunlight, adorned with a necklace of vine shadow against a clear white skin, incredibly banal and gloom-infested on cloudy days, when every pimple of plaster shows up in all its ugly pretension. The designers of this twentieth-century bazaar have been resourceful and have kept the comfort of the people in mind. Experience has taught them much. The modern technique of sight-seeing is this: you sit in a chair (wired for sound) or stand on a platform (movable, glass-embowered) and while sitting, standing, you are brought mysteriously and reverently into easy view of what you want to see. There is no shoving in the exhibit hall of Tomorrow. There is no loitering and there is usually no smoking. Even in the girl show in the amusement area, the sailor is placed in a rather astringent attitude, behind glass, for the adoration of the female form. It is all rather serious-minded, this World of Tomorrow, and extremely impersonal. A ride on the Futurama of General Motors induces approximately the same emotional response as a trip through the Cathedral of St. John the Divine. The countryside unfolds before you in five-million-dollar micro-loveliness, conceived in motion and executed by Norman Bel Geddes. The voice is a voice of utmost respect, of complete religious faith in the eternal benefaction of faster travel. The highways unroll in ribbons of perfection through the fertile and rejuvenated America of 1960—a vision of the day to come, the unobstructed left turn, the vanished grade crossing, the town which beckons but does not impede, the millennium of passionless motion. When night falls in the General Motors exhibit and you lean back in the cushioned chair (yourself in motion and the world so still) and hear (from the depths of the chair) the soft electric assurance of a better life—the life which rests on wheels alone—there is a strong, sweet poison which infects the blood. I didn't want to wake up. I liked 1960 in purple light, going a hundred miles an hour around impossible turns ever onward toward the certified cities of the flawless future. It wasn't till I passed an apple orchard and saw the trees, each blooming under its own canopy of glass, that I perceived that even the General Motors dream, as dreams so often do, left some questions unanswered about the future. The apple tree of Tomorrow, abloom under its inviolate hood, makes you stop and wonder. How will the little boy climb it? Where will the little bird build its nest?

I made a few notes at the Fair, a few hints of what you may expect of Tomorrow, its appointments, its characteristics.

In Tomorrow, people and objects are lit not from above but from below. Trees are lit from below. Even the cow on the rotolactor appears to be lit from below—the buried flood lamp illuminates the distended udder.

In Tomorrow one voice does for all. But it is a little unsure of itself; it keeps testing itself; it says, "Hello! One, two, three, four. Hello! One, two, three, four."

Rugs do not slip in Tomorrow, and the bassinets of newborn infants are wired against kidnappers.

There is no talking back in Tomorrow. You are expected to take it or leave it alone. There are sailors there (which makes you feel less lonely) and the sound of music.

The living room of Tomorrow contains the following objects: a broadloom carpet, artificial carnations, a television radio victrola incessantly producing an image of someone or something which is somewhere else, a glass bird, a chrome steel lamp, a terra-cotta zebra, some veneered book cabinets containing no visible books, another cabinet out of which a small newspaper slowly pours in a never-ending ribbon, and a small plush love seat in the shape of a new moon.

In Tomorrow, most sounds are not the sounds themselves but a memory of sounds, or an electrification. In the case of a cow, the moo will come to you not from the cow but from a small aperture above your head.

Tomorrow is a little on the expensive side. I checked this with my cabdriver in Manhattan to make sure. He was full of praise about the Fair, but said he hadn't seen it and might, in fact, never see it. "I hack out there, but I got it figured that for me and the wife to go all through and do it right—no cheapskate stuff

—it would break the hell out of a five-dollar bill. In my racket, I can't afford it."

Tomorrow does not smell. The World's Fair of 1939 has taken the body odor out of man, among other things. It is all rather impersonal, this dream. The country fair manages better, where you can hang over the rail at the ox-pulling and smell the ox. It's not only that the sailors can't get at the girls through the glass, but even so wholesome an exhibit as Swift's Premium Bacon produces twenty lovesick maidens in a glass pit hermetically sealed from the ultimate consumer.

The voice of Mr. Kaltenborn in the City of Man says, "They come with joyous song," but the truth is there is very little joyous song in the Fair grounds. There is a great deal of electrically transmitted joy, but very little spontaneous joy. Tomorrow's music, I noticed, came mostly from Yesterday's singer. In fact, if Mr. Whalen wants a suggestion from me as to how to improve his show (and I am reasonably confident he doesn't), it would be to snip a few wires, hire a couple of bands, and hand out ticklers. Gaiety is not the keynote in Tomorrow. I finally found it at the tag end of a chilly evening, far along in the Amusement Area, in a tent with some colored folks. There was laughing and shouting there, and a beautiful brown belly-dancer.

Another gay spot, to my surprise, was the American Telephone & Telegraph Exhibit. It took the old Telephone Company to put on the best show of all. To anyone who draws a lucky number, the company grants the privilege of making a long-distance call. This call can be to any point in the United States, and the bystanders have the exquisite privilege of listening in through earphones and of laughing unashamed. To understand the full wonder of this, you must reflect that there are millions of people who have never either made or received a long-distance call, and that when Eddie Pancha, a waiter in a restaurant in El Paso, Texas, hears the magic words "New York is calling . . . Go ahead, please," he is transfixed in holy dread and excitement. I listened for two hours and ten minutes to this show, and I'd be there this minute if I were capable of standing up. I had the good luck to be listening at the earphone when a little boy named David Wagstaff won the toss and put in a call to tell his father in Springfield, Mass., what a good time he was having at the World's Fair. David walked resolutely to the glass booth before the assembled kibitzers and in a tiny, timid voice gave the operator his call, his little new cloth hat set all nicely on his head. But his father wasn't there, and David was suddenly confronted with the necessity of telling his story to a man named Mr. Henry, who happened to answer the phone and who, on hearing little David Wagstaff's voice calling from New York, must surely have thought that David's mother had been run down in the B.-M. T. and that David was doing the manly thing.

"Yes, David," he said, tensely.

"Tell my father this," began David, slowly, carefully, determined to go through with the halcyon experience of winning a lucky call at the largest Fair the world had yet produced.

"Yes, David."

"We got on the train, and . . . and . . . had a nice trip, and at New Haven, when they were taking off the car and putting another car on, it was *awfully* funny because the car gave a great —big—BUMP!"

Then followed David's three-minute appreciation of the World of Tomorrow and the Citadel of Light, phrased in the crumbling remnants of speech that little boys are left with when a lot of people are watching, and when their thoughts begin to run down, and when Perispheres begin to swim mistily in time. Mr. Henry—the invisible and infinitely surprised Mr. Henry—maintained a respectful and indulgent silence. I don't know what he was thinking, but I would swap the Helicline for a copy of his attempted transcription of David's message to his father.

My own memory of the Fair, like David's, has begun to dim. From so much culture, from so much concentrated beauty and progress, one can retain only a fragment. I remember the trees at night, shivering in their burlap undershirts, the eerie shadows clinging to the wrong side of their branches. I remember the fountains playing in the light, I remember the girl who sat so still, so clean, so tangible, producing with the tips of her fingers the synthetic speech—but the words were not the words she wanted to say, they were not the words that were in her mind.

I remember the little old Stourbridge Lion, puffing in under its own steam to start the railroads bursting across America. But mostly the Fair has vanished, leaving only the voice of little David Wagstaff and the rambling ecstasy of his first big trip away from home; so many million dollars spent on the idea that our trains and our motorcars should go fast and smoothly, and the child remembering, not the smoothness, but the great—big—BUMP.

So (as the voice says) man dreams on. And the dream is still a contradiction and an enigma—the biologist peeping at bacteria through his microscope, the sailor peeping at the strip queen through binoculars, the eyes so watchful, and the hopes so high. Out in the honky-tonk section, in front of the Amazon show, where the ladies exposed one breast in deference to the fleet, kept one concealed in deference to Mr. Whalen, there was an automaton—a giant man in white tie and tails, with enormous rubber hands. At the start of each show, while the barker was drumming up trade, a couple of the girls would come outside and sit in the robot's lap. The effect was peculiarly lascivious—the extra-size man, exploring with his gigantic rubber hands the breasts of the little girls, the girls with their own small hands (by comparison so small, by comparison so terribly real) restrainingly on his, to check the unthinkable impact of his mechanical passion. Here was the Fair, all fairs, in pantomime; and here the strange mixed dream that made the Fair: the heroic man, bloodless and perfect and enormous, created in his own image, and in his hand (rubber, aseptic) the literal desire, the warm and living breast.

1939

WALDEN

Miss Nims, take a letter to Henry David Thoreau. Dear Henry: I thought of you the other afternoon as I was approaching Concord doing fifty on Route 62. That is a high speed at which to hold a philosopher in one's mind, but in this century we are a nimble bunch.

On one of the lawns in the outskirts of the village a woman was cutting the grass with a motorized lawn mower. What made me think of you was that the machine had rather got away from her, although she was game enough, and in the brief glimpse I had of the scene it appeared to me that the lawn was mowing the lady. She kept a tight grip on the handles, which throbbed violently with every explosion of the one-cylinder motor, and as she sheered around bushes and lurched along at a reluctant trot behind her impetuous servant, she looked like a puppy who had grabbed something that was too much for him. Concord hasn't changed much, Henry; the farm implements and the animals still have the upper hand.

I may as well admit that I was journeying to Concord with the deliberate intention of visiting your woods; for although I have never knelt at the grave of a philosopher nor placed wreaths on moldy poets, and have often gone a mile out of my way to avoid some place of historical interest, I have always wanted to see Walden Pond. The account which you left of your sojourn there is, you will be amused to learn, a document of increasing pertinence; each year it seems to gain a little headway, as the world loses ground. We may all be transcendental yet, whether we like it or not. As our common complexities increase, any tale of individual simplicity (and yours is the best written and the cockiest) acquires a new fascination; as our goods accumulate, but not our well-being, your report of an existence without material adornment takes on a certain awkward credibility.

My purpose in going to Walden Pond, like yours, was not to live cheaply or to live dearly there, but to transact some private business with the fewest obstacles. Approaching Concord, doing forty, doing forty-five, doing fifty, the steering wheel held snug in my palms, the highway held grimly in my vision, the crown of the road now serving me (on the righthand curves), now defeating me (on the lefthand curves), I began to rouse myself from the stupefaction which a day's motor journey induces. It was a delicious evening, Henry, when the whole body is one sense, and imbibes delight through every pore, if I may coin a phrase. Fields were richly brown where the harrow, drawn by the stripped Ford, had lately sunk its teeth; pastures were green; and overhead the sky had that same everlasting great look which you will find on Page 144 of the Oxford pocket edition. I could feel the road entering me, through tire, wheel, spring, and cushion; shall I not have intelligence with earth too? Am I not partly leaves and vegetable mold myself?—a man of infinite horsepower, yet partly leaves.

Stay with me on 62 and it will take you into Concord. As I say, it was a delicious evening. The snake had come forth to die in a bloody S on the highway, the wheel upon its head, its bowels flat now and exposed. The turtle had come up too to cross the road and die in the attempt, its hard shell smashed under the rubber blow, its intestinal yearning (for the other side of the road) forever squashed. There was a sign by the wayside which announced that the road had a "cotton surface." You wouldn't know what that is, but neither, for that matter, did I. There is a cryptic ingredient in many of our modern improvements—we are awed and pleased without knowing quite what we are enjoying. It is something to be traveling on a road with a cotton surface.

The civilization round Concord today is an odd distillation of city, village, farm, and manor. The houses, yards, fields look not quite suburban, not quite rural. Under the bronze beech and the blue spruce of the departed baron grazes the milch goat of the heirs. Under the porte-cochère stands the reconditioned station wagon; under the grape arbor sit the puppies for sale. (But why do men degenerate ever? What makes families run out?)

It was June and everywhere June was publishing her immemorial stanza; in the lilacs, in the syringa, in the freshly edged paths and the sweetness of moist beloved gardens, and the little wire wickets that preserve the tulips' front. Farmers were already moving the fruits of their toil into their yards, arranging the rhubarb, the asparagus, the strictly fresh eggs on the painted stands under the little shed roofs with the patent shingles. And though it was almost a hundred years since you had taken your ax and started cutting out your home on Walden Pond, I was interested to observe that the philosophical spirit was still alive in Massachusetts: in the center of a vacant lot some boys were assembling the framework of the rude shelter, their whole mind and skill concentrated in the rather inauspicious helter-skeleton of studs and rafters. They too were escaping from town, to live naturally, in a rich blend of savagery and philosophy.

That evening, after supper at the inn, I strolled out into the twilight to dream my shapeless transcendental dreams and see that the car was locked up for the night (first open the right front door, then reach over, straining, and pull up the handles of the left rear and the left front till you hear the click, then the handle of the right rear, then shut the right front but open it again remembering that the key is still in the ignition switch, remove the key, shut the right front again with a bang, push the tiny keyhole cover to one side, insert key, turn, and withdraw). It is what we all do, Henry. It is called locking the car. It is said to confuse thieves and keep them from making off with the laprobe. Four doors to lock behind one robe. The driver himself never uses a laprobe, the free movement of his legs being vital to the operation of the vehicle; so that when he locks the car it is a pure and unselfish act. I have in my life gained very little essential heat from laprobes, yet I have ever been at pains to lock them up.

The evening was full of sounds, some of which would have stirred your memory. The robins still love the elms of New England villages at sundown. There is enough of the thrush in them to make song inevitable at the end of day, and enough of the tramp to make them hang round the dwellings of men. A robin, like many another American, dearly loves a white house with green blinds. Concord is still full of them.

Your fellow-townsmen were stirring abroad—not many afoot, most of them in their cars; and the sound which they made in Concord at evening was a rustling and a whispering. The sound lacks steadfastness and is wholly unlike that of a train. A train, as you know who lived so near the Fitchburg line, whistles once or twice sadly and is gone, trailing a memory in smoke, soothing to ear and mind. Automobiles, skirting a village green, are like flies that have gained the inner ear—they buzz, cease, pause, start, shift, stop, halt, brake, and the whole effect is a nervous polytone curiously disturbing.

As I wandered along, the toc toc of ping pong balls drifted from an attic window. In front of the Reuben Brown house a Buick was drawn up. At the wheel, motionless, his hat upon his head, a man sat, listening to Amos and Andy on the radio (it is a drama of many scenes and without an end). The deep voice of Andrew Brown, emerging from the car, although it originated more than two hundred miles away, was unstrained by distance. When you used to sit on the shore of your pond on Sunday morning, listening to the church bells of Acton and Concord, you were aware of the excellent filter of the intervening atmosphere. Science has attended to that, and sound now maintains its intensity without regard for distance. Properly sponsored, it goes on forever.

A fire engine, out for a trial spin, roared past Emerson's house, hot with readiness for public duty. Over the barn roofs the martins dipped and chittered. A swarthy daughter of an asparagus grower, in culottes, shirt, and bandanna, pedalled past on her bicycle. It was indeed a delicious evening, and I returned to the inn (I believe it was your house once) to rock with the old ladies on the concrete veranda.

Next morning early I started afoot for Walden, out Main Street and down Thoreau, past the depot and the Minuteman Chevrolet Company. The morning was fresh, and in a bean field along the way I flushed an agriculturalist, quietly studying his beans. Thoreau Street soon joined Number 126, an artery of the State. We number our highways nowadays, our speed being so great we can remember little of their quality or character and are lucky to remember their number. (Men have an indistinct notion that if they keep up this activity long enough all will at length ride somewhere, in next to no time.) Your pond is on 126.

I knew I must be nearing your woodland retreat when the Golden Pheasant lunchroom came into view—Sealtest ice cream, toasted sandwiches, hot frankfurters, waffles, tonics, and lunches. Were I the proprietor, I should add rice, Indian meal, and molasses—just for old time's sake. The Pheasant, incidentally, is for sale: a chance for some nature lover who wishes to set himself up beside a pond in the Concord atmosphere and live deliberately, fronting only the essential facts of life on Number 126. Beyond the Pheasant was a place called Walden Breezes, an oasis whose porch pillars were made of old green shutters sawed into lengths. On the porch was a distorting mirror, to give the traveler a comical image of himself, who had miraculously learned to gaze in an ordinary glass without smiling. Behind the Breezes, in a sun-parched clearing, dwelt your philosophical descendants in their trailers, each trailer the size of your hut, but all grouped together for the sake of congeniality. Trailer people leave the city, as you did, to discover solitude and in any weather, at any hour of the day or night, to improve the nick of time; but they soon collect in villages and get bogged deeper in the mud than ever. The camp behind Walden Breezes was just rousing itself to the morning. The ground was packed hard under the heel, and the sun came through the clearing to bake the soil and enlarge the wry smell of cramped housekeeping. Cushman's bakery truck had stopped to deliver an early basket of rolls. A camp dog, seeing me in the road, barked petulantly. A man emerged from one of the trailers and set forth with a bucket to draw water from some forest tap.

Leaving the highway I turned off into the woods toward the pond, which was apparent through the foliage. The floor of the forest was strewn with dried old oak leaves and *Transcripts.* From beneath the flattened popcorn wrapper (*granum explosum*) peeped the frail violet. I followed a footpath and descended to the water's edge. The pond lay clear and blue in the morning light, as you have seen it so many times. In the shallows a man's waterlogged shirt undulated gently. A few flies came out to greet me and convoy me to your cove, past the No Bathing signs on which the fellows and the girls had scrawled their names. I felt strangely excited suddenly to be snooping around your premises, tiptoeing along watchfully, as though not to tread by mistake upon the intervening century. Before I got to the cove I heard something which seemed to me quite wonderful: I heard your frog, a full, clear *troonk*, guiding me, still hoarse and solemn, bridging the years as the robins had bridged them in the sweetness of the village evening. But he soon quit, and I came on a couple of young boys throwing stones at him.

Your front yard is marked by a bronze tablet set in a stone. Four small granite posts, a few feet away, show where the house was. On top of the tablet was a pair of faded blue bathing trunks with a white stripe. Back of it is a pile of stones, a sort of cairn, left by your visitors as a tribute I suppose. It is a rather ugly little heap of stones, Henry. In fact the hillside itself seems faded, browbeaten; a few tall skinny pines, bare of lower limbs, a smattering of young maples in suitable green, some birches and oaks, and a number of trees felled by the last big wind. It was from the bole of one of these fallen pines, torn up by the roots, that I extracted the stone which I added to the cairn—a sentimental act in which I was interrupted by a small terrier from a nearby picnic group, who confronted me and wanted to know about the stone.

I sat down for a while on one of the posts of your house to listen to the bluebottles and the dragonflies. The invaded glade sprawled shabby and mean at my feet, but the flies were tuned to the old vibration. There were the remains of a fire in your ruins, but I doubt that it was yours; also two beer bottles trodden into the soil and become part of earth. A young oak had taken root in your house, and two or three ferns, unrolling like the ticklers at a banquet. The only other furnishings were a DuBarry pattern sheet, a page torn from a picture magazine, and some crusts in wax paper.

Before I quit I walked clear round the pond and found the place where you used to sit on the northeast side to get the sun in the fall, and the beach where you got sand for scrubbing your floor. On the eastern side of the pond, where the highway borders it, the State has built dressing rooms for swimmers, a float with diving towers, drinking fountains of porcelain, and rowboats for hire. The pond is in fact a State Preserve, and carries a twenty-dollar fine for picking wild flowers, a decree signed in all solemnity by your fellow-citizens Walter C. Wardwell, Erson B. Barlow, and Nathaniel I. Bowditch. There was a smell of creosote where they had been building a wide wooden stairway to the road and the parking area. Swimmers and boaters were arriving; bodies plunged vigorously into the water and emerged wet and beautiful in the bright air. As I left, a boatload of town boys were splashing about in mid-pond, kidding and fooling, the young fellows singing at the tops of their lungs in a wild chorus:

Amer-ica, Amer-ica, God shed his grace on thee,
And crown thy good with brotherhood
From sea to shi-ning sea!

I walked back to town along the railroad, following your custom. The rails were expanding noisily in the hot sun, and on the slope of the roadbed the wild grape and the blackberry sent up their creepers to the track.

The expense of my brief sojourn in Concord was:

Canvas shoes	$1.95	
Baseball bat	.25	gifts to take back to a boy
Left-handed fielder's glove	1.25	
Hotel and meals	4.25	
In all	$7.70	

As you see, this amount was almost what you spent for food for eight months. I cannot defend the shoes or the expenditure for shelter and food: they reveal a meanness and grossness in my nature which you would find contemptible. The baseball equipment, however, is the kind of impediment with which you were never on even terms. You must remember that the house where you practiced the sort of economy which I respect was haunted only by mice and squirrels. You never had to cope with a shortstop.

1939

ONCE MORE TO THE LAKE

One summer, along about 1904, my father rented a camp on a lake in Maine and took us all there for the month of August. We all got ringworm from some kittens and had to rub Pond's Extract on our arms and legs night and morning, and my father rolled over in a canoe with all his clothes on; but outside of that the vacation was a success and from then on none of us ever thought there was any place in the world like that lake in Maine. We returned summer after summer—always on August 1st for one month. I have since become a salt-water man, but sometimes in summer there are days when the restlessness of the tides and the fearful cold of the sea water and the incessant wind which blows across the afternoon and into the evening make me wish for the placidity of a lake in the woods. A few weeks ago this feeling got so strong I bought myself a couple of bass hooks and a spinner and returned to the lake where we used to go, for a week's fishing and to revisit old haunts.

I took along my son, who had never had any fresh water up his nose and who had seen lily pads only from train windows. On the journey over to the lake I began to wonder what it would be like. I wondered how time would have marred this unique, this holy spot—the coves and streams, the hills that the sun set behind, the camps and the paths behind the camps. I was sure that the tarred road would have found it out and I wondered in what other ways it would be desolated. It is strange how much you can remember about places like that once you allow your mind to return into the grooves which lead back. You remember one thing, and that suddenly reminds you of another thing. I guess I remembered clearest of all the early mornings, when the lake was cool and motionless, remembered how the bedroom smelled of the lumber it was made of and of the wet woods whose scent entered through the screen. The partitions in the camp were thin and did not extend clear to the top of the rooms, and as I was always the first up I would dress softly so as not to wake the others, and sneak out into the sweet outdoors and start out in the canoe, keeping close along the shore in the long shadows of the pines. I remembered being very careful never to rub my paddle against the gunwale for fear of disturbing the stillness of the cathedral.

The lake had never been what you would call a wild lake. There were cottages sprinkled around the shores, and it was in farming country although the shores of the lake were quite heavily wooded. Some of the cottages were owned by nearby farmers, and you would live at the shore and eat your meals at the farmhouse. That's what our family did. But although it wasn't wild, it was a fairly large and undisturbed lake and there were places in it which, to a child at least, seemed infinitely remote and primeval.

I was right about the tar: it led to within half a mile of the shore. But when I got back there, with my boy, and we settled into a camp near a farmhouse and into the kind of summertime I had known, I could tell that it was going to be pretty much the same as it had been before—I knew it, lying in bed the first morning, smelling the bedroom, and hearing the boy sneak quietly out and go off along the shore in a boat. I began to sustain the illusion that he was I, and therefore, by simple transposition, that I was my father. This sensation persisted, kept cropping up all the time we were there. It was not an entirely new feeling, but in this setting it grew much stronger. I seemed to be living a dual existence. I would be in the middle of some simple act, I would be picking up a bait box or laying down a table fork, or I would be saying something, and suddenly it would be not I but my father who was saying the words or making the gesture. It gave me a creepy sensation.

We went fishing the first morning. I felt the same damp moss covering the worms in the bait can, and saw the dragonfly alight on the tip of my rod as it hovered a few inches from the surface of the water. It was the arrival of this fly that convinced me beyond any doubt that everything was as it always had been, that the years were a mirage and there had been no years. The small waves were the same, chucking the rowboat under the chin as we fished at anchor, and the boat was the same boat, the same color green and the ribs broken in the same places, and under the floor-boards the same fresh-water leavings and debris—the dead helgramite, the wisps of moss, the rusty discarded fishhook, the dried blood from yesterday's catch. We stared silently at the tips of our rods, at the dragonflies that came and went. I lowered the top of mine into the water, tentatively, pensively dislodging the fly, which darted two feet away, poised, darted two feet back, and came to rest again a little farther up the rod. There had been no years between the ducking of this dragonfly and the other one—the one that was part of memory. I looked at the boy, who was silently watching his fly, and it was my hands that held his rod, my eyes watching. I felt dizzy and didn't know which rod I was at the end of.

We caught two bass, hauling them in briskly as though they were mackerel, pulling them over the side of the boat in a business-like manner without any landing net, and stunning them with a blow on the back of the head. When we got back for a swim before lunch, the lake was exactly where we had left it, the same number of inches from the dock, and there was only the merest suggestion of a breeze. This seemed an utterly enchanted sea, this lake you could leave to its own devices for a few hours and come back to, and find that it had not stirred, this constant and trustworthy body of water. In the shallows, the dark, water-soaked sticks and twigs, smooth and old, were undulating in clusters on the bottom against the clean ribbed sand, and the track of the mussel was plain. A school of minnows swam by, each minnow with its small individual shadow, doubling the attendance, so clear and sharp in the sunlight. Some of the other campers were in swimming, along the shore, one of them with a cake of soap, and the water felt thin and clear and unsubstantial. Over the years there had been this person with the cake of soap, this cultist, and here he was. There had been no years.

Up to the farmhouse to dinner through the teeming, dusty field, the road under our sneakers was only a two-track road. The middle track was missing, the one with the marks of the hooves and the splotches of dried, flaky manure. There had always been three tracks to choose from in choosing which track to walk in; now the choice was narrowed down to two. For a moment I missed terribly the middle alternative. But the way led past the tennis court, and something about the way it lay there in the sun reassured me; the tape had loosened along the backline, the alleys were green with plantains and other weeds, and the net (installed in June and removed in September) sagged in the dry noon, and the whole place steamed with midday heat and hunger and emptiness. There was a choice of pie for dessert, and one was blueberry and one was apple, and the waitresses were the same country girls, there having been no passage of time, only the illusion of it as in a dropped curtain—the waitresses were still fifteen; their hair had been washed, that was the only difference—they had been to the movies and seen the pretty girls with the clean hair.

Summertime, oh summertime, pattern of life indelible, the fade-proof lake, the woods unshatterable, the pasture with the sweetfern and the juniper forever and ever, summer without end; this was the background, and the life along the shore was the design, the cottages with their innocent and tranquil design, their tiny docks with the flagpole and the American flag floating against the white clouds in the blue sky, the little paths over the roots of the trees leading from camp to camp and the paths leading back to the outhouses and the can of lime for sprinkling, and at the souvenir counters at the store the miniature birch-bark canoes and the post cards that showed things looking a little better than they looked. This was the American family at play, escaping the city heat, wondering whether the newcomers in the camp at the head of the cove were "common" or "nice," wondering whether it was true that the people who drove up for Sunday dinner at the farmhouse were turned away because there wasn't enough chicken.

It seemed to me, as I kept remembering all this, that those times and those summers had been infinitely precious and worth saving. There had been jollity and peace and goodness. The arriving (at the beginning of August) had been so big a business in itself, at the railway station the farm wagon drawn up, the first smell of the pine-laden air, the first glimpse of the smiling farmer, and the great importance of the trunks and your father's enormous authority in such matters, and the feel of the wagon under you for the long ten-mile haul, and at the top of the last long hill catching the first view of the lake after eleven months of not seeing this cherished body of water. The shouts and cries of the other campers when they saw you, and the trunks to be unpacked, to give up their rich burden. (Arriving was less exciting nowadays, when you sneaked up in your car and parked it under a tree near the camp and took out the bags and in five minutes it was all over, no fuss, no loud wonderful fuss about trunks.)

Peace and goodness and jollity. The only thing that was wrong now, really, was the sound of the place, an unfamiliar nervous sound of the outboard motors. This was the note that jarred, the one thing that would sometimes break the illusion and set the years moving. In those other summertimes all motors were inboard; and when they were at a little distance, the noise they made was a sedative, an ingredient of summer sleep. They were one-cylinder and two-cylinder engines, and some were make-and-break and some were jump-spark, but they all made a sleepy sound across the lake. The one-lungers throbbed and fluttered, and the twin-cylinder ones purred and purred, and that was a quiet sound too. But now the campers all had outboards. In the daytime, in the hot mornings, these motors made a petulant, irritable sound; at night, in the still evening when the afterglow lit the water, they whined about one's ears like mosquitoes. My boy loved our rented outboard, and his great desire was to achieve singlehanded mastery over it, and authority, and he soon learned the trick of choking it a little (but not too much), and the adjustment of the needle valve. Watching him I would remember the things you could do with the old one-cylinder engine with the heavy flywheel, how you could have it eating out of your hand if you got really close to it spiritually. Motor boats in those days didn't have clutches, and you would make a landing by shutting off the motor at the proper time and coasting in with a dead rudder. But there was a way of reversing them, if you learned the trick, by cutting the switch and putting it on again exactly on the final dying revolution of the flywheel, so that it would kick back against compression and begin reversing. Approaching a dock in a strong following breeze, it was difficult to slow up sufficiently by the ordinary coasting method, and if a boy felt he had complete mastery over his motor, he was tempted to keep it running beyond its time and then reverse it a few feet from the dock. It took a cool nerve, because if you threw the switch a twentieth of a second too soon you would catch the flywheel when it still had speed enough to go up past center, and the boat would leap ahead, charging bull-fashion at the dock.

We had a good week at the camp. The bass were biting well and the sun shone endlessly, day after day. We would be tired at night and lie down in the accumulated heat of the little bedrooms after the long hot day and the breeze would stir almost imperceptibly outside and the smell of the swamp drift in through the rusty screens. Sleep would come easily and in the morning the red squirrel would be on the roof, tapping out his gay routine. I kept remembering everything, lying in bed in the mornings—the small steamboat that had a long rounded stern like the lip of a Ubangi, and how quietly she ran on the moonlight sails, when the older boys played their mandolins and the girls sang and we ate doughnuts dipped in sugar, and how sweet the music was on the water in the shining night, and what it had felt like to think about girls then. After breakfast we would go up to the store and the things were in the same place—the minnows in a bottle, the plugs and spinners disarranged and pawed over by the youngsters from the boys' camp, the fig newtons and the Beeman's gum. Outside, the road was tarred and cars stood in front of the store. Inside, all was just as it had always been, except there was more Coca-Cola and not so much Moxie and root beer and birch beer and sarsaparilla. We would walk out with a bottle of pop apiece and sometimes the pop would backfire up our noses and hurt. We explored the streams, quietly, where the turtles slid off the sunny logs and dug their way into the soft bottom; and we lay on the town wharf and fed worms to the tame bass. Everywhere we went I had trouble making out which was I, the one walking at my side, the one walking in my pants.

One afternoon while we were there at that lake a thunderstorm came up. It was like the revival of an old melodrama that I had seen long ago with childish awe. The second-act climax of the drama of the electrical disturbance over a lake in America had not changed in any important respect. This was the big scene, still the big scene. The whole thing was so familiar, the first feeling of oppression and heat and a general air around camp of not wanting to go very far away. In midafternoon (it was all the same) a curious darkening of the sky, and a lull in everything that had made life tick; and then the way the boats suddenly swung the other way at their moorings with the coming of a breeze out of the new quarter, and the premonitory rumble. Then the kettle drum, then the snare, then the bass drum and cymbals, then crackling light against the dark, and the gods grinning and licking their chops in the hills. Afterward the calm, the rain steadily rustling in the calm lake, the return of light and hope and spirits, and the campers running out in joy and relief to go swimming in the rain, their bright cries perpetuating the deathless joke about how they were getting simply drenched, and the children screaming with delight at the new sensation of bathing in the rain, and the joke about getting drenched linking the generations in a strong indestructible chain. And the comedian who waded in carrying an umbrella.

When the others went swimming my son said he was going in too. He pulled his dripping trunks from the line where they had hung all through the shower, and wrung them out. Languidly, and with no thought of going in, I watched him, his hard little body, skinny and bare, saw him wince slightly as he pulled up around his vitals the small, soggy, icy garment. As he buckled the swollen belt suddenly my groin felt the chill of death.

1941

AFTERNOON OF AN AMERICAN BOY

When I was in my teens, I lived in Mount Vernon, in the same block with J. Parnell Thomas, who grew up to become chairman of the House Committee on Un-American Activities. I lived on the corner of Summit and East Sidney, at No. 101 Summit

Avenue, and Parnell lived four or five doors north of us on the same side of the avenue, in the house the Diefendorfs used to live in.

Parnell was not a playmate of mine, as he was a few years older, but I used to greet him as he walked by our house on his way to and from the depot. He was a good-looking young man, rather quiet and shy. Seeing him, I would call "Hello, Parnell!" and he would smile and say "Hello, Elwyn!" and walk on. Once I remember dashing out of our yard on roller skates and executing a rink turn in front of Parnell, to show off, and he said, "Well! Quite an artist, aren't you?" I remember the words. I was delighted at praise from an older man and sped away along the flagstone sidewalk, dodging the cracks I knew so well.

The thing that made Parnell a special man in my eyes in those days was not his handsome appearance and friendly manner but his sister. Her name was Eileen. She was my age and she was a quiet, nice-looking girl. She never came over to my yard to play, and I never went over there, and, considering that we lived so near each other, we were remarkably uncommunicative; nevertheless, she was the girl I singled out, at one point, to be of special interest to me. Being of special interest to me involved practically nothing on a girl's part—it simply meant that she was under constant surveillance. On my own part, it meant that I suffered an astonishing disintegration when I walked by her house, from embarrassment, fright, and the knowledge that I was in enchanted territory.

In the matter of girls, I was different from most boys of my age. I admired girls a lot, but they terrified me. I did not feel that I possessed the peculiar gifts or accomplishments that girls liked in their male companions—the ability to dance, to play football, to cut up a bit in public, to smoke, and to make small talk. I couldn't do any of these things successfully, and seldom tried. Instead, I stuck with the accomplishments I was sure of: I rode my bicycle sitting backward on the handle bars, I made up poems, I played selections from *Aïda* on the piano. In winter, I tended goal in the hockey games on the frozen pond in the dell. None of these tricks counted much with girls. In the four years I was in the Mount Vernon High School, I never went to a school dance and I never took a girl to a drugstore for a soda or to the

Westchester Playhouse or to Proctor's. I wanted to do these things but did not have the nerve. What I finally did manage to do, however, and what is the subject of this memoir, was far brassier, far gaudier. As an exhibit of teen-age courage and ineptitude, it never fails to amaze me in retrospect. I am not even sure it wasn't un-American.

My bashfulness and backwardness annoyed my older sister very much, and at about the period of which I am writing she began making strong efforts to stir me up. She was convinced that I was in a rut, socially, and she found me a drag in her own social life, which was brisk. She kept trying to throw me with girls, but I always bounced. And whenever she saw a chance she would start the phonograph and grab me, and we would go charging around the parlor in the toils of the one-step, she gripping me as in a death struggle, and I hurling her finally away from me through greater strength. I was a skinny kid but my muscles were hard, and it would have taken an unusually powerful woman to have held me long in the attitude of the dance.

One day, through a set of circumstances I have forgotten, my sister managed to work me into an afternoon engagement she had with some others in New York. To me, at that time, New York was a wonderland largely unexplored. I had been to the Hippodrome a couple of times with my father, and to the Hudson-Fulton Celebration, and to a few matinées; but New York, except as a setting for extravaganzas, was unknown. My sister had heard tales of tea-dancing at the Plaza Hotel. She and a girl friend of hers and another fellow and myself went there to give it a try. The expedition struck me as a slick piece of arrangement on her part. I was the junior member of the group and had been roped in, I imagine, to give symmetry to the occasion. Or perhaps Mother had forbidden my sister to go at all unless another member of the family was along. Whether I was there for symmetry or for decency I can't really remember, but I was there.

The spectacle was a revelation to me. However repulsive the idea of dancing was, I was filled with amazement at the setup. Here were tables where a fellow could sit so close to the dance floor that he was practically on it. And you could order cinnamon toast and from the safety of your chair observe girls and men in close embrace, swinging along, the music playing while you ate the toast, and the dancers so near to you that they almost brushed the things off your table as they jogged by. I was impressed. Dancing or no dancing, this was certainly high life, and I knew I was witnessing a scene miles and miles ahead of anything that took place in Mount Vernon. I had never seen anything like it, and a ferment must have begun working in me that afternoon.

Incredible as it seems to me now, I formed the idea of asking Parnell's sister Eileen to accompany me to a tea dance at the Plaza. The plan shaped up in my mind as an expedition of unparalleled worldliness, calculated to stun even the most blasé girl. The fact that I didn't know how to dance must have been a powerful deterrent, but not powerful enough to stop me. As I look back on the affair, it's hard to credit my own memory, and I sometimes wonder if, in fact, the whole business isn't some dream that has gradually gained the status of actuality. A boy with any sense, wishing to become better acquainted with a girl who was "of special interest," would have cut out for himself a more modest assignment to start with—a soda date or a movie date—something within reasonable limits. Not me. I apparently became obsessed with the notion of taking Eileen to the Plaza and not to any darned old drugstore. I had learned the location of the Plaza, and just knowing how to get to it gave me a feeling of confidence. I had learned about cinnamon toast, so I felt able to cope with the waiter when he came along. And I banked heavily on the general splendor of the surroundings and the extreme sophistication of the function to carry the day, I guess.

I was three days getting up nerve to make the phone call. Meantime, I worked out everything in the greatest detail. I heeled myself with a safe amount of money. I looked up trains. I overhauled my clothes and assembled an outfit I believed would meet the test. Then, one night at six o'clock, when Mother and Father went downstairs to dinner, I lingered upstairs and entered the big closet off my bedroom where the wall phone was. There I stood for several minutes, trembling, my hand on the receiver, which hung upside down on the hook. (In our family, the receiver always hung upside down, with the big end up.)

I had rehearsed my first line and my second line. I planned to say, "Hello, can I please speak to Eileen?" Then when she came to the phone, I planned to say, "Hello, Eileen, this is Elwyn White." From there on, I figured I could ad-lib it.

At last, I picked up the receiver and gave the number. As I had suspected, Eileen's mother answered.

"Can I please speak to Eileen?" I asked, in a low, troubled voice.

"Just a minute," said her mother. Then, on second thought, she asked, "Who is it, please?"

"It's Elwyn," I said.

She left the phone, and after quite a while Eileen's voice said, "Hello, Elwyn." This threw my second line out of whack, but I stuck to it doggedly.

"Hello, Eileen, this is Elwyn White," I said.

In no time at all I laid the proposition before her. She seemed dazed and asked me to wait a minute. I assume she went into a huddle with her mother. Finally, she said yes, she would like to go tea-dancing with me at the Plaza, and I said fine, I would call for her at quarter past three on Thursday afternoon, or whatever afternoon it was—I've forgotten.

I do not know now, and of course did not know then, just how great was the mental and physical torture Eileen went through that day, but the incident stacks up as a sort of unintentional un-American activity, for which I was solely responsible. It all went off as scheduled: the stately walk to the depot; the solemn train ride, during which we sat staring shyly into the seat in front of us; the difficult walk from Grand Central across Forty-second to Fifth, with pedestrians clipping us and cutting in between us; the bus ride to Fifty-ninth Street; then the Plaza itself, and the cinnamon toast, and the music, and the excitement. The thundering quality of the occasion must have delivered a mental shock to me, deadening my recollection, for I have only the dimmest memory of leading Eileen onto the dance floor to execute two or three unspeakable rounds, in which I vainly tried to adapt my violent sister-and-brother wrestling act into something graceful and appropriate. It must have been awful. And at six o'clock, emerging, I gave no thought to any further entertainment, such as dinner in town. I simply herded

Eileen back all the long, dreary way to Mount Vernon and deposited her, a few minutes after seven, on an empty stomach, at her home. Even if I had attempted to dine her, I don't believe it would have been possible; the emotional strain of the afternoon had caused me to perspire uninterruptedly, and any restaurant would have been justified in rejecting me solely on the ground that I was too moist.

Over the intervening years, I've often felt guilty about my afternoon at the Plaza, and many years ago, during Parnell's investigation of writers, my feeling sometimes took the form of a guilt sequence in which I imagined myself on the stand, in the committee room, being questioned. It went something like this:

PARNELL: Have you ever written for the screen, Mr. White?

ME: No, sir.

PARNELL: Have you ever been, or are you now, a member of the Screen Writers' Guild?

ME: No, sir.

PARNELL: Have you ever been, or are you now, a member of the Communist Party?

ME: No, sir.

Then, in this imaginary guilt sequence of mine, Parnell digs deep and comes up with the big question, calculated to throw me.

PARNELL: Do you recall an afternoon, along about the middle of the second decade of this century, when you took my sister to the Plaza Hotel for tea under the grossly misleading and false pretext that you knew how to dance?

And as my reply comes weakly, "Yes, sir," I hear the murmur run through the committee room and see reporters bending over their notebooks, scribbling hard. In my dream, I am again seated with Eileen at the edge of the dance floor, frightened, stunned, and happy—in my ears the intoxicating drumbeat of the dance, in my throat the dry, bittersweet taste of cinnamon.

I don't know about the guilt, really. I guess a good many girls might say that an excursion such as the one I conducted Eileen on belongs in the un-American category. But there must be millions of aging males, now slipping into their anecdotage, who recall their Willie Baxter period with affection, and who remember some similar journey into ineptitude, in that precious, brief moment in life before love's pages, through constant reference, had become dog-eared, and before its narrative, through sheer competence, had lost the first, wild sense of derring-do.

1947

DEATH OF A PIG

I spent several days and nights in mid-September with an ailing pig and I feel driven to account for this stretch of time, more particularly since the pig died at last, and I lived, and things might easily have gone the other way round and none left to do the accounting. Even now, so close to the event, I cannot recall the hours sharply and am not ready to say whether death came on the third night or the fourth night. This uncertainty afflicts me with a sense of personal deterioration; if I were in decent health I would know how many nights I had sat up with a pig.

The scheme of buying a spring pig in blossomtime, feeding it through summer and fall, and butchering it when the solid cold weather arrives, is a familiar scheme to me and follows an antique pattern. It is a tragedy enacted on most farms with perfect fidelity to the original script. The murder, being premeditated, is in the first degree but is quick and skillful, and the smoked bacon and ham provide a ceremonial ending whose fitness is seldom questioned.

Once in a while something slips—one of the actors goes up in his lines and the whole performance stumbles and halts. My pig simply failed to show up for a meal. The alarm spread rapidly. The classic outline of the tragedy was lost. I found myself cast suddenly in the role of pig's friend and physician—a farcical character with an enema bag for a prop. I had a presentiment, the very first afternoon, that the play would never regain its balance and that my sympathies were now wholly with the pig. This was slapstick—the sort of dramatic treatment that instantly appealed to my old dachshund, Fred, who joined the vigil, held the bag, and, when all was over, presided at the interment. When we slid the body into the grave, we both were shaken to the core. The loss we felt was not the loss of ham but the loss of pig. He had evidently become precious to me, not that he represented a distant nourishment in a hungry time, but that he had suffered in a suffering world. But I'm running ahead of my story and shall have to go back.

My pigpen is at the bottom of an old orchard below the house. The pigs I have raised have lived in a faded building that once was an icehouse. There is a pleasant yard to move about in, shaded by an apple tree that overhangs the low rail fence. A pig couldn't ask for anything better—or none has, at any rate. The sawdust in the icehouse makes a comfortable bottom in which to root, and a warm bed. This sawdust, however, came under suspicion when the pig took sick. One of my neighbors said he thought the pig would have done better on new ground—the same principle that applies in planting potatoes. He said there might be something unhealthy about that sawdust, that he never thought well of sawdust.

It was about four o'clock in the afternoon when I first noticed that there was something wrong with the pig. He failed to appear at the trough for his supper, and when a pig (or a child) refuses supper a chill wave of fear runs through any household, or icehousehold. After examining my pig, who was stretched out in the sawdust inside the building, I went to the phone and cranked it four times. Mr. Dameron answered. "What's good for a sick pig?" I asked. (There is never any identification needed on a country phone; the person on the other end knows who is talking by the sound of the voice and by the character of the question.)

"I don't know, I never had a sick pig," said Mr. Dameron, "but I can find out quick enough. You hang up and I'll call Henry."

Mr. Dameron was back on the line again in five minutes. "Henry says roll him over on his back and give him two ounces of castor oil or sweet oil, and if that doesn't do the trick give him an injection of soapy water. He says he's almost sure the pig's plugged up, and even if he's wrong, it can't do any harm."

I thanked Mr. Dameron. I didn't go right down to the pig, though. I sank into a chair and sat still for a few minutes to think about my troubles, and then I got up and went to the barn, catching up on some odds and ends that needed tending to. Unconsciously I held off, for an hour, the deed by which I would officially recognize the collapse of the performance of raising a pig; I wanted no interruption in the regularity of feeding, the steadiness of growth, the even succession of days. I wanted no interruption, wanted no oil, no deviation. I just wanted to keep on raising a pig, full meal after full meal, spring into summer into fall. I didn't even know whether there were two ounces of castor oil on the place.

Shortly after five o'clock I remembered that we had been invited out to dinner that night and realized that if I were to dose a pig there was no time to lose. The dinner date seemed a familiar conflict: I move in a desultory society and often a week or two will roll by without my going to anybody's house to dinner or anyone's coming to mine, but when an occasion does arise, and I am summoned, something usually turns up (an hour or two in advance) to make all human intercourse seem vastly inappropriate. I have come to believe that there is in hostesses a special power of divination, and that they deliberately arrange dinners to coincide with pig failure or some other sort of failure. At any rate, it was after five o'clock and I knew I could put off no longer the evil hour.

When my son and I arrived at the pigyard, armed with a small bottle of castor oil and a length of clothesline, the pig had emerged from his house and was standing in the middle of his yard, listlessly. He gave us a slim greeting. I could see that he felt uncomfortable and uncertain. I had brought the clothesline thinking I'd have to tie him (the pig weighed more than a hundred pounds) but we never used it. My son reached down, grabbed both front legs, upset him quickly, and when he opened his mouth to scream I turned the oil into his throat—a pink, corrugated area I had never seen before. I had just time to read the label while the neck of the bottle was in his mouth. It said Pure-test. The screams, slightly muffled by oil, were pitched in the hysterically high range of pigsound, as though torture were being carried out, but they didn't last long: it was all over rather suddenly, and, his legs released, the pig righted himself.

In the upset position the corners of his mouth had been turned down, giving him a frowning expression. Back on his feet again, he regained the set smile that a pig wears even in sickness. He stood his ground, sucking slightly at the residue of oil; a few drops leaked out of his lips while his wicked eyes, shaded by their coy little lashes, turned on me in disgust and hatred. I scratched him gently with oily fingers and he remained quiet, as though trying to recall the satisfaction of being scratched when in health, and seeming to rehearse in his mind the indignity to which he had just been subjected. I noticed, as I stood there, four or five small dark spots on his back near the tail end, reddish brown in color, each about the size of a housefly. I could not make out what they were. They did not look troublesome but at the same time they did not look like mere surface bruises or chafe marks. Rather they seemed blemishes of internal origin. His stiff white bristles almost completely hid them and I had to part the bristles with my fingers to get a good look.

Several hours later, a few minutes before midnight, having dined well and at someone else's expense, I returned to the pighouse with a flashlight. The patient was asleep. Kneeling, I felt his ears (as you might put your hand on the forehead of a child) and they seemed cool, and then with the light made a careful examination of the yard and the house for a sign that the oil had worked. I found none and went to bed.

We had been having an unseasonable spell of weather—hot, close days, with the fog shutting in every night, scaling for a few hours in midday, then creeping back again at dark, drifting in first over the trees on the point, then suddenly blowing across the fields, blotting out the world and taking possession of houses, men, and animals. Everyone kept hoping for a break, but the break failed to come. Next day was another hot one. I visited the pig before breakfast and tried to tempt him with a little milk in his trough. He just stared at it, while I made a sucking sound through my teeth to remind him of past pleasures of the feast. With very small, timid pigs, weanlings, this ruse is often quite successful and will encourage them to eat; but with a large, sick pig the ruse is senseless and the sound I made must have made him feel, if anything, more miserable. He not only did not crave food, he felt a positive revulsion to it. I found a place under the apple tree where he had vomited in the night.

At this point, although a depression had settled over me, I didn't suppose that I was going to lose my pig. From the lustiness of a healthy pig a man derives a feeling of personal lustiness; the stuff that goes into the trough and is received with such enthusiasm is an earnest of some later feast of his own, and when this suddenly comes to an end and the food lies stale and untouched, souring in the sun, the pig's imbalance becomes the man's vicariously, and life seems insecure, displaced, transitory.

As my own spirits declined, along with the pig's, the spirits of my vile old dachshund rose. The frequency of our trips down the footpath through the orchard to the pigyard delighted him, although he suffers greatly from arthritis, moves with difficulty, and would be bedridden if he could find anyone willing to serve him meals on a tray.

He never missed a chance to visit the pig with me, and he made many professional calls on his own. You could see him down there at all hours, his white face parting the grass along the fence as he wobbled and stumbled about, his stethoscope dangling—a happy quack, writing his villainous prescriptions and grinning his corrosive grin. When the enema bag appeared, and the bucket of warm suds, his happiness was complete, and he managed to squeeze his enormous body between the two lowest rails of the yard and then assumed full charge of the irrigation. Once, when I lowered the bag to check the flow, he reached in and hurriedly drank a few mouthfuls of the suds to test their potency. I have noticed that Fred will feverishly consume any substance that is associated with trouble—the bitter flavor is to his liking. When the bag was above reach, he concentrated on the pig and was everywhere at once, a tower of strength and inconvenience. The pig, curiously enough, stood rather quietly through this colonic carnival, and the enema, though ineffective, was not as difficult as I had anticipated.

I discovered, though, that once having given a pig an enema

there is no turning back, no chance of resuming one of life's more stereotyped roles. The pig's lot and mine were inextricably bound now, as though the rubber tube were the silver cord. From then until the time of his death I held the pig steadily in the bowl of my mind; the task of trying to deliver him from his misery became a strong obsession. His suffering soon became the embodiment of all earthly wretchedness. Along toward the end of the afternoon, defeated in physicking, I phoned the veterinary twenty miles away and placed the case formally in his hands. He was full of questions, and when I casually mentioned the dark spots on the pig's back, his voice changed its tone.

"I don't want to scare you," he said, "but when there are spots, erysipelas has to be considered."

Together we considered erysipelas, with frequent interruptions from the telephone operator, who wasn't sure the connection had been established.

"If a pig has erysipelas can he give it to a person?" I asked.

"Yes, he can," replied the vet.

"Have they answered?" asked the operator.

"Yes, they have," I said. Then I addressed the vet again. "You better come over here and examine this pig right away."

"I can't come myself," said the vet, "but McFarland can come this evening if that's all right. Mac knows more about pigs than I do anyway. You needn't worry too much about the spots. To indicate erysipelas they would have to be deep hemorrhagic infarcts."

"Deep hemorrhagic what?" I asked.

"Infarcts," said the vet.

"Have they answered?" asked the operator

"Well," I said, "I don't know what you'd call these spots, except they're about the size of a housefly. If the pig has erysipelas I guess I have it, too, by this time, because we've been very close lately."

"McFarland will be over," said the vet.

I hung up. My throat felt dry and I went to the cupboard and got a bottle of whiskey. Deep hemorrhagic infarcts—the phrase began fastening its hooks in my head. I had assumed that there could be nothing much wrong with a pig during the months it was being groomed for murder; my confidence in the essential health and endurance of pigs had been strong and deep, particularly in the health of pigs that belonged to me and that were part of my proud scheme. The awakening had been violent and I minded it all the more because I knew that what could be true of my pig could be true also of the rest of my tidy world. I tried to put this distasteful idea from me, but it kept recurring. I took a short drink of the whiskey and then, although I wanted to go down to the yard and look for fresh signs, I was scared to. I was certain I had erysipelas.

It was long after dark and the supper dishes had been put away when a car drove in and McFarland got out. He had a girl with him. I could just make her out in the darkness—she seemed young and pretty. "This is Miss Owen," he said. "We've been having a picnic supper on the shore, that's why I'm late."

McFarland stood in the driveway and stripped off his jacket, then his shirt. His stocky arms and capable hands showed up in my flashlight's gleam as I helped him find his coverall and get zipped up. The rear seat of his car contained an astonishing amount of paraphernalia, which he soon overhauled, selecting a chain, a syringe, a bottle of oil, a rubber tube, and some other things I couldn't identify. Miss Owen said she'd go along with us and see the pig. I led the way down the warm slope of the orchard, my light picking out the path for them, and we all three climbed the fence, entered the pighouse, and squatted by the pig while McFarland took a rectal reading. My flashlight picked up the glitter of an engagement ring on the girl's hand.

"No elevation," said McFarland, twisting the thermometer in the light. "You needn't worry about erysipelas." He ran his hand slowly over the pig's stomach and at one point the pig cried out in pain.

"Poor piggledy-wiggledy!" said Miss Owen.

The treatment I had been giving the pig for two days was then repeated, somewhat more expertly, by the doctor, Miss Owen and I handing him things as he needed them—holding the chain that he had looped around the pig's upper jaw, holding the syringe, holding the bottle stopper, the end of the tube, all of us working in darkness and in comfort, working with the instinctive teamwork induced by emergency conditions, the pig unprotesting, the house shadowy, protecting, intimate. I went to bed tired but with a feeling of relief that I had turned over part of the responsibility of the case to a licensed doctor. I was beginning to think, though, that the pig was not going to live.

He died twenty-four hours later, or it might have been forty-eight—there is a blur in time here, and I may have lost or picked up a day in the telling and the pig one in the dying. At intervals during the last day I took cool fresh water down to him and at such times as he found the strength to get to his feet he would stand with head in the pail and snuffle his snout around. He drank a few sips but no more; yet it seemed to comfort him to dip his nose in water and bobble it about, sucking in and blowing out through his teeth. Much of the time, now, he lay indoors half buried in sawdust. Once, near the last, while I was attending him I saw him try to make a bed for himself but he lacked the strength, and when he set his snout into the dust he was unable to plow even the little furrow he needed to lie down in.

He came out of the house to die. When I went down, before going to bed, he lay stretched in the yard a few feet from the door. I knelt, saw that he was dead, and left him there: his face had a mild look, expressive neither of deep peace nor of deep suffering, although I think he had suffered a good deal. I went back up to the house and to bed, and cried internally—deep hemorrhagic intears. I didn't wake till nearly eight the next morning, and when I looked out the open window the grave was already being dug, down beyond the dump under a wild apple. I could hear the spade strike against the small rocks that blocked the way. Never send to know for whom the grave is dug, I said to myself, it's dug for thee. Fred, I well knew, was supervising the work of digging, so I ate breakfast slowly.

It was a Saturday morning. The thicket in which I found the gravediggers at work was dark and warm, the sky overcast. Here, among alders and young hackmatacks, at the foot of the apple tree, Lennie had dug a beautiful hole, five feet long, three feet wide, three feet deep. He was standing in it, removing the last spadefuls of earth while Fred patrolled the brink in simple but impressive circles, disturbing the loose earth of the mound so that it trickled back in. There had been no rain in weeks and the soil, even three feet down, was dry and powdery. As I stood and stared, an enormous earthworm which had been partially exposed by the spade at the bottom dug itself deeper and made a slow withdrawal, seeking even remoter moistures at even lonelier depths. And just as Lennie stepped out and rested his spade against the tree and lit a cigarette, a small green apple separated itself from a branch overhead and fell into the hole. Everything about this last scene seemed over-written—the dismal sky, the shabby woods, the imminence of rain, the worm (legendary bedfellow of the dead), the apple (conventional garnish of a pig).

But even so, there was a directness and dispatch about animal burial, I thought, that made it a more decent affair than human burial: there was no stopover in the undertaker's foul parlor, no wreath nor spray; and when we hitched a line to the pig's hind legs and dragged him swiftly from his yard, throwing our weight into the harness and leaving a wake of crushed grass and smoothed rubble over the dump, ours was a businesslike procession, with Fred, the dishonorable pallbearer, staggering along in the rear, his perverse bereavement showing in every seam in his face; and the post mortem performed handily and swiftly right at the edge of the grave, so that the innards that had caused the pig's death preceded him into the ground and he lay at last resting squarely on the cause of his own undoing.

I threw in the first shovelful, and then we worked rapidly and without talk, until the job was complete. I picked up the rope, made it fast to Fred's collar (he is a notorious ghoul), and we all three filed back up the path to the house, Fred bringing up the rear and holding back every inch of the way, feigning unusual stiffness. I noticed that although he weighed far less than the pig, he was harder to drag, being possessed of the vital spark.

The news of the death of my pig traveled fast and far, and I received many expressions of sympathy from friends and neighbors, for no one took the event lightly and the premature expiration of a pig is, I soon discovered, a departure which the community marks solemnly on its calendar, a sorrow in which it feels fully involved. I have written this account in penitence and in grief, as a man who failed to raise his pig, and to explain my deviation from the classic course of so many raised pigs. The grave in the woods is unmarked, but Fred can direct the mourner to it unerringly and with immense good will, and I know he and

I shall often revisit it, singly and together, in seasons of reflection and despair, on flagless memorial days of our own choosing.

1948

THE RING OF TIME

After the lions had returned to their cages, creeping angrily through the chutes, a little bunch of us drifted away and into an open doorway nearby, where we stood for a while in semidarkness, watching a big brown circus horse go harumphing around the practice ring. His trainer was a woman of about forty, and the two of them, horse and woman, seemed caught up in one of those desultory treadmills of afternoon from which there is no apparent escape. The day was hot, and we kibitzers were grateful to be briefly out of the sun's glare. The long rein, or tape, by which the woman guided her charge counterclockwise in his dull career formed the radius of their private circle, of which she was the revolving center; and she, too, stepped a tiny circumference of her own, in order to accommodate the horse and allow him his maximum scope. She had on a short-skirted costume and a conical straw hat. Her legs were bare and she wore high heels, which probed deep into the loose tanbark and kept her ankles in a state of constant turmoil. The great size and meekness of the horse, the repetitious exercise, the heat of the afternoon, all exerted a hypnotic charm that invited boredom; we spectators were experiencing a languor—we neither expected relief nor felt entitled to any. We had paid a dollar to get into the grounds, to be sure, but we had got our dollar's worth a few minutes before, when the lion trainer's whiplash had got caught around a toe of one of the lions. What more did we want for a dollar?

Behind me I heard someone say, "Excuse me, please," in a low voice. She was halfway into the building when I turned and saw her—a girl of sixteen or seventeen, politely threading her way through us onlookers who blocked the entrance. As she emerged in front of us, I saw that she was barefoot, her dirty little feet fighting the uneven ground. In most respects she was like any of two or three dozen showgirls you encounter if you wander about in the winter quarters of Mr. John Ringling North's circus, in Sarasota—cleverly proportioned, deeply browned by the sun, dusty, eager, and almost naked. But her grave face and the naturalness of her manner gave her a sort of quick distinction and brought a new note into the gloomy octagonal building where we had all cast our lot for a few moments. As soon as she had squeezed through the crowd, she spoke a word or two to the older woman, whom I took to be her mother, stepped to the ring, and waited while the horse coasted to a stop in front of her. She gave the animal a couple of affectionate swipes on his enormous neck and then swung herself aboard. The horse immediately resumed his rocking canter, the woman goading him on, chanting something that sounded like "Hop! Hop!"

In attempting to recapture this mild spectacle, I am merely acting as recording secretary for one of the oldest of societies—the society of those who, at one time or another, have surrendered, without even a show of resistance, to the bedazzlement of a circus rider. As a writing man, or secretary, I have always felt charged with the safekeeping of all unexpected items of worldly or unworldly enchantment, as though I might be held personally responsible if even a small one were to be lost. But it is not easy to communicate anything of this nature. The circus comes as close to being the world in microcosm as anything I know; in a way, it puts all the rest of show business in the shade. Its magic is universal and complex. Out of its wild disorder comes order; from its rank smell rises the good aroma of courage and daring; out of its preliminary shabbiness comes the final splendor. And buried in the familiar boasts of its advance agents lies the modesty of most of its people. For me the circus is at its best before it has been put together. It is at its best at certain moments when it comes to a point, as through a burning glass, in the activity and destiny of a single performer out of so many. One ring is always bigger than three. One rider, one aerialist, is always greater than six. In short, a man has to catch the circus unawares to experience its full impact and share its gaudy dream.

The ten-minute ride the girl took achieved—as far as I was concerned, who wasn't looking for it, and quite unbeknownst to her, who wasn't even striving for it—the thing that is sought by performers everywhere, on whatever stage, whether struggling in the tidal currents of Shakespeare or bucking the difficult motion of a horse. I somewhat got the idea she was just cadging a ride, improving a shining ten minutes in the diligent way all serious artists seize free moments to hone the blade of their talent and keep themselves in trim. Her brief tour included only elementary postures and tricks, perhaps because her warmup at this hour was unscheduled and the ring was not rigged for a real practice session. She swung herself off and on the horse several times, gripping his mane. She did a few knee-stands—or whatever they are called—dropping to her knees and quickly bouncing back up on her feet again. Most of the time she simply rode in a standing position, well aft on the beast, her hands hanging easily at her sides, her head erect, her straw-colored ponytail lightly brushing her shoulders, the blood of exertion showing faintly through the tan of her skin. Twice she managed a one-foot stance—a sort of ballet pose, with arms out-stretched. At one point the neck strap of her bathing suit broke and she went twice around the ring in the classic attitude of a woman making minor repairs to a garment. The fact that she was standing on the back of a moving horse while doing this invested the matter with a clownish significance that perfectly fitted the spirit of the circus—jocund, yet charming. She just rolled the strap into a neat ball and stowed it inside her bodice while the horse rocked and rolled beneath her in dutiful innocence. The bathing suit proved as self-reliant as its owner and stood up well enough without benefit of strap.

The richness of the scene was in its plainness, its natural condition—of horse, of ring, of girl, even to the girl's bare feet that gripped the bare back of her proud and ridiculous mount. The enchantment grew not out of anything that happened or was performed but out of something that seemed to go round and around and around with the girl, attending her, a steady gleam in the shape of a circle—a ring of ambition, of happiness, of youth. (And the positive pleasures of equilibrium under difficulties.) In a week or two, all would be changed, all (or almost all) lost: the girl would wear makeup, the horse would wear gold, the ring would be painted, the bark would be clean for the feet of the horse, the girl's feet would be clean for the slippers that she'd wear. All, all would be lost.

As I watched with the others, our jaws adroop, our eyes alight, I became painfully conscious of the element of time. Everything in the hideous old building seemed to take the shape of a circle, conforming to the course of the horse. The rider's gaze, as she peered straight ahead, seemed to be circular, as though bent by force of circumstance; then time itself began running in circles, and so the beginning was where the end was, and the two were the same, and one thing ran into the next and time went round and around and got nowhere. The girl wasn't so young that she did not know the delicious satisfaction of having a perfectly behaved body and the fun of using it to do a trick most people can't do, but she was too young to know that time does not really move in a circle at all. I thought: "She will never be as beautiful as this again"—a thought that made me acutely unhappy—and in a flash my mind (which is too much of a busybody to suit me) had projected her twenty-five years ahead, and she was now in the center of the ring, on foot, wearing a conical hat and high-heeled shoes, the image of the older woman, holding the long rein, caught in the treadmill of an afternoon long in the future. "She is at that enviable moment in life [I thought] when she believes she can go once around the ring, make one complete circuit, and at the end be exactly the same age as at the start." Everything in her movements, her expression, told you that for her the ring of time was perfectly formed, changeless, predictable, without beginning or end, like the ring in which she was travelling at this moment with the horse that wallowed under her. And then I slipped back into my trance, and time was circular again—time, pausing quietly with the rest of us, so as not to disturb the balance of a performer.

Her ride ended as casually as it had begun. The older woman stopped the horse, and the girl slid to the ground. As she walked toward us to leave, there was a quick, small burst of applause. She smiled broadly, in surprise and pleasure; then her face suddenly regained its gravity and she disappeared through the door.

It has been ambitious and plucky of me to attempt to describe what is indescribable, and I have failed, as I knew I would. But I have discharged my duty to my society; and besides, a writer, like an acrobat, must occasionally try a stunt that is too much for him. At any rate, it is worth reporting that long before the circus comes to town, its most notable performances have already been given. Under the bright lights of the finished show, a performer need only reflect the electric candle power that is directed upon him; but in the dark and dirty old training rings and in the make-shift cages, whatever light is generated, whatever excitement, whatever beauty, must come from original sources—from internal fires of professional hunger and delight, from the exuberance and gravity of youth. It is the difference between planetary light and the combustion of stars.

1956

Lewis Thomas

A DISTINGUISHED MEDICAL RESEARCHER AND ADMINISTRATOR, dean of the School of Medicine at Yale University and author of over two hundred highly specialized papers in the fields of immunology and pathology, Dr. Lewis Thomas was invited in 1971 to write a monthly column for the prestigious *New England Journal of Medicine*. Given a free hand with everything but length (the column was limited to 1,200 words), he called it simply "Notes of a Biology-Watcher" and once a month presented a brief overview of recent research or some current issue in the biological sciences. Hardly the sort of stuff to appeal to a wide audience, one would think; but Dr. Thomas wrote with such grace, wit, and wisdom, such clarity and *style*, that soon he had a following well beyond the medical profession. This led, in 1974, to the publication of twenty-nine of Dr. Thomas's columns in a book. To his great surprise, *The Lives of a Cell* not only became a bestseller, it received the National Book Award for Arts and Letters. Somewhat embarrassed by his sudden eminence as a writer, Dr. Thomas commented: "I mean it's not really fair to have a book with a cover and everything when you never wrote a book, except in such little tiny bits. I love having it, but it doesn't seem as though I'd earned it."

Lewis Thomas was born in Flushing, New York, on November 25, 1913, the son of a general practitioner. After graduating from a private school in Manhattan, he entered Princeton, intent on becoming a doctor; but exposure to the poetry of T. S. Eliot and Ezra Pound awakened his literary interests, and he published in the college literary magazine. A course in advanced biology during his senior year drew him back to medicine as a career, but he continued to write. Graduating from Harvard Medical School in 1937, Thomas interned at Boston City Hospital. A poem written during this period was published in the *Atlantic Monthly*.

Following his residency at the Neurological Institute in New

York City, Dr. Thomas was called into the navy in 1941. As a lieutenant commander doing research in tropical diseases, he took part in the invasion of Okinawa. "I went over the side of a troop transport with a case on my shoulder containing fifty white mice, bedded in white toilet paper. One soldier who watched me wade ashore with this load said, 'Now I've seen everything.' "

In 1946 Thomas returned to the academic world of teaching and research, first at Johns Hopkins, then at Tulane and the University of Minnesota, moving steadily up through the academic ranks and into administration. From 1954 to 1969 Dr. Thomas was successively head of the Department of Pathology, director of University Hospital, and dean of the School of Medicine at New York University. Then he moved to Yale, where he became dean of the medical school. Since 1973 Dr. Thomas has been president and chief executive officer of Memorial Sloan-Kettering Cancer Center in New York City. Throughout this exceptional career Dr. Thomas has served on numerous scientific panels, committees, and commissions.

When Lewis Thomas took on the added responsibility of writing a monthly column for the *New England Journal of Medicine* in 1971, it was clearly a labor of love, an opportunity to speak to his profession about the matters that most deeply concerned him. What these came down to was a highly optimistic view of the beneficent complexity of nature, a world of endless wonder that is strange beyond imagination, yet all to the good. "Most of the associations between the living things we know about are essentially cooperative ones, symbiotic in one degree or another. . . . Every creature is, in some degree, connected to and dependent on the rest."

Thomas took the phenomenon of symbiosis—the mutually beneficial relationship between organisms—for the title of his second collection of essays, *The Medusa and the Snail: More Notes of a Biology Watcher,* published in 1979. Bolder and wider-ranging in subject matter than *The Lives of a Cell,* it celebrates the diversity of life in terms at once serious and humorous, mystical and precise. Close scientific observation and the wildest flights of fancy are linked through subtle uses of paradox. In an essay on warts, Thomas wonders at the complex processes by which warts can be removed by hypnotic suggestion. "Not everyone believes this, but the evidence goes back a long way and is persuasive. Generations of internists and dermatologists, and their grandmothers for that matter, have been convinced of the phenomenon."

As a stylist, Lewis Thomas writes in the great tradition of the informal essay. His manner is casual, offhand, seemingly spontaneous, his model the preeminent sixteenth-century French essayist, Michel de Montaigne. In an essay entitled "Why Montaigne Is Not a Bore," Thomas describes Montaigne as he himself might be described: "He is, of course, a moralist and, like all the greatest moralists, also a humorist." Like Montaigne, Lewis Thomas is not an absolutist, but only, he hopes, an ordinary man who tries to persuade you "of his ordinariness on every page. You cannot help but believe him in this; he is, above all else, an honest and candid man. And there is the marvel of his book: if Montaigne is an ordinary man, then what an encouragement, what a piece of work is, after all, an ordinary man!" Though Lewis Thomas would deny any comparison to Montaigne, it is indeed that same quality one admires in him, and it is a quality only achieved slowly by careful attention to detail, whether looking through a microscope or applying pencil to paper.

AUTONOMY

Working a typewriter by touch, like riding a bicycle or strolling on a path, is best done by not giving it a glancing thought. Once you do, your fingers fumble and hit the wrong keys. To do things involving practiced skills, you need to turn loose the systems of muscles and nerves responsible for each maneuver, place them on their own, and stay out of it. There is no real loss of authority in this, since you get to decide whether to do the thing or not, and you can intervene and embellish the technique any time you like; if you want to ride a bicycle backward, or walk with an eccentric loping gait giving a little skip every fourth step, whistling at the same time, you can do that. But if you concentrate your attention on the details, keeping in touch with each muscle, thrusting yourself into a free fall with each step and catching yourself at the last moment by sticking out the other foot in time to break the fall, you will end up immobilized, vibrating with fatigue.

It is a blessing to have options for choice and change in the learning of such unconsciously coordinated acts. If we were born with all these knacks inbuilt, automated like ants, we would surely miss the variety. It would be a less interesting world if we all walked and skipped alike, and never fell from bicycles. If we were all genetically programmed to play the piano deftly from birth, we might never learn to understand music.

The rules are different for the complicated, coordinated, fantastically skilled manipulations we perform with our insides. We do not have to learn anything. Our smooth-muscle cells are born with complete instructions, in need of no help from us, and they work away on their own schedules, modulating the lumen of blood vessels, moving things through intestines, opening and closing tubules according to the requirements of the entire system. Secretory cells elaborate their products in privacy; the heart contracts and relaxes; hormones are sent off to react silently with cell membranes, switching adenyl cyclase, prostaglandin, and other signals on and off; cells communicate with each other by simply touching; organelles send messages to other organelles; all this goes on continually, without ever a personal word from us. The arrangement is that of an ecosystem, with the operation of each part being governed by the state and function of all the other parts. When things are going well, as they generally are, it is an infallible mechanism.

But now the autonomy of this interior domain, long regarded as inviolate, is open to question. The experimental psychologists have recently found that visceral organs can be taught to do various things, as easily as a boy learns to ride a bicycle, by the instrumental techniques of operant conditioning. If a thing is done in the way the teacher wants, at a signal, and a suitable reward given immediately to reinforce the action, it becomes learned. Rats, rewarded by stimulation of their cerebral "pleasure centers," have been instructed to speed up or slow down their hearts at a signal, or to alter their blood pressures, or switch off certain waves in their electroencephalograms and switch on others.

The same technology has been applied to human beings, with other kinds of rewards, and the results have been startling. It is claimed that you can teach your kidneys to change the rate of urine formation, raise or lower your blood pressure, change your heart rate, write different brain waves, at will.

There is already talk of a breakthrough in the prevention and treatment of human disease. According to proponents, when the technology is perfected and extended it will surely lead to new possibilities for therapy. If a rat can be trained to dilate the blood vessels of one of his ears more than those of the other, as has been reported, what rich experiences in self-control and self-operation may lie just ahead for man? There are already cryptic advertisements in the Personal columns of literary magazines, urging the purchase of electronic headsets for the training and regulation of one's own brain waves, according to one's taste.

You can have it.

Not to downgrade it. It is extremely important, I know, and one ought to feel elated by the prospect of taking personal charge, calling the shots, running one's cells around like toy trains. Now that we know that viscera can be taught, the thought comes naturally that we've been neglecting them all these years, and by judicious application of human intelligence, these primitive structures can be trained to whatever standards of behavior we wish to set for them.

My trouble, to be quite candid, is a lack of confidence in myself. If I were informed tomorrow that I was in direct communication with my liver, and could now take over, I would become deeply depressed. I'd sooner be told, forty thousand feet over Denver, that the 747 jet in which I had a coach seat was now mine to operate as I pleased; at least I would have the hope of bailing out, if I could find a parachute and discover quickly how to open a door. Nothing would save me and my liver, if I were in charge. For I am, to face the facts squarely, considerably less intelligent than my liver. I am, moreover, constitutionally unable to make hepatic decisions, and I prefer not to be obliged to, ever. I would not be able to think of the first thing to do.

I have the same feeling about the rest of my working parts. They are all better off without my intervention, in whatever they do. It might be something of a temptation to take over my brain, on paper, but I cannot imagine doing so in real life. I would lose track, get things mixed up, turn on wrong cells at wrong times, drop things. I doubt if I would ever be able to think up my own thoughts. My cells were born, or differentiated anyway, knowing how to do this kind of thing together. If I moved in to organize them they would resent it, perhaps become frightened, perhaps swarm out into my ventricles like bees.

Although it is, as I say, a temptation. I have never really been satisfied with the operation of my brain, and it might be fun to try running it myself, just once. There are several things I would change, given the opportunity: certain memories that tend to slip away unrecorded, others I've had enough of and would prefer to delete, certain notions I'd just as soon didn't keep popping in, trains of thought that go round and round without getting anywhere, rather like this one. I've always suspected that some of the cells in there are fluffing off much of the time, and I'd like to see a little more attention and real work. Also, while I'm about it, I could do with a bit more respect.

On balance, however, I think it best to stay out of this business. Once you began, there would be no end to the responsibilities. I'd rather leave all my automatic functions with as much autonomy as they please, and hope for the best. Imagine having to worry about running leukocytes, keeping track, herding them here and there, listening for signals. After the first flush of pride in ownership, it would be exhausting and debilitating, and there would be no time for anything else.

What to do, then? It cannot simply be left there. If we have learned anything at all in this century, it is that all new technologies will be put to use, sooner or later, for better or worse, as it is in our nature to do. We cannot expect an exception for the instrumental conditioning of automatic functions. We will be driven to make use of it, trying to communicate with our internal environment, to meddle, and it will consume so much of our energy that we will end up even more cut off from things outside, missing the main sources of the sensation of living.

I have a suggestion for a way out. Given the capacity to control autonomic functions, modulate brain waves, run cells, why shouldn't it be possible to employ exactly the same technology to go in precisely the opposite direction? Instead of getting in there and taking things over, couldn't we learn to disconnect altogether, uncouple, detach, and float free? You would only need to be careful, if you tried it, that you let go of the right end.

Of course, people have been trying to do this sort of thing for a long time, by other techniques and with varying degrees of luck. This is what Zen archery seems to be about, come to think of it. You learn, after long months of study under a master, to release the arrow without releasing it yourself. Your fingers must do the releasing, on their own, remotely, like the opening of a flower. When you have learned this, no matter where the arrow goes, you have it made. You can step outside for a look around.

1972

A FEAR OF PHEROMONES

What are we going to do if it turns out that we have pheromones? What on earth would we be doing with such things? With the richness of speech, and all our new devices for communication, why would we want to release odors into the air to convey information about anything? We can send notes, telephone, whisper cryptic invitations, announce the giving of parties, even bounce words off the moon and make them carom around the planets. Why a gas, or droplets of moisture made to be deposited on fence posts?

Comfort has recently reviewed the reasons for believing that we are, in fact, in possession of anatomic structures for which there is no rational explanation except as sources of pheromones —tufts of hair, strategically located apocrine glands, unaccountable areas of moisture. We even have folds of skin here and there designed for the controlled nurture of bacteria, and it is known that certain microbes eke out a living, like eighteenth-century musicians, producing chemical signals by ornamenting the products of their hosts.

Most of the known pheromones are small, simple molecules, active in extremely small concentrations. Eight or ten carbon atoms in a chain are all that are needed to generate precise, unequivocal directions about all kinds of matters—when and where to cluster in crowds, when to disperse, how to behave to the opposite sex, how to ascertain what *is* the opposite sex, how to organize members of a society in the proper ranking orders of dominance, how to mark out exact boundaries of real estate, and how to establish that one is, beyond argument, one's self. Trails can be laid and followed, antagonists frightened and confused, friends attracted and enchanted.

The messages are urgent, but they may arrive, for all we know, in a fragrance of ambiguity. "At home, 4 p.m. today," says the female moth, and releases a brief explosion of bombykol, a single molecule of which will tremble the hairs of any male within miles and send him driving upwind in a confusion of ardor. But it is doubtful if he has an awareness of being caught in an aerosol of chemical attractant. On the contrary, he probably finds suddenly that it has become an excellent day, the weather remarkably bracing, the time appropriate for a bit of exercise of the old wings, a brisk turn upwind. En route, traveling the gradient of bombykol, he notes the presence of other males, heading in the same direction, all in a good mood, inclined to race for the sheer sport of it. Then, when he reaches his destination, it may seem to him the most extraordinary of coincidences, the greatest piece of luck: "Bless my soul, what have we here!"

It has been soberly calculated that if a single female moth were to release all the bombykol in her sac in a single spray, all at once, she could theoretically attract a trillion males in the instant. This is, of course, not done.

Fish make use of chemical signals for the identification of individual members of a species, and also for the announcement of changes in the status of certain individuals. A catfish that has had a career as a local leader smells one way, but as soon as he is displaced in an administrative reorganization, he smells differently, and everyone recognizes the loss of standing. A bullhead can immediately identify the water in which a recent adversary has been swimming, and he can distinguish between this fish and all others in the school.

There is some preliminary, still fragmentary evidence for important pheromones in primates. Short-chain aliphatic compounds are elaborated by female monkeys in response to estradiol, and these are of consuming interest to the males. Whether there are other sorts of social communication by pheromones among primates is not known.

The possibility that human beings are involved in this sort of thing has not attracted much attention until recently. It is still too early to say how it will come out. Perhaps we have inherited only vestiges of the organs needed, only antique and archaic traces of the fragrance, and the memory may be forever gone. We may remain safe from this new challenge to our technology, and, while the twentieth century continues to run out in concentric circles down the drain, we may be able to keep our attention concentrated on how to get energy straight from the sun.

But there are just the slightest suggestions, hints of what may be ahead. Last year it was observed that young women living at close quarters in dormitories tended to undergo spontaneous synchronization of their menstrual cycles. A paper in *Nature* reported the personal experience of an anonymous, quantitatively minded British scientist who lived for long stretches in isolation on an offshore island, and discovered, by taking the dry weight of the hairs trapped by his electric razor every day, that his beard grew much more rapidly each time he returned to the mainland and encountered girls. Schizophrenic patients are reported to have a special odor to their sweat, traced to trans-3-methylhexanoic acid.

The mind, already jelled by the advances in modern communication so that further boggling is impossible, twitches. One can imagine whole new industries springing up to create new perfumes ("A Scientific Combination of Primer and Releaser"), and other, larger corporations raising new turrets with flames alight at their tops on the Jersey flats, for the production of phenolic, anesthetic, possibly bright green sprays to cover, mask, or suppress all pheromones ("Don't Let On"). Gas chromatography of air samples might reveal blips of difference between substances released over a Glasgow football match, a committee meeting on academic promotions, and a summer beach on Saturday afternoon, all highly important. One can even imagine agitated conferences in the Pentagon, new agreements in Geneva.

It is claimed that a well-trained tracking hound can follow with accuracy the trail of a man in shoes, across open ground marked by the footsteps of any number of other people, provided the dog is given an item of the man's clothing to smell beforehand. If one had to think up an R&D program for a National Institute of Human Fragrance (to be created by combining the budgets of the FDA and FCC), this would be a good problem to start with. It might also provide the kind of secondary, spin-off items of science that we like to see in federally supported research. If it is true, as the novels say, that an intelligent dog can tell the difference between one human being and any other by detecting differences in their scents, an explanation might be geometric differences in 10-carbon molecules, or perhaps differences in the relative concentrations of several pheromones in a medley. If this is a fact, it should be of interest to the immunologic community, which has long since staked out claims on the mechanisms involved in the discrimination between self and nonself. Perhaps the fantastically sensitive and precise immunologic mechanisms for the detection of small molecules such as haptenes represent another way of sensing the same markers. Man's best friend might be used to sniff out histocompatible donors. And so forth. If we could just succeed in maintaining the research activity at this level, perhaps diverting everyone's attention from all other aspects by releasing large quantities of money, we might be able to stay out of trouble.

1971

ON CLONING A HUMAN BEING

It is now theoretically possible to recreate an identical creature from any animal or plant, from the DNA contained in the nucleus of any somatic cell. A single plant root-tip cell can be teased and seduced into conceiving a perfect copy of the whole plant; a frog's intestinal epithelial cell possesses the complete instructions needed for a new, same frog. If the technology were further advanced, you could do this with a human being, and there are now startled predictions all over the place that this will in fact be done, someday, in order to provide a version of immortality for carefully selected, especially valuable people.

The cloning of humans is on most of the lists of things to worry about from Science, along with behavior control, genetic engineering, transplanted heads, computer poetry, and the unrestrained growth of plastic flowers.

Cloning is the most dismaying of prospects, mandating as it does the elimination of sex with only a metaphoric elimination of death as compensation. It is almost no comfort to know that one's cloned, identical surrogate lives on, especially when the living will very likely involve edging one's real, now aging self off to the side, sooner or later. It is hard to imagine anything like filial affection or respect for a single, unmated nucleus; harder still to think of one's new, self-generated self as anything but an absolute, desolate orphan. Not to mention the complex interpersonal relationship involved in raising one's self from infancy, teaching the language, enforcing discipline, instilling good manners, and the like. How would you feel if you became an incorrigible juvenile delinquent by proxy, at the age of fifty-five?

The public questions are obvious. Who is to be selected, and on what qualifications? How to handle the risks of misused technology, such as self-determined cloning by the rich and powerful but socially objectionable, or the cloning by governments of dumb, docile masses for the world's work? What will be the effect on all the uncloned rest of us of human sameness? After all, we've accustomed ourselves through hundreds of millennia to the continual exhilaration of uniqueness; each of us is totally different, in a fundamental sense, from all the other four billion. Selfness is an essential fact of life. The thought of human nonselfness, precise sameness, is terrifying, when you think about it.

Well, don't think about it, because it isn't a probable possibility, not even as a long shot for the distant future, in my opinion. I agree that you might clone some people who would look amazingly like their parental cell donors, but the odds are that they'd be almost as different as you or me, and certainly more different than any of today's identical twins.

The time required for the experiment is only one of the problems, but a formidable one. Suppose you wanted to clone a prominent, spectacularly successful diplomat, to look after the Middle East problems of the distant future. You'd have to catch him and persuade him, probably not very hard to do, and extirpate a cell. But then you'd have to wait for him to grow up through embryonic life and then for at least forty years more, and you'd have to be sure all observers remained patient and unmeddlesome through his unpromising, ambiguous childhood and adolescence.

Moreover, you'd have to be sure of recreating his environment, perhaps down to the last detail. "Environment" is a word which really means people, so you'd have to do a lot more cloning than just the diplomat himself.

This is a very important part of the cloning problem, largely overlooked in our excitement about the cloned individual himself. You don't have to agree all the way with B. F. Skinner to acknowledge that the environment does make a difference, and when you examine what we really mean by the word "environment" it comes down to other human beings. We use euphemisms and jargon for this, like "social forces," "cultural influences," even Skinner's "verbal community," but what is meant is the dense crowd of nearby people who talk to, listen to, smile or frown at, give to, withhold from, nudge, push, caress, or flail out at the individual. No matter what the genome says, these people have a lot to do with shaping a character. Indeed, if all you had was the genome, and no people around, you'd grow a sort of vertebrate plant, nothing more.

So, to start with, you will undoubtedly need to clone the parents. No question about this. This means the diplomat is out, even in theory, since you couldn't have gotten cells from both his parents at the time when he was himself just recognizable as an early social treasure. You'd have to limit the list of clones to people already certified as sufficiently valuable for the effort, with both parents still alive. The parents would need cloning and, for consistency, their parents as well. I suppose you'd also need the usual informed-consent forms, filled out and signed, not easy to get if I know parents, even harder for grandparents.

But this is only the beginning. It is the whole family that really influences the way a person turns out, not just the parents, according to current psychiatric thinking. Clone the family.

Then what? The way each member of the family develops has already been determined by the environment set around him, and this environment is more people, people outside the family, schoolmates, acquaintances, lovers, enemies, car-pool partners, even, in special circumstances, peculiar strangers across the aisle on the subway. Find them, and clone them.

But there is no end to the protocol. Each of the outer contacts has his own surrounding family, and his and their outer contacts. Clone them all.

To do the thing properly, with any hope of ending up with a genuine duplicate of a single person, you really have no choice. You must clone the world, no less.

We are not ready for an experiment of this size, nor, I should think, are we willing. For one thing, it would mean replacing today's world by an entirely identical world to follow immediately, and this means no new, natural, spontaneous, random, chancy children. No children at all, except for the manufactured doubles of those now on the scene. Plus all those identical adults, including all of today's politicians, all seen double. It is too much to contemplate.

Moreover, when the whole experiment is finally finished, fifty years or so from now, how could you get a responsible scientific reading on the outcome? Somewhere in there would be the original clonee, probably lost and overworked, now well into middle age, but everyone around him would be precise duplicates of today's everyone. It would be today's same world, filled to overflowing with duplicates of today's people and their same, duplicated problems, probably all resentful at having had to go through our whole thing all over, sore enough at the clone to make endless trouble for him, if they found him.

And obviously, if the whole thing were done precisely right, they would still be casting about for ways to solve the problem of universal dissatisfaction, and sooner or later they'd surely begin to look around at each other, wondering who should be cloned for his special value to society, to get us out of all this. And so it would go, in regular cycles, perhaps forever.

I once lived through a period when I wondered what Hell could be like, and I stretched my imagination to try to think of a perpetual sort of damnation. I have to confess, I never thought of anything like this.

I have an alternative suggestion, if you're looking for a way out. Set cloning aside, and don't try it. Instead, go in the other direction. Look for ways to get mutations more quickly, new variety, different songs. Fiddle around, if you must fiddle, but never with ways to keep things the same, no matter who, not even yourself. Heaven, somewhere ahead, has got to be a change.

1974

ON NATURAL DEATH

There are so many new books about dying that there are now special shelves set aside for them in bookshops, along with the health-diet and home-repair paperbacks and the sex manuals. Some of them are so packed with detailed information and step-by-step instructions for performing the function that you'd think this was a new sort of skill which all of us are now required to learn. The strongest impression the casual reader gets, leafing through, is that proper dying has become an extraordinary, even an exotic experience, something only the specially trained get to do.

Also, you could be led to believe that we are the only creatures capable of the awareness of death, that when all the rest of nature is being cycled through dying, one generation after another, it is a different kind of process, done automatically and trivially, more "natural," as we say.

An elm in our backyard caught the blight this summer and dropped stone dead, leafless, almost overnight. One weekend it was a normal-looking elm, maybe a little bare in spots but nothing alarming, and the next weekend it was gone, passed over, departed, taken. Taken is right, for the tree surgeon came by yesterday with his crew of young helpers and their cherry picker, and took it down branch by branch and carted it off in the back of a red truck, everyone singing.

The dying of a field mouse, at the jaws of an amiable household cat, is a spectacle I have beheld many times. It used to make me wince. Early in life I gave up throwing sticks at the cat to make him drop the mouse, because the dropped mouse regularly went ahead and died anyway, but I always shouted unaffections at the cat to let him know the sort of animal he had become. Nature, I thought, was an abomination.

Recently I've done some thinking about that mouse, and I wonder if his dying is necessarily all that different from the passing of our elm. The main difference, if there is one, would be in the matter of pain. I do not believe that an elm tree has pain receptors, and even so, the blight seems to me a relatively painless way to go even if there were nerve endings in a tree, which there are not. But the mouse dangling tail-down from the teeth of a gray cat is something else again, with pain beyond bearing, you'd think, all over his small body.

There are now some plausible reasons for thinking it is not like that at all, and you can make up an entirely different story about the mouse and his dying if you like. At the instant of being trapped and penetrated by teeth, peptide hormones are released by cells in the hypothalamus and the pituitary gland; instantly these substances, called endorphins, are attached to the surface of other cells responsible for pain perception; the hormones have the pharmacologic properties of opium; there is no pain. Thus it is that the mouse seems always to dangle so languidly from the jaws, lies there so quietly when dropped, dies of his injuries without a struggle. If a mouse could shrug, he'd shrug.

I do not know if this is true or not, nor do I know how to prove it if it is true. Maybe if you could get in there quickly enough and administer naloxone, a specific morphine antagonist, you could turn off the endorphins and observe the restoration of pain, but this is not something I would care to do or see. I think I will leave it there, as a good guess about the dying of a cat-chewed mouse, perhaps about dying in general.

Montaigne had a hunch about dying, based on his own close call in a riding accident. He was so badly injured as to be believed dead by his companions, and was carried home with lamentations, "all bloody, stained all over with the blood I had thrown up." He remembers the entire episode, despite having been "dead, for two full hours," with wonderment:

> It seemed to me that my life was hanging only by the tip of my lips. I closed my eyes in order, it seemed to me, to help push it out, and took pleasure in growing languid and letting myself go. It was an idea that was only floating on the surface of my soul, as delicate and feeble as all the rest, but in truth not only free from distress but mingled with that sweet feeling that people have who have let themselves slide into sleep. I believe that this is the same state in which people find themselves whom we see fainting in the agony of death, and I maintain that we pity them without cause. . . . In order to get used to the idea of death, I find there is nothing like coming close to it.

Later, in another essay, Montaigne returns to it:

> If you know not how to die, never trouble yourself; Nature will in a moment fully and sufficiently instruct you; she will exactly do that business for you; take you no care for it.

The worst accident I've ever seen was in Okinawa, in the early days of the invasion, when a jeep ran into a troop carrier and was crushed nearly flat. Inside were two young MPs, trapped in bent steel, both mortally hurt, with only their heads and shoulders visible. We had a conversation while people with the right tools were prying them free. Sorry about the accident, they said. No, they said, they felt fine. Is everyone else okay, one of them said. Well, the other one said, no hurry now. And then they died.

Pain is useful for avoidance, for getting away when there's time to get away, but when it is end game, and no way back, pain is likely to be turned off, and the mechanisms for this are wonderfully precise and quick. If I had to design an ecosystem in which creatures had to live off each other and in which dying was an indispensable part of living, I could not think of a better way to manage.

1979

ON EMBRYOLOGY

A short while ago, in mid-1978, the newest astonishment in medicine, covering all the front pages, was the birth of an English baby nine months after conception in a dish. The older surprise, which should still be fazing us all, is that a solitary sperm and a single egg can fuse and become a human being under any circumstance, and that, however implanted, a mere cluster of the progeny of this fused cell affixed to the uterine wall will grow and differentiate into eight pounds of baby; this has been going on under our eyes for so long a time that we've gotten used to it; hence the outcries of amazement at this really minor technical modification of the general procedure—nothing much, really, beyond relocating the beginning of the process from the fallopian tube to a plastic container and, perhaps worth mentioning, the exclusion of the father from any role likely to add, with any justification, to his vanity.

There is, of course, talk now about extending the technology beyond the act of conception itself, and predictions are being made that the whole process of embryonic development, all nine months of it, will ultimately be conducted in elaborate plastic flasks. When this happens, as perhaps it will someday, it will be another surprise, with more headlines. Everyone will say how marvelously terrifying is the new power of science, and arguments over whether science should be stopped in its tracks will preoccupy senatorial subcommittees, with more headlines. Meanwhile, the sheer incredibility of the process itself, whether it occurs in the uterus or *in* some sort of *vitro*, will probably be overlooked as much as it is today.

For the real amazement, if you want to be amazed, is the process. You start out as a single cell derived from the coupling of a sperm and an egg, this divides into two, then four, then eight, and so on, and at a certain stage there emerges a single cell which will have as all its progeny the human brain. The mere existence of that cell should be one of the great astonishments of the earth. People ought to be walking around all day, all through their waking hours, calling to each other in endless wonderment, talking of nothing except that cell. It is an unbelievable thing, and yet there it is, popping neatly into its place amid the jumbled cells of every one of the several billion human embryos around the planet, just as if it were the easiest thing in the world to do.

If you like being surprised, there's the source. One cell is switched on to become the whole trillion-cell, massive apparatus for thinking and imagining and, for that matter, being surprised. All the information needed for learning to read and write, playing the piano, arguing before senatorial subcommittees, walking across a street through traffic, or the marvelous human act of putting out one hand and leaning against a tree, is contained in that first cell. All of grammar, all syntax, all arithmetic, all music.

It is not known how the switching on occurs. At the very beginning of an embryo, when it is still nothing more than a cluster of cells, all of this information and much more is latent inside every cell in the cluster. When the stem cell for the brain emerges, it could be that the special quality of brainness is simply switched on. But it could as well be that everything else, every other potential property, is switched off, so that this most specialized of all cells no longer has its precursors' option of being a thyroid or a liver or whatever, only a brain.

No one has the ghost of an idea how this works, and nothing else in life can ever be so puzzling. If anyone does succeed in explaining it, within my lifetime, I will charter a skywriting airplane, maybe a whole fleet of them, and send them aloft to write one great exclamation point after another, around the whole sky, until all my money runs out.

1979

MEDICAL LESSONS FROM HISTORY

It is customary to place the date for the beginnings of modern medicine somewhere in the mid-1930s, with the entry of sulfonamides and penicillin into the pharmacopoeia, and it is usual to ascribe to these events the force of a revolution in medical practice. This is what things seemed like at the time. Medicine was upheaved, revolutionized indeed. Therapy had been discovered for great numbers of patients whose illnesses had previously been untreatable. Cures were now available. As we saw it then, it seemed a totally new world. Doctors could now *cure* disease, and this was astonishing, most of all to the doctors themselves.

It was, no doubt about it, a major occurrence in medicine, and a triumph for biological science applied to medicine but perhaps not a revolution after all, looking back from this distance. For the real revolution in medicine, which set the stage for antibiotics and whatever else we have in the way of effective therapy today, had already occurred one hundred years before penicillin. It did not begin with the introduction of science into medicine. That came years later. Like a good many revolutions, this one began with the destruction of dogma. It was discovered, sometime in the 1830s, that the greater part of medicine was nonsense.

The history of medicine has never been a particularly attractive subject in medical education, and one reason for this is that it is so unrelievedly deplorable a story. For century after century, all the way into the remote millennia of its origins, medicine got along by sheer guesswork and the crudest sort of empiricism. It is hard to conceive of a less scientific enterprise among human endeavors. Virtually anything that could be thought up for the treatment of disease was tried out at one time or another, and, once tried, lasted decades or even centuries before being given up. It was, in retrospect, the most frivolous and irresponsible kind of human experimentation, based on nothing but trial and error, and usually resulting in precisely that sequence. Bleeding, purging, cupping, the administration of infusions of every known plant, solutions of every known metal, every conceivable diet including total fasting, most of these based on the weirdest imaginings about the cause of disease, concocted out of nothing but thin air—this was the heritage of medicine up until a little over a century ago. It is astounding that the profession survived so long, and got away with so much with so little outcry. Almost everyone seems to have been taken in. Evidently one had to be a born skeptic, like Montaigne, to see through the old nonsense; but even Montaigne, who wrote scathingly about the illnesses caused by doctoring centuries before Ivan Illich, had little effect. Most people were convinced of the magical powers of medicine and put up with it.

Then, sometime in the early nineteenth century, it was realized by a few of the leading figures in medicine that almost all of the complicated treatments then available for disease did not really work, and the suggestion was made by several courageous physicians, here and abroad, that most of them actually did more harm than good. Simultaneously, the surprising discovery was made that certain diseases were self-limited, got better by themselves, possessed, so to speak, a "natural history." It is hard for us now to imagine the magnitude of this discovery and its effect on the practice of medicine. The long habit of medicine, extending back into the distant past, had been to treat everything with something, and it was taken for granted that every disease demanded treatment and might in fact end fatally if not treated. In a sober essay written on this topic in 1876, Professor Edward H. Clarke of Harvard reviewed what he regarded as the major scientific accomplishment of medicine in the preceding fifty years, which consisted of studies proving that patients with typhoid and typhus fever could recover all by themselves, without medical intervention, and often did better for being untreated than when they received the bizarre herbs, heavy metals, and fomentations that were popular at that time. Delirium tremens, a disorder long believed to be fatal in all cases unless subjected to constant and aggressive medical intervention, was observed to subside by itself more readily in patients left untreated, with a substantially improved rate of survival.

Gradually, over the succeeding decades, the traditional therapeutic ritual of medicine was given up, and what came to be called the "art of medicine" emerged to take its place. In retrospect, this art was really the beginning of the science of medicine. It was based on meticulous, objective, even cool observations of sick people. From this endeavor we learned the details of the natural history of illness, so that, for example, it came to be understood that typhoid and typhus were really two entirely separate, unrelated disorders, with quite different causes. Accurate diagnosis became the central purpose and justification for medicine, and as the methods for diagnosis improved, accurate prognosis also became possible, so that patients and their families could be told not only the name of the illness but also, with some reliability, how it was most likely to turn out. By the time this century had begun, these were becoming generally accepted as the principal responsibilities of the physician. In addition, a new kind of much less ambitious and flamboyant therapy began to emerge, termed "supportive treatment" and consisting in large part of plain common sense: good nursing care, appropriate bed rest, a sensible diet, avoidance of traditional nostrums and patent medicine, and a measured degree of trust that nature, in taking its course, would very often bring things to a satisfactory conclusion.

The doctor became a considerably more useful and respected professional. For all his limitations, and despite his inability to do much in the way of preventing or terminating illness, he could be depended on to explain things, to relieve anxieties, and to be on hand. He was trusted as an adviser and guide in difficult times, including the time of dying.

Meanwhile, starting in the last decade of the nineteenth century, the basic science needed for a future science of medicine got under way. The role of bacteria and viruses in illness was discerned, and research on the details of this connection began in earnest. The major pathogenic organisms, most notably the tubercle bacillus and the syphilis spirochete, were recognized for what they were and did. By the late 1930s this research had already paid off; the techniques of active and passive immunization had been worked out for diphtheria, tetanus, lobar pneumonia, and a few other bacterial infections; the taxonomy of infectious disease had become an orderly discipline; and the time was ready for sulfanilamide, penicillin, streptomycin, and all the rest. But it needs emphasizing that it took about fifty years of concentrated effort in basic research to reach this level; if this research had not been done we could not have guessed that streptococci and pneumococci exist, and the search for antibiotics would have made no sense at all. Without the long, painstaking research on the tubercle bacillus, we would still be thinking that tuberculosis was due to night air and we would still be trying to cure it by sunlight.

At that time, after almost a century of modified skepticism about therapy amounting finally to near nihilism, we abruptly entered a new era in which, almost overnight, it became possible with antibiotics to cure outright some of the most common and lethal illnesses of human beings—lobar pneumonia, meningitis, typhoid, typhus, tuberculosis, septicemias of various types. Only the virus diseases lay beyond reach, and even some of these were shortly to come under control—as in poliomyelitis and measles—by new techniques for making vaccines.

These events were simply overwhelming when they occurred. I was a medical student at the time of sulfanilamide and penicillin, and I remember the earliest reaction of flat disbelief concerning such things. We had given up on therapy, a century earlier. With a few exceptions which we regarded as anomalies, such as vitamin B for pellagra, liver extract for pernicious anemia, and insulin for diabetes, we were educated to be skeptical about the treatment of disease. Miliary tuberculosis and subacute bacterial endocarditis were fatal in 100 percent of cases, and we were convinced that the course of master diseases like these could never be changed, not in our lifetime or in any other.

Overnight, we became optimists, enthusiasts. The realization that disease could be turned around by treatment, provided that one knew enough about the underlying mechanism, was a totally new idea just forty years ago.

Most people have forgotten about that time, or are too young to remember it, and tend now to take such things for granted. They were born knowing about antibiotics, or the drugs simply fell by luck into their laps. We need reminding, now more than ever, that the capacity of medicine to deal with infectious disease was not a lucky fluke, nor was it something that happened simply as the result of the passage of time. It was the direct outcome of many years of hard work, done by imaginative and skilled scientists, none of whom had the faintest idea that penicillin and streptomycin lay somewhere in the decades ahead. It was basic science of a very high order, storing up a great mass of interesting knowledge for its own sake, creating, so to speak, a bank of information, ready for drawing on when the time for intelligent use arrived.

For example, it took a great deal of time, and work, before it could be understood that there were such things as hemolytic streptococci, that there were more than forty different serological types of the principal streptococcal species responsible for human disease, and that some of these were responsible for rheumatic fever and valvular heart disease. The bacteriology and immunology had to be done first, over decades, and by the early 1930s the work had progressed just far enough so that the connection between streptococcal infection and rheumatic fever could be perceived.

Not until this information was at hand did it become a certainty that rheumatic fever could be prevented, and with it a large amount of the chief heart disease affecting young people, if only a way could be found to prevent streptococcal infection. Similarly, the identification of the role of pneumococci in lobar pneumonia, of brucellae in undulant fever, typhoid bacilli in typhoid fever, the meningococci in epidemic meningitis, required the sorting out and analysis of what seemed at the time an immensely complicated body of information. Most of the labor in infectious-disease laboratories went into work of this kind in the first third of this century. When it was finished, the scene was ready for antibiotics.

What was not realized then and is not fully realized even now was how difficult it would be to accomplish the same end for the other diseases of man. We still have heart disease, cancer, stroke, schizophrenia, arthritis, kidney failure, cirrhosis, and the degenerative diseases associated with aging. All told, there is a list of around twenty-five major afflictions of man in this country, and a still more formidable list of parasitic, viral, and nutritional diseases in the less developed countries of the world, which make up the unfinished agenda of modern biomedical science.

How does one make plans for science policy with such a list?

The quick and easy way is to conclude that these diseases, not yet mastered, are simply beyond our grasp. The thing to do is to settle down with today's versions of science and technology, and make sure that our health-care system is equipped to do the best it can in an imperfect world. The trouble with this approach is that we cannot afford it. The costs are already too high, and they escalate higher each year. Moreover, the measures available are simply not good enough. We cannot go on indefinitely trying to cope with heart disease by open-heart surgery, carried out at formidable expense after the disease has run its destructive course. Nor can we postpone such issues by oversimplifying the problems, which is what we do, in my opinion, by attributing so much of today's chronic and disabling disease to the environment, or to wrong ways of living. The plain fact of the matter is that we do not know enough about the facts of the matter, and we should be more open about our ignorance.

At the same time, and this will have a paradoxical sound, there has never been a period in medicine when the future has looked so bright. There is within medicine, somewhere beneath the pessimism and discouragement resulting from the disarray of the health-care system and its stupendous cost, an undercurrent of almost outrageous optimism about what may lie ahead for the treatment of human disease if we can only keep learning. The scientists who do research on the cardiovascular system are entirely confident that they will soon be working close to the center of things, and they no longer regard the mechanisms of heart disease as impenetrable mysteries. The cancer scientists, for all their public disagreements about how best to organize their research, are in possession of insights into the intimate functioning of normal and neoplastic cells that were unimaginable a few years back. The eukaryotic cell, the cell with a true nucleus, has itself become a laboratory instrument almost as neat and handy as the bacterial cell became in the early 1950s, ready now to be used for elucidating the mechanisms by which genes are switched on or off as developing cells differentiate or, as in the case of cancer cells, dedifferentiate. The ways in which carcinogenic substances, or viruses, or other factors still unrecognized intervene in the regulation of cell behavior represent problems still unsolved, but the problems themselves now appear to be approachable; with what has been learned in the past decade, they can now be worked on.

The neurobiologists can do all sorts of things in their investigation, and the brain is an organ different from what it seemed twenty-five years ago. Far from being an intricate but ultimately simplifiable mass of electronic circuitry governed by wiring diagrams, it now has the aspect of a fundamentally endocrine tissue, in which the essential reactions, the internal traffic of nerve impulses, are determined by biochemical activators and their suppressors. The technologies available for quantitative study of individual nerve cells are powerful and precise, and the work is now turning toward the functioning of collections of cells, the centers for visual and auditory perception and the like, because work at this level can now be done. It is difficult to think of problems that cannot be studied, ever. The matter of consciousness is argued over, naturally, as a candidate for perpetual unapproachability, but this has more the sound of a philosophical discussion. Nobody has the feeling any longer, as we used to believe, that we can never find out how the brain works.

The immunologists, the molecular biochemists, and the new generation of investigators obsessed with the structure and function of cell membranes have all discovered that they are really working together, along with the geneticists, on a common set of problems: how do cells and tissues become labeled for what they are, what are the forces that govern the orderly development and differentiation of tissues and organs, and how are errors in the process controlled?

There has never been a time like it, and I find it difficult to imagine that this tremendous surge of new information will terminate with nothing more than an understanding of how normal cells and tissues, and organisms, function. I regard it as a certainty that there will be uncovered, at the same time, detailed information concerning the mechanisms of disease.

The record of the past half century has established, I think, two general principles about human disease. First, it is necessary to know a great deal about underlying mechanisms before one can really act effectively; one had to know that the pneumococcus causes lobar pneumonia before one could begin thinking about antibiotics. One did not have to know all the details, not even how the pneumococcus does its damage to the lungs, but one had to know that it was there, and in charge.

Second, for every disease there is a single key mechanism that dominates all others. If one can find it, and then think one's way around it, one can control the disorder. This generalization is harder to prove, and arguable—it is more like a strong hunch than a scientific assertion—but I believe that the record thus far tends to support it. The most complicated, multicell, multitissue, and multiorgan diseases I know of are tertiary syphilis, chronic tuberculosis, and pernicious anemia. In each, there are at least five major organs and tissues involved, and each appears to be affected by a variety of environmental influences. Before they came under scientific appraisal each was thought to be what we now call a "multifactorial" disease, far too complex to allow for any single causative mechanism. And yet, when all the necessary facts were in, it was clear that by simply switching off one thing—the spirochete, the tubercle bacillus, or a single vitamin deficiency—the whole array of disordered and seemingly unrelated pathologic mechanisms could be switched off, at once.

I believe that a prospect something like this is the likelihood for the future of medicine. I have no doubt that there will turn out to be dozens of separate influences that can launch cancer, including all sorts of environmental carcinogens and very likely many sorts of virus, but I think there will turn out to be a single switch at the center of things, there for the finding. I think that schizophrenia will turn out to be a neurochemical disorder, with some central, single chemical event gone wrong. I think there is a single causative agent responsible for rheumatoid arthritis, which has not yet been found. I think that the central vascular abnormalities that launch coronary occlusion and stroke have not yet been glimpsed, but they are there, waiting to be switched on or off.

In short, I believe that the major diseases of human beings have become approachable biological puzzles, ultimately solvable. It follows from this that it is now possible to begin thinking about a human society relatively free of disease. This would surely have been an unthinkable notion a half century ago, and oddly enough it has a rather apocalyptic sound today. What will we do about dying, and about all that population, if such things were to come about? What can we die of, if not disease?

My response is that it would not make all that much difference. We would still age away and wear out, on about the same schedule as today, with the terminal event being more like the sudden disintegration and collapse all at once of Oliver Wendell Holmes's well-known one-hoss shay. The main effect, almost pure benefit it seems to me, would be that we would not be beset and raddled by disease in the last decades of life, as most of us are today. We could become a healthy species, not all that different from the healthy stocks of domestic plants and animals that we already take for granted. Strokes, and senile dementia, and cancer, and arthritis are not natural aspects of the human condition, and we ought to rid ourselves of such impediments as quickly as we can.

There is another argument against this view of the future which needs comment. It is said that we are fundamentally fallible as organisms, prone to failure, and if we succeed in getting rid of one set of ailments there will always be other new diseases, now waiting out in the forest, ready to take their places. I do not know why this is said, for I can see no evidence that such a thing has ever happened. To be sure, we have a higher incidence of chronic illness among older people than we had in the early years of this century, but that is because more of us have survived to become older people. No new disease, so far as I know, has come in to take the place of diphtheria, or smallpox, or whooping cough, or poliomyelitis. Nature being inventive, we will probably always have the odd new illness turning up, but not in order to fill out some ordained, predestined quota of human maladies.

Indeed, the official public-health tables of morbidity and mortality seem to be telling us this sort of thing already, even though, in all our anxiety, we seem unwilling to accept the news. We have already become in the Western world, on the record, the healthiest society in the history of human-kind. Compared with a century ago, when every family was obliged to count on losing members throughout the early years of life, we are in a new world. A death in a young family has become a rare and dreadful catastrophe, no longer a commonplace event. Our estimated life expectancy, collectively, is longer this year than ever before in history. Part of this general and gradual improvement in health and survival is thanks to sanitary engineering, better housing, and, probably, more affluence, but a substantial part is also attributable, in recent years, to biomedical science. We have not done badly at all, and having begun so well, I see no reason why we should not do even better in the future.

My argument about how to do this will come as no surprise. I say that we must continue doing biomedical research, on about the same scale and scope as in the past twenty years, with expansion and growth of the enterprise being dependent on where new leads seem to be taking us. It is an expensive undertaking, but still it is less than 3 percent of the total annual cost of today's health industry, which at last count was over $140 billion, and it is nothing like as expensive as trying to live with the halfway technologies we are obliged to depend on in medicine today; if we try to stay with these for the rest of the century the costs will go through the ionosphere.

But I should like to insert a qualification in this argument, which may be somewhat more of a surprise, coming from a doctor. I believe that the major research effort, and far and away the greatest investment for the future, must be in the broad area of basic biological science. Here and there, to be sure, there will be opportunities for productive applied science, comparable, say, to the making of polio vaccine or the devising of multidrug therapy for childhood leukemia, but these opportunities will not come often, nor can they be forced into existence before their time. The great need now, for the medicine of the future, is for more information at the most fundamental levels of the living process. We are nowhere near ready for large-scale programs of applied science in medicine, for we do not yet know enough.

Good applied science in medicine, as in physics, requires a high degree of certainty about the basic facts at hand, and especially about their meaning, and we have not yet reached this point for most of medicine. Nor can we predict at this stage, with much confidence, which particular items of new information, from which fields, are the likeliest to be relevant to particular disease problems. In this circumstance there has to be a certain amount of guessing, even gambling, and my own view is that the highest yield for the future will come from whatever fields are generating the most interesting, exciting, and surprising sorts of information, most of all, surprising.

It seems to me that the safest and most prudent of bets to lay money on is surprise. There is a very high probability that whatever astonishes us in biology today will turn out to be usable, and useful, tomorrow. This, I think, is the established record of science itself, over the past two hundred years, and we ought to have more confidence in the process. It worked this way for the beginnings of chemistry; we obtained electricity in this manner; using surprise as a guide, we progressed from Newtonian physics to electromagnetism, to quantum mechanics and contemporary geophysics and cosmology. In biology, evolution and genetics were the earliest big astonishments, but what has been going on in the past quarter century is simply flabbergasting. For medicine, the greatest surprises lie still ahead of us, but they are there, waiting to be discovered or stumbled over, sooner or later.

I am arguing this way from the most practical, down-to-earth, pragmatic point of view. This kind of science is most likely, in the real world, to lead to significant improvements in human health, and at low cost. This is a point worth further emphasis, by the way. When medicine has really succeeded brilliantly in technology, as in immunization, for example, or antibiotics, or nutrition, or endocrine-replacement therapy, so that the therapeutic measures can be directed straight at the underlying disease mechanism and are decisively effective, the cost is likely to be very low indeed. It is when our technologies have to be applied halfway along against the progress of disease, or must be brought in after the fact to shore up the loss of destroyed tissue, that health care becomes enormously expensive. The deeper our understanding of a disease mechanism, the greater are our chances of devising direct and decisive measures to prevent disease, or to turn it around before it is too late.

So much for the practical side of the argument. We need much more basic science for the future of human health, and I will leave the matter there.

But I have one last thing to say about biological science. Even if I should be wrong about some of these predictions, and it turns out that we can blunder our way into treating or preventing one disease or another without understanding the process (which I will not believe until it happens), and if we continue to invest in biological science anyway, we cannot lose. Congress, in its wisdom, cannot lose. The public cannot lose.

Here is what I have in mind.

These ought to be the best of times for the human mind, but it is not so. All sorts of things seem to be turning out wrong, and the century seems to be slipping through our fingers here at the end, with almost all promises unfulfilled. I cannot begin to guess at all the causes of our cultural sadness, not even the most important ones, but I can think of one thing that is wrong with us and eats away at us: we do not know enough about ourselves. We are ignorant about how we work, about where we fit in, and most of all about the enormous, imponderable system of life in which we are embedded as working parts. We do not really understand nature, at all. We have come a long way indeed, but just enough to become conscious of our ignorance. It is not so bad a thing to be totally ignorant; the hard thing is to be partway along toward real knowledge, far enough to be aware of being ignorant. It is embarrassing and depressing, and it is one of our troubles today.

It is a new experience for all of us. Only two centuries ago we could explain everything about everything, out of pure reason, and now most of that elaborate and harmonious structure has come apart before our eyes. We are *dumb*.

This is, in a certain sense, a health problem after all. For as long as we are bewildered by the mystery of ourselves, and confused by the strangeness of our uncomfortable connection to all the rest of life, and dumbfounded by the inscrutability of our own minds, we cannot be said to be healthy animals in today's world.

We need to know more. To come to realize this is what this seemingly inconclusive century has been all about. We have discovered how to ask important questions, and now we really do need, as an urgent matter, for the sake of our civilization, to obtain some answers. We now know that we cannot do this any longer by searching our minds, for there is not enough there to search, nor can we find the truth by guessing at it or by making up stories for ourselves. We cannot stop where we are, stuck with today's level of understanding, nor can we go back. I do not see that we have a real choice in this, for I can see only the one way ahead. We need science, more and better science, not for its technology, not for leisure, not even for health or longevity, but for the hope of wisdom which our kind of culture must acquire for its survival.

1977

James Baldwin

JAMES BALDWIN was born in the Harlem section of New York City on August 2, 1924. The eldest of nine children, his childhood was, in his own words, a "bleak fantasy" of poverty, hopelessness, the violence of Harlem's streets, and—overshadowing it all—the grim religious fanaticism of his father, a lay preacher in an evangelical church. By the time he was fourteen Baldwin saw that only two possible ways lay open to him: either he would sink into the abyss of liquor, sex, drugs, and crime that was already beginning to claim many of his friends; or he would find himself a "gimmick," some role or position that would make him less susceptible to the frustrations of Harlem. The gimmick he found was religion, and for the next three years Baldwin was a Young Minister in a store-front church. He finally abandoned religion as a result of the books he was reading, especially Dostoevsky, and his growing confidence that what he most wanted to do was write.

Following his graduation from DeWitt Clinton High School in 1942, Baldwin began that succession of odd jobs that characterizes the modern, moneyless writer learning his craft. Then, in 1945, he received his first grant, a Saxton Fellowship for an unfinished novel, and since that time he has had to do very little nonliterary work. (Baldwin is a good example of the twentieth century artist who is supported by foundations: between the years 1948 and 1959 he received grants or fellowships from the *Partisan Review*, the National Institute of Arts and Letters, and the Rosenwald, Guggenheim, and Ford Foundations.)

In 1948 he left America for Europe, and for the next nine years lived mainly in Paris on the fringe of a colony of Negro artists that included Richard Wright and Chester Himes. Gradually he began to publish essays in magazines such as *Commentary*, *Harper's*, and *Partisan Review*, and in 1953 his first novel, *Go Tell It on the Mountain*, was published. Largely autobiographical, it describes a climactic day in the life of a Harlem family, during which each of the principal characters reviews his life at the same time that the oldest son of the family is experiencing his soul's salvation. In 1955 Baldwin published *Notes of a Native Son*, a collection of essays, and, in the following year, a second novel, *Giovanni's Room*. The latter is interesting primarily for the way in which it reveals Baldwin's attempt to follow Ralph Ellison's advice that he not confine himself to writing about Negroes (there are none in the book), and in the fact that it deals with homosexuality without capitalizing on its more sensational aspects.

Upon returning to the United States in 1958, Baldwin took up residence in Greenwich Village (where he had lived before going to Europe), and since then has published another collection of essays, *Nobody Knows My Name* (1961), a novel. *Another Country* (1962), and a long essay prophesying racial conflict in America, *The Fire Next Time* (1963). In 1964 his play *Blues for Mister Charlie* was produced by the Actor's Studio in New York, and a year later an earlier play, *The Amen Corner* (written in 1953), was produced on Broadway. Although Baldwin has published a number of books in recent years—among them his first collection of short stories, *Going to Meet the Man* (1965); another novel, *Tell Me How Long the Train's Been Gone* (1968); and a long, autobiographical essay on his involvement in black militancy, *No Name in the Street* (1972)—none of it has been as good as his early essays. His most recent novels have been *If Beale Street Could Talk* (1974) and *Just Above My Head* (1979).

It is impossible to know what readers one or two generations from now will think of James Baldwin, whether he will still be read or simply dismissed as a minor novelist and interesting polemicist during a special period of our history, for nothing is more transitory than social-political issues. At the same time, *all* works of art reflect the age in which they are written, and everything, in a sense, is political. Those which survive do so because they manage to transcend the purely temporal aspects of their subjects: they reveal problems—relationships between people—that exist from generation to generation and from nation to nation. Thus, if an essay such as "Notes of a Native Son" lasts beyond our own time, it will most likely be not solely because of what it tells us about Black–White relations, but rather, for what it says about the relationship between fathers and sons. And surely this is what Baldwin had in mind when he said that he did not wish to become "merely a Negro writer." He added, "I wanted to find out in what way the *specialness* of my experience could be made to connect me with other people instead of dividing me from them."

Fortunately, as an essayist Baldwin has developed a style that is both clear and forceful, that draws its strength not from eccentricities but from its combination of candor and a strict adherence to logic. Baldwin recognizes both its strengths and weaknesses when he describes his style as being a mixture of "the King James Bible, the rhetoric of the store-front church, something ironic and violent and perpetually understated in Negro speech—and something of Dickens' love of bravura." It seems perfectly suited to the things he writes about: bitterness, self-pity, rage, and—above all—the struggle to be a man.

NOTES OF A NATIVE SON

On the 29th of July, in 1943, my father died. On the same day, a few hours later, his last child was born. Over a month before this, while all our energies were concentrated in waiting for these events, there had been, in Detroit, one of the bloodiest race riots of the century. A few hours after my father's funeral, while he lay in state in the undertaker's chapel, a race riot broke out in Harlem. On the morning of the 3rd of August, we drove my father to the graveyard through a wilderness of smashed plate glass.

The day of my father's funeral had also been my nineteenth birthday. As we drove him to the graveyard, the spoils of injustice, anarchy, discontent, and hatred were all around us. It seemed to me that God himself had devised, to mark my father's end, the most sustained and brutally dissonant of codas. And it seemed to me, too, that the violence which rose all about us as my father left the world had been devised as a corrective for the pride of his eldest son. I had declined to believe in that apocalypse which had been central to my father's vision; very well, life seemed to be saying, here is something that will certainly pass for an apocalypse until the real thing comes along. I had inclined to be contemptuous of my father for the conditions of his life, for the conditions of our lives. When his life had ended I began to wonder about that life and also, in a new way, to be apprehensive about my own.

I had not known my father very well. We had got on badly, partly because we shared, in our different fashions, the vice of stubborn pride. When he was dead I realized that I had hardly ever spoken to him. When he had been dead a long time I began to wish I had. It seems to be typical of life in America, where opportunities, real and fancied, are thicker than anywhere else on the globe, that the second generation has no time to talk to the first. No one, including my father, seems to have known exactly how old he was, but his mother had been born during slavery. He was of the first generation of free men. He, along with thousands of other Negroes, came North after 1919 and I was part of that generation which had never seen the landscape of what Negroes sometimes call the Old Country.

He had been born in New Orleans and had been a quite young man there during the time that Louis Armstrong, a boy, was running errands for the dives and honky-tonks of what was always presented to me as one of the most wicked of cities—to this day, whenever I think of New Orleans, I also helplessly think of Sodom and Gomorrah. My father never mentioned Louis Armstrong, except to forbid us to play his records; but there was a picture of him on our wall for a long time. One of my father's strong-willed female relatives had placed it there and forbade my father to take it down. He never did, but he eventually maneuvered her out of the house and when, some years later, she was in trouble and near death, he refused to do anything to help her.

He was, I think, very handsome. I gather this from photographs and from my own memories of him, dressed in his Sunday best and on his way to preach a sermon somewhere, when I was little. Handsome, proud, and ingrown, "like a toe-nail," somebody said. But he looked to me, as I grew older, like pictures I had seen of African tribal chieftains: he really should have been naked, with war-paint on and barbaric mementos, standing among spears. He could be chilling in the pulpit and indescribably cruel in his personal life and he was certainly the most bitter man I have ever met; yet it must be said that there was something else in him, buried in him, which lent him his tremendous power and, even, a rather crushing charm. It had something to do with his blackness, I think—he was very black—with his blackness and his beauty, and with the fact that he knew that he was black but did not know that he was beautiful. He claimed to be proud of his blackness but it had also been the cause of much humiliation and it had fixed bleak boundaries to his life. He was not a young man when we were growing up and he had already suffered many kinds of ruin; in his outrageously demanding and protective way he loved his children, who were black like him and menaced, like him; and all these things sometimes showed in his face when he tried, never to my knowledge with any success, to establish contact with any of us. When he took one of his children on his knee to play, the child always became fretful and began to cry; when he tried to help one of us with our homework the absolutely unabating tension which emanated from him caused our minds and our tongues to become paralyzed, so that he, scarcely knowing why, flew into a rage and the child, not knowing why, was punished. If it ever entered his head to bring a surprise home for his children, it was, almost unfailingly, the wrong surprise and even the big watermelons he often brought home on his back in the summertime led to the most appalling scenes. I do not remember, in all those years, that one of his children was ever glad to see him come home. From what I was able to gather of his early life, it seemed that this inability to establish contact with other people had always marked him and had been one of the things which had driven him out of New Orleans. There was something in him, therefore, groping and tentative, which was never expressed and which was buried with him. One saw it most clearly when he was facing new people and hoping to impress them. But he never did, not for long. We went from church to smaller and more improbable church, he found himself in less and less demand as a minister, and by the time he died none of his friends had come to see him for a long time. He had lived and died in an intolerable bitterness of spirit and it frightened me, as we drove him to the graveyard through those unquiet, ruined streets, to see how powerful and overflowing this bitterness could be and to realize that this bitterness now was mine.

When he died I had been away from home for a little over a year. In that year I had had time to become aware of the meaning of all my father's bitter warnings, had discovered the secret of his proudly pursed lips and rigid carriage: I had discovered the weight of white people in the world. I saw that this had been for my ancestors and now would be for me an awful thing to live with and that the bitterness which had helped to kill my father could also kill me.

He had been ill a long time—in the mind, as we now realized, reliving instances of his fantastic intransigence in the new light of his affliction and endeavoring to feel a sorrow for him which never, quite, came true. We had not known that he was being eaten up by paranoia, and the discovery that his cruelty, to our bodies and our minds, had been one of the symptoms of his illness was not, then, enough to enable us to forgive him. The younger children felt, quite simply, relief that he would not be coming home anymore. My mother's observation that it was he, after all, who had kept them alive all these years meant nothing because the problems of keeping children alive are not real for children. The older children felt, with my father gone, that they could invite their friends to the house without fear that their friends would be insulted or, as had sometimes happened with me, being told that their friends were in league with the devil and intended to rob our family of everything we owned. (I didn't fail to wonder, and it made me hate him, what on earth we owned that anybody else would want.)

His illness was beyond all hope of healing before anyone realized that he was ill. He had always been so strange and had lived, like a prophet, in such unimaginably close communion with the Lord that his long silences which were punctuated by moans and hallelujahs and snatches of old songs while he sat at the living room window never seemed odd to us. It was not until he refused to eat because, he said, his family was trying to poison him that my mother was forced to accept as a fact what had, until then, been only an unwilling suspicion. When he was committed, it was discovered that he had tuberculosis and, as it turned out, the disease of his mind allowed the disease of his body to destroy him. For the doctors could not force him to eat, either, and, though he was fed intravenously, it was clear from the beginning that there was no hope for him.

In my mind's eye I could see him, sitting at the window, locked up in his terrors; hating and fearing every living soul including his children who had betrayed him, too, by reaching towards the world which had despised him. There were nine of us. I began to wonder what it could have felt like for such a man to have had nine children whom he could barely feed. He used to make little jokes about our poverty, which never, of course, seemed very funny to us; they could not have seemed very funny to him, either, or else our all too feeble response to them would never have caused such rages. He spent great energy and achieved, to our chagrin, no small amount of success in keeping us away from the people who surrounded us, people who had all-night rent parties to which we listened when we should have been sleeping, people who cursed and drank and flashed razor blades on Lenox Avenue. He could not understand why, if they had so much energy to spare, they could not use it to make their lives better. He treated almost everybody on our block with a most uncharitable asperity and neither they, nor, of course, their children were slow to reciprocate.

The only white people who came to our house were welfare workers and bill collectors. It was almost always my mother who dealt with them, for my father's temper, which was at the mercy of his pride, was never to be trusted. It was clear that he felt their very presence in his home to be a violation: this was conveyed by his carriage, almost ludicrously stiff, and by his voice, harsh and vindictively polite. When I was around nine or ten I wrote a play which was directed by a young, white schoolteacher, a woman, who then took an interest in me, and gave me books to read and, in order to corroborate my theatrical bent, decided to take me to see what she somewhat tactlessly referred to as "real" plays. Theater-going was forbidden in our house, but, with the really cruel intuitiveness of a child, I suspected that the color of this woman's skin would carry the day for me. When, at school, she suggested taking me to the theater, I did not, as I might have done if she had been a Negro, find a way of discouraging her, but agreed that she should pick me up at my house one evening. I then, very cleverly, left all the rest to my mother, who suggested to my father, as I knew she would, that it would not be very nice to let such a kind woman make the trip for nothing. Also, since it was a schoolteacher, I imagine that my mother countered the idea of sin with the idea of "education," which word, even with my father, carried a kind of bitter weight.

Before the teacher came my father took me aside to ask *why* she was coming, what *interest* she could possibly have in our house, in a boy like me. I said I didn't know but I, too, suggested that it had something to do with education. And I understood that my father was waiting for me to say something—I didn't quite know what; perhaps that I wanted his protection against this teacher and her "education." I said none of these things and the teacher came and we went out. It was clear, during the brief interview in our living room, that my father was agreeing very much against his will and that he would have refused permission if he had dared. The fact that he did not dare caused me to despise him: I had no way of knowing that he was facing in that living room a wholly unprecedented and frightening situation.

Later, when my father had been laid off from his job, this woman became very important to us. She was really a very sweet and generous woman and went to a great deal of trouble to be of help to us, particularly during one awful winter. My mother called her by the highest name she knew: she said she was a "christian." My father could scarcely disagree but during the four or five years of our relatively close association he never trusted her and was always trying to surprise in her open, Midwestern face the genuine, cunningly hidden, and hideous motivation. In later years, particularly when it began to be clear that this "education" of mine was going to lead me to perdition, he became more explicit and warned me that my white friends in high school were not really my friends and that I would see, when I was older, how white people would do anything to keep a Negro down. Some of them could be nice, he admitted, but none of them were to be trusted and most of them were not even nice. The best thing was to have as little to do with them as possible. I did not feel this way and I was certain, in my innocence, that I never would.

But the year which preceded my father's death had made a great change in my life. I had been living in New Jersey, working in defense plants, working and living among southerners, white and black. I knew about the south, of course, and about how southerners treated Negroes and how they expected them to behave, but it had never entered my mind that anyone would look at me and expect *me* to behave that way. I learned in New Jersey that to be a Negro meant, precisely, that one was never looked at but was simply at the mercy of the reflexes the color of one's skin caused in other people. I acted in New Jersey as I had always acted, that is as though I thought a great deal of myself—I had to *act* that way—with results that were, simply, unbelievable. I had scarcely arrived before I had earned the enmity, which was extraordinarily ingenious, of all my superiors and nearly all my co-workers. In the beginning, to make matters worse, I simply did not know what was happening. I did not know what I had done, and I shortly began to wonder what *anyone* could possibly do, to bring about such unanimous, active, and unbearably vocal hostility. I knew about jim-crow but I had never experienced it. I went to the same self-service restaurant three times and stood with all the Princeton boys before the counter, waiting for a hamburger and coffee; it was always an extraordinarily long time before anything was set before me; but it was not until the fourth visit that I learned that, in fact, nothing had ever been set before me: I had simply picked something up. Negroes were not served there, I was told, and they had been waiting for me to realize that I was always the only Negro present. Once I was told this, I determined to go there all the time. But now they were ready for me and, though some dreadful scenes were subsequently enacted in that restaurant, I never ate there again.

It was the same story all over New Jersey, in bars, bowling alleys, diners, places to live. I was always being forced to leave, silently, or with mutual imprecations. I very shortly became notorious and children giggled behind me when I passed and their elders whispered or shouted—they really believed that I was mad. And it did begin to work on my mind, of course; I began to be afraid to go anywhere and to compensate for this I went places to which I really should not have gone and where, God knows, I had no desire to be. My reputation in town naturally enhanced my reputation at work and my working day became one long series of acrobatics designed to keep me out of trouble. I cannot say that these acrobatics succeeded. It began to seem that the machinery of the organization I worked for was turning over, day and night, with but one aim: to eject me. I was fired once, and contrived, with the aid of a friend from New York, to get back on the payroll; was fired again, and bounced back again. It took a while to fire me for the third time, but the third time took. There were no loopholes anywhere. There was not even any way of getting back inside the gates.

That year in New Jersey lives in my mind as though it were the year during which, having an unsuspected predilection for it, I first contracted some dread, chronic disease, the unfailing symptom of which is a kind of blind fever, a pounding in the skull and fire in the bowels. Once this disease is contracted, one can never be really carefree again, for the fever, without an instant's warning, can recur at any moment. It can wreck more important things than race relations. There is not a Negro alive who does not have this rage in his blood—one has the choice, merely, of living with it consciously or surrendering to it. As for me, this fever has recurred in me, and does, and will until the day I die.

My last night in New Jersey, a white friend from New York took me to the nearest big town, Trenton, to go to the movies and have a few drinks. As it turned out, he also saved me from, at the very least, a violent whipping. Almost every detail of that night stands out very clearly in my memory. I even remember the name of the movie we saw because its title impressed me as being so patly ironical. It was a movie about the German occupation of France, starring Maureen O'Hara and Charles Laughton and called *This Land Is Mine*. I remember the name of the diner we walked into when the movie ended: it was the "American Diner." When we walked in the counterman asked what we wanted and I remember answering with the casual sharpness which had become my habit: "We want a hamburger and a cup of coffee, what do you think we want?" I do not know why, after a year of such rebuffs, I so completely failed to anticipate his answer, which was, of course, "We don't serve Negroes here." This reply failed to discompose me, at least for the moment. I made some sardonic comment about the name of the diner and we walked out into the streets.

This was the time of what was called the "brown-out," when the lights in all American cities were very dim. When we re-entered the streets something happened to me which had the force of an optical illusion, or a nightmare. The streets were very crowded and I was facing north. People were moving in every direction but it seemed to me, in that instant, that all of the people I could see, and many more than that, were moving toward me, against me, and that everyone was white. I remember how their faces gleamed. And I felt, like a physical sensation, a *click* at the nape of my neck as though some interior string connecting my head to my body had been cut. I began to walk.

I heard my friend call after me, but I ignored him. Heaven only knows what was going on in his mind, but he had the good sense not to touch me—I don't know what would have happened if he had—and to keep me in sight. I don't know what was going on in my mind, either; I certainly had no conscious plan. I wanted to do something to crush these white faces, which were crushing me. I walked for perhaps a block or two until I came to an enormous, glittering, and fashionable restaurant in which I knew not even the intercession of the Virgin would cause me to be served. I pushed through the doors and took the first vacant seat I saw, at a table for two, and waited.

I do not know how long I waited and I rather wonder, until today, what I could possibly have looked like. Whatever I looked like, I frightened the waitress who shortly appeared, and the moment she appeared all my fury flowed towards her. I hated her for her white face, and for her great, astounded, frightened eyes. I felt that if she found a black man so frightening I would make her fright worth-while.

She did not ask me what I wanted, but repeated, as though she had learned it somewhere, "We don't serve Negroes here." She did not say it with the blunt, derisive hostility to which I had grown so accustomed, but, rather, with a note of apology in her voice, and fear. This made me colder and more murderous than ever. I felt I had to do something with my hands. I wanted her to come close enough for me to get her neck between my hands.

So I pretended not to have understood her, hoping to draw her closer. And she did step a very short step closer, with her pencil poised incongruously over her pad, and repeated the formula: ". . . don't serve Negroes here."

Somehow, with the repetition of that phrase, which was already ringing in my head like a thousand bells of a nightmare, I realized that she would never come any closer and that I would have to strike from a distance. There was nothing on the table but an ordinary water-mug half full of water, and I picked this up and hurled it with all my strength at her. She ducked and it missed her and shattered against the mirror behind the bar. And, with that sound, my frozen blood abruptly thawed, I returned from wherever I had been, I *saw*, for the first time, the restaurant, the people with their mouths open, already, as it seemed to me, rising as one man, and I realized what I had done, and where I was, and I was frightened. I rose and began running for the door. A round, pot-bellied man grabbed me by the nape of the neck just as I reached the doors and began to beat me about the face. I kicked him and got loose and ran into the streets. My friend whispered, "*Run!*" and I ran.

My friend stayed outside the restaurant long enough to misdirect my pursuers and the police, who arrived, he told me, at once. I do not know what I said to him when he came to my room that night. I could not have said much. I felt, in the oddest, most awful way, that I had somehow betrayed him. I lived it over and over and over again, the way one relives an automobile accident after it has happened and one finds oneself alone and safe. I could not get over two facts, both equally difficult for the imagination to grasp, and one was that I could have been murdered. But the other was that I had been ready to commit murder. I saw nothing very clearly but I did see this: that my life, my *real* life, was in danger, and not from anything other people might do but from the hatred I carried in my own heart.

[2]

I had returned home around the second week in June—in great haste because it seemed that my father's death and my mother's confinement were both but a matter of hours. In the case of my mother, it soon became clear that she had simply made a miscalculation. This had always been her tendency and I don't believe that a single one of us arrived in the world, or has since arrived anywhere else, on time. But none of us dawdled so intolerably about the business of being born as did my baby sister. We sometimes amused ourselves, during those endless, stifling weeks, by picturing the baby sitting within in the safe, warm dark, bitterly regretting the necessity of becoming a part of our chaos and stubbornly putting it off as long as possible. I understood her perfectly and congratulated her on showing such good sense so soon. Death, however, sat as purposefully at my father's bedside as life stirred within my mother's womb and it was harder to understand why he so lingered in that long shadow. It seemed that he had bent, and for a long time, too, all of his energies towards dying. Now death was ready for him but my father held back.

All of Harlem, indeed, seemed to be infected by waiting. I had never before known it to be so violently still. Racial tensions throughout this country were exacerbated during the early years of the war, partly because the labor market brought together hundreds of thousands of ill-prepared people and partly because Negro soldiers, regardless of where they were born, received their military training in the south. What happened in defense plants and army camps had repercussions, naturally, in every Negro ghetto. The situation in Harlem had grown bad enough for clergymen, policemen, educators, politicians, and social workers to assert in one breath that there was no "crime wave" and to offer, in the very next breath, suggestions as to how to combat it. These suggestions always seemed to involve playgrounds, despite the fact that racial skirmishes were occurring in the playgrounds, too. Playground or not, crime wave or not, the Harlem police force had been augmented in March, and the unrest grew—perhaps, in fact, partly as a result of the ghetto's instinctive hatred of policemen. Perhaps the most revealing news item, out of the steady parade of reports of muggings, stabbings, shootings, assaults, gang wars, and accusations of police brutality, is the item concerning six Negro girls who set upon a white girl in the subway because, as they all too accurately put it, she was stepping on their toes. Indeed she was, all over the nation.

I had never before been so aware of policemen, on foot, on horseback, on corners, everywhere, always two by two. Nor had I ever been so aware of small knots of people. They were on stoops and on corners and in doorways, and what was striking about them, I think, was that they did not seem to be talking. Never, when I passed these groups, did the usual sound of a curse or a laugh ring out and neither did there seem to be any hum of gossip. There was certainly, on the other hand, occurring between them communication extraordinarily intense. Another thing that was striking was the unexpected diversity of the people who made up these groups. Usually, for example, one would see a group of sharpies standing on the street corner, jiving the passing chicks; or a group of older men, usually, for some reason, in the vicinity of a barber shop, discussing baseball scores, or the numbers, or making rather chilling observations about women they had known. Women, in a general way, tended to be seen less often together—unless they were church women, or very young girls, or prostitutes met together for an unprofessional instant. But that summer I saw the strangest combinations: large, respectable, churchly matrons standing on the stoops or the corners with their hair tied up, together with a girl in sleazy satin whose face bore the marks of gin and the razor, or heavy-set, abrupt, no-nonsense older men, in company with the most disreputable and fanatical "race" men, or these same "race" men with the sharpies, or these sharpies with the churchly women. Seventh Day Adventists and Methodists and Spiritualists seemed to be hobnobbing with Holyrollers and they were all, alike, entangled with the most flagrant disbelievers; something heavy in their stance seemed to indicate that they had all, incredibly, seen a common vision, and on each face there seemed to be the same strange, bitter shadow.

The churchly women and the matter-of-fact, no-nonsense men had children in the Army. The sleazy girls they talked to had lovers there, the sharpies and the "race" men had friends and brothers there. It would have demanded an unquestioning patriotism, happily as uncommon in this country as it is undesirable, for these people not to have been disturbed by the bitter letters they received, by the newspaper stories they read, not to have been enraged by the posters, then to be found all over New York, which described the Japanese as "yellow-bellied Japs." It was only the "race" men, to be sure, who spoke ceaselessly of being revenged—how this vengeance was to be exacted was not clear—for the indignities and dangers suffered by Negro boys in uniform; but everybody felt a directionless, hopeless bitterness, as well as that panic which can scarcely be suppressed when one knows that a human being one loves is beyond one's reach, and in danger. This helplessness and this gnawing uneasiness does something, at length, to even the toughest mind. Perhaps the best way to sum all this up is to say that the people I knew felt, mainly, a peculiar kind of relief when they knew that their boys were being shipped out of the south, to do battle overseas. It was, perhaps, like feeling that the most dangerous part of a dangerous journey had been passed and that now, even if death should come, it would come with honor and without the complicity of their countrymen. Such a death would be, in short, a fact with which one could hope to live.

It was on the 28th of July, which I believe was a Wednesday, that I visited my father for the first time during his illness and for the last time in his life. The moment I saw him I knew why I had put off this visit so long. I had told my mother that I did not want to see him because I hated him. But this was not true. It was only that I *had* hated him and I wanted to hold on to this hatred. I did not want to look on him as a ruin: it was not a ruin I had hated. I imagine that one of the reasons people cling to their hates so stubbornly is because they sense, once hate is gone, that they will be forced to deal with pain.

We traveled out to him, his older sister and myself, to what seemed to be the very end of a very Long Island. It was hot and dusty and we wrangled, my aunt and I, all the way out, over the fact that I had recently begun to smoke and, as she said, to give myself airs. But I knew that she wrangled with me because she could not bear to face the fact of her brother's dying. Neither could I endure the reality of her despair, her unstated bafflement as to what had happened to her brother's life, and her own. So we wrangled and I smoked and from time to time she fell into a heavy reverie. Covertly, I watched her face, which was the face of an old woman; it had fallen in, the eyes were sunken and lightless; soon she would be dying, too.

In my childhood—it had not been so long ago—I had thought her beautiful. She had been quick-witted and quick-moving and very generous with all the children and each of her visits had been an event. At one time one of my brothers and myself had thought of running away to live with her. Now she could no longer produce out of her handbag some unexpected and yet familiar delight. She made me feel pity and revulsion and fear. It was awful to realize that she no longer caused me to feel affection. The closer we came to the hospital the more querulous she became and at the same time, naturally, grew more dependent on me. Between pity and guilt and fear I began to feel that there was another me trapped in my skull like a jack-in-the-box who might escape my control at any moment and fill the air with screaming.

She began to cry the moment we entered the room and she saw him lying there, all shriveled and still, like a little black monkey. The great, gleaming apparatus which fed him and would have compelled him to be still even if he had been able to move brought to mind, not beneficence, but torture; the tubes entering his arm made me think of pictures I had seen, when a child, of Gulliver, tied down by the pygmies on that island. My aunt wept and wept, there was a whistling sound in my father's throat; nothing was said; he could not speak. I wanted to take his hand, to say something. But I do not know what I could have said, even if he could have heard me. He was not really in that room with us, he had at last really embarked on his journey; and though my aunt told me that he said he was going to meet Jesus, I did not hear anything except that whistling in his throat. The doctor came back and we left, into that unbearable train again, and home. In the morning came the telegram saying that he was dead. Then the house was suddenly full of relatives, friends, hysteria, and confusion and I quickly left my mother and the children to the care of those impressive women, who, in Negro communities at least, automatically appear at times of bereavement armed with lotions, proverbs, and patience, and an ability to cook. I went downtown. By the time I returned, later the same day, my mother had been carried to the hospital and the baby had been born.

[3]

For my father's funeral I had nothing black to wear and this posed a nagging problem all day long. It was one of those problems, simple, or impossible of solution, to which the mind insanely clings in order to avoid the mind's real trouble. I spent most of that day at the downtown apartment of a girl I knew, celebrating my birthday with whiskey and wondering what to wear that night. When planning a birthday celebration one naturally does not expect that it will be up against competition from a funeral and this girl had anticipated taking me out that night, for a big dinner and a night club afterwards. Sometime during the course of that long day we decided that we would go out anyway, when my father's funeral service was over. I imagine *I* decided it, since, as the funeral hour approached, it became clearer and clearer to me that I would not know what to do with myself when it was over. The girl, stifling her very lively concern as to the possible effects of the whiskey on one of my father's chief mourners, concentrated on being conciliatory and practically helpful. She found a black shirt for me somewhere and ironed it and, dressed in the darkest pants and jacket I owned, and slightly drunk, I made my way to my father's funeral.

The chapel was full, but not packed, and very quiet. There were, mainly, my father's relatives, and his children, and here and there I saw faces I had not seen since childhood, the faces of my father's one-time friends. They were very dark and solemn now, seeming somehow to suggest that they had known all along that something like this would happen. Chief among the mourners was my aunt, who had quarreled with my father all his life; by which I do not mean to suggest that her mourning was insincere or that she had not loved him. I suppose that she was one of the few people in the world who had, and their incessant quarreling proved precisely the strength of the tie that bound them. The only other person in the world, as far as I knew, whose relationship to my father rivaled my aunt's in depth was my mother, who was not there.

It seemed to me, of course, that it was a very long funeral. But it was, if anything, a rather shorter funeral than most, nor, since there were no overwhelming uncontrollable expressions of grief, could it be called—if I dare to use the word—successful. The minister who preached my father's funeral sermon was one of the few my father had still been seeing as he neared his end. He presented to us in his sermon a man whom none of us had ever seen—a man thoughtful, patient, and forbearing, a Christian inspiration to all who knew him, and a model for his children. And no doubt the children, in their disturbed and guilty state, were almost ready to believe this; he had been remote enough to be anything and, anyway, the shock of the incontrovertible, that it was really our father lying up there in that casket, prepared the mind for anything. His sister moaned and this grief-stricken moaning was taken as corroboration. The other faces held a dark, non-committal thoughtfulness. This was not the man they had known, but they had scarcely expected to be confronted with *him;* this was, in a sense deeper than questions of fact, the man they had not known, and the man they had not known may have been the real one. The real man, whoever he had been, had suffered and now he was dead: this was all that was sure and all that mattered now. Every man in the chapel hoped that when his hour came he, too, would be eulogized, which is to say forgiven, and that all of his lapses, greeds, errors, and strayings from the truth would be invested with coherence and looked upon with charity. This was perhaps the last thing human beings could give each other and it was what they demanded, after all, of the Lord. Only the Lord saw the midnight tears, only He was present when one of His children, moaning and wringing hands, paced up and down the room. When one slapped one's child in anger the recoil in the heart reverberated through heaven and became part of the pain of the universe. And when the children were hungry and sullen and distrustful and one watched them, daily, growing wilder, and further away, and running headlong into danger, it was the Lord who knew what the charged heart endured as the strap was laid to the backside; the Lord alone who knew what one *would* have said if one had had, like the Lord, the gift of the living word. It was the Lord who knew of the impossibility every parent in that room faced: how to prepare the child for the day when the child would be despised and how to *create* in the child—by what means?—a stronger antidote to this poison than one had found for oneself. The avenues, side streets, bars, billiard halls, hospitals, police stations, and even the playgrounds of Harlem—not to mention the houses of correction, the jails, and the morgue—testified to the potency of the poison while remaining silent as to the efficacy of whatever antidote, irresistibly raising the question of whether or not such an antidote existed; raising, which was worse, the question of whether or not an antidote was desirable; perhaps poison should be fought with poison. With these several schisms in the mind and with more terrors in the heart than could be named, it was better not to judge the man who had gone down under an impossible burden. It was better to remember: *Thou knowest this man's fall; but thou knowest not his wrassling.*

While the preacher talked and I watched the children—years of changing their diapers, scrubbing them, slapping them, taking them to school, and scolding them had had the perhaps inevitable result of making me love them, though I am not sure I knew this then—my mind was busily breaking out with a rash of disconnected impressions. Snatches of popular songs, indecent jokes, bits of books I had read, movie sequences, faces, voices, political issues—I thought I was going mad; all these impressions suspended, as it were, in the solution of the faint nausea produced in me by the heat and liquor. For a moment I had the impression that my alcoholic breath, inefficiently disguised with chewing gum, filled the entire chapel. Then someone began singing one of my father's favorite songs and, abruptly, I was with him, sitting on his knee, in the hot, enormous, crowded church which was the first church we attended. It was the Abyssinia Baptist Church on 138th Street. We had not gone there long. With this image, a host of others came. I had forgotten, in the rage of my growing up, how proud my father had been of me when I was little. Apparently, I had had a voice and my father had liked to show me off before the members of the church. I had forgotten what he had looked like when he was pleased but now I remembered that he had always been grinning with pleasure when my solos ended. I even remembered certain expressions on his face when he teased my mother—had he loved her? I would never know. And when had it all begun to change? For now it seemed that he had not always been cruel. I remembered being taken for a haircut and scraping my knee on the footrest of the barber's chair and I remembered my father's face as he soothed my crying and applied the stinging iodine. Then I remembered our fights, fights which had been of the worst possible kind because my technique had been silence.

I remembered the one time in all our life together when we had really spoken to each other.

It was on a Sunday and it must have been shortly before I left home. We were walking, just the two of us, in our usual silence, to or from church. I was in high school and had been doing a lot of writing and I was, at about this time, the editor of the high school magazine. But I had also been a Young Minister and had been preaching from the pulpit. Lately, I had been taking fewer engagements and preached as rarely as possible. It was said in the church, quite truthfully, that I was "cooling off."

My father asked me abruptly, "You'd rather write than preach, wouldn't you?"

I was astonished at his question—because it was a real question. I answered, "Yes."

That was all we said. It was awful to remember that that was all we had *ever* said.

The casket now was opened and the mourners were being led up the aisle to look for the last time on the deceased. The assumption was that the family was too overcome with grief to be allowed to make this journey alone and I watched while my aunt was led to the casket and, muffled in black, and shaking, led back to her seat. I disapproved of forcing the children to look on their dead father, considering that the shock of his death, or, more truthfully, the shock of death as a reality, was already a little more than a child could bear, but my judgment in this matter had been overruled and there they were, bewildered and frightened and very small, being led, one by one, to the casket. But there is also something very gallant about children at such moments. It has something to do with their silence and gravity and with the fact that one cannot help them. Their legs, somehow, seem *exposed*, so that it is at once incredible and terribly clear that their legs are all they have to hold them up.

I had not wanted to go to the casket myself and I certainly had not wished to be led there, but there was no way of avoiding either of these forms. One of the deacons led me up and I looked on my father's face. I cannot say that it looked like him at all. His blackness had been equivocated by powder and there was no suggestion in that casket of what his power had or could have been. He was simply an old man dead, and it was hard to believe that he had ever given anyone either joy or pain. Yet, his life filled that room. Further up the avenue his wife was holding his newborn child. Life and death so close together, and love and hatred, and right and wrong, said something to me which I did not want to hear concerning man, concerning the life of man.

After the funeral, while I was downtown desperately celebrating my birthday, a Negro soldier, in the lobby of the Hotel Braddock, got into a fight with a white policeman over a Negro girl. Negro girls, white policemen, in or out of uniform, and Negro males—in or out of uniform—were part of the furniture of the lobby of the Hotel Braddock and this was certainly not the first time such an incident had occurred. It was destined, however, to receive an unprecedented publicity, for the fight between the policeman and the soldier ended with the shooting of the soldier. Rumor, flowing immediately to the streets outside, stated that the soldier had been shot in the back, an instantaneous and revealing invention, and that the soldier had died protecting a Negro woman. The facts were somewhat different—for example, the soldier had not been shot in the back, and was not dead, and the girl seems to have been as dubious a symbol of womanhood as her white counterpart in Georgia usually is, but no one was interested in the facts. They preferred the invention because this invention expressed and corroborated their hates and fears so perfectly. It is just as well to remember that people are always doing this. Perhaps many of those legends, including Christianity, to which the world clings began their conquest of the world with just some such concerted surrender to distortion. The effect, in Harlem, of this particular legend was like the effect of a lit match in a tin of gasoline. The mob gathered before the doors of the Hotel Braddock simply began to swell and to spread in every direction, and Harlem exploded.

The mob did not cross the ghetto lines. It would have been easy, for example, to have gone over to Morningside Park on the west side or to have crossed the Grand Central railroad tracks at 125th Street on the east side, to wreak havoc in white neighborhoods. The mob seems to have been mainly interested in something more potent and real than the white face, that is, in white power, and the principal damage done during the riot of the summer of 1943 was to white business establishments in Harlem. It might have been a far bloodier story, of course, if, at the hour the riot began, these establishments had still been open. From the Hotel Braddock the mob fanned out, east and west along 125th Street, and for the entire length of Lenox, Seventh, and Eighth avenues. Along each of these avenues, and along each major side street—116th, 125th, 135th, and so on—bars, stores, pawnshops, restaurants, even little luncheonettes had been smashed open and entered and looted—looted, it might be added, with more haste than efficiency. The shelves really looked as though a bomb had struck them. Cans of beans and soup and dog food, along with toilet paper, corn flakes, sardines, and milk tumbled every which way, and abandoned cash registers and cases of beer leaned crazily out of the splintered windows and were strewn along the avenues. Sheets, blankets, and clothing of every description formed a kind of path, as though people had dropped them while running. I truly had not realized that Harlem *had* so many stores until I saw them all smashed open; the first time the word *wealth* ever entered my mind in relation to Harlem was when I saw it scattered in the streets. But one's first, incongruous impression of plenty was countered immediately by an impression of waste. None of this was doing anybody any good. It would have been better to have left the plate glass as it had been and the goods lying in the stores.

It would have been better, but it would also have been intolerable, for Harlem had needed something to smash. To smash something is the ghetto's chronic need. Most of the time it is the members of the ghetto who smash each other, and themselves. But as long as the ghetto walls are standing there will always come a moment when these outlets do not work. That summer, for example, it was not enough to get into a fight on Lenox Avenue, or curse out one's cronies in the barber shops. If ever, indeed, the violence which fills Harlem's churches, pool halls, and bars erupts outward in a more direct fashion, Harlem and its citizens are likely to vanish in an apocalyptic flood. That this is not likely to happen is due to a great many reasons, most hidden and powerful among them the Negro's real relation to the white American. This relation prohibits, simply, anything as uncomplicated and satisfactory as pure hatred. In order really to hate white people, one has to blot so much out of the mind—and the heart—that this hatred itself becomes an exhausting and self-destructive pose. But this does not mean, on the other hand, that love comes easily: the white world is too powerful, too complacent, too ready with gratuitous humiliation, and, above all, too ignorant and too innocent for that. One is absolutely forced to make perpetual qualifications and one's own reactions are always canceling each other out. It is this, really, which has driven so many people mad, both white and black. One is always in the position of having to decide between amputation and gangrene. Amputation is swift but time may prove that the amputation was not necessary—or one may delay the amputation too long. Gangrene is slow, but it is impossible to be sure that one is reading one's symptoms right. The idea of going through life as a cripple is more than one can bear, and equally unbearable is the risk of swelling up slowly, in agony, with poison. And the trouble, finally, is that the risks are real even if the choices do not exist.

"But as for me and my house," my father had said, "we will serve the Lord." I wondered, as we drove him to his resting place, what this line had meant for him. I had heard him preach it many times. I had preached it once myself, proudly giving it an interpretation different from my father's. Now the whole thing came back to me, as though my father and I were on our way to Sunday school and I were memorizing the golden text: *And if it seem evil unto you to serve the Lord, choose you this day whom you will serve; whether the gods which your fathers served that were on the other side of the flood, or the gods of the Amorites, in whose land ye dwell: but as for me and my house, we will serve the Lord.* I suspected in these familiar lines a meaning which had never been there for me before. All of my father's texts and songs, which I had decided were meaningless, were arranged before me at his death like empty bottles, waiting to hold the meaning which life would give them for me. This was his legacy: nothing is ever escaped. That bleakly memorable morning I hated the unbelievable streets and the Negroes and whites who had, equally, made them that way. But I knew that it was folly, as my father would have said, this bitterness was folly. It was necessary to hold on to the things that mattered. The dead man mattered, the new life mattered; blackness and whiteness did not matter; to believe that they did was to acquiesce in one's own destruction. Hatred, which could destroy so much, never failed to destroy the man who hated and this was an immutable law.

It began to seem that one would have to hold in the mind forever two ideas which seemed to be in opposition. The first idea was acceptance, the acceptance, totally without rancor, of life as it is, and men as they are: in the light of this idea, it goes without saying that injustice is a commonplace. But this did not mean that one could be complacent, for the second idea was of equal power: that one must never, in one's own life, accept these injustices as commonplace but must fight them with all one's strength. This fight begins, however, in the heart and it now had been laid to my charge to keep my own heart free of hatred and despair. This intimation made my heart heavy and, now that my father was irrecoverable, I wished that he had been beside me so that I could have searched his face for the answers which only the future would give me now.

1955

EQUAL IN PARIS

On the 19th of December, in 1949, when I had been living in Paris for a little over a year, I was arrested as a receiver of stolen goods and spent eight days in prison. My arrest came about through an American tourist whom I had met twice in New York, who had been given my name and address and told to look me up. I was then living on the top floor of a ludicrously grim hotel on the rue du Bac, one of those enormous dark, cold, and hideous establishments in which Paris abounds that seem to breathe forth, in their airless, humid, stone-cold halls, the weak light, scurrying chambermaids, and creaking stairs, an odor of gentility long long dead. The place was run by an ancient Frenchman dressed in an elegant black suit which was green with age, who cannot properly be described as bewildered or even as being in a state of shock, since he had really stopped breathing around 1910. There he sat at his desk in the weirdly lit, fantastically furnished lobby, day in and day out, greeting each one of his extremely impoverished and *louche* lodgers with a stately inclination of the head that he had no doubt been taught in some impossibly remote time was the proper way for a *propriétaire* to greet his guests. If it had not been for his daughter, an extremely hardheaded *tricoteuse*—the inclination of *her* head was chilling and abrupt, like the downbeat of an ax—the hotel would certainly have gone bankrupt long before. It was said that this old man had not gone farther than the door of his hotel for thirty years, which was not at all difficult to believe. He looked as though the daylight would have killed him.

I did not, of course, spend much of my time in this palace. The moment I began living in French hotels I understood the necessity of French cafés. This made it rather difficult to look me up, for as soon as I was out of bed I hopefully took notebook and fountain pen off to the upstairs room of the Flore, where I consumed rather a lot of coffee and, as evening approached, rather a lot of alcohol, but did not get much writing done. But one night, in one of the cafés of St. Germain des Près, I was discovered by this New Yorker and only because we found ourselves in Paris we immediately established the illusion that we had been fast friends back in the good old U.S.A. This illusion proved itself too thin to support an evening's drinking, but by that time it was too late. I had committed myself to getting him a room in my hotel the next day, for he was living in one of the nest of hotels near the Gare St. Lazare, where, he said, the *propriétaire* was a thief, his wife a repressed nymphomaniac, the chambermaids "pigs," and the rent a crime. Americans are always talking this way about the French and so it did not occur to me that he meant what he said or that he would take into his own hands the means of avenging himself on the French Republic. It did not occur to me, either, that the means which he *did* take could possibly have brought about such dire results, results which were not less dire for being also comic-opera.

It came as the last of a series of disasters which had perhaps been made inevitable by the fact that I had come to Paris originally with a little over forty dollars in my pockets, nothing in the bank, and no grasp whatever of the French language. It developed, shortly, that I had no grasp of the French character either. I considered the French an ancient, intelligent, and cultured race, which indeed they are. I did not know, however, that ancient glories imply, at least in the middle of the present century, present fatigue and, quite probably, paranoia; that there is a limit to the role of the intelligence in human affairs; and that no people come into possession of a culture without having paid a heavy price for it. This price they cannot, of course, assess, but it is revealed in their personalities and in their institutions. The very word "institutions," from my side of the ocean, where, it seemed to me, we suffered so cruelly from the lack of them, had a pleasant ring, as of safety and order and common sense; one had to come into contact with these institutions in order to understand that they were also outmoded, exasperating, completely impersonal, and very often cruel. Similarly, the personality which had seemed from a distance to be so large and free had to be dealt with before one could see that, if it was large, it was also inflexible and, for the foreigner, full of strange, high, dusty rooms which could not be inhabited. One had, in short, to come into contact with an alien culture in order to understand that a culture was not a community basket-weaving project, nor yet an act of God; was something neither desirable nor undesirable in itself, being inevitable, being nothing more or less than the recorded and visible effects on a body of people of the vicissitudes with which they had been forced to deal. And their great men are revealed as simply another of these vicissitudes, even if, quite against their will, the brief battle of their great men with them has left them richer.

When my American friend left his hotel to move to mine, he took with him, out of pique, a bedsheet belonging to the hotel and put it in his suitcase. When he arrived at my hotel I borrowed the sheet, since my own were filthy and the chambermaid showed no sign of bringing me any clean ones, and put it on my bed. The sheets belonging to *my* hotel I put out in the hall, congratulating myself on having thus forced on the attention of the Grand Hôtel du Bac the unpleasant state of its linen. Thereafter, since, as it turned out, we kept very different hours—I got up at noon, when, as I gathered by meeting him on the stairs one day, he was only just getting in—my new-found friend and I saw very little of each other.

On the evening of the 19th I was sitting thinking melancholy thoughts about Christmas and staring at the walls of my room. I imagine that I had sold something or that someone had sent me a Christmas present, for I remember that I had a little money. In those days in Paris, though I floated, so to speak, on a sea of acquaintances, I knew almost no one. Many people were eliminated from my orbit by virtue of the fact that they had more money than I did, which placed me, in my own eyes, in the humiliating role of a free-loader; and other people were eliminated by virtue of the fact that they enjoyed their poverty, shrilly insisting that this wretched round of hotel rooms, bad food, humiliating concierges, and unpaid bills was the Great Adventure. It couldn't, however, for me, end soon enough, this Great Adventure; there was a real question in my mind as to which would end soonest, the Great Adventure or me. This meant, however, that there were many evenings when I sat in my room, knowing that I couldn't work there, and not knowing what to do, or whom to see. On this particular evening I went down and knocked on the American's door.

There were two Frenchmen standing in the room, who immediately introduced themselves to me as policemen; which did not worry me. I had got used to policemen in Paris bobbing up at the most improbable times and places, asking to see one's *carte d'identité*. These policemen, however, showed very little interest in my papers. They were looking for something else. I could not imagine what this would be and, since I knew I certainly didn't have it, I scarcely followed the conversation they were having with my friend. I gathered that they were looking for some kind of gangster and since I wasn't a gangster and knew that gangsterism was not, insofar as he had one, my friend's style, I was sure that the two policemen would presently bow and say *Merci, messieurs,* and leave. For by this time, I remember very clearly, I was dying to have a drink and go to dinner.

I did not have a drink or go to dinner for many days after this, and when I did my outraged stomach promptly heaved everything up again. For now one of the policemen began to exhibit the most vivid interest in me and asked, very politely, if he might see my room. To which we mounted, making, I remember, the most civilized small talk on the way and even continuing it for some moments after we were in the room in which there was certainly nothing to be seen but the familiar poverty and disorder of that precarious group of people of whatever age, race, country, calling, or intention which Paris recognizes as *les étudiants* and sometimes, more ironically and precisely, as *les nonconformistes.* Then he moved to my bed, and in a terrible flash, not quite an instant before he lifted the bedspread, I understood what he was looking for. We looked at the sheet, on which I read, for the first time, lettered in the most brilliant scarlet I have ever seen, the name of the hotel from which it had been stolen. It was the first time the word *stolen* entered my mind. I had certainly seen the hotel monogram the day I put the sheet on the bed. It had simply meant nothing to me. In New York I had seen hotel monograms on everything from silver to soap and towels. Taking things from New York hotels was practically a custom, though, I suddenly realized, I had never known anyone to take a *sheet.* Sadly, and without a word to me, the inspector took the sheet from the bed, folded it under his arm, and we started back downstairs. I understood that I was under arrest.

And so we passed through the lobby, four of us, two of us very clearly criminal, under the eyes of the old man and his daughter, neither of whom said a word, into the streets where a light rain was falling. And I asked, in French, "But is this very serious?"

For I was thinking, it is, after all, only a sheet, not even new.

"No," said one of them. "It's not serious."

"It's nothing at all," said the other.

I took this to mean that we would receive a reprimand at the police station and be allowed to go to dinner. Later on I concluded that they were not being hypocritical or even trying to comfort us. They meant exactly what they said. It was only that they spoke another language.

In Paris everything is very slow. Also, when dealing with the bureaucracy, the man you are talking to is never the man you have to see. The man you have to see has just gone off to Belgium, or is busy with his family, or has just discovered that he is a cuckold; he will be in next Tuesday at three o'clock, or sometime in the course of the afternoon, or possibly tomorrow, or, possibly, in the next five minutes. But if he is coming in the next five minutes he will be far too busy to be able to see you today. So that I suppose I was not really astonished to learn at the commissariat that nothing could possibly be done about us before The Man arrived in the morning. But no, we could not go off and have dinner and come back in the morning. Of course he knew that we *would* come back—that was not the question. Indeed, there was no question; we would simply have to stay there for the night. We were placed in a cell which rather resembled a chicken coop. It was now about seven in the evening and I relinquished the thought of dinner and began to think of lunch.

I discouraged the chatter of my New York friend and this left me alone with my thoughts. I was beginning to be frightened and I bent all my energies, therefore, to keeping my panic under control. I began to realize that I was in a country I knew nothing about, in the hands of a people I did not understand at all. In a similar situation in New York I would have had some idea of what to do because I would have had some idea of what to expect. I am not speaking now of legality which, like most of the poor, I had never for an instant trusted, but of the temperament of the people with whom I had to deal. I had become very accomplished in New York at guessing and, therefore, to a limited extent manipulating to my advantage the reactions of the white world. But this was not New York. None of my old weapons could serve me here. I did not know what they saw when they looked at me. I knew very well what Americans saw when they looked at me and this allowed me to play endless and sinister variations on the role which they had assigned me; since I knew that it was, for them, of the utmost importance that they never be confronted with what, in their own personalities, made this role so necessary and gratifying to them, I knew that they could never call my hand or, indeed, afford to know what I was doing; so that I moved into every crucial situation with the deadly and rather desperate advantage of bitterly accumulated perception, of pride and contempt. This is an awful sword and shield to carry through the world, and the discovery that, in the game I was playing, I did myself a violence of which the world, at its most ferocious, would scarcely have been capable, was what had driven me out of New York. It was a strange feeling, in this situation, after a year in Paris, to discover that my weapons would never again serve me as they had.

It was quite clear to me that the Frenchmen in whose hands I found myself were no better or worse than their American counterparts. Certainly their uniforms frightened me quite as much, and their impersonality, and the threat, always very keenly felt by the poor, of violence, was as present in that commissariat as it had ever been for me in any police station. And I had seen, for example, what Paris policemen could do to Arab peanut vendors. The only difference here was that I did not understand these people, did not know what techniques their cruelty took, did not know enough about their personalities to see danger coming, to ward it off, did not know on what ground to meet it. That evening in the commissariat I was not a despised black man. They would simply have laughed at me if I had behaved like one. For them, I was an American. And here it was they who had the advantage, for that word, *Américain*, gave them some idea, far from inaccurate, of what to expect from me. In order to corroborate none of their ironical expectations I said nothing and did nothing—which was not the way any Frenchman, white or black, would have reacted. The question thrusting up from the bottom of my mind was not *what* I was, but *who*. And this question, since a *what* can get by with skill but a *who* demands resources, was my first real intimation of what humility must mean.

In the morning it was still raining. Between nine and ten o'clock a black Citroën took us off to the Ile de la Cité, to the great, gray Préfecture. I realize now that the questions I put to the various policemen who escorted us were always answered in such a way as to corroborate what I wished to hear. This was not out of politeness, but simply out of indifference—or, possibly, an ironical pity—since each of the policemen knew very well that nothing would speed or halt the machine in which I had become entangled. They knew I did not know this and there was certainly no point in their telling me. In one way or another I would certainly come out at the other side—for they also knew that being found with a stolen bedsheet in one's possession was not a crime punishable by guillotine. (They had the advantage over me there, too, for there were certainly moments later on when I was not so sure.) If I did *not* come out at the other side—well, that was just too bad. So, to my question, put while we were in the Citroën—"Will it be over today?"—I received a "*Oui, bien sûr.*" He was not lying. As it turned out, the *procès-verbal* was over that day. Trying to be realistic, I dismissed, in the Citroën, all thoughts of lunch and pushed my mind ahead to dinner.

At the Préfecture we were first placed in a tiny cell, in which it was almost impossible either to sit or to lie down. After a couple of hours of this we were taken down to an office, where, for the first time, I encountered the owner of the bedsheet and where the *procès-verbal* took place. This was simply an interrogation, quite chillingly clipped and efficient (so that there was, shortly, no doubt in one's own mind that one *should* be treated as a criminal), which was recorded by a secretary. When it was over, this report was given to us to sign. One had, of course, no choice but to sign it, even though my mastery of written French was very far from certain. We were being held, according to the law in France, incommunicado, and all my angry demands to be allowed to speak to my embassy or to see a lawyer met with a stony "*Oui, oui. Plus tard.*" The *procès-verbal* over, we were taken back to the cell, before which, shortly, passed the owner of the bedsheet. He said he hoped we had slept well, gave a vindictive wink, and disappeared.

By this time there was only one thing clear: that we had no way of controlling the sequence of events and could not possibly guess what this sequence would be. It seemed to me, since what I regarded as the high point—the *procès-verbal*—had been passed and since the hotel-keeper was once again in possession of his sheet, that we might reasonably expect to be released from police custody in a matter of hours. We had been detained now for what would soon be twenty-four hours, during which time I had learned only that the official charge against me was *receleur*. My mental shifting, between lunch and dinner, to say nothing of the physical lack of either of these delights, was beginning to make me dizzy. The steady chatter of my friend from New York, who was determined to keep my spirits up, made me feel murderous; I was praying that some power would release us from this freezing pile of stone before the impulse became the act.

And I was beginning to wonder what was happening in that beautiful city, Paris, which lived outside these walls. I wondered how long it would take before anyone casually asked, "But where's Jimmy? He hasn't been around"—and realized, knowing the people I knew, that it would take several days.

Quite late in the afternoon we were taken from our cells; handcuffed, each to a separate officer; led through a maze of steps and corridors to the top of the building; fingerprinted; photographed. As in movies I had seen, I was placed against a wall, facing an old-fashioned camera, behind which stood one of the most completely cruel and indifferent faces I had ever seen, while someone next to me and, therefore, just outside my line of vision, read off in a voice from which all human feeling, even feeling of the most base description, had long since fled, what must be called my public characteristics—which, at that time and in that place, seemed anything but that. He might have been roaring to the hostile world secrets which I could barely, in the privacy of midnight, utter to myself. But he was only reading off my height, my features, my approximate weight, my color—that color which, in the United States, had often, odd as it may sound, been my salvation—the color of my hair, my age, my nationality. A light then flashed, the photographer and I staring at each other as though there was murder in our hearts, and then it was over. Handcuffed again, I was led downstairs to the bottom of the building, into a great enclosed shed in which had been gathered the very scrapings off the Paris streets. Old, old men, so ruined and old that life in them seemed really to prove the miracle of the quickening power of the Holy Ghost—for clearly their life was no longer their affair, it was no longer even their burden, they were simply the clay which had once been touched. And men not so old, with faces the color of lead and the consistency of oatmeal, eyes that made me think of stale *café-au-lait* spiked with arsenic, bodies which could take in food and water—any food and water—and pass it out, but which could not do anything more, except possibly, at midnight, along the riverbank where rats scurried, rape. And young men, harder and crueler than the Paris stones, older by far than I, their chronological senior by some five to seven years. And North Africans, old and young, who seemed the only living people in this place because they yet retained the grace to be bewildered. But they were not bewildered by being in this shed: they were simply bewildered because they were no longer in North Africa. There was a great hole in the center of this shed, which was the common toilet. Near it, though it was impossible to get very far from it, stood an old man with white hair, eating a piece of camembert. It was at this point, probably, that thought, for me, stopped, that physiology, if one may say so, took over. I found myself incapable of saying a word, not because I was afraid I would cry but because I was afraid I would vomit. And I did not think any longer of the city of Paris but my mind flew back to that home from which I had fled. I was sure that I would never see it any more. And it must have seemed to me that my flight from home was the cruelest trick I had ever played on myself, since it had led me here, down to a lower point than any I could ever in my life have imagined—lower, far, than anything I had seen in that Harlem which I had so hated and so loved, the escape from which had soon become the greatest direction of my life. After we had been here an hour or so a functionary came and opened the door and called out our names. And I was sure that *this* was my release. But I was handcuffed again and led out of the Préfecture into the streets—it was dark now, it was still raining—and before the steps of the Préfecture stood the great police wagon, doors facing me, wide open. The handcuffs were taken off, I entered the wagon, which was peculiarly constructed. It was divided by a narrow aisle, and on each side of the aisle was a series of narrow doors. These doors opened on a narrow cubicle, beyond which was a door which opened onto another narrow cubicle: three or four cubicles, each private, with a locking door. I was placed in one of them; I remember there was a small vent just above my head which let in a little light. The door of my cubicle was locked from the outside. I had no idea where this wagon was taking me and, as it began to move, I began to cry. I suppose I cried all the way to prison, the prison called Fresnes, which is twelve kilometers outside of Paris.

For reasons I have no way at all of understanding, prisoners whose last initial is A, B, or C are always sent to Fresnes; everybody else is sent to a prison called, rather cynically it seems to me, La Santé. I will, obviously, never be allowed to enter La Santé, but I was told by people who certainly seemed to know that it was infinitely more unbearable than Fresnes. This arouses in me, until today, a positive storm of curiosity concerning what I promptly began to think of as The Other Prison. My colleague in crime, occurring lower in the alphabet, had been sent there and I confess that the minute he was gone I missed him. I missed him because he was not French and because he was the only person in the world who knew that the story I told was true.

For, once locked in, divested of shoelaces, belt, watch, money, papers, nailfile, in a freezing cell in which both the window and the toilet were broken, with six other adventurers, the story I told of *l'affaire du drap de lit* elicited only the wildest amusement or the most suspicious disbelief. Among the people who shared my cell the first three days no one, it is true, had been arrested for anything much more serious—or, at least, not serious in my eyes. I remember that there was a boy who had stolen a knitted sweater from a *monoprix*, who would probably, it was agreed, receive a six-month sentence. There was an older man there who had been arrested for some kind of petty larceny. There were two North Africans, vivid, brutish, and beautiful, who alternated between gaiety and fury, not at the fact of their arrest but at the state of the cell. None poured as much emotional energy into the fact of their arrest as I did; they took it, as I would have liked to take it, as simply another unlucky happening in a very dirty world. For, though I had grown accustomed to thinking of myself as looking upon the world with a hard, penetrating eye, the truth was that they were far more realistic about the world than I, and more nearly right about it. The gap between us, which only a gesture I made could have bridged, grew steadily, during thirty-six hours, wider. I could not make any gesture simply because they frightened me. I was unable to accept my imprisonment as a fact, even as a temporary fact. I could not, even for a moment, accept my present companions as *my* companions. And they, of course, felt this and put it down, with perfect justice, to the fact that I was an American.

There was nothing to do all day long. It appeared that we would one day come to trial but no one knew when. We were awakened at seven-thirty by a rapping on what I believe is called the Judas, that small opening in the door of the cell which allows the guards to survey the prisoners. At this rapping we rose from the floor—we slept on straw pallets and each of us was covered with one thin blanket—and moved to the door of the cell. We peered through the opening into the center of the prison, which was, as I remember, three tiers high, all gray stone and gunmetal steel, precisely that prison I had seen in movies, except that, in the movies, I had not known that it was cold in prison. I had not known that when one's shoelaces and belt have been removed one is, in the strangest way, demoralized. The necessity of shuffling and the necessity of holding up one's trousers with one hand turn one into a rag doll. And the movies fail, of course, to give one any idea of what prison food is like. Along the corridor, at seven-thirty, came three men, each pushing before him a great garbage can, mounted on wheels. In the garbage can of the first was the bread—this was passed to one through the small opening in the door. In the can of the second was the coffee. In the can of the third was what was always called *la soupe*, a pallid paste of potatoes which had certainly been bubbling on the back of the prison stove long before that first, so momentous revolution. Naturally, it was cold by this time and, starving as I was, I could not eat it. I drank the coffee—which was not coffee—because it was hot, and spent the rest of the day, huddled in my blanket, munching on the bread. It was not the French bread one bought in bakeries. In the evening the same procession returned. At ten-thirty the lights went out. I had a recurring dream, each night, a nightmare which always involved my mother's fried chicken. At the moment I was about to eat it came the rapping at the door. Silence is really all I remember of those first three days, silence and the color gray.

I am not sure now whether it was on the third or the fourth day that I was taken to trial for the first time. The days had nothing, obviously, to distinguish them from one another. I remember that I was very much aware that Christmas Day was approaching and I wondered if I was really going to spend Christmas Day in prison. And I remember that the first trial came the day before Christmas Eve.

On the morning of the first trial I was awakened by hearing

my name called. I was told, hanging in a kind of void between my mother's fried chicken and the cold prison floor, "*Vous préparez. Vous êtes extrait*"—which simply terrified me, since I did not know what interpretation to put on the word "*extrait,*" and since my cellmates had been amusing themselves with me by telling terrible stories about the inefficiency of French prisons, an inefficiency so extreme that it had often happened that someone who was supposed to be taken out and tried found himself on the wrong line and was guillotined instead. The best way of putting my reaction to this is to say that, though I knew they were teasing me, it was simply not possible for me to totally *dis*believe them. As far as I was concerned, once in the hands of the law in France, anything could happen. I shuffled along with the others who were *extrait* to the center of the prison, trying, rather, to linger in the office, which seemed the only warm spot in the whole world, and found myself again in that dreadful wagon, and was carried again to the Ile de la Cité, this time to the Palais de Justice. The entire day, except for ten minutes, was spent in one of the cells, first waiting to be tried, then waiting to be taken back to prison.

For I was *not* tried that day. By and by I was handcuffed and led through the halls, upstairs to the courtroom where I found my New York friend. We were placed together, both stage-whisperingly certain that this was the end of our ordeal. Nevertheless, while I waited for our case to be called, my eyes searched the courtroom, looking for a face I knew, hoping, anyway, that there was someone there who knew *me*, who would carry to someone outside the news that I was in trouble. But there was no one I knew there and I had had time to realize that there was probably only one man in Paris who could help me, an American patent attorney for whom I had worked as an office boy. He could have helped me because he had a quite solid position and some prestige and would have testified that, while working for him, I had handled large sums of money regularly, which made it rather unlikely that I would stoop to trafficking in bedsheets. However, he was somewhere in Paris, probably at this very moment enjoying a snack and a glass of wine and as far as the possibility of reaching him was concerned, he might as well have been on Mars. I tried to watch the proceedings and to make my mind a blank. But the proceedings were not reassuring. The boy, for example, who had stolen the sweater *did* receive a six-month sentence. It seemed to me that all the sentences meted out that day were excessive; though, again, it seemed that all the people who were sentenced that day had made, or clearly were going to make, crime their career. This seemed to be the opinion of the judge, who scarcely looked at the prisoners or listened to them; it seemed to be the opinion of the prisoners, who scarcely bothered to speak in their own behalf; it seemed to be the opinion of the lawyers, state lawyers for the most part, who were defending them. The great impulse of the courtroom seemed to be to put these people where they could not be seen—and not because they were offended at the crimes, unless, indeed, they were offended that the crimes were so petty, but because they did not wish to know that their society could be counted on to produce, probably in greater and greater numbers, a whole body of people for whom crime was the only possible career. Any society inevitably produces its criminals, but a society at once rigid and unstable can do nothing whatever to alleviate the poverty of its lowest members, cannot present to the hypothetical young man at the crucial moment that so-well-advertised right path. And the fact, perhaps, that the French are the earth's least sentimental people and must also be numbered among the most proud aggravates the plight of their lowest, youngest, and unluckiest members, for it means that the idea of rehabilitation is scarcely real to them. I confess that this attitude on their part raises in me sentiments of exasperation, admiration, and despair, revealing as it does, in both the best and the worst sense, their renowned and spectacular hard-headedness.

Finally our case was called and we rose. We gave our names. At the point that it developed that we were American the proceedings ceased, a hurried consultation took place between the judge and what I took to be several lawyers. Someone called out for an interpreter. The arresting officer had forgotten to mention our nationalities and there was, therefore, no interpreter in the court. Even if our French had been better than it was we would not have been allowed to stand trial without an interpreter. Before I clearly understood what was happening, I was handcuffed again and led out of the courtroom. The trial had been set back for the 27th of December.

I have sometimes wondered if I would *ever* have got out of prison if it had not been for the older man who had been arrested for the mysterious petty larceny. He was acquitted that day and when he returned to the cell—for he could not be released until morning—he found me sitting numbly on the floor, having just been prevented, by the sight of a man, all blood, being carried back to *his* cell on a stretcher, from seizing the bars and screaming until they let me out. The sight of the man on the stretcher proved, however, that screaming would not do much for me. The petty-larceny man went around asking if he could do anything in the world outside for those he was leaving behind. When he came to me I, at first, responded, "No, nothing"—for I suppose I had by now retreated into the attitude, the earliest I remember, that of my father, which was simply (since I had lost his God) that nothing could help me. And I suppose I will remember with gratitude until I die the fact that the man now insisted: *"Mais, êtes-vous sûr?"* Then it swept over me that he was going *outside* and he instantly became my first contact since the Lord alone knew how long with the outside world. At the same time, I remember, I did not really believe that he would help me. There was no reason why he should. But I gave him the phone number of my attorney friend and my own name.

So, in the middle of the next day, Christmas Eve, I shuffled downstairs again, to meet my visitor. He looked extremely well fed and sane and clean. He told me I had nothing to worry about any more. Only not even he could do anything to make the mill of justice grind any faster. He would, however, send me a lawyer of his acquaintance who would defend me on the 27th, and he would himself, along with several other people, appear as a character witness. He gave me a package of Lucky Strikes (which the turnkey took from me on the way upstairs) and said that, though it was doubtful that there would be any celebration in the prison, he would see to it that I got a fine Christmas dinner when I got out. And this, somehow, seemed very funny. I remember being astonished at the discovery that I was actually laughing. I was, too, I imagine, also rather disappointed that my hair had not turned white, that my face was clearly not going to bear any marks of tragedy, disappointed at bottom, no doubt, to realize, facing him in that room, that far worse things had happened to most people and that, indeed, to paraphrase my mother, if this was the worst thing that ever happened to me I could consider myself among the luckiest people ever to be born. He injected—my visitor—into my solitary nightmare common sense, the world, and the hint of blacker things to come.

The next day, Christmas, unable to endure my cell, and feeling that, after all, the day demanded a gesture, I asked to be allowed to go to Mass, hoping to hear some music. But I found myself, for a freezing hour and a half, locked in exactly the same kind of cubicle as in the wagon which had first brought me to prison, peering through a slot placed at the level of the eye at an old Frenchman, hatted, overcoated, muffled, and gloved, preaching in this language which I did not understand, to this row of wooden boxes, the story of Jesus Christ's love for men.

The next day, the 26th, I spent learning a peculiar kind of game, played with match-sticks, with my cellmates. For, since I no longer felt that I would stay in this cell forever, I was beginning to be able to make peace with it for a time. On the 27th I went again to trial and, as had been predicted, the case against us was dismissed. The story of the *drap de lit*, finally told, caused great merriment in the courtroom, whereupon my friend decided that the French were "great." I was chilled by their merriment, even though it was meant to warm me. It could only remind me of the laughter I had often heard at home, laughter which I had sometimes deliberately elicited. This laughter is the laughter of those who consider themselves to be at a safe remove from all the wretched, for whom the pain of the living is not real. I had heard it so often in my native land that I had resolved to find a place where I would never hear it any more. In some deep, black, stony, and liberating way, my life, in my own eyes, began during that first year in Paris, when it was borne in on me that this laughter is universal and never can be stilled.

1955

STRANGER IN THE VILLAGE

From all available evidence no black man had ever set foot in this tiny Swiss village before I came. I was told before arriving that I would probably be a "sight" for the village; I took this to mean that people of my complexion were rarely seen in Switzerland, and also that city people are always something of a "sight" outside of the city. It did not occur to me—possibly because I am an American—that there could be people anywhere who had never seen a Negro.

It is a fact that cannot be explained on the basis of the inaccessibility of the village. The village is very high, but it is only four hours from Milan and three hours from Lausanne. It is true that it is virtually unknown. Few people making plans for a holiday would elect to come here. On the other hand, the villagers are able, presumably, to come and go as they please—which they do: to another town at the foot of the mountain, with a population of approximately five thousand, the nearest place to see a movie or go to the bank. In the village there is no movie house, no bank, no library, no theater; very few radios, one jeep, one station wagon; and, at the moment, one typewriter, mine, an invention which the woman next door to me here had never seen. There are about six hundred people living here, all Catholic—I conclude this from the fact that the Catholic church is open all year round, whereas the Protestant chapel, set off on a hill a little removed from the village, is open only in the summertime when the tourists arrive. There are four or five hotels, all closed now, and four or five *bistros,* of which, however, only two do any business during the winter. These two do not do a great deal, for life in the village seems to end around nine or ten o'clock. There are a few stores, butcher, baker, *épicerie,* a hardware store, and a money-changer—who cannot change travelers' checks, but must send them down to the bank, an operation which takes two or three days. There is something called the *Ballet Haus,* closed in the winter and used for God knows what, certainly not ballet, during the summer. There seems to be only one schoolhouse in the village, and this for the quite young children; I suppose this to mean that their older brothers and sisters at some point descend from these mountains in order to complete their education —possibly, again, to the town just below. The landscape is absolutely forbidding, mountains towering on all four sides, ice and snow as far as the eye can reach. In this white wilderness, men and women and children move all day, carrying washing, wood, buckets of milk or water, sometimes skiing on Sunday afternoons. All week long boys and young men are to be seen shoveling snow off the rooftops, or dragging wood down from the forest in sleds.

The village's only real attraction, which explains the tourist season, is the hot spring water. A disquietingly high proportion of these tourists are cripples, or semi-cripples, who come year after year—from other parts of Switzerland, usually—to take the waters. This lends the village, at the height of the season, a rather terrifying air of sanctity, as though it were a lesser Lourdes. There is often something beautiful, there is always something awful, in the spectacle of a person who has lost one of his faculties, a faculty he never questioned until it was gone, and who struggles to recover it. Yet people remain people, on crutches or indeed on deathbeds; and wherever I passed, the first summer I was here, among the native villagers or among the lame, a wind passed with me—of astonishment, curiosity, amusement, and outrage. That first summer I stayed two weeks and never intended to return. But I did return in the winter, to work; the village offers, obviously, no distractions whatever and has the further advantage of being extremely cheap. Now it is winter again, a year later, and I am here again. Everyone in the village knows my name, though they scarcely ever use it, knows that I come from America —though, this, apparently, they will never really believe: black men come from Africa—and everyone knows that I am the friend of the son of a woman who was born here, and that I am staying in their chalet. But I remain as much a stranger today as I was the first day I arrived, and the children shout *Neger! Neger!* as I walk along the streets.

It must be admitted that in the beginning I was far too shocked to have any real reaction. In so far as I reacted at all, I reacted by trying to be pleasant—it being a great part of the

American Negro's education (long before he goes to school) that he must make people "like" him. This smile-and-the-world-smiles-with-you routine worked about as well in this situation as it had in the situation for which it was designed, which is to say that it did not work at all. No one, after all, can be liked whose human weight and complexity cannot be, or has not been, admitted. My smile was simply another unheard-of phenomenon which allowed them to see my teeth—they did not, really, see my smile and I began to think that, should I take to snarling, no one would notice any difference. All of the physical characteristics of the Negro which had caused me, in America, a very different and almost forgotten pain were nothing less than miraculous—or infernal—in the eyes of the village people. Some thought my hair was the color of tar, that it had the texture of wire, or the texture of cotton. It was jocularly suggested that I might let it all grow long and make myself a winter coat. If I sat in the sun for more than five minutes some daring creature was certain to come along and gingerly put his fingers on my hair, as though he were afraid of an electric shock, or put his hand on my hand, astonished that the color did not rub off. In all of this, in which it must be conceded there was the charm of genuine wonder and in which there was certainly no element of intentional unkindness, there was yet no suggestion that I was human: I was simply a living wonder.

I knew that they did not mean to be unkind, and I know it now; it is necessary, nevertheless, for me to repeat this to myself each time I walk out of the chalet. The children who shout *Neger!* have no way of knowing the echoes this sound raises in me. They are brimming with good humor and the more daring swell with pride when I stop to speak with them. Just the same, there are days when I cannot pause and smile, when I have no heart to play with them; when, indeed, I mutter sourly to myself, exactly as I muttered on the streets of a city these children have never seen, when I was no bigger than these children are now: *Your* mother *was a nigger.* Joyce is right about history being a nightmare—but it may be the nightmare from which no one *can* awaken. People are trapped in history and history is trapped in them.

There is a custom in the village—I am told it is repeated in many villages—of "buying" African natives for the purpose of converting them to Christianity. There stands in the church all year round a small box with a slot for money, decorated with a black figurine, and into this box the villagers drop their francs. During the *carnaval* which precedes Lent, two village children have their faces blackened—out of which bloodless darkness their blue eyes shine like ice—and fantastic horsehair wigs are placed on their blond heads; thus disguised, they solicit among the villagers for money for the missionaries in Africa. Between the box in the church and the blackened children, the village "bought" last year six or eight African natives. This was reported to me with pride by the wife of one of the *bistro* owners and I was careful to express astonishment and pleasure at the solicitude shown by the village for the souls of black folk. The *bistro* owner's wife beamed with a pleasure far more genuine than my own and seemed to feel that I might now breathe more easily concerning the souls of at least six of my kinsmen.

I tried not to think of these so lately baptized kinsmen, of the price paid for them, or the peculiar price they themselves would pay, and said nothing about my father, who having taken his own conversion too literally never, at bottom, forgave the white world (which he described as heathen) for having saddled him with a Christ in whom, to judge at least from their treatment of him, they themselves no longer believed. I thought of white men arriving for the first time in an African village, strangers there, as I am a stranger here, and tried to imagine the astounded populace touching their hair and marveling at the color of their skin. But there is a great difference between being the first white man to be seen by Africans and being the first black man to be seen by whites. The white man takes the astonishment as tribute, for he arrives to conquer and to convert the natives, whose inferiority in relation to himself is not even to be questioned; whereas I, without a thought of conquest, find myself among a people whose culture controls me, has even, in a sense, created me, people who have cost me more in anguish and rage than they will ever know, who yet do not even know of my existence. The astonishment with which I might have greeted them, should they have stumbled into my African village a few hundred years ago, might have rejoiced their hearts. But the astonishment with which they greet me today can only poison mine.

And this is so despite everything I may do to feel differently, despite my friendly conversations with the *bistro* owner's wife, despite their three-year-old son who has at last become my friend, despite the *saluts* and *bonsoirs* which I exchange with people as I walk, despite the fact that I know that no individual can be taken to task for what history is doing, or has done. I say that the culture of these people controls me—but they can scarcely be held responsible for European culture. America comes out of Europe, but these people have never seen America, nor have most of them seen more of Europe than the hamlet at the foot of their mountain. Yet they move with an authority which I shall never have; and they regard me, quite rightly, not only as a stranger in their village but as a suspect latecomer, bearing no credentials, to everything they have—however unconsciously—inherited.

For this village, even were it incomparably more remote and incredibly more primitive, is the West, the West onto which I have been so strangely grafted. These people cannot be, from the point of view of power, strangers anywhere in the world; they have made the modern world, in effect, even if they do not know it. The most illiterate among them is related, in a way that I am not, to Dante, Shakespeare, Michelangelo, Aeschylus, Da Vinci, Rembrandt, and Racine; the cathedral at Chartres says something to them which it cannot say to me, as indeed would New York's Empire State Building, should anyone here ever see it. Out of their hymns and dances come Beethoven and Bach. Go back a few centuries and they are in their full glory—but I am in Africa, watching the conquerors arrive.

The rage of the disesteemed is personally fruitless, but it is also absolutely inevitable; this rage, so generally discounted, so little understood even among the people whose daily bread it is, is one of the things that makes history. Rage can only with difficulty, and never entirely, be brought under the domination of the intelligence and is therefore not susceptible to any arguments whatever. This is a fact which ordinary representatives of the *Herrenvolk*, having never felt this rage and being unable to imagine it, quite fail to understand. Also, rage cannot be hidden, it can only be dissembled. This dissembling deludes the thoughtless, and strengthens rage and adds, to rage, contempt. There are, no doubt, as many ways of coping with the resulting complex of tensions as there are black men in the world, but no black man can hope ever to be entirely liberated from this internal warfare —rage, dissembling, and contempt having inevitably accompanied his first realization of the power of white men. What is crucial here is that, since white men represent in the black man's world so heavy a weight, white men have for black men a reality which is far from being reciprocal; and hence all black men have toward all white men an attitude which is designed, really, either to rob the white man of the jewel of his naïveté, or else to make it cost him dear.

The black man insists, by whatever means he finds at his disposal, that the white man cease to regard him as an exotic rarity and recognize him as a human being. This is a very charged and difficult moment, for there is a great deal of will power involved in the white man's naïveté. Most people are not naturally reflective any more than they are naturally malicious, and the white man prefers to keep the black man at a certain human remove because it is easier for him thus to preserve his simplicity and avoid being called to account for crimes committed by his forefathers, or his neighbors. He is inescapably aware, nevertheless, that he is in a better position in the world than black men are, nor can he quite put to death the suspicion that he is hated by black men therefor. He does not wish to be hated, neither does he wish to change places, and at this point in his uneasiness he can scarcely avoid having recourse to those legends which white men have created about black men, the most usual effect of which is that the white man finds himself enmeshed, so to speak, in his own language which describes hell, as well as the attributes which lead one to hell, as being as black as night.

Every legend, moreover, contains its residuum of truth, and the root function of language is to control the universe by describing it. It is of quite considerable significance that black men remain, in the imagination, and in overwhelming numbers in fact, beyond the disciplines of salvation; and this despite the fact that the West has been "buying" African natives for centuries. There is, I should hazard, an instantaneous necessity to be divorced from this so visibly unsaved stranger, in whose heart, moreover, one cannot guess what dreams of vengeance are being nourished; and, at the same time, there are few things on earth more attractive than the idea of the unspeakable liberty which is allowed the unredeemed. When, beneath the black mask, a human being begins to make himself felt one cannot escape a certain awful wonder as to what kind of human being it is. What one's imagination makes of other people is dictated, of course, by the laws of one's own personality and it is one of the ironies of black-white relations that, by means of what the white man imagines the black man to be, the black man is enabled to know who the white man is.

I have said, for example, that I am as much a stranger in this village today as I was the first summer I arrived, but this is not quite true. The villagers wonder less about the texture of my hair than they did then, and wonder rather more about me. And the fact that their wonder now exists on another level is reflected in their attitudes and in their eyes. There are the children who make those delightful, hilarious, sometimes astonishing grave overtures of friendship in the unpredictable fashion of children; other children, having been taught that the devil is a black man, scream in genuine anguish as I approach. Some of the older women never pass without a friendly greeting, never pass, indeed, if it seems that they will be able to engage me in conversation; other women look down or look away or rather contemptuously smirk. Some of the men drink with me and suggest that I learn how to ski—partly, I gather, because they cannot imagine what I would look like on skis—and want to know if I am married, and ask questions about my *métier*. But some of the men have accused *le sale nègre*—behind my back—of stealing wood and there is already in the eyes of some of them that peculiar intent, paranoiac malevolence which one sometimes surprises in the eyes of American white men when, out walking with their Sunday girl, they see a Negro male approach.

There is a dreadful abyss between the streets of this village and the streets of the city in which I was born, between the children who shout *Neger!* today and those who shouted *Nigger!* yesterday—the abyss is experience, the American experience. The syllable hurled behind me today expresses, above all, wonder: I am a stranger here. But I am not a stranger in America and the same syllable riding on the American air expresses the war my presence has occasioned in the American soul.

For this village brings home to me this fact: that there was a day, and not really a very distant day, when Americans were scarcely Americans at all but discontented Europeans, facing a great unconquered continent and strolling, say, into a market-place and seeing black men for the first time. The shock this spectacle afforded is suggested, surely, by the promptness with which they decided that these black men were not really men but cattle. It is true that the necessity on the part of the settlers of the New World of reconciling their moral assumptions with the fact—and the necessity—of slavery enhanced immensely the charm of this idea, and it is also true that this idea expresses, with a truly American bluntness, the attitude which to varying extents all masters have had toward all slaves.

But between all former slaves and slave-owners and the drama which begins for Americans over three hundred years ago at Jamestown, there are at least two differences to be observed. The American Negro slave could not suppose, for one thing, as slaves in past epochs had supposed and often done, that he would ever be able to wrest the power from his master's hands. This was a supposition which the modern era, which was to bring about such vast changes in the aims and dimensions of power, put to death; it only begins, in unprecedented fashion, and with dreadful implications, to be resurrected today. But even had this supposition persisted with undiminished force, the American Negro slave could not have used it to lend his condition dignity, for the reason that this supposition rests on another: that the slave in exile yet remains related to his past, has some means—if only in memory—of revering and sustaining the forms of his former life, is able, in short, to maintain his identity.

This was not the case with the American Negro slave. He is unique among the black men of the world in that his past was taken from him, almost literally, at one blow. One wonders what on earth the first slave found to say to the first dark child he bore. I am told that there are Haitians able to trace their ancestry back to African kings, but any American Negro wishing to go back so far will find his journey through time abruptly arrested by the signature on the bill of sale which served as the entrance paper for his ancestor. At the time—to say nothing of the circumstances—of the enslavement of the captive black man who was to become the American Negro, there was not the remotest possibility that he would ever take power from his master's hands. There was no reason to suppose that his situation would ever change, nor was there, shortly, anything to indicate that his situation had ever been different. It was his necessity, in the words of E. Franklin Frazier, to find a "motive for living under American culture or die." The identity of the American Negro comes out of this extreme situation, and the evolution of this identity was a source of the most intolerable anxiety in the minds and the lives of his masters.

For the history of the American Negro is unique also in this: that the question of his humanity, and of his rights therefore as a human being, became a burning one for several generations of Americans, so burning a question that it ultimately became one of those used to divide the nation. It is out of this argument that the venom of the epithet *Nigger!* is derived. It is an argument which Europe has never had, and hence Europe quite sincerely fails to understand how or why the argument arose in the first place, why its effects are so frequently disastrous and always so unpredictable, why it refuses until today to be entirely settled. Europe's black possessions remained—and do remain—in Europe's colonies, at which remove they represented no threat to European identity. If they posed any problem at all for the European conscience, it was a problem which remained comfortingly abstract: in effect, the black man, *as a man,* did not exist for Europe. But in America, even as a slave, he was an inescapable part of the general social fabric and no American could escape having an attitude toward him. Americans attempt until today to make an abstraction of the Negro, but the very nature of these abstractions reveals the tremendous effects the presence of the Negro has had on the American character.

When one considers the history of the Negro in America it is of the greatest importance to recognize that the moral beliefs of a person, or a people, are never really as tenuous as life—which is not moral—very often causes them to appear; these create for them a frame of reference and a necessary hope, the hope being that when life has done its worst they will be enabled to rise above themselves and to triumph over life. Life would scarcely be bearable if this hope did not exist. Again, even when the worst has been said, to betray a belief is not by any means to have put oneself beyond its power; the betrayal of a belief is not the same thing as ceasing to believe. If this were not so there would be no moral standards in the world at all. Yet one must also recognize that morality is based on ideas and that all ideas are dangerous—dangerous because ideas can only lead to action and where the action leads no man can say. And dangerous in this respect: that confronted with the impossibility of remaining faithful to one's beliefs, and the equal impossibility of becoming free of them, one can be driven to the most inhuman excesses. The ideas on which American beliefs are based are not, though Americans often seem to think so, ideas which originated in America. They came out of Europe. And the establishment of democracy on the American continent was scarcely as radical a break with the past as was the necessity, which Americans faced, of broadening this concept to include black men.

This was, literally, a hard necessity. It was impossible, for one thing, for Americans to abandon their beliefs, not only because these beliefs alone seemed able to justify the sacrifices they had endured and the blood that they had spilled, but also because these beliefs afforded them their only bulwark against a moral chaos as absolute as the physical chaos of the continent it was their destiny to conquer. But in the situation in which Americans found themselves, these beliefs threatened an idea which, whether or not one likes to think so, is the very warp and woof of the heritage of the West, the idea of white supremacy.

Americans have made themselves notorious by the shrillness and the brutality with which they have insisted on this idea, but they did not invent it; and it has escaped the world's notice that those very excesses of which Americans have been guilty imply a certain, unprecedented uneasiness over the idea's life and power, if not, indeed, the idea's validity. The idea of white supremacy rests simply on the fact that white men are the creators of civilization (the present civilization, which is the only one that matters; all previous civilizations are simply "contributions" to our own) and are therefore civilization's guardians and defenders. Thus it was impossible for Americans to accept the black man as one of themselves, for to do so was to jeopardize their status as white men. But not so to accept him was to deny his human reality, his human weight and complexity, and the strain of denying the overwhelmingly undeniable forced Americans into rationalizations so fantastic that they approached the pathological.

At the root of the American Negro problem is the necessity of the American white man to find a way of living with the Negro in order to be able to live with himself. And the history of this problem can be reduced to the means used by Americans—lynch law and law, segregation and legal acceptance, terrorization and concession—either to come to terms with this necessity, or to find a way around it, or (most usually) to find a way of doing both these things at once. The resulting spectacle, at once foolish and dreadful, led someone to make the quite accurate observation that "the Negro-in-America is a form of insanity which overtakes white men."

In this long battle, a battle by no means finished, the unforeseeable effects of which will be felt by many future generations, the white man's motive was the protection of his identity; the black man was motivated by the need to establish an identity. And despite the terrorization which the Negro in America endured and endures sporadically until today, despite the cruel and totally inescapable ambivalence of his status in his country, the battle for his identity has long ago been won. He is not a visitor to the West, but a citizen there, an American; as American as the Americans who despise him, the Americans who fear him, the Americans who love him—the Americans who became less than themselves, or rose to be greater than themselves by virtue of the fact that the challenge he represented was inescapable. He is perhaps the only black man in the world whose relationship to white men is more terrible, more subtle, and more meaningful than the relationship of bitter possessed to uncertain possessor. His survival depended, and his development depends, on his ability to turn his peculiar status in the Western world to his own advantage and, it may be, to the very great advantage of that world. It remains for him to fashion out of his experience that which will give him sustenance, and a voice.

The cathedral of Chartres, I have said, says something to the people of this village which it cannot say to me; but it is important to understand that this cathedral says something to me which it cannot say to them. Perhaps they are struck by the power of the spires, the glory of the windows; but they have known God, after all, longer than I have known him, and in a different way, and I am terrified by the slippery bottomless well to be found in the crypt, down which heretics were hurled to death, and by the obscene, inescapable gargoyles jutting out of the stone and seeming to say that God and the devil can never be divorced. I doubt that the villagers think of the devil when they face a cathedral because they have never been identified with the devil. But I must accept the status which myth, if nothing else, gives me in the West before I can hope to change the myth.

Yet, if the American Negro has arrived at his identity by virtue of the absoluteness of his estrangement from his past, American white men still nourish the illusion that there is some means of recovering the European innocence, of returning to a state in which black men do not exist. This is one of the greatest errors Americans can make. The identity they fought so hard to protect has, by virtue of that battle, undergone a change: Americans are as unlike any other white people in the world as it is possible to be. I do not think, for example, that it is too much to suggest that the American vision of the world—which allows so little reality, generally speaking, for any of the darker forces in human life, which tends until today to paint moral issues in glaring black and white—owes a great deal to the battle waged by Americans to maintain between themselves and black men a human separation which could not be bridged. It is only now beginning to be borne in on us—very faintly, it must be admitted, very slowly, and very much against our will—that this vision of the world is dangerously inaccurate, and perfectly useless. For it protects our moral high-mindedness at the terrible expense of weakening our grasp of reality. People who shut their eyes to reality simply invite their own destruction, and anyone who insists on remaining in a state of innocence long after that innocence is dead turns himself into a monster.

The time has come to realize that the interracial drama acted out on the American continent has not only created a new black man, it has created a new white man, too. No road whatever will lead Americans back to the simplicity of this European village where white men still have the luxury of looking on me as a stranger. I am not, really, a stranger any longer for any American alive. One of the things that distinguishes Americans from other people is that no other people has ever been so deeply involved in the lives of black men, and vice versa. This fact faced, with all its implications, it can be seen that the history of the American Negro problem is not merely shameful, it is also something of an achievement. For even when the worst has been said, it must also be added that the perpetual challenge posed by this problem was always, somehow, perpetually met. It is precisely this black-white experience which may prove of indispensable value to us in the world we face today. This world is white no longer, and it will never be white again.

1953

Joan Didion

JOAN DIDION was born in Sacramento, California, on December 5, 1934, a fifth-generation descendant of pioneers who had helped settle the Sacramento Valley in the 1840s. In her autobiographical essays she frequently points out how different Sacramento is from the California most people think of: Hollywood, freeways, surfers, religious cults. Sacramento has always been farming country; Didion's family were landowners, their politics Republican, their religion Episcopal. She grew up in a world where the middle-class values of character, morality, and economy were firmly established.

During World War II her family was temporarily uprooted as they followed her father, an officer in the air corps, to air bases around the country, celebrating "makeshift Christmases in rented rooms." But with the end of the war they returned to Sacramento and a settled life again, where there were "teacups hand-painted with cabbage roses and signed 'E.M.,' my grandmother's initials" and they visited "the great-aunts on Sundays." After graduating from the local high school, Didion went to the University of California at Berkeley (A.B., 1956) and from there to New York, where she was an associate feature editor for *Vogue* for seven years. (As a senior at Berkeley she had won *Vogue's Prix de Paris.*) In 1964 she married John Gregory Dunne, a writer for *Time*, and a few months later they left New York for Los Angeles, intending to stay only six months; it was one of those leaves of absence from frustrating security that writers often take in order to see if they can make it on their own, just writing.

Fortunately, within a year Didion and Dunne had both established freelance associations with *The Saturday Evening Post*, and by the end of 1966 they shared a regular *Post* column entitled "Points West." (The two have also collaborated on the screenplays for *The Panic in Needle Park*, 1971, and *A Star Is Born*, 1976.) In 1968 Didion published *Slouching Towards Bethlehem*, a collection of her essays for the *Post* and other magazines, and she began receiving serious attention from literary critics. (An earlier novel, *Run River*, 1963, written while she was at *Vogue* and during a brief residency at the Bread Loaf Writers' Conference, had gone largely unnoticed.) What critics admired in *Slouching Towards Bethlehem* were Didion's economical style, her autobiographical honesty, and the intense clarity with which she reported some of the most grotesque aspects of life in America in the late sixties.

In 1970 Joan Didion published *Play It as It Lays*, a novel of apocalyptic vision reminiscent of Nathanael West's *The Day of the Locust*. A depressing tale of abortion, divorce, and suicide in Hollywood and Las Vegas, *Play It as It Lays* is also, in the end, a story of survival: despite all that happens to her, the central character, Maria Wyeth, does not give up. As she says at the end, "I know what 'nothing' means, and keep on playing."

In her next novel, *A Book of Common Prayer* (1977), Didion again portrays a woman who attempts to survive a catastrophic life. Charlotte Douglas, like Maria Wyeth, lacks heroic qualities; in many ways she is shallow, foolish, weak. Coming out of a protected, monied background, her ability to cope with life's difficulties is as ritualized as the public responses codified in the Episcopal Church's *Book of Common Prayer*—not enough, Didion might say, in a world as deceptively evil as ours. And yet, again, in the novel's moral complexity, Charlotte Douglas ends up being a deeply sympathetic character and a hero of sorts.

In 1979 a second collection of essays, entitled *The White Album*, was published. Further elaborating images of personal and cultural breakdown, Didion writes with painful honesty about the difficulty of maintaining a sense of meaningful purpose in a fragmented world. In the essay "On the Morning After the Sixties" she explains the difference between the private values of her own generation and the collective beliefs of young people in the late sixties and early seventies: "If I could believe that going to a barricade would affect man's fate in the slightest I would go to that barricade, and often wish that I could, but it would be less than honest to say that I expect to happen on such a happy ending."

As a writer Joan Didion is bringing us reports from the

"front," as she says in "Why I Write," and therefore she will write "in a no-nonsense way." It is a style of ellipses and fragments, of sharp images and paradoxical juxtapositions, as different as one could imagine from the style of an E. B. White or Lewis Thomas, and yet as appropriate to her themes as their styles are to their themes, and no doubt just as carefully crafted. Didion indicates what an extremely conscious understanding of style she has when she says: "To shift the structure of a sentence alters the meaning of that sentence, as definitely and inflexibly as the position of a camera alters the meaning of the object photographed. Many people know about camera angles now, but not so many know about sentences."

ON MORALITY

As it happens I am in Death Valley, in a room at the Enterprise Motel and Trailer Park, and it is July, and it is hot. In fact it is 119°. I cannot seem to make the air conditioner work, but there is a small refrigerator, and I can wrap ice cubes in a towel and hold them against the small of my back. With the help of the ice cubes I have been trying to think, because *The American Scholar* asked me to, in some abstract way about "morality," a word I distrust more every day, but my mind veers inflexibly toward the particular.

Here are some particulars. At midnight last night, on the road in from Las Vegas to Death Valley Junction, a car hit a shoulder and turned over. The driver, very young and apparently drunk, was killed instantly. His girl was found alive but bleeding internally, deep in shock. I talked this afternoon to the nurse who had driven the girl to the nearest doctor, 185 miles across the floor of the Valley and three ranges of lethal mountain road. The nurse explained that her husband, a talc miner, had stayed on the highway with the boy's body until the coroner could get over the mountains from Bishop, at dawn today. "You can't just leave a body on the highway," she said. "It's immoral."

It was one instance in which I did not distrust the word, because she meant something quite specific. She meant that if a body is left alone for even a few minutes on the desert, the coyotes close in and eat the flesh. Whether or not a corpse is torn apart by coyotes may seem only a sentimental consideration, but of course it is more: one of the promises we make to one another is that we will try to retrieve our casualties, try not to abandon our dead to the coyotes. If we have been taught to keep our promises—if, in the simplest terms, our upbringing is good enough—we stay with the body, or have bad dreams.

I am talking, of course, about the kind of social code that is sometimes called, usually pejoratively, "wagon-train morality." In fact that is precisely what it is. For better or worse, we are what we learned as children: my own childhood was illuminated by graphic litanies of the grief awaiting those who failed in their loyalties to each other. The Donner-Reed Party, starving in the Sierra snows, all the ephemera of civilization gone save that one vestigial taboo, the provision that no one should eat his own blood kin. The Jayhawkers, who quarreled and separated not far from where I am tonight. Some of them died in the Funerals and some of them died down near Badwater and most of the rest of them died in the Panamints. A woman who got through gave the Valley its name. Some might say that the Jayhawkers were killed by the desert summer, and the Donner Party by the mountain winter, by circumstances beyond control; we were taught instead that they had somewhere abdicated their responsibilities, somehow breached their primary loyalties, or they would not have found themselves helpless in the mountain winter or the desert summer, would not have given way to acrimony, would not have deserted one another, would not have *failed.* In brief, we heard such stories as cautionary tales, and they still suggest the only kind of "morality" that seems to me to have any but the most potentially mendacious meaning.

You are quite possibly impatient with me by now; I am talking, you want to say, about a "morality" so primitive that it scarcely deserves the name, a code that has as its point only survival, not the attainment of the ideal good. Exactly. Particularly out here tonight, in this country so ominous and terrible that to live in it is to live with antimatter, it is difficult to believe that "the good" is a knowable quantity. Let me tell you what it is like out here tonight. Stories travel at night on the desert. Someone gets in his pickup and drives a couple of hundred miles for a beer, and he carries news of what is happening, back wherever he came from. Then he drives another hundred miles for another beer, and passes along stories from the last place as well as from the one before; it is a network kept alive by people whose instincts tell them that if they do not keep moving at night in the desert they will lose all reason. Here is a story that is going around the desert tonight: over across the Nevada line, sheriff's deputies are diving in some underground pools, trying to retrieve a couple of bodies known to be in the hole. The widow of one of the drowned boys is over there; she is eighteen, and pregnant, and is said not to leave the hole. The divers go down and come up, and she just stands there and stares into the water. They have been diving for ten days but have found no bottom to the caves, no bodies and no trace of them, only the black 90° water going down and down and down, and a single translucent fish, not classified. The story tonight is that one of the divers has been hauled up incoherent, out of his head, shouting—until they got him out of there so that the widow could not hear—about water that got hotter instead of cooler as he went down, about light flickering through the water, about magma, about underground nuclear testing.

That is the tone stories take out here, and there are quite a few of them. And it is more than the stories alone. Across the road at the Faith Community Church a couple of dozen old people, come here to live in trailers and die in the sun, are holding a prayer sing. I cannot hear them and do not want to. What I can hear are occasional coyotes and a constant chorus of "Baby the Rain Must Fall" from the jukebox in the Snake Room next door, and if I were also to hear those dying voices, those Midwestern voices drawn to this lunar country for some unimaginable atavistic rites, *rock of ages cleft for me*, I think I would lose my own reason. Every now and then I imagine I hear a rattlesnake, but my husband says that it is a faucet, a paper rustling, the wind. Then he stands by a window, and plays a flashlight over the dry wash outside.

What does it mean? It means nothing manageable. There is some sinister hysteria in the air out here tonight, some hint of the monstrous perversion to which any human idea can come. "I followed my own conscience." "I did what I thought was right." How many madmen have said it and meant it? How many murderers? Klaus Fuchs said it, and the men who committed the Mountain Meadows Massacre said it, and Alfred Rosenberg said it. And, as we are rotely and rather presumptuously reminded by those who would say it now, Jesus said it. Maybe we have all said it, and maybe we have been wrong. Except on that most primitive level—our loyalties to those we love—what could be more arrogant than to claim the primacy of personal conscience? ("Tell me," a rabbi asked Daniel Bell when he said, as a child, that he did not believe in God. "Do you think God cares?") At least some of the time, the world appears to me as a painting by Hieronymous Bosch; were I to follow my conscience then, it would lead me out onto the desert with Marion Faye, out to where he stood in *The Deer Park* looking east to Los Alamos and praying, as if for rain, that it would happen: ". . . *let it come and clear the rot and the stench and the stink, let it come for all of everywhere, just so it comes and the world stands clear in the white dead dawn.*"

Of course you will say that I do not have the right, even if I had the power, to inflict that unreasonable conscience upon you; nor do I want you to inflict your conscience, however reasonable, however enlightened, upon me. ("We must be aware of the dangers which lie in our most generous wishes," Lionel Trilling once wrote. "Some paradox of our nature leads us, when once we have made our fellow men the objects of our enlightened interest, to go on to make them the objects of our pity, then of our wisdom, ultimately of our coercion.") That the ethic of conscience is intrinsically insidious seems scarcely a revelatory point, but it is one raised with increasing infrequency; even those who do raise it tend to *segue* with troubling readiness into the quite contradictory position that the ethic of conscience is dangerous when it is "wrong," and admirable when it is "right."

You see I want to be quite obstinate about insisting that we have no way of knowing—beyond that fundamental loyalty to the social code—what is "right" and what is "wrong," what is "good" and what "evil." I dwell so upon this because the most disturbing aspect of "morality" seems to me to be the frequency with which the word now appears; in the press, on television, in the most perfunctory kinds of conversation. Questions of straightforward power (or survival) politics, questions of quite indifferent public policy, questions of almost anything: they are all assigned these factitious moral burdens. There is something facile going on, some self-indulgence at work. Of course we would all like to "believe" in something, like to assuage our private guilts in public causes, like to lose our tiresome selves; like, perhaps, to transform the white flag of defeat at home into the brave white banner of battle away from home. And of course it is all right to do that; that is how, immemorially, things have gotten done. But I think it is all right only so long as we do not delude ourselves about what we are doing, and why. It is all right only so long as we remember that all the *ad hoc* committees, all the picket lines, all the brave signatures in *The New York Times*, all the tools of agitprop straight across the spectrum, do not confer upon anyone any *ipso facto* virtue. It is all right only so long as we recognize that the end may or may not be expedient, may or may not be a good idea, but in any case has nothing to do with "morality." Because when we start deceiving ourselves into thinking not that we want something or need something, not that it is a pragmatic necessity for us to have it, but that it is a *moral imperative* that we have it, then is when we join the fashionable madmen, and then is when the thin whine of hysteria is heard in the land, and then is when we are in bad trouble. And I suspect we are already there.

1965

GOODBYE TO ALL THAT

How many miles to Babylon?
Three score miles and ten—
Can I get there by candlelight?
Yes, and back again—
If your feet are nimble and light
You can get there by candlelight.

It is easy to see the beginnings of things, and harder to see the ends. I can remember now, with a clarity that makes the nerves in the back of my neck constrict, when New York began for me, but I cannot lay my finger upon the moment it ended, can never cut through the ambiguities and second starts and broken resolves to the exact place on the page where the heroine is no longer as optimistic as she once was. When I first saw New York I was twenty, and it was summertime, and I got off a DC-7 at the old Idlewild temporary terminal in a new dress which had seemed very smart in Sacramento but seemed less smart already, even in the old Idlewild temporary terminal, and the warm air smelled of mildew and some instinct, programmed by all the movies I had ever seen and all the songs I had ever heard sung and all the stories I had ever read about New York, informed me that it would never be quite the same again. In fact it never was. Some time later there was a song on all the jukeboxes on the upper East Side that went "but where is the schoolgirl who used to be me," and if it was late enough at night I used to wonder that. I know now that almost everyone wonders something like that, sooner or later and no matter what he or she is doing, but one of the mixed blessings of being twenty and twenty-one and even twenty-three is the conviction that nothing like this, all evidence to the contrary notwithstanding, has ever happened to anyone before.

Of course it might have been some other city, had circumstances been different and the time been different and had I been different, might have been Paris or Chicago or even San Francisco, but because I am talking about myself I am talking here about New York. That first night I opened my window on the bus into town and watched for the skyline, but all I could see were the wastes of Queens and the big signs that said MIDTOWN TUNNEL THIS LANE and then a flood of summer rain (even that seemed remarkable and exotic, for I had come out of the West where there was no summer rain), and for the next three days I sat wrapped in blankets in a hotel room air-conditioned to 35° and tried to get over a bad cold and a high fever. It did not occur to me to call a doctor, because I knew none, and although it did occur to me to call the desk and ask that the air conditioner be turned off, I never called, because I did not know how much to tip whoever might come—was anyone ever so young? I am here to tell you that someone was. All I could do during those three days was talk long-distance to the boy I already knew I would never marry in the spring. I would stay in New York, I told him, just six months, and I could see the

Brooklyn Bridge from my window. As it turned out the bridge was the Triborough, and I stayed eight years.

In retrospect it seems to me that those days before I knew the names of all the bridges were happier than the ones that came later, but perhaps you will see that as we go along. Part of what I want to tell you is what it is like to be young in New York, how six months can become eight years with the deceptive ease of a film dissolve, for that is how those years appear to me now, in a long sequence of sentimental dissolves and old-fashioned trick shots—the Seagram Building fountains dissolve into snowflakes, I enter a revolving door at twenty and come out a good deal older, and on a different street. But most particularly I want to explain to you, and in the process perhaps to myself, why I no longer live in New York. It is often said that New York is a city for only the very rich and the very poor. It is less often said that New York is also, at least for those of us who came there from somewhere else, a city for only the very young.

I remember once, one cold bright December evening in New York, suggesting to a friend who complained of having been around too long that he come with me to a party where there would be, I assured him with the bright resourcefulness of twenty-three, "new faces." He laughed literally until he choked, and I had to roll down the taxi window and hit him on the back. "New faces," he said finally, "don't tell me about *new faces.*" It seemed that the last time he had gone to a party where he had been promised "new faces," there had been fifteen people in the room, and he had already slept with five of the women and owed money to all but two of the men. I laughed with him, but the first snow had just begun to fall and the big Christmas trees glittered yellow and white as far as I could see up Park Avenue and I had a new dress and it would be a long while before I would come to understand the particular moral of the story.

It would be a long while because, quite simply, I was in love with New York. I do not mean "love" in any colloquial way, I mean that I was in love with the city, the way you love the first person who ever touches you and never love anyone quite that way again. I remember walking across Sixty-second Street one twilight that first spring, or the second spring, they were all alike for a while. I was late to meet someone but I stopped at Lexington Avenue and bought a peach and stood on the corner eating it and knew that I had come out of the West and reached the mirage. I could taste the peach and feel the soft air blowing from a subway grating on my legs and I could smell lilac and garbage and expensive perfume and I knew that it would cost something sooner or later—because I did not belong there, did not come from there—but when you are twenty-two or twenty-three, you figure that later you will have a high emotional balance, and be able to pay whatever it costs. I still believed in possibilities then, still had the sense, so peculiar to New York, that something extraordinary would happen any minute, any day, any month. I was making only $65 or $70 a week then ("Put yourself in Hattie Carnegie's hands," I was advised without the slightest trace of irony by an editor of the magazine for which I worked), so little money that some weeks I had to charge food at Bloomingdale's gourmet shop in order to eat, a fact which went unmentioned in the letters I wrote to California. I never told my father that I needed money because then he would have sent it, and I would never know if I could do it by myself. At that time making a living seemed a game to me, with arbitrary but quite inflexible rules. And except on a certain kind of winter evening—six-thirty in the Seventies, say, already dark and bitter with a wind off the river, when I would be walking very fast toward a bus and would look in the bright windows of brownstones and see cooks working in clean kitchens and imagine women lighting candles on the floor above and beautiful children being bathed on the floor above that—except on nights like those, I never felt poor; I had the feeling that if I needed money I could always get it. I could write a syndicated column for teenagers under the name "Debbi Lynn" or I could smuggle gold into India or I could become a $100 call girl, and none of it would matter.

Nothing was irrevocable; everything was within reach. Just around every corner lay something curious and interesting, something I had never before seen or done or known about. I could go to a party and meet someone who called himself Mr. Emotional Appeal and ran The Emotional Appeal Institute or Tina

Onassis Blandford or a Florida cracker who was then a regular on what he called "the Big C," the Southampton–El Morocco circuit ("I'm well-connected on the Big C, honey," he would tell me over collard greens on his vast borrowed terrace), or the widow of the celery king of the Harlem market or a piano salesman from Bonne Terre, Missouri, or someone who had already made and lost two fortunes in Midland, Texas. I could make promises to myself and to other people and there would be all the time in the world to keep them. I could stay up all night and make mistakes, and none of it would count.

You see I was in a curious position in New York: it never occurred to me that I was living a real life there. In my imagination I was always there for just another few months, just until Christmas or Easter or the first warm day in May. For that reason I was most comfortable in the company of Southerners. They seemed to be in New York as I was, on some indefinitely extended leave from wherever they belonged, disinclined to consider the future, temporary exiles who always knew when the flights left for New Orleans or Memphis or Richmond or, in my case, California. Someone who lives always with a plane schedule in the drawer lives on a slightly different calendar. Christmas, for example, was a difficult season. Other people could take it in stride, going to Stowe or going abroad or going for the day to their mothers' places in Connecticut; those of us who believed that we lived somewhere else would spend it making and canceling airline reservations, waiting for weatherbound flights as if for the last plane out of Lisbon in 1940, and finally comforting one another, those of us who were left, with the oranges and mementos and smoked-oyster stuffings of childhood, gathering close, colonials in a far country.

Which is precisely what we were. I am not sure that it is possible for anyone brought up in the East to appreciate entirely what New York, the idea of New York, means to those of us who came out of the West and the South. To an Eastern child, particularly a child who has always had an uncle on Wall Street and who has spent several hundred Saturdays first at F. A. O. Schwarz and being fitted for shoes at Best's and then waiting under the Biltmore clock and dancing to Lester Lanin, New York is just a city, albeit *the* city, a plausible place for people to live. But to those of us who came from places where no one had heard of Lester Lanin and Grand Central Station was a Saturday radio program, where Wall Street and Fifth Avenue and Madison Avenue were not places at all but abstractions ("Money," and "High Fashion," and "The Hucksters"), New York was no mere city. It was instead an infinitely romantic notion, the mysterious nexus of all love and money and power, the shining and perishable dream itself. To think of "living" there was to reduce the miraculous to the mundane; one does not "live" at Xanadu.

In fact it was difficult in the extreme for me to understand those young women for whom New York was not simply an ephemeral Estoril but a real place, girls who bought toasters and installed new cabinets in their apartments and committed themselves to some reasonable future. I never bought any furniture in New York. For a year or so I lived in other people's apartments; after that I lived in the Nineties in an apartment furnished entirely with things taken from storage by a friend whose wife had moved away. And when I left the apartment in the Nineties (that was when I was leaving everything, when it was all breaking up) I left everything in it, even my winter clothes and the map of Sacramento County I had hung on the bedroom wall to remind me who I was, and I moved into a monastic four-room floor-through on Seventy-fifth Street. "Monastic" is perhaps misleading here, implying some chic severity; until after I was married and my husband moved some furniture in, there was nothing at all in those four rooms except a cheap double mattress and box springs, ordered by telephone the day I decided to move, and two French garden chairs lent me by a friend who imported them. (It strikes me now that the people I knew in New York all had curious and self-defeating sidelines. They imported garden chairs which did not sell very well at Hammacher Schlemmer or they tried to market hair straighteners in Harlem or they ghosted exposés of Murder Incorporated for Sunday supplements. I think that perhaps none of us was very serious, *engagé* only about our most private lives.)

All I ever did to that apartment was hang fifty yards of yellow theatrical silk across the bedroom windows, because I had some idea that the gold light would make me feel better, but I did not bother to weight the curtains correctly and all that summer the long panels of transparent golden silk would blow out the windows and get tangled and drenched in the afternoon thunderstorms. That was the year, my twenty-eighth, when I was discovering that not all of the promises would be kept, that some things are in fact irrevocable and that it had counted after all, every evasion and every procrastination, every mistake, every word, all of it.

That is what it was all about, wasn't it? Promises? Now when New York comes back to me it comes in hallucinatory flashes, so clinically detailed that I sometimes wish that memory would effect the distortion with which it is commonly credited. For a lot of the time I was in New York I used a perfume called *Fleurs de Rocaille,* and then *L'Air du Temps,* and now the slightest trace of either can short-circuit my connections for the rest of the day. Nor can I smell Henri Bendel jasmine soap without falling back into the past, or the particular mixture of spices used for boiling crabs. There were barrels of crab boil in a Czech place in the Eighties where I once shopped. Smells, of course, are notorious memory stimuli, but there are other things which affect me the same way. Blue-and-white striped sheets. Vermouth cassis. Some faded nightgowns which were new in 1959 or 1960, and some chiffon scarves I bought about the same time.

I suppose that a lot of us who have been young in New York have the same scenes on our home screens. I remember sitting in a lot of apartments with a slight headache about five o'clock in the morning. I had a friend who could not sleep, and he knew a few other people who had the same trouble, and we would watch the sky lighten and have a last drink with no ice and then go home in the early morning light, when the streets were clean and wet (had it rained in the night? we never knew) and the few cruising taxis still had their headlights on and the only color was the red and green of traffic signals. The White Rose bars opened very early in the morning; I recall waiting in one of them to watch an astronaut go into space, waiting so long that at the moment it actually happened I had my eyes not on the television screen but on a cockroach on the tile floor. I liked the bleak branches above Washington Square at dawn, and the monochromatic flatness of Second Avenue, the fire escapes and the grilled storefronts peculiar and empty in their perspective.

It is relatively hard to fight at six-thirty or seven in the morning, without any sleep, which was perhaps one reason we stayed up all night, and it seemed to me a pleasant time of day. The windows were shuttered in that apartment in the Nineties and I could sleep a few hours and then go to work. I could work then on two or three hours' sleep and a container of coffee from Chock Full O' Nuts. I liked going to work, liked the soothing and satisfactory rhythm of getting out a magazine, liked the orderly progression of four-color closings and two-color closings and black-and-white closings and then The Product, no abstraction but something which looked effortlessly glossy and could be picked up on a newsstand and weighed in the hand. I liked all the minutiae of proofs and layouts, liked working late on the nights the magazine went to press, sitting and reading *Variety* and waiting for the copy desk to call. From my office I could look across town to the weather signal on the Mutual of New York Building and the lights that alternately spelled out TIME and LIFE above Rockefeller Plaza; that pleased me obscurely, and so did walking uptown in the mauve eight o'clocks of early summer evenings and looking at things, Lowestoft tureens in Fifty-seventh Street windows, people in evening clothes trying to get taxis, the trees just coming into full leaf, the lambent air, all the sweet promises of money and summer.

Some years passed, but I still did not lose that sense of wonder about New York. I began to cherish the loneliness of it, the sense that at any given time no one need know where I was or what I was doing. I liked walking, from the East River over to the Hudson and back on brisk days, down around the Village on warm days. A friend would leave me the key to her apartment in the West Village when she was out of town, and sometimes I would just move down there, because by that time the telephone was beginning to bother me (the canker, you see, was already in the rose) and not many people had that number. I remember one day when someone who did have the West Village number came to pick me up for lunch there, and we both had hangovers, and I cut my finger opening him a beer and burst into tears, and we walked to a Spanish restaurant and drank Bloody Marys and *gazpacho* until we felt better. I was not then guilt-ridden about spending afternoons that way, because I still had all the afternoons in the world.

And even that late in the game I still liked going to parties, all parties, bad parties, Saturday-afternoon parties given by recently married couples who lived in Stuyvesant Town, West Side parties given by unpublished or failed writers who served cheap red wine and talked about going to Guadalajara, Village parties where all the guests worked for advertising agencies and voted for Reform Democrats, press parties at Sardi's, the worst kinds of parties. You will have perceived by now that I was not one to profit by the experience of others, that it was a very long time indeed before I stopped believing in new faces and began to understand the lesson in that story, which was that it is distinctly possible to stay too long at the Fair.

I could not tell you when I began to understand that. All I know is that it was very bad when I was twenty-eight. Everything that was said to me I seemed to have heard before, and I could no longer listen. I could no longer sit in little bars near Grand Central and listen to someone complaining of his wife's inability to cope with the help while he missed another train to Connecticut. I no longer had any interest in hearing about the advances other people had received from their publishers, about plays which were having second-act trouble in Philadelphia, or about people I would like very much if only I would come out and meet them. I had already met them, always. There were certain parts of the city which I had to avoid. I could not bear upper Madison Avenue on weekday mornings (this was a particularly inconvenient aversion, since I then lived just fifty or sixty feet east of Madison), because I would see women walking Yorkshire terriers and shopping at Gristede's, and some Veblenesque gorge would rise in my throat. I could not go to Times Square in the afternoon, or to the New York Public Library for any reason whatsoever. One day I could not go into a Schrafft's; the next day it would be Bonwit Teller.

I hurt the people I cared about, and insulted those I did not. I cut myself off from the one person who was closer to me than any other. I cried until I was not even aware when I was crying and when I was not, cried in elevators and in taxis and in Chinese laundries, and when I went to the doctor he said only that I seemed to be depressed, and should see a "specialist." He wrote down a psychiatrist's name and address for me, but I did not go.

Instead I got married, which as it turned out was a very good thing to do but badly timed, since I still could not walk on upper Madison Avenue in the mornings and still could not talk to people and still cried in Chinese laundries. I had never before understood what "despair" meant, and I am not sure that I understand now, but I understood that year. Of course I could not work. I could not even get dinner with any degree of certainty, and I would sit in the apartment on Seventy-fifth Street paralyzed until my husband would call from his office and say gently that I did not have to get dinner, that I could meet him at Michael's Pub or at Toots Shor's or at Sardi's East. And then one morning in April (we had been married in January) he called and told me that he wanted to get out of New York for a while, that he would take a six-month leave of absence, that we would go somewhere.

It was three years ago that he told me that, and we have lived in Los Angeles since. Many of the people we knew in New York think this a curious aberration, and in fact tell us so. There is no possible, no adequate answer to that, and so we give certain stock answers, the answers everyone gives. I talk about how difficult it would be for us to "afford" to live in New York right now, about how much "space" we need. All I mean is that I was very young in New York, and that at some point the golden rhythm was broken, and I am not that young any more. The last time I was in New York was in a cold January, and everyone was ill and tired. Many of the people I used to know there had moved to Dallas or had gone on Antabuse or had bought a farm in New Hampshire. We stayed ten days, and then we took an afternoon flight back to Los Angeles, and on the way home from the airport that night I could see the moon on the Pacific and smell jasmine all around and we both knew that there was no longer any point in keeping the apartment we still kept in New York. There were years when I called Los Angeles "the Coast," but they seem a long time ago.

1967

ON GOING HOME

I am home for my daughter's first birthday. By "home" I do not mean the house in Los Angeles where my husband and I and the baby live, but the place where my family is, in the Central Valley of California. It is a vital although troublesome distinction. My husband likes my family but is uneasy in their house, because once there I fall into their ways, which are difficult, oblique, deliberately inarticulate, not my husband's ways. We live in dusty houses ("D-U-S-T," he once wrote with his finger on surfaces all over the house, but no one noticed it) filled with mementos quite without value to him (what could the Canton dessert plates mean to him? how could he have known about the assay scales, why should he care if he did know?), and we appear to talk exclusively about people we know who have been committed to mental hospitals, about people we know who have been booked on drunk-driving charges, and about property, particularly about property, land, price per acre and C-2 zoning and assessments and freeway access. My brother does not understand my husband's inability to perceive the advantage in the rather common real-estate transaction known as "sale-leaseback," and my husband in turn does not understand why so many of the people he hears about in my father's house have recently been committed to mental hospitals or booked on drunk-driving charges. Nor does he understand that when we talk about sale-leasebacks and right-of-way condemnations we are talking in code about the things we like best, the yellow fields and the cottonwoods and the rivers rising and falling and the mountain roads closing when the heavy snow comes in. We miss each other's points, have another drink and regard the fire. My brother refers to my husband, in his presence, as "Joan's husband." Marriage is the classic betrayal.

Or perhaps it is not any more. Sometimes I think that those of us who are now in our thirties were born into the last generation to carry the burden of "home," to find in family life the source of all tension and drama. I had by all objective accounts a "normal" and a "happy" family situation, and yet I was almost thirty years old before I could talk to my family on the telephone without crying after I had hung up. We did not fight. Nothing was wrong. And yet some nameless anxiety colored the emotional charges between me and the place that I came from. The question of whether or not you could go home again was a very real part of the sentimental and largely literary baggage with which we left home in the fifties; I suspect that it is irrelevant to the children born of the fragmentation after World War II. A few weeks ago in a San Francisco bar I saw a pretty young girl on crystal take off her clothes and dance for the cash prize in an "amateur-topless" contest. There was no particular sense of moment about this, none of the effect of romantic degradation, of "dark journey," for which my generation strived so assiduously. What sense could that girl possibly make of, say, *Long Day's Journey into Night*? Who is beside the point?

That I am trapped in this particular irrelevancy is never more apparent to me than when I am home. Paralyzed by the neurotic lassitude engendered by meeting one's past at every turn, around every corner, inside every cupboard, I go aimlessly from room to room. I decide to meet it head-on and clean out a drawer, and I spread the contents on the bed. A bathing suit I wore the summer I was seventeen. A letter of rejection from *The Nation*, an aerial photograph of the site for a shopping center my father did not build in 1954. Three teacups hand-painted with cabbage roses and signed "E.M.," my grandmother's initials. There is no final solution for letters of rejection from *The Nation* and teacups hand-painted in 1900. Nor is there any answer to snapshots of one's grandfather as a young man on skis, surveying around Donner Pass in the year 1910. I smooth out the snapshot and look into his face, and do and do not see my own. I close the drawer, and have another cup of coffee with my mother. We get along very well, veterans of a guerrilla war we never understood.

Days pass. I see no one. I come to dread my husband's evening call, not only because he is full of news of what by now seems to me our remote life in Los Angeles, people he has seen, letters which require attention, but because he asks what I have been doing, suggests uneasily that I get out, drive to San Francisco or Berkeley. Instead I drive across the river to a family graveyard. It has been vandalized since my last visit and the monuments are broken, overturned in the dry grass. Because I once saw a rattlesnake in the grass I stay in the car and listen to a country-and-Western station. Later I drive with my father to a ranch he has in the foothills. The man who runs his cattle on it asks us to the roundup, a week from Sunday, and although I know that I will be in Los Angeles I say, in the oblique way my family talks, that I will come. Once home I mention the broken monuments in the graveyard. My mother shrugs.

I go to visit my great-aunts. A few of them think now that I am my cousin, or their daughter who died young. We recall an anecdote about a relative last seen in 1948, and they ask if I still like living in New York City. I have lived in Los Angeles for three years, but I say that I do. The baby is offered a horehound drop, and I am slipped a dollar bill "to buy a treat." Questions trail off, answers are abandoned, the baby plays with the dust motes in a shaft of afternoon sun.

It is time for the baby's birthday party: a white cake, strawberry-marshmallow ice cream, a bottle of champagne saved from another party. In the evening, after she has gone to sleep, I kneel beside the crib and touch her face, where it is pressed against the slats, with mine. She is an open and trusting child, unprepared for and unaccustomed to the ambushes of family life, and perhaps it is just as well that I can offer her little of that life. I would like to give her more. I would like to promise her that she will grow up with a sense of her cousins and of rivers and of her great-grandmother's teacups, would like to pledge her a picnic on a river with fried chicken and her hair uncombed, would like to give her *home* for her birthday, but we live differently now and I can promise her nothing like that. I give her a xylophone and a sundress from Madeira, and promise to tell her a funny story.

1967

ON THE MORNING AFTER THE SIXTIES

I am talking here about being a child of my time. When I think about the Sixties now I think about an afternoon not of the Sixties at all, an afternoon early in my sophomore year at Berkeley, a bright autumn Saturday in 1953. I was lying on a leather couch in a fraternity house (there had been a lunch for the alumni, my date had gone on to the game, I do not now recall why I had stayed behind), lying there alone reading a book by Lionel Trilling and listening to a middle-aged man pick out on a piano in need of tuning the melodic line to "Blue Room." All that afternoon he sat at the piano and all that afternoon he played "Blue Room" and he never got it right. I can hear and see it still, the wrong note in "We will thrive on / Keep alive on," the sunlight falling through the big windows, the man picking up his drink and beginning again and telling me, without ever saying a word, something I had not known before about bad marriages and wasted time and looking backward. That such an afternoon would now seem implausible in every detail—the idea of having had a "date" for a football lunch now seems to me so exotic as to be almost czarist—suggests the extent to which the narrative on which many of us grew up no longer applies.

The distance we have come from the world in which I went to college was on my mind quite a bit during those seasons when not only Berkeley but dozens of other campuses were periodically shut down, incipient battlegrounds, their borders sealed. To think of Berkeley as it was in the Fifties was not to think of barricades and reconstituted classes. "Reconstitution" would have sounded to us then like Newspeak, and barricades are never personal. We were all very personal then, sometimes relentlessly so, and, at that point where we either act or do not act, most of us are still. I suppose I am talking about just that: the ambiguity of belonging to a generation distrustful of political highs, the historical irrelevancy of growing up convinced that the heart of darkness lay not in some error of social organization but in man's own blood. If man was bound to err, then any social organization was bound to be in error. It was a premise which still seems to me accurate enough, but one which robbed us early of a certain capacity for surprise.

At Berkeley in the Fifties no one was surprised by anything at all, a *donnée* which tended to render discourse less than spirited, and debate nonexistent. The world was by definition imperfect, and so of course was the university. There was some talk even then about IBM cards, but on balance the notion that free education for tens of thousands of people might involve automation did not seem unreasonable. We took it for granted that the Board of Regents would sometimes act wrongly. We simply avoided those students rumored to be FBI informers. We were that generation called "silent," but we were silent neither, as some thought, because we shared the period's official optimism nor, as others thought, because we feared its official repression. We were silent because the exhilaration of social action seemed to many of us just one more way of escaping the personal, of masking for a while that dread of the meaningless which was man's fate.

To have assumed that particular fate so early was the peculiarity of my generation. I think now that we were the last generation to identify with adults. That most of us have found adulthood just as morally ambiguous as we expected it to be falls perhaps into the category of prophecies self-fulfilled: I am simply not sure. I am telling you only how it was. The mood of Berkeley in those years was one of mild but chronic "depression," against which I remember certain small things that seemed to me somehow explications, dazzling in their clarity, of the world I was about to enter: I remember a woman picking daffodils in the rain one day when I was walking in the hills. I remember a teacher who drank too much one night and revealed his fright and bitterness. I remember my real joy at discovering for the first time how language worked, at discovering, for example, that the central line of *Heart of Darkness* was a postscript. All such images were personal, and the personal was all that most of us expected to find. We would make a separate peace. We would do graduate work in Middle English, we would go abroad. We would make some money and live on a ranch. We would survive outside history, in a kind of *idée fixe* referred to always, during the years I spent at Berkeley, as "some little town with a decent beach."

As it worked out I did not find or even look for the little town with the decent beach. I sat in the large bare apartment in which I lived my junior and senior years (I had lived awhile in a sorority, the Tri Delt house, and had left it, typically, not over any "issue" but because I, the implacable "I," did not like living with sixty people) and I read Camus and Henry James and I watched a flowering plum come in and out of blossom and at night, most nights, I walked outside and looked up to where the cyclotron and the bevatron glowed on the dark hillside, unspeakable mysteries which engaged me, in the style of my time, only personally. Later I got out of Berkeley and went to New York and later I got out of New York and came to Los Angeles. What I have made for myself is personal, but is not exactly peace. Only one person I knew at Berkeley later discovered an ideology, dealt himself into history, cut himself loose from both his own dread and his own time. A few of the people I knew at Berkeley killed themselves not long after. Another attempted suicide in Mexico and then, in a recovery which seemed in many ways a more advanced derangement, came home and joined the Bank of America's three-year executive-training program. Most of us live less theatrically, but remain the survivors of a peculiar and inward time. If I could believe that going to a barricade would affect man's fate in the slightest I would go to that barricade, and quite often I wish that I could, but it would be less than honest to say that I expect to happen upon such a happy ending.

1970

WHY I WRITE

Of course I stole the title for this talk from George Orwell. One reason I stole it was that I like the sound of the words: *Why I Write.* There you have three short unambiguous words that share a sound, and the sound they share is this:

I
I
I

In many ways writing is the act of saying *I*, of imposing oneself upon other people, of saying *listen to me, see it my way, change your mind.* It's an aggressive, even a hostile act. You can disguise its aggressiveness all you want with veils of subordinate clauses and qualifiers and tentative subjunctives, with ellipses and evasions—with the whole manner of intimating rather than claiming, of alluding rather than stating—but there's no getting around the fact that setting words on paper is the tactic of a secret bully, an invasion, an imposition of the writer's sensibility on the reader's most private space.

I stole the title not only because the words sounded right but because they seemed to sum up, in a no-nonsense way, all I have to tell you. Like many writers I have only this one "subject," this one "area": the act of writing. I can bring you no reports from any other front. I may have other interests: I am "interested," for example, in marine biology, but I don't flatter myself that you would come out to hear me talk about it. I am not a scholar. I am not in the least an intellectual, which is not to say that when I hear the word "intellectual" I reach for my gun, but only to say that I do not think in abstracts. During the years when I was an undergraduate at Berkeley I tried, with a kind of hopeless late-adolescent energy, to buy some temporary visa into the world of ideas, to forge for myself a mind that could deal with the abstract.

In short I tried to think. I failed. My attention veered inexorably back to the specific, to the tangible, to what was generally considered, by everyone I knew then and for that matter have known since, the peripheral. I would try to contemplate the Hegelian dialectic and would find myself concentrating instead on a flowering pear tree outside my window and the particular way the petals fell on my floor. I would try to read linguistic theory and would find myself wondering instead if the lights were on in the bevatron up the hill. When I say that I was wondering if the lights were on in the bevatron you might immediately suspect, if you deal in ideas at all, that I was registering the bevatron as a political symbol, thinking in shorthand about the military-industrial complex and its role in the university community, but you would be wrong. I was only wondering if the lights were on in the bevatron, and how they looked. A physical fact.

I had trouble graduating from Berkeley, not because of this inability to deal with ideas—I was majoring in English, and I could locate the house-and-garden imagery in *The Portrait of a Lady* as well as the next person, "imagery" being by definition the kind of specific that got my attention—but simply because I had neglected to take a course in Milton. For reasons which now sound baroque I needed a degree by the end of that summer, and the English department finally agreed, if I would come down from Sacramento every Friday and talk about the cosmology of *Paradise Lost*, to certify me proficient in Milton. I did this. Some Fridays I took the Greyhound bus, other Fridays I caught the Southern Pacific's City of San Francisco on the last leg of its transcontinental trip. I can no longer tell you whether Milton put the sun or the earth at the center of his universe in *Paradise Lost*, the central question of at least one century and a topic about which I wrote 10,000 words that summer, but I can still recall the exact rancidity of the butter in the City of San Francisco's dining car, and the way the tinted windows on the Greyhound bus cast the oil refineries around Carquinez Straits into a grayed and obscurely sinister light. In short my attention was always on the periphery, on what I would see and taste and touch, on the butter, and the Greyhound bus. During those years I was traveling on what I knew to be a very shaky passport, forged papers: I knew that I was no legitimate resident in any world of ideas. I knew I couldn't think. All I knew then was what I couldn't do. All I knew then was what I wasn't, and it took me some years to discover what I was.

Which was a writer.

By which I mean not a "good" writer or a "bad" writer but simply a writer, a person whose most absorbed and passionate hours are spent arranging words on pieces of paper. Had my credentials been in order I would never have become a writer. Had I been blessed with even limited access to my own mind there would have been no reason to write. I write entirely to find out what I'm thinking, what I'm looking at, what I see and what it means. What I want and what I fear. Why did the oil refineries around Carquinez Straits seem sinister to me in the summer of 1956? Why have the night lights in the bevatron burned in my mind for twenty years? *What is going on in these pictures in my mind?*

When I talk about pictures in my mind I am talking, quite specifically, about images that shimmer around the edges. There used to be an illustration in every elementary psychology book showing a cat drawn by a patient in varying stages of schizophrenia. This cat had a shimmer around it. You could see the molecular structure breaking down at the very edges of the cat: the cat became the background and the background the cat, everything interacting, exchanging ions. People on hallucinogens describe the same perception of objects. I'm not a schizophrenic, nor do I take hallucinogens, but certain images do shimmer for me. Look hard enough, and you can't miss the shimmer. It's there. You can't think too much about these pictures that shimmer. You just lie low and let them develop. You stay quiet. You don't talk to many people and you keep your nervous system from shorting out and you try to locate the cat in the shimmer, the grammar in the picture.

Just as I meant "shimmer" literally I mean "grammar" literally. Grammar is a piano I play by ear, since I seem to have been out of school the year the rules were mentioned. All I know about grammar is its infinite power. To shift the structure of a sentence alters the meaning of that sentence, as definitely and inflexibly as the position of a camera alters the meaning of the object photographed. Many people know about camera angles now, but not so many know about sentences. The arrangement of the words matters, and the arrangement you want can be found in the picture in your mind. The picture dictates the arrangement. The picture dictates whether this will be a sentence with or without clauses, a sentence that ends hard or a dying-fall sentence, long or short, active or passive. The picture tells you how to arrange the words and the arrangement of the words tells you, or tells me, what's going on in the picture. *Nota bene*:

It tells you.

You don't tell it.

Let me show you what I mean by pictures in the mind. I began *Play It as It Lays* just as I have begun each of my novels, with no notion of "character" or "plot" or even "incident." I had only two pictures in my mind, more about which later, and a technical intention, which was to write a novel so elliptical and fast that it would be over before you noticed it, a novel so fast that it would scarcely exist on the page at all. About the pictures: the first was of white space. Empty space. This was clearly the picture that dictated the narrative intention of the book—a book in which anything that happened would happen off the page, a "white" book to which the reader would have to bring his or her own bad dreams—and yet this picture told me no "story," suggested no situation. The second picture did. This second picture was of something actually witnessed. A young woman with long hair and a short white halter dress walks through the casino at the Riviera in Las Vegas at one in the morning. She crosses the casino alone and picks up a house telephone. I watch her because I have heard her paged, and recognize her name: she is a minor actress I see around Los Angeles from time to time, in places like

Jax and once in a gynecologist's office in the Beverly Hills Clinic, but have never met. I know nothing about her. Who is paging her? Why is she here to be paged? How exactly did she come to this? It was precisely this moment in Las Vegas that made *Play It as It Lays* begin to tell itself to me, but the moment appears in the novel only obliquely, in a chapter which begins:

> Maria made a list of things she would never do. She would never: walk through the Sands or Caesar's alone after midnight. She would never: ball at a party, do S-M unless she wanted to, borrow furs from Abe Lipsey, deal. She would never: carry a Yorkshire in Beverly Hills.

That is the beginning of the chapter and that is also the end of the chapter, which may suggest what I meant by "white space."

I recall having a number of pictures in my mind when I began the novel I just finished, *A Book of Common Prayer.* As a matter of fact one of these pictures was of that bevatron I mentioned, although I would be hard put to tell you a story in which nuclear energy figured. Another was a newspaper photograph of a hijacked 707 burning on the desert in the Middle East. Another was the night view from a room in which I once spent a week with paratyphoid, a hotel room on the Colombian coast. My husband and I seemed to be on the Colombian coast representing the United States of America at a film festival (I recall invoking the name "Jack Valenti" a lot, as if its reiteration could make me well), and it was a bad place to have fever, not only because my indisposition offended our hosts but because every night in this hotel the generator failed. The lights went out. The elevator stopped. My husband would go to the event of the evening and make excuses for me and I would stay alone in this hotel room, in the dark. I remember standing at the window trying to call Bogotá (the telephone seemed to work on the same principle as the generator) and watching the night wind come up and wondering what I was doing eleven degrees off the equator with a fever of 103. The view from that window definitely figures in *A Book of Common Prayer,* as does the burning 707, and yet none of these pictures told me the story I needed.

The picture that did, the picture that shimmered and made

these other images coalesce, was the Panama airport at 6 A.M. I was in this airport only once, on a plane to Bogotá that stopped for an hour to refuel, but the way it looked that morning remained superimposed on everything I saw until the day I finished *A Book of Common Prayer.* I lived in that airport for several years. I can still feel the hot air when I step off the plane, can see the heat already rising off the tarmac at 6 A.M. I can feel my skirt damp and wrinkled on my legs. I can feel the asphalt stick to my sandals. I remember the big tail of a Pan American plane floating motionless down at the end of the tarmac. I remember the sound of a slot machine in the waiting room. I could tell you that I remember a particular woman in the airport, an American woman, a *norteamericana,* a thin *norteamericana* about 40 who wore a big square emerald in lieu of a wedding ring, but there was no such woman there.

I put this woman in the airport later. I made this woman up, just as I later made up a country to put the airport in, and a family to run the country. This woman in the airport is neither catching a plane nor meeting one. She is ordering tea in the airport coffee shop. In fact she is not simply "ordering" tea but insisting that the water be boiled, in front of her, for twenty minutes. Why is this woman in this airport? Why is she going nowhere, where has she been? Where did she get that big emerald? What derangement, or disassociation, makes her believe that her will to see the water boiled can possibly prevail?

> She had been going to one airport or another for four months, one could see it, looking at the visas on her passport. All those airports where Charlotte Douglas's passport had been stamped would have looked alike. Sometimes the sign on the tower would say "Bienvenidos" and sometimes the sign on the tower would say "Bienvenue," some places were wet and hot and others dry and hot, but at each of these airports the pastel concrete walls would rust and stain and the swamp off the runway would be littered with the fuselages of cannibalized Fairchild F-227's and the water would need boiling.
>
> "I knew why Charlotte went to the airport even if Victor did not.
>
> "I knew about airports."

These lines appear about halfway through *A Book of Common Prayer,* but I wrote them during the second week I worked on the book, long before I had any idea where Charlotte Douglas had been or why she went to airports. Until I wrote these lines I had no character called "Victor" in mind: the necessity for mentioning a name, and the name "Victor," occurred to me as I wrote the sentence. *I knew why Charlotte went to the airport* sounded incomplete. *I knew why Charlotte went to the airport even if Victor did not* carried a little more narrative drive. Most important of all, until I wrote these lines I did not know who "I" was, who was telling the story. I had intended until that moment that the "I" be no more than the voice of the author, a 19th-century omniscient narrator. But there it was:

> "I knew why Charlotte went to the airport even if Victor did not.
> "I knew about airports."

This "I" was the voice of no author in my house. This "I" was someone who not only knew why Charlotte went to the airport but also knew someone called "Victor." Who was Victor? Who was this narrator? Why was this narrator telling me this story? Let me tell you one thing about why writers write: had I known the answer to any of these questions I would never have needed to write a novel.

1976

ON THE ROAD

Where are we heading, they asked in all the television and radio studios. They asked it in New York and Los Angeles and they asked it in Boston and Washington and they asked it in Dallas and Houston and Chicago and San Francisco. Sometimes they made eye contact as they asked it. Sometimes they closed their eyes as they asked it. Quite often they wondered not just where we were heading but where we were heading "as Americans," or "as concerned Americans," or "as American women," or, on one occasion, "as the American guy and the American woman." I never learned the answer, nor did the answer matter, for one of the eerie and liberating aspects of broadcast discourse is that nothing one says will alter in the slightest either the form or the length of the conversation. Our voices in the studios were those of manic actors assigned to do three-minute, four-minute, seven-minute improvs. Our faces on the monitors were those of concerned Americans. On my way to one of those studios in Boston I had seen the magnolias bursting white down Marlborough Street. On my way to another in Dallas I had watched the highway lights blazing and dimming pink against the big dawn sky. Outside one studio in Houston the afternoon heat was sinking into the deep primeval green of the place and outside the next, that night in Chicago, snow fell and glittered in the lights along the lake. Outside all these studios America lay in all its exhilaratingly volatile weather and eccentricity and specificity, but inside the studios we shed the specific and rocketed on to the general, for they were The Interviewers and I was The Author and the single question we seemed able to address together was *where are we heading.*

> *"8:30 A.M. to 9:30 A.M.: LIVE: on WFSB TV/THIS MORNING.*
> *"10 A.M. to 10:30 A.M.: LIVE on WINF AM/THE WORLD TODAY.*
> *"10:45 A.M. to 11:45 A.M.: PRESS INTERVIEW with HARTFORD COURANT.*
> *"12 noon to 1:30 P.M.: AUTOGRAPHING at BARNES AND NOBLE.*
> *"2 P.M. to 2:30 P.M.: TAPE at WDRC AM/FM.*
> *"3 P.M. to 3:30 P.M.: PRESS INTERVIEW with THE HILL INK.*
> *"7:30 P.M. to 9 P.M.: TAPE at WHNB TV/WHAT ABOUT WOMEN."*

From 12 noon to 1:30 P.M., that first day in Hartford, I talked to a man who had cut a picture of me from a magazine in 1970 and had come round to Barnes and Noble to see what I looked like in 1977. From 2 P.M. to 2:30 P.M., that first day in Hartford, I listened to the receptionists at WDRC AM/FM talk about the new records and I watched snow drop from the pine boughs in the cemetery across the street. The name of the cemetery was Mt. St. Benedict and my husband's father had been buried there. "Any Steely Dan come in?" the receptionists kept asking. From 8:30 A.M. until 9 P.M., that first day in Hartford, I neglected to mention the name of the book I was supposed to be promoting. It was my fourth book but I had never before done what is called in the trade a book tour. I was not sure what I was doing or why I was doing it. I had left California equipped with two "good" suits, a box of unanswered mail, Elizabeth Hardwick's *Seduction and Betrayal*, Edmund Wilson's *To the Finland Station*, six Judy Blume books and my eleven-year-old daughter. The Judy Blume books were along to divert my daughter. My daughter was along to divert me. Three days into the tour I sent home the box of unanswered mail to make room for a packet of Simon and Schuster press releases describing me in favorable terms. Four days into the tour I sent home *Seduction and Betrayal* and *To the Finland Station* to make room for a thousand-watt hair blower. By the time I reached Boston, ten days into the tour, I knew that I had never before heard and would possibly never again hear America singing at precisely this pitch: ethereal, speedy, an angel choir on Dexamyl.

Where were we heading. The set for this discussion was always the same: a cozy oasis of wicker and ferns in the wilderness of cables and cameras and Styrofoam coffee cups that was the actual studio. On wicker settees across the nation I expressed my conviction that we were heading "into an era" of whatever the clock seemed to demand. In green rooms across the nation I listened to other people talk about where we were heading, and also about their vocations, avocations, and secret interests. I discussed L-dopa and biorhythm with a woman whose father invented prayer breakfasts. I exchanged makeup tips with a former Mouseketeer. I stopped reading newspapers and started relying on bulletins from limo drivers, from Mouseketeers, from the callers-in on call-in shows and from the closed-circuit screens in airports that flashed random stories off the wire ("CARTER

URGES BARBITURATE BAN" is one that got my attention at La Guardia) between advertisements for *Shenandoah.* I gravitated to the random. I swung with the non-sequential.

I began to see America as my own, a child's map over which my child and I could skim and light at will. We spoke not of cities but of airports. If rain fell at Logan we could find sun at Dulles. Bags lost at O'Hare could be found at Dallas/Fort Worth. In the first-class cabins of the planes on which we traveled we were often, my child and I, the only female passengers, and I apprehended for the first time those particular illusions of mobility which power American business. Time was money. Motion was progress. Decisions were snap and the ministrations of other people were constant. Room service, for example, assumed paramount importance. We needed, my eleven-year-old and I, instant but erratically timed infusions of consommé, oatmeal, crab salad and asparagus vinaigrette. We needed Perrier water and tea to drink when we were working. We needed bourbon on the rocks and Shirley Temples to drink when we were not. A kind of irritable panic came over us when room service went off, and also when no one answered in the housekeeping department. In short we had fallen into the peculiar hormonal momentum of business travel, and I had begun to understand the habituation many men and a few women have to planes and telephones and schedules. I had begun to regard my own schedule—a sheaf of thick cream-colored pages printed with the words "SIMON & SCHUSTER/A DIVISION OF GULF & WESTERN CORPORATION"—with a reverence approaching the mystical. We wanted 24-hour room service. We wanted direct-dial telephones. We wanted to stay on the road forever.

We saw air as our element. In Houston the air was warm and rich and suggestive of fossil fuel and we pretended we owned a house in River Oaks. In Chicago the air was brilliant and thin and we pretended we owned the 27th floor of the Ritz. In New York the air was charged and crackling and shorting out with opinions, and we pretended we had some. Everyone in New York had opinions. Opinions were demanded in return. The absence of opinion was construed as opinion. Even my daughter was developing opinions. "Had an interesting talk with Carl Bernstein," she noted in the log she had been assigned to keep for her fifth-grade teacher in Malibu, California. Many of these New York opinions seemed intended as tonic revisions, bold corrections to opinions in vogue during the previous week, but since I had just dropped from the sky it was difficult for me to distinguish those opinions which were "bold" and "revisionist" from those which were merely "weary" and "rote." At the time I left New York many people were expressing a bold belief in "joy"—joy in children, joy in wedlock, joy in the dailiness of life—but joy was trickling down fast to show-business personalities. Mike Nichols, for example, was expressing his joy in the pages of *Newsweek*, and also his weariness with "lapidary bleakness." Lapidary bleakness was definitely rote.

We were rethinking the Sixties that week, or Morris Dickstein was.

We were taking another look at the Fifties that week, or Hilton Kramer was.

I agreed passionately. I disagreed passionately. I called room service on one phone and listened attentively on the other to people who seemed convinced that the "texture" of their lives had been agreeably or adversely affected by conversion to the politics of joy, by regression to lapidary bleakness, by the Sixties, by the Fifties, by the recent change in administrations and by the sale of *The Thorn Birds* to paper for one-million-nine.

I lost track of information.

I was blitzed by opinion.

I began to see opinions arcing in the air, intersecting flight patterns. The Eastern shuttle was cleared for landing and so was lapidary bleakness. John Leonard and joy were on converging vectors. I began to see the country itself as a projection on air, a kind of hologram, an invisible grid of image and opinion and electronic impulse. There were opinions in the air and there were planes in the air and there were even people in the air: one afternoon in New York my husband saw a man jump from a window and fall to the sidewalk outside the Yale Club. I mentioned this to a *Daily News* photographer who was taking my picture. "You have to catch a jumper in the act to make the paper," he advised me. He had caught two in the act but only the first had made the paper. The second was a better picture but coincided with the crash of a DC-10 at Orly. "They're all over town," the photographer said. "Jumpers. A lot of them aren't even jumpers. They're window washers. Who fall."

What does that say about us as a nation, I was asked the next day when I mentioned the jumpers and window washers on the air. *Where are we headed.* On the 27th floor of the Ritz in Chicago my daughter and I sat frozen at the breakfast table until the window washers glided safely out of sight. At a call-in station in Los Angeles I was told by the guard that there would be a delay because they had a jumper on the line. "I say let him jump," the guard said to me. I imagined a sky dense with jumpers and fallers and DC-10s. I held my daughter's hand at take-off and landing and watched for antennae on the drive into town. The big antennae with the pulsing red lights had been for a month our landmarks. The big antennae with the pulsing red lights had in fact been for a month our destinations. "Out I-10 to the antenna" was the kind of direction we had come to understand, for we were on the road, on the grid, on the air and also in it. *Where were we heading.* I don't know where you're heading, I said in the studio attached to the last of these antennae, my eyes fixed on still another of the neon FLEETWOOD MAC signs that flickered that spring in radio stations from coast to coast, but I'm heading home.

1977

An Appendix on Style

Ben Jonson
Of Style

Jonathan Swift
from *A Letter to a Young Gentleman*

William Hazlitt
Of Familiar Style

Alexander Smith
from *On the Writing of Essays*

F. L. Lucas
On the Fascination of Style

BEN JONSON

Of Style

For a man to write well, there are required three necessaries—to read the best authors, observe the best speakers, and much exercise of his own style. In style, to consider what ought to be written, and after what manner, he must first think and excogitate his matter, then choose his words and examine the weight of either. Then take care, in placing and ranking both matter and words, that the composition be comely; and to do this with diligence and often. No matter how slow the style be at first, so it be labored and accurate; seek the best, and be not glad of the forward conceits or first words that offer themselves to us, but judge of what we invent, and order what we approve. Repeat often what we have formerly written; which beside that it helps the consequence, and makes the juncture better, it quickens the heat of imagination, that often cools in the time of setting down, and gives it new strength, as if it grew lustier by the going back. As we see in the contention of leaping, they jump farthest that fetch their race largest; or, as in throwing a dart or javelin, we force back our arms to make our loose the stronger. Yet, if we have a fair gale of wind, I forbid not the steering out of our sail, so the favor of the gale deceive us not. For all that we invent doth please us in the conception of birth, else we would never set it down. But the safest is to return to our judgment, and handle over again those things the easiness of which might make them justly suspected. So did the best writers in their beginnings; they imposed upon themselves care and industry; they did nothing rashly: they obtained first to write well, and then custom made it easy and a habit. By little and little their matter showed itself to them more plentifully; their words answered, their composition followed; and all, as in a well-ordered family, presented itself in the place. So that the sum of all is, ready writing makes not good writing, but good writing brings on ready writing. Yet, when we think we have got the faculty, it is even then good to resist it, as to give a horse a check sometimes with a bit, which doth not so much stop his course as stir his mettle. Again, whether a man's genius is best able to reach, thither it should more and more contend, lift and dilate itself; as men of low stature raise themselves on their toes, and so oft-times get even, if not eminent. Besides, as it is fit for grown and able writers to stand of themselves, and work with their own strength, to trust and endeavor by their own faculties, so it is fit for the beginner and learner to study others and the best. For the mind and memory are more sharply exercised in comprehending another man's things than our own; and such as accustom themselves and are familiar with the best authors shall ever and anon find somewhat of them in themselves, and in the expression of their minds, even when they feel it not, be able to utter something like theirs, which hath an authority above their own. Nay, sometimes it is the reward of a man's study, the praise of quoting another man fitly; and though a man be more prone and able for one kind of writing than another, yet he must exercise all. For as in an instrument, so in style, there must be harmony and consent of parts.

1640

JONATHAN SWIFT

from *A Letter to a Young Gentleman*

LATELY ENTERED INTO HOLY ORDERS

By a Person of QUALITY

January 9, 1720

Sir,

Although it was against my knowledge or advice, that you entered into holy orders, under the present dispositions of mankind toward the Church, yet since it is now supposed too late to recede (at least according to the general practice and opinion), I cannot forbear offering my thoughts to you upon this new condition of life you are engaged in.

I could heartily wish that the circumstances of your fortune had enabled you to have continued some years longer in the university, at least until you were ten years' standing; to have laid in a competent stock of human learning, and some knowledge in divinity, before you attempted to appear in the world: for I cannot but lament the common course, which at least nine in ten of those who enter into the ministry are obliged to run. When they have taken a degree, and are consequently grown a burden to their friends, who now think themselves fully discharged, they get into orders as soon as they can (upon which I shall make no remarks), first solicit a readership, and if they be very fortunate, arrive in time to a curacy here in town; or else are sent to be assistants in the country, where they probably continue several years (many of them their whole lives), with thirty or forty pounds a year for their support, until some bishop, who happens to be not overstocked with relations, or attached to favorites, or is content to supply his diocese without colonies from England, bestows upon them some inconsiderable benefice, when it is odds they are already encumbered with a numerous family. I would be glad to know what intervals of life such persons can possibly set apart for improvements of their minds; or which way they could be furnished with books, the library they brought with them from their college being usually not the most numerous, or judiciously chosen. If such gentlemen arrive to be great scholars, it must, I think, be either by means supernatural, or by a method altogether out of any road yet known to the learned. But I conceive the fact directly otherwise, and that many of them lose the greatest part of the small pittance they received at the university.

I take it for granted, that you intend to pursue the beaten track, and are already desirous to be seen in a pulpit; only I hope you will think it proper to pass your quarantine among some of the desolate churches five miles round this town, where you may at least learn to *read* and to *speak* before you venture to expose your parts in a city congregation; not that these are better judges, but because, if a man must needs expose his folly, it is more safe and discreet to be so before few witnesses, and in a scattered neighborhood. And you will do well if you can prevail upon some intimate and judicious friend to be your constant hearer, and allow him with the utmost freedom to give you notice of whatever he shall find amiss either in your voice or gesture; for want of which early warning, many clergymen continue defective, and sometimes ridiculous, to the end of their lives; neither is it rare to observe among excellent and learned divines, a certain ungracious manner, or an unhappy tone of voice, which they never have been able to shake off.

I could likewise have been glad if you had applied yourself a little more to the study of the English language, than I fear you have done; the neglect whereof is one of the most general defects among the scholars of this kingdom, who seem to have not the least conception of a style, but run on in a flat kind of phraseology, often mingled with barbarous terms and expressions, peculiar to the nation. Neither do I perceive that any person either finds or acknowledges his wants upon this head, or in the least desires to have them supplied. Proper words in proper places, makes the true definition of a style. But this would require too ample a disquisition to be now dwelt on: however, I shall venture to name one or two faults, which are easy to be remedied, with a very small portion of abilities.

The first is the frequent use of obscure terms, which by the women are called *hard words*, and by the better sort of vulgar, *fine language*; than which I do not know a more universal, inexcusable, and unnecessary mistake, among the clergy of all distinctions, but especially the younger practitioners. I have been curious enough to take a list of several hundred words in a sermon of a new beginner, which not one of his hearers among a hundred could possibly understand; neither can I easily call to mind any clergyman of my own acquaintance who is wholly exempt from this error, although many of them agree with me in the dislike of the thing. But I am apt to put myself in the place of the vulgar, and think many words difficult or obscure, which the preacher will not allow to be so, because those words are obvious to scholars. I believe the method observed by the famous Lord Falkland in some of his writings, would not be an ill one for young divines: I was assured by an old person of quality who knew him well, that when he doubted whether a word was perfectly intelligible or no, he used to consult one of his lady's chambermaids (not the waiting woman, because it was possible she might be conversant in romances), and by her judgment was guided whether to receive or reject it. And if that great person thought such a caution necessary in treatises offered to the learned world, it will be sure at least as proper in sermons, where the meanest hearer is supposed to be concerned, and where very often a lady's chambermaid may be allowed to equal half the congregation, both as to quality and understanding. But I know not how it comes to pass, that professors in most arts and sciences are generally the worst qualified to explain their meanings to those who are not of their tribe. A common farmer shall make you understand in three words, *that his foot is out of joint, or his collarbone broken*, wherein a surgeon, after a hundred terms of art, if you are not a scholar, shall leave you to seek. It is frequently the same case in law, physic, and even many of the meaner arts.

And upon this account it is, that among *hard words*, I number likewise those which are peculiar to divinity as it is a science; because I have observed several clergymen, otherwise little fond of obscure terms, yet in their sermons very liberal of those which they find in ecclesiastical writers, as if it were our duty to understand them; which I am sure it is not. And I defy the greatest divine to produce any law either of God or man, which obliges me to comprehend the meaning of *omniscience, omnipresence, ubiquity, attribute, beatific vision,* with a thousand others so frequent in pulpits, any more than that of *eccentric, idiosyncracy, entity,* and the like. I believe I may venture to insist further, that many terms used in Holy Writ, particularly by St. Paul, might with more discretion be changed into plainer speech, except when they are introduced as part of a quotation.

I am the more earnest in this matter, because it is a general complaint, and the justest in the world. For a divine has nothing to say to the wisest congregation of any parish in this kingdom, which he may not express in a manner to be understood by the meanest among them. And this assertion must be true, or else God requires from us more than we are able to perform. However, not to contend whether a logician might possibly put a case that would serve for an exception, I will appeal to any man of letters, whether at least nineteen in twenty of those perplexing words might not be changed into easy ones, such as naturally first occur to ordinary men, and probably did so at first to those very gentlemen who are so fond of the former.

We are often reproved by divines from the pulpits, on account of our ignorance in things sacred, and perhaps with justice enough. However, it is not very reasonable for them to expect, that *common men* should understand expressions which are never made use of in *common life.* No gentleman thinks it safe or prudent to send a servant with a message, without repeating it more than once, and endeavoring to put it into terms brought down to the capacity of the bearer. Yet after all this care, it is frequent for servants to mistake, and sometimes to occasion misunderstandings between friends, although the common domestics in some gentlemen's families may have more opportunities of improving their minds than the ordinary sort of tradesmen.

It is usual for clergymen who are taxed with this learned defect, to quote Dr. Tillotson, and other famous divines, in their defense, without considering the difference between elaborate discourses upon important occasions, delivered to princes or parliaments, written with a view to being made public, and a plain sermon intended for the middle or lower size of people. Neither do they seem to remember the many alterations, additions, and expungings, made by great authors in those treatises which they prepare for the public. Besides, that excellent prelate above-mentioned, was known to preach after a much more popular manner in the city congregations: and if in those parts of his works he be anywhere too obscure for the understandings of many who may be supposed to have been his hearers, it ought to be numbered among his omissions.

The fear of being thought pedants hath been of pernicious consequence to young divines. This hath wholly taken many of them off from their severer studies in the university, which they have exchanged for plays, poems, and pamphlets, in order to qualify them for tea tables and coffee-houses. This they usually call *polite conversation*; *knowing the world*; and *reading men instead of books*. These accomplishments when applied in the pulpit, appear by a quaint, terse, florid style, rounded into periods and cadences, commonly without either propriety or meaning. I have listened with my utmost attention for half an hour to an orator of this species, without being able to understand, much less to carry away one single sentence out of a whole sermon. Others, to show that their studies have not been confined to sciences, or ancient authors, will talk in the style of a gaming ordinary, and Whitefriars, where I suppose the hearers can be little edified by the terms of *palming, shuffling, biting, bamboozling,* and the like, if they have not been sometimes conversant among pickpockets and sharpers. And truly, as they say, a man is known by his company, so it should seem that a man's company may be known by his manner of expressing himself, either in public assemblies, or private conversations.

It would be endless to run over the several defects of style among us; I shall therefore say nothing of the *mean* and *paltry* (which are usually attended by the *fustian*), much less of the *slovenly* or *indecent.* Two things I will just warn you against: the first is the frequency of flat unnecessary epithets; and the other is the folly of using old threadbare phrases, which will often make you go out of your way to find and apply them, are nauseous to rational hearers, and will seldom express your meaning as well as your own natural words.

Although, as I have already observed, our English tongue is too little cultivated in this kingdom, yet the faults are nine in ten owing to affectation, and not to the want of understanding. When a man's thoughts are clear, the properest words will generally offer themselves first, and his own judgment will direct him in what order to place them, so as they may be best understood. Where men err against this method, it is usually on purpose, and to show their learning, their oratory, their politeness, or their knowledge of the world. In short, that simplicity without which no human performance can arrive to any great perfection, is nowhere more eminently useful than in this.

1720

WILLIAM HAZLITT

Of Familiar Style

It is not easy to write a familiar style. Many people mistake a familiar for a vulgar style, and suppose that to write without affectation is to write at random. On the contrary, there is nothing that requires more precision, and, if I may so say, purity of expression, than the style I am speaking of. It utterly rejects not only all unmeaning pomp, but all low, cant phrases, and loose, unconnected, *slipshod* allusions. It is not to take the first word that offers, but the best word in common use; it is not to throw words together in any combinations we please, but to follow and avail ourselves of the true idiom of the language. To write a genuine familiar or truly English style, is to write as any one would speak in common conversation, who had a thorough command and choice of words, or who could discourse with ease, force, and perspicuity, setting aside all pedantic and oratorical flourishes. Or to give another illustration, to write naturally is the same thing in regard to common conversation, as to read naturally is in regard to common speech. It does not follow that it is an easy thing to give the true accent and inflection to the words you utter, because you do not attempt to rise above the level of ordinary life and colloquial speaking. You do not assume indeed the solemnity of the pulpit, or the tone of stage declamation: neither are you at liberty to gabble on at a venture, without emphasis or discretion, or to resort to vulgar dialect or clownish pronunciation. You must steer a middle course. You are tied down to a given and appropriate articulation, which is determined by the habitual associations between sense and sound, and which you can only hit by entering into the author's meaning, as you must find the proper words and style to express yourself by fixing your thoughts on the subject you have to write about. Any one may mouth out a passage with a theatrical cadence, or get upon stilts to tell his thoughts: but to speak or write with propriety and simplicity is a more difficult task. Thus it is easy to affect a pompous style, to use a word twice as big as the thing you want to express: it is not so easy to pitch upon the very word that exactly fits it. Out of eight or ten words equally common, equally intelligible, with nearly equal pretensions, it is a matter of some nicety and discrimination to pick out the very one, the preferableness of which is scarcely perceptible, but decisive. The reason why I object to Dr. Johnson's style is, that there is no discrimination, no variety in it. He uses none but "tall, opaque words," taken from the "first row of the rubric": words with the greatest number of syllables, or Latin phrases with merely English terminations. If a fine style depended on this sort of arbitrary pretension, it would be fair to judge of an author's elegance by the measurement of his words, and the substitution of foreign circumlocutions (with no precise associations) for the mother tongue. How simple it is to be dignified without ease, to be pompous without meaning! Surely, it is but a mechanical rule for avoiding what is low to be always pedantic and affected. It is clear you cannot use a vulgar English word, if you never use a common English word at all. A fine tact is shown in adhering to those which are perfectly common, and yet never falling into any expressions which are debased by disgusting circumstances, or which owe their signification and point to technical or professional allusions. A truly natural or familiar style can never be quaint or vulgar, for this reason, that it is of universal force and applicability, and that quaintness and vulgarity arise out of the immediate connection of certain words with coarse and disagreeable, or with confined ideas. The last form what we understand by *cant* or *slang* phrases. To give an example of what is not very clear in the general statement, I should say that the phrase *To cut with a knife,* or *To cut a piece of wood,* is perfectly free from vulgarity, because it is perfectly common: but to *cut an acquaintance* is not quite unexceptionable, because it is not perfectly common or intelligible, and has hardly yet escaped out of the limits of slang phraseology. I should hardly therefore use the word in this sense without putting it in italics as a license of expression, to be received *cum grano salis.* All provincial or bye-phrases come under the same mark of reprobation—all such as the writer transfers to the page from his fireside or a particular *coterie,* or that he invents for his own sole use and convenience. I conceive that words are like money, not the worse for being common, but that it is the stamp of custom alone that gives them circulation or value. I am fastidious in this respect, and would almost as soon coin the currency of the realm as counterfeit the King's English. I never invented or gave a new and unauthorized meaning to any word but one single one (the term *impersonal* applied to feelings) and that was in an abstruse metaphysical discussion to express a very difficult distinction. I have been (I know) loudly accused of reveling in vulgarisms and broken English. I cannot speak to that point: but so far I plead guilty to the determined use of acknowledged idioms and common elliptical expressions. I am not sure that the critics in question know the one from the other, that is, can distinguish any medium between formal pedantry and the most barbarous solecism. As an author, I endeavor to employ plain words and popular modes of construction, as were I a chapman and dealer, I should common weights and measures.

The proper force of words lies not in the words themselves, but in their application. A word may be a fine-sounding word of an unusual length, and very imposing from its learning and novelty, and yet in the connection in which it is introduced, may be quite pointless and irrelevant. It is not pomp or pretension, but the adaptation of the expression to the idea that clenches a writer's meaning: as it is not the size or glossiness of the materials, but their being fitted each to its place, that gives strength to the arch; or as the pegs and nails are as necessary to the support of the building as the large timbers, and more so than the mere showy, unsubstantial ornaments. I hate any thing that occupies more space than it is worth. I hate to see a load of band-boxes go along the street, and I hate to see a parcel of big words without any thing in them. A person who does not deliberately dispose of all his thoughts alike in cumbrous draperies and flimsy disguises, may strike out twenty varieties of familiar everyday language, each coming somewhat nearer to the feeling he wants to convey, and at last not hit upon that particular and only one, which may be said to be identical with the exact expression in his mind. This would seem to show that Mr. Cobbett is hardly right in saying that the first word that occurs is always the best. It may be a very good one; and yet a better may present itself on reflection or from time to time. It should be suggested naturally, however, and spontaneously, from a fresh and lively conception of the subject. We seldom succeed by trying at improvement, or by merely substituting one word for another that we are not satisfied with, as we cannot recollect the name of a place or person by merely plaguing ourselves about it. We wander farther from the point by persisting in a wrong scent, but it starts up accidentally in the memory when we least expected it, by touching some link in the chain of previous association.

There are those who hoard up and make a cautious display of nothing but rich and rare phraseology: ancient medals, obscure coins, and Spanish pieces of eight. They are very curious to inspect; but I myself would neither offer nor take them in the course of exchange. A sprinkling of archaisms is not amiss; but a tissue of obsolete expressions is more fit *for keep than wear.* I do not say I would not use any phrase that had been brought into fashion before the middle or the end of the last century; but I should be shy of using any that had not been employed by any approved author during the whole of that time. Words, like clothes, get old-fashioned, or mean and ridiculous, when they have been for some time laid aside. Mr. Lamb is the only imitator of old English style I can read with pleasure; and he is so thoroughly imbued with the spirit of his authors, that the idea of imitation is almost done away. There is an inward unction, a marrowy vein both in the thought and feeling, an intuition, deep and lively, of his subject, that carries off any quaintness or awkwardness arising from an antiquated style and dress. The matter is completely his own, though the manner is assumed. Perhaps his ideas are altogether so marked and individual, as to require their point and pungency to be neutralized by the affectation of a singular but traditional form of conveyance. Tricked out in the prevailing costume, they would probably seem more startling and out of the way. The old English authors, Burton, Fuller, Coryate, Sir Thomas Browne, are a kind of mediators between us and the more eccentric and whimsical modern, reconciling us to his peculiarities. I do not, however, know how far this is the case or not, till he condescends to write like one of us. I must confess that what I like best of his papers under the signature of Elia (still I do not presume, amidst such excellence, to decide what is most excellent) is the account of *Mrs. Battle's Opinions on Whist,* which is also the most free from obsolete allusions and turns of expressions—

A well of native English undefiled.

To those acquainted with his admired prototypes, these *Essays* of the ingenious and highly gifted author have the same sort of charm and relish that Erasmus's *Colloquies* or a fine piece of modern Latin have to the classical scholar. Certainly, I do not know any borrowed pencil that has more power or felicity of execution than the one of which I have here been speaking.

It is as easy to write a gaudy style without ideas as it is to spread a pallet of showy colors, or to smear in a flaunting transparency. "What do you read?"—"Words, words, words."—"What is the matter?"—"*Nothing,*" it might be answered. The florid style is the reverse of the familiar. The last is employed as an unvarnished medium to convey ideas; the first is resorted to as a spangled veil to conceal the want of them. When there is nothing to be set down but words, it costs little to have them fine. Look through the dictionary, and cull out a *florilegium,* rival the *tulipomania. Rouge* high enough, and never mind the natural complexion. The vulgar, who are not in the secret, will admire the look of preternatural health and vigor; and the fashionable, who regard only appearances, will be delighted with the imposition. Keep to your sounding generalities, your tinkling phrases, and all will be well. Swell out an unmeaning truism to a perfect tympany of style. A thought, a distinction is the rock on which all this brittle cargo of verbiage splits at once. Such writers have merely *verbal* imaginations, that retain nothing but words. Or their puny thoughts have dragonwings, all green and gold. They soar far above the vulgar failing of the *Sermo humi obrepens*—their most ordinary speech is never short of an hyperbole, splendid, imposing, vague, incomprehensible, magniloquent, a cento of sounding commonplaces. If some of us, whose "ambition is more lowly," pry a little too narrowly into nooks and corners to pick up a number of "unconsidered trifles," they never once direct their eyes or lift their hands to seize on any but the most gorgeous, tarnished, threadbare patchwork set of phrases, the left-off finery of poetic extravagance, transmitted down through successive generations of barren pretenders. If they criticize actors and actresses, a huddled phantasmagoria of feathers, spangles, floods of light, and oceans of sound float before their morbid sense, which they paint in the style of Ancient Pistol. Not a glimpse can you get of the merits or defects of the performers: they are hidden in a profusion of barbarous epithets and willful rhodomontade. Our hypercritics are not thinking of these little fantoccini beings —

> That strut and fret their hour upon the stage—

but of tall phantoms of words, abstractions, *genera* and *species*, sweeping clauses, periods that unite the Poles, forced alliterations, astounding antitheses—

> And on their pens *Fustian* sits plumed.

If they describe kings and queens, it is an Eastern pageant. The Coronation at either House is nothing to it. We get at four repeated images—a curtain, a throne, a scepter, and a footstool. These are with them the wardrobe of a lofty imagination; and they turn their service strains to servile uses. Do we read a description of pictures? It is not a reflection of tones and hues which "nature's own sweet and cunning hand laid on," but piles of precious stones, rubies, pearls, emeralds, Golconda's mines, and all the blazonry of art. Such persons are in fact besotted with words, and their brains are turned with the glittering, but empty and sterile phantoms of things. Personifications, capital letters, seas of sunbeams, visions of glory, shining inscriptions, the figures of a transparency, Britannia with her shield, or Hope leaning on an anchor, make up their stock in trade. They may be considered as *hieroglyphical* writers. Images stand out in their minds isolated and important merely in themselves, without any groundwork of feeling—there is no context in their imaginations. Words affect them in the same way, by the mere sound, that is, by their possible, not by their actual application to the subject in hand. They are fascinated by first appearances, and have no sense of consequences. Nothing more is meant by them than meets the ear: they understand or feel nothing more than meets their eye. The web and texture of the universe, and of the heart of man, is a mystery to them: they have no faculty that strikes a chord in unison with it. They cannot get beyond the daubings of fancy, the varnish of sentiment. Objects are not linked to feelings, words to things, but images revolve in splendid mockery, words represent themselves in their strange rhapsodies. The categories of such a mind are pride and ignorance—pride in outside show, to which they sacrifice every thing, and ignorance of the true worth and hidden structure both of words and things. With a sovereign contempt for what is familiar and natural, they are the slaves of vulgar affection—of a routine of highflown phrases. Scorning to imitate realities, they are unable to invent anything, to strike out one original idea. They are not copyists of nature, it is true; but they are the poorest of all plagiarists, the plagiarists of words. All is farfetched, dear-bought, artificial, oriental in subject and allusion: all is mechanical, conventional, vapid, formal, pedantic in style and execution. They startle and confound the understanding of the reader, by the remoteness and obscurity of their illustrations: they soothe the ear by the monotony of the same everlasting round of circuitous metaphors. They are the *mock-school* in poetry and prose. They flounder about between fustian in expression, and bathos in sentiment. They tantalize the fancy but never reach the head nor touch the heart. Their Temple of Fame is like a shadowy structure raised by Dullness to Vanity, or like Cowper's description of the Empress of Russia's palace of ice, as "worthless as in show 'twas glittering"—

It smiled, and it was cold!

1821

ALEXANDER SMITH

from *On the Writing of Essays*

. . . Giddy people may think the life I lead here staid and humdrum, but they are mistaken. It is true, I hear no concerts, save those in which the thrushes are performers in the spring mornings. I see no pictures, save those painted on the wide sky-canvas with the colors of sunrise and sunset. I attend neither rout nor ball; I have no deeper dissipation than the tea-table; I hear no gossip. Yet I enjoy my concerts more than I would the great London ones. I like the pictures I see, and think them better painted, too, than those which adorn the walls of the Royal Academy; and the village gossip is more after my turn of mind than the scandals that convulse the clubs. It is wonderful how the whole world reflects itself in the simple village life. The people around me are full of their own affairs and interests; were they of imperial magnitude, they could not be excited more strongly. Farmer Worthy is anxious about the next market; the likelihood of a fall in the price of butter and eggs hardly allows him to sleep o' nights. The village doctor—happily we have only one—skirrs hither and thither in his gig, as if man could neither die nor be born without his assistance. He is continually standing on the confines of existence, welcoming the new comer, bidding farewell to the goer-away. And the robustious fellow who sits at the head of the table when the Jolly Swillers meet at the Blue Lion on Wednesday evenings is a great politician, sound of lung metal, and wields the village in the taproom, as my Lord Palmerston wields the nation in the House. His listeners think him a wiser personage than the Premier, and he is inclined to lean to that opinion himself. I find everything here that other men find in the big world. London is but a magnified Dreamthorp.

And just as the Rev. Mr. White took note of the ongoings of the seasons in and around Hampshire Selborne, watched the colonies of the rooks in the tall elms, looked after the swallows in the cottage and rectory eaves, played the affectionate spy on the private lives of chaffinch and hedge-sparrow, was eavesdropper to the solitary cuckoo; so here I keep eye and ear open; take note of man, woman, and child; find many a pregnant text imbedded in the commonplace of village life; and, out of what I see and hear, weave in my own room my essays as solitarily as the spider weaves his web in the darkened corner. The essay, as a literary form, resembles the lyric, in so far as it is molded by some central mood—whimsical, serious, or satirical. Give the mood, and the essay, from the first sentence to the last, grows around it as the cocoon grows around the silkworm. The essay writer is a chartered libertine, and a law unto himself. A quick ear and eye, an ability to discern the infinite suggestiveness of common things, a brooding meditative spirit, are all that the essayist requires to start business with. Jacques, in "As You Like It," had the makings of a charming essayist. It is not the essayist's duty to inform, to build pathways through metaphysical morasses, to cancel abuses, any more than it is the duty of the poet to do these things. Incidentally he may do something in that way, just as the poet may, but it is not his duty, and should not be expected of him. Skylarks are primarily created to sing, although a whole choir of them may be baked in pies and brought to table; they were born to make music, although they may incidentally stay the pangs of vulgar hunger. The essayist is a kind of poet in prose, and if questioned harshly as to his uses, he might be unable to render a better apology for his existence than a flower might. The essay should be pure literature as the poem is pure literature. The essayist wears a lance, but he cares more for the sharpness of its point than for the pennon that flutters on it, than for the banner of the captain under whom he serves. He plays with death as Hamlet plays with Yorick's skull, and he reads the morals—strangely stern, often, for such fragrant lodging—which are folded up in the bosoms of roses. He has no pride, and is deficient in a sense of the congruity and fitness of things. He lifts a pebble from the ground, and puts it aside more carefully than any gem; and on a nail in a cottage door he will hang the mantle of his thought, heavily brocaded with the gold of rhetoric. He finds his way into the Elysian fields through portals the most shabby and commonplace.

The essayist plays with his subject, now in whimsical, now in grave, now in melancholy mood. He lies upon the idle grassy bank, like Jacques, letting the world flow past him, and from this thing and the other he extracts his mirth and his moralities. His main gift is an eye to discover the suggestiveness of common things; to find a sermon in the most unpromising texts. Beyond the vital hint, the first step, his discourses are not beholden to their titles. Let him take up the most trivial subject, and it will lead him away to the great questions over which the serious imagination loves to brood—fortune, mutability, death—just as inevitably as the runnel, trickling among the summer hills, on which sheep are bleating, leads you to the sea; or as, turning down the first street you come to in the city, you are led finally, albeit by many an intricacy, out into the open country, with its waste places and its woods, where you are lost in a sense of strangeness and solitariness. The world is to the meditative man what the mulberry plant is to the silkworm. The essay writer has no lack of subject matter. He has the day that is passing over his head; and, if unsatisfied with that, he has the world's six thousand years to depasture his gay or serious humor upon. I idle away my time here, and I am finding new subjects every hour. Everything I see or hear is an essay in bud. The world is everywhere whispering essays, and one need only be the world's amanuensis. The proverbial expression which last evening the clown dropped as he trudged homeward to supper, the light of the setting sun on his face, expands before me to a dozen pages. The coffin of the pauper, which today I saw carried carelessly along, is as good a subject as the funeral procession of an emperor. Craped drum and banner add nothing to death; penury and disrespect take nothing away. Incontinently my thought moves like a slow-paced hearse with sable nodding plumes. Two rustic lovers, whispering between the darkening hedges, is as potent to project my mind into the tender passion as if I had seen Romeo touch the cheek of Juliet in the moonlight garden. Seeing a curly-headed child asleep in the sunshine before a cottage door is sufficient excuse for a discourse on childhood; quite as good as if I had seen infant Cain asleep in the lap of Eve with Adam looking on. A lark cannot rise to heaven without raising as many thoughts as there are notes in its song. Dawn cannot pour its white light on my village without starting from their dim lair a hundred reminiscences; nor can sunset burn above yonder trees in the west without attracting to itself the melancholy of a lifetime. When spring unfolds her green leaves I would be provoked to indite an essay on hope and youth, were it not that it is already writ in the carols of the birds; and I might be tempted in autumn to improve the occasion, were it not for the rustle of the withered leaves as I walk through the woods. Compared with that simple music, the saddest-cadenced words have but a shallow meaning.

The essayist who feeds his thoughts upon the segment of the world which surrounds him cannot avoid being an egotist; but then his egotism is not unpleasing. If he be without taint of boastfulness, of self-sufficiency, of hungry vanity, the world will not press the charge home. If a man discourses continually of his wines, his plate, his titled acquaintances, the number and quality of his horses, his men-servants and maid-servants, he must discourse very skillfully indeed if he escapes being called a coxcomb. If a man speaks of death—tells you that the idea of it continually haunts him, that he has the most insatiable curiosity as to death and dying, that his thought mines in churchyards like a "demon-mole"—no one is specially offended, and that this is a dull fellow is the hardest thing likely to be said of him. Only, the egotism that over-crows you is offensive, that exalts trifles and takes pleasure in them, that suggests superiority in matters of equipage and furniture; and the egotism is offensive, because it runs counter to and jostles your self-complacency. The egotism which rises no higher than the grave is of a solitary and a hermit kind—it crosses no man's path, it disturbs no man's *amour propre.*

You may offend a man if you say you are as rich as he, as wise as he, as handsome as he. You offend no man if you tell him that, like him, you have to die. The king, in his crown and coronation robes, will allow the beggar to claim that relationship with him. To have to die is a distinction of which no man is proud. The speaking about one's self is not necessarily offensive. A modest, truthful man speaks better about himself than about anything else, and on that subject his speech is likely to be most profitable to his hearers. Certainly, there is no subject with which he is better acquainted, and on which he has a better title to be heard. And it is this egotism, this perpetual reference to self, in which the charm of the essayist resides. If a man is worth knowing at all, he is worth knowing well. The essayist gives you his thoughts, and lets you know, in addition, how he came by them. He has nothing to conceal; he throws open his doors and windows, and lets him enter who will. You like to walk round peculiar or important men as you like to walk round a building, to view it from different points, and in different lights. Of the essayist, when his mood is communicative, you obtain a full picture. You are made his contemporary and familiar friend. You enter into his humors and his seriousness. You are made heir of his whims, prejudices, and playfulness. You walk through the whole nature of him, as you walk through the streets of Pompeii, looking into the interior of stately mansions, reading the satirical scribblings on the walls. And the essayist's habit of not only giving you his thoughts, but telling you how he came by them, is interesting, because it shows you by what alchemy the ruder world becomes transmuted into the finer. We like to know the lineage of ideas, just as we like to know the lineage of great earls and swift race horses. We like to know that the discovery of the law of gravitation was born of the fall of an apple in an English garden on a summer afternoon. Essays written after this fashion are racy of the soil in which they grow, as you taste the lava in the vines grown on the slopes of Etna, they say. There is a healthy Gascon flavor in Montaigne's Essays; and Charles Lamb's are scented with the primrose of Covent Garden.

The essayist does not usually appear early in the literary history of a country: he comes naturally after the poet and the chronicler. His habit of mind is leisurely; he does not write from any special stress of passionate impulse; he does not create material so much as he comments upon material already existing. It is essential for him that books should have been written, and that they should, at least to some extent, have been read and digested. He is usually full of allusions and references, and these his reader must be able to follow and understand. And in this literary walk, as in most others, the giants came first: Montaigne and Lord Bacon were our earliest essayists, and, as yet, they are our best. In point of style, these essays are different from anything that could now be produced. Not only is the thinking different—the manner of setting forth the thinking is different also. We despair of reaching the language. We can no more bring back their turns of sentence than we can bring back their tournaments. Montaigne, in his serious moods, has a curiously rich and intricate eloquence; and Bacon's sentence bends beneath the weight of its fruit. Bacon seems to have written his essays with Shakespeare's pen. There is a certain want of ease about the old writers which has an irresistible charm. The language flows like a stream over a pebbled bed, with propulsion, eddy, and sweet recoil—the pebbles, if retarding movement, giving ring and dimple to the surface, and breaking the whole into babbling music. There is a ceremoniousness in the mental habits of these ancients. Their intellectual garniture is picturesque, like the garniture of their bodies. Their thoughts are courtly and high-mannered. A singular analogy exists between the personal attire of a period and its written style. The peaked beard, the starched collar, the quilted doublet, have their correspondences in the high sentence and elaborate ornament (worked upon the thought like figures upon tapestry) of Sidney and Spenser. In Pope's day men wore rapiers, and their weapons they carried with them into literature, and frequently unsheathed them too. They knew how to stab to the heart with an epigram. Style went out with the men who wore knee breeches and buckles in their shoes. We write more easily now; but in our easy writing there is ever a taint of flippancy: our writing is to theirs, what shooting coat and wideawake are to doublet and plumed hat.

Montaigne and Bacon are our earliest and greatest essayists, and likeness and unlikeness exist between the men. Bacon was constitutionally the graver nature. He writes like one on whom presses the weight of affairs, and he approaches a subject always on its serious side. He lives amongst great ideas, as with great nobles, with whom he dare not be too familiar. In the tone of his mind there is ever something imperial. When he writes on building, he speaks of a palace with spacious entrances, and courts, and banqueting halls; when he writes on gardens, he speaks of alleys and mounts, waste places and fountains, of a garden "which is indeed princelike." To read over his table of contents, is like reading over a roll of peers' names. We have, taking them as they stand, essays treating *Of Great Place, Of Boldness, Of Goodness, and Goodness of Nature, Of Nobility, Of Seditions and Troubles, Of Atheism, Of Superstition, Of Travel, Of Empire, Of Counsel*—a book plainly to lie in the closets of statesmen and princes, and designed to nurture the noblest natures. Bacon always seems to write with his ermine on. Montaigne was different from all this. His table of contents reads in comparison like a medley, or a catalogue of an auction. He was quite as wise as Bacon; he could look through men quite as clearly and search them quite as narrowly; certain of his moods were quite as serious, and in one corner of his heart he kept a yet profounder melancholy; but he was volatile, a humorist, and a gossip. He could be dignified enough on great occasions, but dignity and great occasions bored him. He could stand in the presence with propriety enough, but then he got out of the presence as rapidly as possible. When, in the thirty-eighth year of his age, he—somewhat world-weary, and with more scars on his heart than he cared to discover—retired to his chateau, he placed his library "in the great tower overlooking the entrance to the court," and over the central rafter he inscribed in large letters the device—"I DO NOT UNDERSTAND; I PAUSE; I EXAMINE." When he began to write his Essays he had no great desire to shine as an author; he wrote simply to relieve teeming heart and brain. The best method to lay the specters of the mind is to commit them to paper. Speaking of the Essays, he says, "This book has a domestic and private object. It is intended for the use of my relations and friends; so that, when they have lost me, which they will soon do, they may find in it some features of my condition and humors; and by this means keep up more completely, and in a more lively manner, the knowledge they have of me." In his Essays he meant to portray himself, his habits, his modes of thought, his opinions, what fruit of wisdom he had gathered from experience sweet and bitter; and the task he has executed with wonderful fidelity. He does not make himself a hero. Cromwell would have his warts painted; and Montaigne paints his, and paints them too with a certain fondness. He is perfectly tolerant of himself and of everybody else. Whatever be the subject, the writing flows on easy, equable, self-satisfied, almost always with a personal anecdote floating on the surface. Each event of his past life he considers a fact of nature; credible or the reverse, there it is; sometimes to be speculated upon, not in the least to be regretted. If it is worth nothing else, it may be made the subject of an essay, or, at least, be useful as an illustration. . . .

. . . Bacon is the greatest of the serious and stately essayists—Montaigne the greatest of the garrulous and communicative. The one gives you his thoughts on Death, Travel, Government, and the like, and lets you make the best of them; the other gives you his on the same subjects, but he wraps them up in personal gossip and reminiscence. With the last it is never Death or Travel alone; it is always Death one-fourth, and Montaigne three-fourths. He pours his thought into the water of gossip, and gives you to drink. He gilds his pill always, and he always gilds it with himself. The general characteristics of his Essays have been indicated, and it is worth while inquiring what they teach, what positive good they have done, and why for three centuries they have charmed, and still continue to charm.

The Essays contain a philosophy of life, which is not specially high, yet which is certain to find acceptance more or less with men who have passed out beyond the glow of youth, and who have made trial of the actual world. The essence of his philosophy is a kind of cynical common sense. He will ask nothing in life; he will keep to the beaten track; he will not let passion blind or enslave him; he will gather around him what good he can; and will therewith endeavor to be content. He will be, as far as possible, self-sustained; he will not risk his happiness in the hands of man, or of woman either. He is shy of friendship, he fears love, for he knows that both are dangerous. He knows that life is full of bitters, and he holds it wisdom that a man should console himself, as far as possible, with its sweets, the principal of which are peace, travel, leisure, and the writing of essays. He values obtainable Gascon bread and cheese more than the unobtainable stars. He thinks crying for the moon the foolishest thing in the world. He will remain where he is. He will not deny that a new world may exist beyond the sunset, but he knows that to reach the new world there is a troublesome Atlantic to cross; and he is not in the least certain that, putting aside the chance of being drowned on the way, he will be one whit happier in the new world than he is in the old. For his part he will embark with no Columbus. He feels that life is but a sad thing at best; but as he has little hope of making it better, he accepts it, and will not make it worse by murmuring. When the chain galls him, he can at least revenge himself by making jests on it. He will temper the despotism of nature by epigrams. He has read Aesop's fable, and is the last man in the world to relinquish the shabbiest substance to grasp at the finest shadow.

Of nothing under the sun was Montaigne quite certain, except that every man—whatever his station—might travel farther and fare worse; and the playing with his own thoughts, in the shape of essay writing, was the most harmless of amusements. . . .

. . . And on style depends the success of the essayist. Montaigne said the most familiar things in the finest way. Goldsmith could not be termed a thinker; but everything he touched he brightened, as after a month of dry weather, the shower brightens the dusty shrubbery of a suburban villa. The world is not so much in need of new thoughts as that when thought grows old and worn with usage it should, like current coin, be called in, and, from the mint of genius, be reissued fresh and new. Love is an old story enough, but in every generation it is reborn, in the downcast eyes and blushes of young maidens. And so, although he fluttered in Eden, Cupid is young today. If Montaigne had lived in Dreamthorp, as I am now living, had he written essays as I am now writing them, his English Essays would have been as good as his Gascon ones. Looking on, the country cart would not for nothing have passed him on the road to market, the setting sun would be arrested in its splendid colors, the idle chimes of the church would be translated into a thoughtful music. As it is, the village life goes on, and there is no result. My sentences are not much more brilliant than the speeches of the clowns; in my book there is little more life than there is in the market place on the days when there is no market.

1863

F. L. LUCAS

On the Fascination of Style

When it was suggested to Walt Whitman that one of his works should be bound in vellum, he was outraged—"Pshaw!" he snorted, "—hangings, curtains, finger bowls, chinaware, Matthew Arnold!" And he might have been equally irritated by talk of style; for he boasted of "my barbaric yawp"—he would *not* be literary; his readers should touch not a book but a man. Yet Whitman took the pains to rewrite *Leaves of Grass* four times, and his style is unmistakable. Samuel Butler maintained that writers who bothered about their style became unreadable but he bothered about his own. "Style" has got a bad name by growing associated with precious and superior persons who, like Oscar Wilde, spend a morning putting in a comma, and the afternoon (so he said) taking it out again. But such abuse of "style" is misuse of English. For the word means merely "a way of expressing oneself, in language, manner, or appearance"; or, secondly, "a *good* way of so expressing oneself"—as when one says, "Her behavior never lacked style."

Now there is no crime in expressing oneself (though to try to *im*press oneself on others easily grows revolting or ridiculous). Indeed one cannot help expressing oneself, unless one passes one's life in a cupboard. Even the most rigid Communist, or Organization-man, is compelled by Nature to have a unique voice, unique fingerprints, unique handwriting. Even the signature of the letters on your breakfast table may reveal more than their writers guess. There are blustering signatures that swish across the page like cornstalks bowed before a tempest. There are cryptic signatures, like a scrabble of lightning across a cloud, suggesting that behind is a lofty divinity whom all must know, or an aloof divinity whom none is worthy to know (though, as this might be highly inconvenient, a docile typist sometimes interprets the mystery in a bracket underneath). There are impetuous squiggles implying that the author is a sort of strenuous Sputnik streaking round the globe every eighty minutes. There are florid signatures, all curlicues and danglements and flamboyance, like the youthful Disraeli (though these seem rather out of fashion). There are humble, humdrum signatures. And there are also, sometimes, signatures that are courteously clear, yet mindful of a certain simple grace and artistic economy—in short, of style.

Since, then, not one of us can put pen to paper, or even open his mouth, without giving something of himself away to shrewd observers, it seems more common sense to give the matter a little thought. Yet it does not seem very common. Ladies may take infinite pains about having style in their clothes, but many of us remain curiously indifferent about having it in our words. How many women would dream of polishing not only their nails but also their tongues? They may play freely on that perilous little organ, but they cannot often be bothered to tune it. And how many men think of improving their talk as well as their golf handicap?

No doubt strong silent men, speaking only in gruff monosyllables, may despise "mere words." No doubt the world does suffer from an endemic plague of verbal dysentery. But that, precisely, is bad style. And consider the amazing power of mere words. Adolf Hitler was a bad artist, bad statesman, bad general, and bad man. But largely because he could tune his rant, with psychological nicety, to the exact wave length of his audiences and make millions quarrelsome-drunk all at the same time by his command of windy nonsense, skilled statesmen, soldiers, scientists were blown away like chaff, and he came near to rule the world. If Sir

Winston Churchill had been a mere speechifier, we might have lost the war; yet his speeches did quite a lot to win it.

No man was less of a literary aesthete than Benjamin Franklin; yet this tallow-chandler's son, who changed world history, regarded as "a principal means of my advancement" that pungent style which he acquired partly by working in youth over old *Spectators*; but mainly by being Benjamin Franklin. The squinting demagogue, John Wilkes, as ugly as his many sins, had yet a tongue so winning that he asked only half an hour's start (to counteract his face) against any rival for a woman's favor. "Vote for you!" growled a surly elector in his constituency, "I'd sooner vote for the devil!" "But in case your friend should not stand . . . ?" Cleopatra, that ensnarer of world conquerors, owed less to the shape of her nose than to the charm of her tongue. Shakespeare himself has often poor plots and thin ideas; even his mastery of character has been questioned; what does remain unchallenged is his verbal magic. Men are often taken, like rabbits, by the ears. And though the tongue has no bones, it can sometimes break millions of them.

"But," the reader may grumble, "I am neither Hitler, Cleopatra, nor Shakespeare. What is all this to me?" Yet we all talk—often too much; we all have to write letters—often too many. We live not by bread alone but also by words. And not always with remarkable efficiency. Strikes, lawsuits, divorces, all sorts of public nuisance and private misery, often come just from the gaggling incompetence with which we express ourselves. Americans and British get at cross-purposes because they use the same words with different meanings. Men have been hanged on a comma in a statute. And in the valley of Balaclava a mere verbal ambiguity, about *which* guns were to be captured, sent the whole Light Brigade to futile annihilation.

Words can be more powerful, and more treacherous, than we sometimes suspect; communication more difficult than we may think. We are all serving life sentences of solitary confinement within our own bodies; like prisoners, we have, as it were, to tap in awkward code to our fellow men in their neighboring cells. Further, when A and B converse, there take part in their dialogue not two characters, as they suppose, but six. For there is A's real self—call it A_1; there is also A's picture of himself—A_2; there is also B's picture of A—A_3. And there are three corresponding personalities of B. With six characters involved even in a simple tête-à-tête, no wonder we fall into muddles and misunderstandings.

Perhaps, then, there are five main reasons for trying to gain some mastery of language:

We have no other way of understanding, informing, misinforming, or persuading one another.

Even alone, we think mainly in words; if our language is muddy, so will our thinking be.

By our handling of words we are often revealed and judged. "Has he written anything?" said Napoleon of a candidate for an appointment. "Let me see his *style*."

Without a feeling for language one remains half-blind and deaf to literature.

Our mother tongue is bettered or worsened by the way each generation uses it. Languages evolve like species. They can degenerate; just as oysters and barnacles have lost their heads. Compare ancient Greek with modern. A heavy responsibility, though often forgotten.

Why and how did I become interested in style? The main answer, I suppose, is that I was born that way. Then I was, till ten, an only child running loose in a house packed with books, and in a world (thank goodness) still undistracted by radio and television. So at three I groaned to my mother, "Oh, I *wish* I could read," and at four I read. Now travel among books is the best travel of all, and the cheapest. (Not that I belittle ordinary travel—which I regard as one of the three main pleasures in life.) One learns to write by reading good books, as one learns to talk by hearing good talkers. And if I have learned anything of writing, it is largely from writers like Montaigne, Dorothy Osborne, Horace Walpole, Johnson, Goldsmith, Montesquieu, Voltaire, Flaubert, and Anatole France. Again, I was reared on Greek and Latin, and one can learn much from translating Homer or the Greek Anthology, Horace or Tacitus, if one is thrilled by the originals and tries, however vainly, to recapture some of the thrill in English.

But at Rugby I could *not* write English essays. I believe it stupid to torment boys to write on topics that they know and care nothing about. I used to rush to the school library and cram the subject, like a python swallowing rabbits; then, still replete as a postprandial python, I would tie myself in clumsy knots to embrace those accursed themes. Bacon was wise in saying that reading makes a full man; talking, a ready one; writing, an exact one. But writing from an empty head is futile anguish.

At Cambridge, my head having grown a little fuller, I suddenly found I *could* write—not with enjoyment (it is always tearing oneself in pieces)—but fairly fluently. Then came the War of 1914–18; and though soldiers have other things than pens to handle, they learn painfully to be clear and brief. Then the late Sir Desmond McCarthy invited me to review for the *New Statesman*; it was a useful apprenticeship, and he was delightful to work for. But I think it was well after a few years to stop; reviewers remain essential, but there are too many books one *cannot* praise, and only the pugnacious enjoy amassing enemies. By then I was an ink-addict—not because writing is much pleasure, but because not to write is pain; just as some smokers do not so much enjoy tobacco as suffer without it. The positive happiness of writing comes, I think, from work well done—decently, one hopes, and not without use—and from the letters of readers which help to reassure, or delude, one that so it is.

But one of my most vivid lessons came, I think, from service in a war department during the Second War. Then, if the matter one sent out was too wordy, the communication channels might choke; yet if it was not absolutely clear, the results might be serious. So I emerged, after six years of it, with more passion than ever for clarity and brevity, more loathing than ever for the obscure and the verbose.

For forty years at Cambridge I have tried to teach young men to write well, and have come to think it impossible. To write really well is a gift inborn; those who have it teach themselves; one can only try to help and hasten the process. After all, the uneducated sometimes express themselves far better than their "betters." In language, as in life, it is possible to be perfectly correct—and yet perfectly tedious, or odious. The illiterate last letter of the doomed Vanzetti was more moving than most professional orators; eighteenth century ladies, who should have been spanked for their spelling, could yet write far better letters than most professors of English; and the talk of Synge's Irish peasants seems to me vastly more vivid than the later style of Henry James. Yet Synge averred that his characters owed far less of their eloquence to what he invented for them than to what he had overheard in the cottages of Wicklow and Kerry:

"*Christy.* 'It's little you'll think if my love's a poacher's, or an earl's itself, when you'll feel my two hands stretched around you, and I squeezing kisses on your puckered lips, till I'd feel a kind of pity for the Lord God is all ages sitting lonesome in His golden chair.'

"*Pegeen.* 'That'll be right fun, Christy Mahon, and any girl would walk her heart out before she'd meet a young man was your like for eloquence, or talk at all.' "

Well she might! It's not like that they talk in universities—more's the pity.

But though one cannot teach people to write well, one can sometimes teach them to write rather better. One can give a certain number of hints, which often seem boringly obvious—only experience shows they are not.

One can say: Beware of pronouns—they are devils. Look at even Addison, describing the type of pedant who chatters of style without having any: "Upon enquiry I found my learned friend had dined that day with Mr. Swan, the famous punster; and desiring *him* to give me some account of Mr. Swan's conversation, *he* told me that *he* generally talked in the Paronomasia, that *he* sometimes gave in to the Plocé, but that in *his* humble opinion, *he* shone most in the Antanaclasis." What a sluttish muddle of *he* and *him* and *his*! It all needs rewording. Far better repeat a noun, or a name, than puzzle the reader, even for a moment, with ambiguous pronouns. Thou shalt not puzzle thy reader.

Or one can say: Avoid jingles. The B.B.C. news bulletins seem compiled by earless persons, capable of crying round the globe: "The enemy is re*port*ed to have seized this im*port*ant *port*, and reinforcements are hurrying up in sup*port*." Any fool, once told, can hear such things to be insupportable.

Or one can say: Be sparing with relative clauses. Don't string them together like sausages, or jam them inside one another like Chinese boxes or the receptacles of Buddha's tooth. Or one can say: Don't flaunt jargon, like Addison's Mr. Swan, or the type of modern critic who gurgles more technical terms in a page than Johnson used in all his *Lives* or Sainte-Beuve in thirty volumes. But dozens of such snippety precepts, though they may sometimes save people from writing badly, will help them little toward writing well. Are there no general rules of a more positive kind, and of more positive use?

Perhaps. There *are* certain basic principles which seem to me observed by many authors I admire, which I think have served me and which may serve others. I am not talking of geniuses, who are a law to themselves (and do not always write a very good style, either); nor of poetry, which has different laws from prose; nor of poetic prose, like Sir Thomas Browne's or De Quincey's, which is often more akin to poetry; but of the plain prose of ordinary books and documents, letters and talk.

The writer should respect truth and himself; therefore honesty. He should respect his readers; therefore courtesy. These are two of the cornerstones of style. Confucius saw it, twenty-five centuries ago; "The Master said, The gentleman is courteous, but not pliable: common men are pliable, but not courteous."

First, honesty. In literature, as in life, one of the fundamentals is to find, and be, one's true self. One's true self may indeed be unpleasant (though one can try to better it); but a false self, sooner or later, becomes disgusting—just as a nice plain woman, painted to the eyebrows, can become horrid. In writing, in the long run, pretense does not work. As the police put it, anything you say may be used as evidence against you. If handwriting reveals character, writing reveals it still more. You cannot fool *all* your judges *all* the time.

Most style is not honest enough. Easy to say, but hard to practice. A writer may take to long words, as young men to beards—to impress. But long words, like long beards, are often the badge of charlatans. Or a writer may cultivate the obscure, to seem profound. But even carefully muddied puddles are soon fathomed. Or he may cultivate eccentricity, to seem original. But really original people do not have to think about being original—they can no more help it than they can help breathing. They do not need to dye their hair green. The fame of Meredith, Wilde or Bernard Shaw might now shine brighter, had they struggled less to be brilliant; whereas Johnson remains great, not merely because his gifts were formidable but also because, with all his prejudice and passion, he fought no less passionately to "clear his mind of cant."

Secondly, courtesy—respect for the reader. From this follow several other basic principles of style. Clarity is one. For it is boorish to make your reader rack his brains to understand. One should aim at being impossible to misunderstand—though men's capacity for misunderstanding approaches infinity. Hence Molière and Po Chu-i tried their work on their cooks; and Swift his on his men servants—"which, if they did not comprehend, he would alter and amend, until they understood it perfectly." Our bureaucrats and pundits, unfortunately, are less considerate.

Brevity is another basic principle. For it is boorish, also, to waste your reader's time. People who would not dream of stealing a penny of one's money turn not a hair at stealing hours of one's life. But that does not make them less exasperating. Therefore there is no excuse for the sort of writer who takes as long as a marching army corps to pass a given point. Besides, brevity is often more effective; the half can say more than the whole, and to imply things may strike far deeper than to state them at length. And because one is particularly apt to waste words on preambles before coming to the substance, there was sense in the Scots professor who always asked his pupils—"Did ye remember to tear up that fir-r-st page?"

Here are some instances that would only lose by lengthening:

It is useless to go to bed to save the light, if the result is twins. (Chinese proverb.)

My barn is burnt down—
Nothing hides the moon. (Complete Japanese poem.)

Je me regrette. (Dying words of the gay Vicomtesse d'Houdetot.)

I have seen their backs before. (Wellington, when French marshals turned their backs on him at a reception.)

Continue until the tanks stop, then get out and walk. (Patton to the Twelfth Corps, halted for fuel supplies at St. Dizier, 8/30/44.)

Or there is the most laconic diplomatic note on record: when Philip of Macedon wrote to the Spartans that if he came within their borders, he would leave not one stone of their city, they wrote back the one word—"If."

Clarity comes before even brevity. But it is a fallacy that wordiness is necessarily clearer. Metternich when he thought something he had written was obscure would simply go through it crossing out everything irrelevant. What remained, he found, often became clear. Wellington, asked to recommend three names for the post of Commander-in-Chief, India, took a piece of paper and wrote three times—"Napier." Pages could not have been clearer—or as forcible. On the other hand the lectures, and the sentences, of Coleridge became at times bewildering because his mind was often "wiggle-waggle"; just as he could not even walk straight on a path.

But clarity and brevity, though a good beginning, are only a beginning. By themselves, they may remain bare and bleak. When Calvin Coolidge, asked by his wife what the preacher had preached on, replied "Sin," and, asked what the preacher had said, replied, "He was against it," he was brief enough. But one hardly envies Mrs. Coolidge.

An attractive style requires, of course, all kinds of further gifts—such as variety, good humor, good sense, vitality, imagination. Variety means avoiding monotony of rhythm, of language, of mood. One needs to vary one's sentence length (this present article has too many short sentences; but so vast a subject grows here as cramped as a djin in a bottle); to amplify one's vocabulary; to diversify one's tone. There are books that petrify one throughout, with the rigidly pompous solemnity of an owl perched on a leafless tree. But ceaseless facetiousness can be as bad; or perpetual irony. Even the smile of Voltaire can seem at times a fixed grin, a disagreeable wrinkle. Constant peevishness is far worse, as often in Swift; even on the stage too much irritable dialogue may irritate an audience, without its knowing why.

Still more are vitality, energy, imagination gifts that must be inborn before they can be cultivated. But under the head of imagination two common devices may be mentioned that have been the making of many a style—metaphor and simile. Why such magic power should reside in simply saying, or implying, that A is like B remains a little mysterious. But even our unconscious seems to love symbols; again, language often tends to lose itself in clouds of vaporous abstraction, and simile or metaphor can bring it back to concrete solidity; and, again, such imagery can gild the gray flats of prose with sudden sun-glints of poetry.

If a foreigner may for a moment be impertinent, I admire the native gift of Americans for imagery as much as I wince at their fondness for slang. (Slang seems to me a kind of linguistic fungus; as poisonous, and as short-lived, as toadstools.) When Matthew Arnold lectured in the United States, he was likened by one newspaper to "an elderly macaw pecking at a trellis of grapes"; he observed, very justly, "How lively journalistic fancy is among the Americans!" General Grant, again, unable to hear him, remarked: "Well, wife, we've paid to see the British lion, but as we can't hear him roar, we'd better go home." By simile and metaphor, these two quotations bring before us the slightly pompous, fastidious, inaudible Arnold as no direct description could have done.

Or consider how language comes alive in the Chinese saying that lending to the feckless is "like pelting a stray dog with dumplings," or in the Arab proverb: "They came to shoe the pasha's horse, and the beetle stretched forth his leg"; in the Greek phrase for a perilous cape—"stepmother of ships"; or the Hebrew adage that "as the climbing up a sandy way is to the feet of the aged, so is a wife full of words to a quiet man"; in Shakespeare's phrase for a little England lost in the world's vastness—"in a great Poole, a Swan's nest"; or Fuller's libel on tall men—"Ofttimes such who are built four stories high are observed to have little in their cockloft"; in Chateaubriand's "I go yawning my life"; or in Jules Renard's portrait of a cat, "well buttoned in her fur." Or, to take a modern instance, there is Churchill on dealings with Russia: "Trying to maintain good relations with a Communist is like wooing a crocodile. You do not know whether to tickle it under the chin or beat it over the head. When it opens its mouth, you cannot tell whether it is trying to smile or preparing to eat you up." What a miracle human speech can be, and how dull is most that one hears! Would one hold one's hearers, it is far less help, I suspect, to read manuals on style than to cultivate one's own imagination and imagery.

I will end with two remarks by two wise old women of the civilized eighteenth century.

The first is from the blind Mme. du Deffand (the friend of Horace Walpole) to that Mlle. De Lespinasse with whom, alas, she was to quarrel so unwisely: "You must make up your mind, my queen, to live with me in the greatest truth and sincerity. You will be charming so long as you let yourself be natural, and remain without pretension and without artifice." The second is from Mme. de Charrière, the Zélide whom Boswell had once loved at Utrecht in vain, to a Swiss girl friend: "Lucinde, my clever Lucinde, while you wait for the Romeos to arrive, you have nothing better to do than become perfect. Have ideas that are clear, and expressions that are simple." ("Ayez des idées nettes et des expressions simples.") More than half the bad writing in the world, I believe, comes from neglecting those two very simple pieces of advice.

In many ways, no doubt, our world grows more and more complex; Sputniks cannot be simple; yet how many of our complexities remain futile, how many of our artificialities false. Simplicity too can be subtle—as the straight lines of a Greek temple, like the Parthenon at Athens, are delicately curved, in order to look straighter still.

1960

"Adolf," "Nottingham and the Mining Countryside," and "Why the Novel Matters" from *Phoenix: The Posthumous Papers of D. H. Lawrence,* edited by Edward D. McDonald. Copyright 1936 by Frieda Lawrence, © renewed 1964 by the Estate of the late Frieda Lawrence Ravagli. Reprinted by permission of Viking Penguin Inc.

"Hymns in a Man's Life," "Insouciance," and "Making Pictures" from *Phoenix II: Uncollected Papers* by D. H. Lawrence, edited by Warren Roberts and Harry T. Moore. Copyright © 1959, 1963, 1968 by the Estate of Frieda Lawrence Ravagli. Reprinted by permission of Viking Penguin Inc.

"Shooting an Elephant," "How the Poor Die," and "Politics and the English Language" from *Shooting an Elephant and Other Essays* by George Orwell, copyright 1950 by Sonia Brownell Orwell; renewed 1978 by Sonia Pitt-Rivers. Reprinted by permission of Harcourt Brace Jovanovich, Inc., Mrs. Sonia Brownell Orwell, and Martin Secker and Warburg Ltd.

"Marrakech" and "Why I Write" from *Such, Such Were the Joys* by George Orwell, copyright 1945, 1952, 1953 by Sonia Brownell Orwell; renewed 1973 by Sonia Pitt-Rivers. Reprinted by permission of Harcourt Brace Jovanovich, Inc., Mrs. Sonia Brownell Orwell, and Martin Secker and Warburg Ltd.

"The World of Tomorrow," copyright 1939 by E. B. White, originally appeared in *The New Yorker*; "Once More to the Lake," copyright 1941 by E. B. White; "Afternoon of an American Boy," copyright 1947 by E. B. White, originally appeared in *The New Yorker*; "Death of A Pig," copyright 1947 by E. B. White; and "The Ring of Time," copyright © 1956 by E. B. White, originally appeared in *The New Yorker*; all from *Essays of E. B. White* (1977) by E. B. White. Reprinted by permission of Harper & Row, Publishers, Inc.

"Walden" from *One Man's Meat* by E. B. White. Copyright 1939 by E. B. White. Reprinted by permission of Harper & Row, Publishers, Inc.

"Autonomy" and "A Fear of Pheromones" from *The Lives of A Cell* by Lewis Thomas. Copyright © 1974 by Lewis Thomas. Originally appeared in *The New England Journal of Medicine.* Reprinted by permission of Viking Penguin Inc.

"On Cloning a Human Being," "On Natural Death," and "On Embryology" from *The Medusa and the Snail* by Lewis Thomas. Copyright © 1979 by Lewis Thomas. "On Cloning a Human Being" originally appeared in *The New England Journal of Medicine.* Reprinted by permission of Viking Penguin Inc.

"Medical Lessons from History" by Lewis Thomas, reprinted by permission of the American Academy of Arts and Sciences from *Daedalus,* Summer 1977. Originally entitled "Biomedical Science and Human Health."

"Notes of a Native Son," "Equal in Paris," and "Stranger in the Village" copyright © 1955 by James Baldwin. Reprinted by permission of Beacon Press.

"On Morality," "Goodbye to All That," and "On Going Home" from *Slouching Towards Bethlehem* by Joan Didion. Copyright © 1965, 1967 by Joan Didion. Reprinted by permission of Farrar, Straus and Giroux, Inc.

"On the Morning After the Sixties" and "On the Road" from *The White Album* by Joan Didion. Copyright © 1979 by Joan Didion. Reprinted by permission of Simon & Schuster, a Division of Gulf & Western Corporation.

"Why I Write" by Joan Didion. Reprinted by permission of Wallace &

Sheil Agency, Inc. Copyright © 1976 by Joan Didion. First appeared in the *New York Times Book Review*.
"On the Fascination of Style" by F. L. Lucas. Reprinted from *Holiday* magazine. Permission granted by *Travel/Holiday*, Travel Building, Floral Park, N.Y. 11001.